AIR POWER

A Centennial Appraisal

Also from Brassey's:

GODDEN
Shield and Storm: Personal Recollections of the Air War in the Gulf

SMALLWOOD
Strike Eagle: Flying the F-15E in the Gulf War

WALKER
Air Superiority Operations (Air Power Technology Series)

ELSAM
Air Defence (Air Power Technology Series)

KNIGHT
Strategic Air Operations (Air Power Technology Series)

Putnam Aeronautical Books:

MASON, FK
The British Bomber Since 1914

MASON, T
British Flight Testing: Martlesham Heath 1920–39

ANDERSSON
Soviet Aircraft and Aviation 1917–1941

BREW
Boulton Paul Aircraft Since 1915

AIR POWER

A Centennial Appraisal

AIR VICE MARSHAL TONY MASON

BRASSEY'S
London • Washington

First English edition 1994
Reprinted 1997

UK editorial offices: Brassey's, 33 John Street, London WC1N 2AT
UK orders: Marston Book Services, PO Box 269, Abingdon OX14 4SD

North American orders: Brassey's Inc., PO Box 960, Herndon, VA 22070, USA

Tony Mason has asserted his moral rights to be identified as
author of this work.

Library of Congress Cataloging in Publication Data
available

British Library Cataloguing in Publication Data
A catalogue record for this book is available
from the British Library

Hardcover 1-85753-069-1

Typeset by M Rules
Printed and bound in Great Britain by
Bookcraft (Bath) Limited

ACKNOWLEDGEMENTS

The author bears sole responsibility for the facts narrated and the conclusions drawn in this study, but he wishes to acknowledge the support and encouragement, in some cases extending over many years, from a number of institutions and individuals.

To the Leverhulme Trust, whose generous Fellowship enabled the research and preparatory work on which this study is based to be carried out; to Marshal of the Royal Air Force Lord Craig of Radley and Professor Sir Michael Howard for their sponsorship, encouragement and inspiration; to Stan Windass, Director of the Foundation for International Security, for his initiation of the Fellowship; to Chris Hobson and his staff at the RAF Staff College Library, Bracknell; to Charles Dick and his research staff at the Conflict Studies Centre Sandhurst; to Bert Cooper and Stanley Sloane of the Congressional Research Service; to Chris Donnelly, Ben Lambeth, Chris Bowie, Ken Brower, Dick Pavlovski, Phil Petersen, Anthony Cordesman, Roy Allison, Jane Sharp, Dick Hallion, Giles Harlow, Wick Murray, David McIsaac, Craig Oliphant, Sasha Kennaway, Edwina Moreton, John Lough, Dennis Marshall-Hasdell, Stuart Croft, Henry Plater-Syberk, Robin Higham, Jacob Kipp, Frank Futrell, Horst Boog, Alex Boyd, Alan Gropman, Olivier De Bouzy, and Sergei Blagovolin: who were always willing to share their research and ideas, as well as being good friends; to Air Commodores Ted Williams and Jasjit Singh, Brigadiers Oded Erez, Giora Furman, Marouf Nadir, V.K.Nair, and Klaus Wittman; to Air Marshal Ray Funnell and his legatees at the Royal Australian Air Force Air Power Studies Centre; to Air Marshal Sir Timothy Garden, Air Commodore Martin van der Veen, Group Captains Andy Vallance and Neil Taylor, Lt.Col.Jim Holcomb: who all illuminated academic rigour with operational awareness; to Marshal of Aviation and Hero of the Soviet Union Alexander Silantiev and Major-General Nikita Chaldymov, whose personal warmth prepared the way for many productive and enjoyable exchanges in Moscow; to Mrs Jean Hollis, on whose patient, painstaking preparation all the research papers and manuscripts depended; to Jenny Shaw and Caroline Bolton at Brassey's, for their highly professional guidance: very many thanks.

CONTENTS

GLOSSARY

AA	Anti Aircraft
AAA	Anti Aircraft Artillery
AAR	Air to Air Refuelling
Ab Initio	Inexperienced Aircrew
AFB	Air Force Base
AFC	Air Force Cross
ARM	Anti Radiation Missile
ATO	Air Tasking Order
ATTU	Atlantic to the Urals
AWACS	Airborne Warning and Control System
BDA	Battle Damage Assessment
C^3	Command, Control and Communication
C^3I	Command, Control, Communication and Intelligence
CAP	Combat Air Patrol
CAS	Chief of the Air Staff
CDE	Conventional Disarmament in Europe
CEE	Central and Eastern Europe
CENTCOM	US Central Command
CEP	Circular Error Probable
CFE	Conventional Forces in Europe
C in C	Commander in Chief
CINCSOUTH	Commander in Chief NATO Southern Europe
CID	Committee for Imperial Defence
CIS	Commonwealth of Independent States
CNN	Cable News Network
CSBM	Confidence and Security Building Measures

CSCE	Conference on Security and Co-operation in Europe
CST	Conventional Stability Talks
DFC	Distinguished Flying Cross
DIA	Defense Intellience Agency
DOD	Department of Defense
EAF	Egyptian Air Force
ECM	Electronic Countermeasures
ELINT	Electronic Intelligence
EW	Electronic Warfare
ET	Emerging Technology
FAC	Forward Air Controller
FEBA	Forward Edge of the Battlefield
FOFA	Follow-on-Forces Attack
GDP	Gross Domestic Product
GDR	German Democratic Republic
GMT	Greenwich Mean Time
GOC	General Officer Commanding
GPS	Global Positioning System
GWAPS	Gulf War Air Power Study
HARM	High Speed Anti-Radiation Missile
HAS	Hardened Aircraft Shelter
HMS	His Majesty's Ship
HMSO	Her Majesty's Stationery Office
IAAC	Inter-allied Aviation Committee
IAF	Israeli Air Force
IDF	Israeli Defence Force
IF	Independent Force
IFF	Identification Friend or Foe
IFR	In-flight Refuelling
INF	Intermediate Nuclear Forces
IQAF	Iraqi Air Force
IR	Infra Red
ISO	International Standard Container
JCS	Joint Chiefs of Staff
JMATO	Joint Military Air Traffic Organisation
JSTARS	Joint Surveillance Target Attack Radar System
JTIDS	Joint Tactical Information Display System
JWAC	Joint War Air Committee
KTO	Kuwait Theatre of Operations
LGB	Laser Guided Bomb
LLAD	Low Level Air Defence
MBFR	Mutual and Balanced Force Reductions

MC	Military Cross
MD	Military District
MEW	Ministry of Economic Warfare
MP	Member of Parliament
MRAF	Marshal of the Royal Air Force
MRLS	Multiple Rocket Launcher System
MT	Mechanised Transport
NACC	North Atlantic Co-operation Council
NAEW	NATO Early Warning
NATO	North Atlantic Treaty Organisation
NAVSTAR	Navigational Satellite System
NSWTO	Non Soviet Warsaw Treaty Organisation
OCA	Offensive Counter Air
OST	Open Skies Treaty
PGM	Precision Guided Munition
PLA	(Chinese) Peoples' Liberation Army
PVO	Air Defence of USSR/Russia
R&D	Research and Development
RFC	Royal Flying Corps
RNAS	Royal Naval Air Service
RSAF	Royal Saudi Air Force
RUSI	Royal United Services Institute
SAC	Strategic Air Command
SACEUR	Supreme Commander Allied Forces Europe
SAD	Surface to Air Defences
SAF	Soviet Air Forces
SAM	Surface to Air Missile
SBAC	Society of British Aircraft Construction (Society of British Aerospace Companies)
SCUD	Soviet designed medium range surface to surface ballistic missile
SIGINT	Signals Intelligence
SOE	Special Operations Executive
TACP	Tactical Air Control Parties
TALD	Tactical Air Launched Decoy
TIALD	Thermal Imaging and Laser Designating
TLAM	Tomahawk Land Attack Missile
TTTE	Tri-National Tornado Training Establishment
TSMA	Theatre of Strategic Military Action
TVD	Theatre of Operations
UAE	United Arab Emirates
UAV	Unmanned Aerial Vehicle

UNPROFOR	United Nations Protection Force in the former Yugoslavia
USAAF	United States Army Air Force
USAF	United States Air Force
USN	United States Navy
V1	German air breathing surface to surface missile
V2	German surface to surface ballistic missile
VPVO	Soviet/Russian Air Defence Ground Forces
VVS	Russian Air Forces
WTO	Warsaw Treaty Organisation

THE AIR POWER PENDULUM

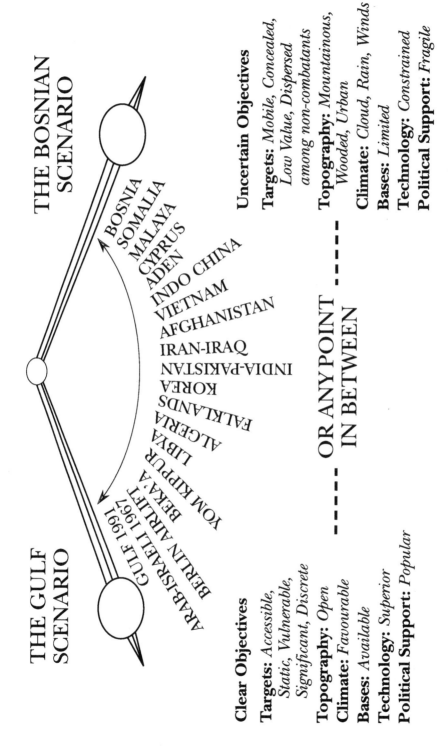

THE BOSNIAN SCENARIO

THE GULF SCENARIO

BOSNIA
SOMALIA
MALAYA
CYPRUS
ADEN
INDO CHINA
VIETNAM
AFGHANISTAN
IRAN-IRAQ
INDIA-PAKISTAN
KOREA
FALKLANDS
ALGERIA
LIBYA
YOM KIPPUR
BEKA'A
BERLIN AIRLIFT 1997
GULF 1991
ARAB-ISRAELI

---- OR ANY POINT
---- IN BETWEEN

Clear Objectives

Targets: *Accessible, Static, Vulnerable, Significant, Discrete*

Topography: *Open*
Climate: *Favourable*

Bases: *Available*

Technology: *Superior*

Political Support: *Popular*

Uncertain Objectives

Targets: *Mobile, Concealed, Low Value, Dispersed among non-combatants*

Topography: *Mountainous, Wooded, Urban*

Climate: *Cloud, Rain, Winds*

Bases: *Limited*

Technology: *Constrained*
Political Support: *Fragile*

REPRODUCED FROM AUTHOR'S PRESENTATION AT THE HIGHER COMMAND AND STAFF COURSE, STAFF COLLEGE, CAMBERLEY, JANUARY 1994 WITH THE COOPERATION OF THE STAFF COLLEGE DRAWING OFFICE

INTRODUCTION

This is a study of the role of air power in the dramatic international environment at the end of east-west confrontation and the re-emergence of strategic unpredictability and uncertainty from 1989 to 1994.

It examines in detail air power in the last years of NATO and the Warsaw Treaty Organisation, the conventional arms limitation process, the Gulf War, peacekeeping operations, the disintegration of the Soviet Air Forces and potential reconstitution of the Russian, and finally looks forward to air power's second century world-wide.

It argues that the longer term significance of these events can best be understood by placing them in the context of the first hundred years of air power theory and application. Consequently, the first two chapters of the book deal, with unashamed hindsight, with a number of specific topics which have relevance to air power in the 1990s. They do not purport to be a history of the evolution of air power, nor even necessarily a chronology of the most important events. Rather they have, in the author's opinion, a particular message for today's military commanders and their civilian masters. In several cases, new original sources have been used.

A generation ago a distinguished airman and air power historian, Robin Higham, wrote: 'The history of air power has been confused by the bragging of its prophets and the derision of its enemies. Too often vision has outrun reality and resulted in disappointment and reaction. As newcomers, forced to plead from a position of weakness, airmen carried arguments to their logical extremes and talked about what air power was going to be able to do, and their listeners tended to forget that these were prognostications, accepting them as imminent realities.'

Fortunately for the course of several wars, the visionaries pushed just hard enough to ensure that the derision of their enemies frequently became muted with relief and appreciation. Today the newcomers are newcomers no longer.

In the 1990s there is a danger that sensible and necessary debates about air power may be threatened by the re-emergence of zealotry on the one hand and obtuseness on the other as resources are reduced, threats diminished and role responsibilities blurred. Now, however, there are one hundred years of theory and practice from which to seek guidance. Indeed, it is now dangerously possible to select a text to fit the sermon rather than vice versa.

Perhaps this study risks prompting exactly that accusation. It covers a century arbitrarily dated from a prophetic address by a British soldier in Chicago in 1893 who provides a link from the early modern visionaries, through the creation of 'air forces' to the apotheosis of air power in *Desert Storm* in 1991. It also argues, however, that it is time to examine air power not just in its own terms of unusual, sometimes unique characteristics, but in the context of warfare as a whole, susceptible to principles and influences akin to those which have affected the evolution of both seapower and land forces. It is hoped thereby that these examples and the analysis may stimulate debate among soldiers and sailors as well as airmen.

'Security' is a complex concept of which the military instrument is only a part. Air power will continue to make a formidable contribution in an age where the only certainty is that force will continue to be an arbiter of international relations. Indeed, it is probable that airpower will make a greater contribution in its second century than it did in its first.

With long reach, rapid response, precise and heavy firepower, impervious to frontiers and coastlines, swiftly inserted and equally easily disengaged, air power already has the capacity to determine the outcome of conflicts. But not necessarily all conflicts. Clausewitz commented on the relationship between policy and the destructive element of war: 'The terrible two-handed sword that should be used with total strength to strike once and no more, becomes the lightest rapier - sometimes even a harmless foil fit only for thrusts and feints and parries.' Air power can offer that wealth of options to the statesman or the defence minister. On other occasions it may be left in its scabbard.

Its relevance to any crisis or conflict, like all other kinds of military power, should be determined by policy. To that end there needs to be an understanding of the resources required to nourish it, the extent of the contribution it can make, and the recurring factors which may tend to constrain it. When air power was first challenged by uncertainty 75 years ago, there was little experience on which to base judgements about the future. This study illustrates the contrast in the 1990s.

CHAPTER 1

INFANCY

The Concept

The first recorded use of the expression 'air power' occurred in H. G. Wells's futuristic novel *The War in the Air*, in 1908 : 'The massed aeronautic park that had been established . . . to give Germany . . . the air power and the empire of the world . . .' [1] The second appeared a year later in F. T. Jane's *All the World's Airships*, 'Air power can hardly be more than one of many factors in deciding the issue of future wars.' [2] It was a coincidence that the two should define the two extremities of contemporary expectation about the new dimension of warfare beginning to lift off above the surface of the earth. A revolutionary force to change the nature of conflict and lay the foundation for world domination? Or simply another technological innovation to take its place alongside new artillery and the new guns for Royal Navy dreadnoughts?

At the end of air power's first 100 years, the debate about its contribution to warfare and hence to international security continued, often in terms which would have been recognisable to Wells and Jane. During the intervening period there was often some disagreement about what 'air power' actually meant. At the opening of the RAF Staff College in 1922 Air Vice Marshal Salmond hoped that officers attending would produce 'new and brilliant ideas for the development of the Air and its power'. [3] It was left to the sub-editor of the report on the occasion to introduce subsequently a side heading 'Air Power', when the speaker was inviting his audience of Staff College students to consider 'whether it is possible for fleets and armies to work, if the command of the air is not assured first, in the same way as it has hitherto been accepted that armies cannot move across the sea unless we have command of the sea. I do not want you to prejudge this

1

question; it must really be carefully studied and investigated.' In the following paragraph Salmond went on to express sentiments which were to
haunt his successors for the next 80 years: 'I now come to another matter
to which it is necessary for you to apply yourselves : the Air as an auxiliary
to the Army and Navy . . . what might be called a subsidiary role . . .'

Winston Churchill observed that 'Air power is the most difficult of all
forms of military force to measure, or even to express in precise terms.'[4] In
its infancy it referred to the military exploitation of the air by soldiers for
soldiers and by sailors for sailors. By the end of air power's first century
there was much greater consensus. The Royal Air Force accepted as a definition 'the ability to use platforms operating in or passing through the air
for military purposes. The means of exercising air power are many and
include any system which can be used to wage warfare in the air : for
example manned and unmanned aircraft (fixed and rotary wing), guided
missiles, balloons and space vehicles.'[5]

Another definition in the 1990s from a small but influential centre for air
power studies was similar but a little wider and more representative of the
evolution of thinking about the subject: 'Air power (which should be
thought of as the sum total of a nation's aviation and related capabilities)
is an extension of the war to the third dimension. Yet the air is used, not
merely as a medium that is traversed by a bullet or other projectile, but as
a medium for manoeuvre, concealment and surprise. So developing the
Mason-Armitage definition,[6] air power represents the ability to project
military force in the third dimension, which includes the environment of
space, by or from a platform above the surface of the earth.'[7]

Since its earliest application air power has been influenced by the
medium below it: umbilically related to all those supporting components
which remain on the surface while the actual 'exploiters' range freely above
them; and continuously harried by surface-to-air defences (SAD). With
the advent of the satellite, air-dependent vehicles have also drawn increasing support from the medium above them: space. Meanwhile
surface-to-surface ballistic missiles have come to traverse both medium
and upper levels and with terminally-guided warheads have become
hybrids. In air power's second century they are likely to impinge more
extensively on the activities of the air-dependent systems. This present
study, however, will concentrate on air power and its interaction with the
surface, minimising examination of both space and ballistic missiles. On
the other hand, it will not emulate the division expressed by Air Vice
Marshal Salmond in 1922. Air power is the specialist responsibility of air
forces, but it has been exploited professionally and successfully on many
occasions by others. But in 1922 it would have been difficult to find many
advocates or exponents who could have agreed with that sentiment.

A Birthday

Examination of the early days of air power has on occasions been misleading. With a few exceptions, of which perhaps the most notable is Robin Higham's *Concise History*,[8] studies of early ideas, experiments in and evolution of air power have concentrated on innovation, technology and controversy rather to the exclusion of the contemporary environment which so strongly influenced all three. Consequently, that early environment has much more in common with events at the close of the first century of air power than may be obvious at first glance. Until the later stages of World War I, air power was a peripheral issue; a topic for a minority of enthusiasts, a marginal figure in defence expenditure and, with occasional dramatic exceptions, not usually the subject of headlines in the world's press.

The arbitrary birthday chosen for the first century of air power is 1893. It could have been 1803, with the creation of a French company of airship balloons; or it could have been 1883, when Albert Robida envisaged a sudden crushing airstrike in his *War in the Twentieth Century*, or it could have been 1903, with the Wright brothers at Kitty Hawk. In 1893 Major J. D. Fullerton of the British Army presented a paper to a meeting of army engineers in Chicago in which he prophesied that the impact of aeronautics foreshadowed 'as great a revolution in the art of war as the discovery of gunpowder', that 'future wars may well start with a great air battle', that 'the arrival over the enemy capital will probably conclude the campaign' and that 'command of the air would be an essential prerequisite for all land and air warfare.'[9]

Fullerton was a senior officer in the Royal Engineers among whom the British Army's first air battalion was formed in February 1911. The Air Battalion evolved into the military wing of the Royal Flying Corps in 1912. In 1918 the Royal Flying Corps was amalgamated with the Royal Naval Air Service to form the Royal Air Force : the first force created for exploitation of air power independent of surface forces. There was a direct link between the advocacy of Fullerton and the advent of organised air power.

International Paternity

There is, however, no record that Fullerton's speech was ever translated into French, Italian, German, or Russian. Too often the coincidence of an idea about air power expressed at one time and applied in another has been elevated to cause and effect. The decades either side of 1900 were marked by the rapid evolution and application of the gasoline internal-combustion engine and many individuals in several countries identified its potential for powered flight. In 1898 the US War Department allocated $50,000 to Samuel P. Langley to produce a flying machine.[10] Between 1892 and 1894

the French War Ministry subsidised the inventor Clement Alder with
550,000 francs to develop a machine capable of carrying passengers or
explosives at 55 km per hour.[11] Both projects were beyond the technical
frontiers of the day.

In 1900 the first powered eponymous airship built by Count Ferdinand
Von Zeppelin flew, albeit for only 18 minutes rather than the 'week' forecast by its inventor several years previously. In Moscow, Nikolai
Zhukovskii built a wind tunnel in 1902 and established the base for Russian
aerodynamic evolution. In Italy in 1900 an army captain named Douhet
was lecturing and writing on military mechanisation and would soon turn
his attention to aeronautics. Before 1903 the Wright brothers had been
kept abreast of international aeronautical advances by Octave Chanute's
Progress in Flying Machines and the three consecutive volumes of James
Means' *Aeronautical Annual*, 1895–97.[12] In 1899 at an international conference at The Hague, the European nations were willing to accept a US
proposal to impose a five-year prohibition against 'the discharge of projectiles or explosives from balloons or by other means of a similar nature',
although the idealism of the agreement was somewhat tempered by a general recognition that the balloons of the day could not do a great deal of
damage.[13]

By the time of the next Hague conference in 1907, however, air power
potential had come to constrain international idealism to a much greater
extent: no powers other than the USA and the UK were willing to extend
the moratorium. The division accurately reflected the growing differences
between Britain and the USA on the one hand, and France and Germany
on the other. French engineers began to establish international pre-eminence in aircraft engines and airframes, securing support in 1905 from
General Joffre. In 1908 Henri Farman took off under his aircraft's own
power, and subsequently flew for 30 km, thereby demonstrating the invention's military potential for reconnaissance.

In that same year the British War Office issued specifications for an aircraft capable of leaving the ground under its own power; British
experiments began with radio communication from airships and Russia
considered buying Wright biplanes. Demonstrations by the Wright brothers in several European countries promoted swift commercial 'adaptation'
of their invention, regardless of the risk of law suits. Meanwhile in
Germany, Zeppelin L24 flew for 240 miles in a flight of 12 hours. Even
though it was subsequently destroyed while on the ground, it stimulated
strong German national support, with both Ludendorff and Von Moltke
encouraging military funding for the airship programme.

Among H.G. Wells's fantasies in his novel *War in the Air* was a very
accurate observation on the inexhaustible military potential of the third

dimension of the skies: 'In the air are no streets, no channels, no point where one can say of an antagonist "If he wants to reach my capital he must come by here". In the air all directions lead everywhere.'[14] After 90 years there is no better definition of air power's potential ubiquity. That potential was now attracting enthusiasm from advocates in several countries. It is easy to forget in the aftermath of the bloody stalemates of World War I, that the preceding period was marked by extended military reforms in Britain and the USA and by a considerable amount of thinking about modern warfare: Repington and Wilkinson in England; Du Picq, Foche and Grandmaison in France; Schlieffen, Von der Goltz and Ludendorff in Germany; Mahan, Tirpitz and Mackinder internationally on seapower. Collectively they produced a body of strategic thought unprecedented in military history. It was no coincidence that the earliest and most permanent air power concept, 'command of the air' had an obvious association with Mahan's 'command of the sea'.

Similarly, there was no monopoly of thinking about the military exploitation of the skies and, as the threat of war in Europe began to take on progressively more substance, so each country kept a close watch on aerial developments and ideas, among potential friend and foe alike. From early 1909, the British military attaché in Berlin began to send a series of reports back to London on German aeronautical developments which were incorporated into annual surveys of military aviation by the War Office. In 1910 the Committee for Imperial Defence was informed that the German government had been experimenting with attacks on airships and attacks by airships dropping bombs, 'with a view to acquiring sufficient precision to enable these bombs to be dropped down the funnels of warships . . .' The Committee recommended 'that the Navy and Military Intelligence Services should take special measures to watch foreign trials, and collect and classify all available information on the subject of aerial navigation, utilising the Secret Service Bureau as may be necessary.'[15]

Meanwhile, military journals in the UK kept a more public eye on aeronautical matters. From them three quite distinct responses to the advent of air power may be identified. First there were those who recognised the technical limitations of contemporary aircraft and airships and failed, for various reasons, to anticipate much improvement. Second were the larger number who saw the potential of air power as an expansion of the two existing military environments on land and at sea. Third were the much smaller and very varied enthusiasts represented by H. G. Wells and visionaries such as Major Fullerton and, in the USA, Major Squier.

Subsequent events have made those who disparaged air power's potential look rather foolish. The Chief of the General Staff, Sir William Nicholson, was associated with a War Office communiqué to the Press in July 1908:

'In the highest military circles in Great Britain it is accepted that so far airships are a failure. The military authorities have had experts employed in watching the flights of the various airships and aeroplanes and the impression is that for a long time to come there is nothing to be feared from them . . .' [16] At the time, this seemed to many to be a more realistic appreciation than that of Wells who referred to German bombers the size of 'mammoth liners'.

In the same year, a Captain Neumann, instructor in the 1st German Airship Battalion, wrote an article in the *Marine-rundschau* which was translated and printed in the *Journal of the Royal United Services Institution* (RUSI). It qualifies as a permanent text for the air power enthusiast:

> The present great interest universally taken in the navigation of the air can only be advantageous for further military development in this direction, provided it does not lead to excessively optimistic expectations, fantastic conclusions and impossible schemes, as now happens occasionally with regard to motor airships. The most ambitious conclusions are at times drawn concerning the future performances and the possibility of making use of motor airships . Their development has however only just successfully commenced. As regards their utilisation in the army and navy, there is a certain danger in the readiness with which too favourable and therefore false suppositions can be made, these being followed by disappointment as a result of which development may easily be undeservedly hampered.[17]

If there is one recurring theme in air power's first century it is the publicity given to the 'promise' of air power technology; not necessarily in the manner of Wells's forecasts, nor even as extreme as the expectations of strategic bombardment between the wars, but to definitions of the potential of new weapons and new aircraft. As a result, as Captain Neumann accurately forecast, air power has frequently been evaluated against its promises rather than on its actual achievements.

A little later, in 1911 a British practitioner, Major C.J. Burke, of the one-month old Air Battalion of the Royal Engineers, wrote an article on 'Aeroplanes of today and their use in war' for the *RUSI Journal*. His view represented that of those soldiers and sailors who had been quick to grasp the potential of air power for their own dimensions of warfare. First, he accurately analysed the inevitable relationship between aerial reconnaissance and combat:

> It cannot be too strongly insisted upon that the great, indeed almost

the only value of the aeroplane for military purposes lies in the amount of good and reliable information it brings back. It is possible that it will be a long time from now before aeroplanes will be utilised as a means of transport for troops, *matériel* or supplies. At present we have the aeroplane as a part of the eyes and ears of the army, as a possible means of transport for staff officers and as a weapon of offence and defence against its own kind.[18]

Therefore, he went on to argue,

As aeroplanes employed on such reconnaissance duties will encounter hostile aeroplanes with a similar mission to themselves, they must be prepared for attack and defence, or in other words, their means of destruction and defence against their own kind must receive consideration from the outset. This must not be taken to mean that fleet actions between aeroplanes are to be expected in the immediate future, but simply that one must be prepared for a struggle between the independent cavalry of two hostile armies.[19]

After considering practical problems of personnel, organisation, training and equipment, Captain Burke extended his reflections more widely, perhaps stimulated by his own previous experience on the ground in the Transvaal and with the West African Frontier Forces. 'Has the aeroplane any particular importance with the British Empire? The writer thinks it has. We have only a small army and nothing must be neglected to make it as efficient as possible. We have not the expertise and strain of conscription and consequently should be able to afford greater expenses in *matériel*, and to give greater facilities to those who take up the duty of defending the Empire. May not the command of the air be as important to us in the future as the command of the sea at the present moment?'[20]

Captain Burke did not live to see his forecast come true in British skies in 1940. He survived two flying accidents before the outbreak of war, then commanded No.2 RFC Squadron in France, was mentioned in Despatches twice, awarded the DSO in 1915, invalided to the UK in 1916 to command the Central Flying School but then went back to France to command a battalion of the East Lancashire Regiment. He was killed in action on the ground in April 1917 at the age of 35. He was an early example of that most valuable genre: the man who brings to the profession of arms both mental strength and military distinction.

A German contemporary of Captain Burke, Major Lieth-Thomson wrote in similar fashion, anticipating the rapid development of the airplane to exceed that of the airship and forecasting that aerial reconnaissance would lead to aerial combat, just as cavalry reconnaissance had led to clashes on the ground.[21] Lieth-Thomson, however, survived to become a chief of German army field aviation and a powerful influence until his retirement in 1919. Meanwhile, in France, in his study *L'Aviation Aux Armees et Aux Colonies*, General Frey posed the question, 'May not the command of the air be of such importance that the power who loses it may be forced to sue for peace?'[22]

These advocates however stopped well short of the 'strategic impact' enthusiasts who envisioned the arrival of aerial battle fleets which reached over armies and masses to strike a government and its heartland direct. As early as 1891 the inventor Hiram Maxim suggested that the first purpose of the flying machine would be as an engine of war, that the destruction by aerial bombardment of primary targets such as bridges, arsenals, factories, railways and utilities could 'paralyse the enemy in a few hours.[23] Almost 20 years later, the then Sir Hiram Maxim was asked by Lord Esher at a secret meeting in London whether he had ever built an aeroplane. 'Oh yes,' he replied, 'I built one in 1894. And all the modern airplanes follow the principles I laid down then.' 'Do you know about airplanes in general?' then asked Lord Esher, prompting the response, 'Oh yes, I know everything on this planet about aeroplanes.' Not surprisingly, Maxim passed into aviation history as 'a pompous old ass' rather than the father of strategic bombardment.[24] The fact that he expressed the idea had no practical consequence.

Nonetheless, Maxim's imagination was widely shared by popular writers before H.G. Wells. They included Jules Verne, Collingwood, Moffatt and Kipling, as well as the authors of several popular boys' papers. 'Such fictions did not exist in a vacuum but both reflected and reinforced popular thinking and had considerable effect on readers, creating an awareness of the importance of the conquest of the air and its future potential.'[25] The general British public tended to make little distinction between the arrival of one Frenchman and the 'imminent threat' of hordes of Germans. In the House of Commons on 2 August 1909, a few days after Bleriot's success, Mr Arthur Lee criticised the government in the first Parliamentary debate on aeronautics: '. . . Frenchmen are landing like migratory birds on our shores . . . I suppose the right hon. Gentleman [R.B. Haldane, Minister for War] would not deny that the moral effect of these [German] airships may be very serious indeed . . . Their power of appearing over such places as the capital of a country, centres of mobilisation, bases of operations . . . at the very commencement of hostilities – indeed, almost before war is declared – at a time when these places are considered to be secure against attack, and dropping explosives and bombs quite at random, must have a very demoralising effect . . . This applies particularly to the possibilities of their use at night.'[26]

It was an historic debate; but 'there was not a large attendance'. [27] When the naval estimates were to be examined, however, or any aspect of comparative seapower, the House would be full. To Britain, the arms race was a naval arms race, to produce more new heavily armed 'dreadnoughts' than Germany, to maintain a two to one ratio despite the expansion of the German Navy led by Tirpitz. Yet the Liberal government of Asquith had been elected on a programme of 'peace, retrenchment and reform', and 'flying machines', no less than artillery or dreadnoughts, had to be justified to a party largely composed of men whose first commitment remained to liberal ideas of social reform and welfare spending. In this context it is not surprising to find even the aircraft-minded Churchill making arrangements as late as December 1913 for the 'compression of the Air Service Vote.'[28] This was the first occasion when British preparation for air warfare was constrained by resource limitation; it would not be the last.

Forecasts of what was to become known as 'strategic bombardment' were not, however, restricted to an excitable general public or to conservative MPs pursuing a convenient congruence of personal concern and political opportunity. Across in the USA, the young Lt. Foulois predicted in 1907 in a student thesis that large fleets in the air would operate well in advance of ground troops and that these opposing air fleets would be the first military forces to engage at the outbreak of war.[29] Two years later, *Flight* reprinted an article by US Major George Squier, later to become commander of the Aeronautical Section of the US Signal Corps, forecasting that in future aerial wars early attack on an enemy's government would induce chaos and weaken his ability to wage war.[30]

In a Belgian aeronautical journal in 1911, Lt. Poutrin suggested that the aerial bombardment of urban centres could disorganise a nation's life and weaken its morale.[31] A German naval officer was reported to have given a lecture at Kiel in 1912 in which he had explained that airships could carry the violence of war to England in a way that no other weapon could. Bombs dropped from airships on targets in England, he suggested, would force the English 'to speak with us on quite different terms.'[32] The audience's response was reported to have been 'enthusiastic'.

Meanwhile, in Italy, the man whose name was to become, with scant justification, synonymous with air power, was also commenting on the infant newcomer to warfare. In an article is 1910 on 'The possibilities of aerial navigation' Guilio Douhet stressed reconnaissance and tactical aspects 'but stopped far short of calling for an independent air arm, or even emphasising the role of strategic bombing.'[33] His articles were not considered significant enough for translation or comment by any of the four regular London monitors of international military aviation: the *RUSI Journal*, *Flight*, *Aeroplane* and *Aeronautical Journal*. Indeed it really

would have been difficult for anyone expressing concern before World
War I about strategic air attack, as opposed to air attack on specific military targets, to avoid being regarded at best as a very far-sighted
visionary.

In February 1911 a realistic appraisal of 'The use of explosives in aerial
warfare' was given to the RUSI in an address by Walter Reid, President of
the Society of Chemical Industry. Ten days later *Flight* magazine highlighted some of his observations.[34] There was no doubt but that in the next
war explosives would be dropped from aeroplanes, and, unless steps were
taken to meet the danger, serious consequences might be anticipated. But
'unless some great change was made in the construction of aerial craft . . .
they would be unable to carry charges of explosives which would do more
than local damage.' He estimated that dirigibles of 500,000 cubic feet
capacity could carry 2–300 lb provided that the bombs were suspended as
near as possible to its centre of gravity. 'He deprecated the hysterical views
as to dirigibles laying towns in waste and playing havoc with the civilised
organisation. He thought that once and for all these views should be
expelled from the public mind.'

Later that year air warfare passed from theory into practice and a habit
was established. The impact of aircraft was analysed not just in terms of
Tripoli in 1911–12, but for its future implications. The two would not
always be separated. Nonetheless, in the Italian-Turkish war a number of
features appeared which did recur in various forms during the following 80
years. For example: the brevity of the official communiqué compared to the
richness of eye witness accounts. On 11 November 1911, *Flight*, with a
touch of self-importance, announced: 'The first *official* [original italics]
communication by one of the belligerents, in regard to the use of aeroplanes in actual warfare, has been issued by the Italian authorities, dated
November 5th from Tripoli. As a matter of historical record, we reproduce
the text in extension as follows:

> Yesterday, Captains Moizo, Piazza and De Rada carried out an aero-
> plane reconnaissance, De Rada successfully trying a new Farman
> military biplane. Moizo, after having located the position of the
> enemy's battery, flew over Ain Zara and dropped two bombs into the
> Arab encampment. He found that the enemy were much diminished
> in numbers since he saw them last time. Piazza dropped two bombs
> on the enemy with effect. The object of the reconnaissance was to dis-
> cover the headquarters of the Arabs and Turkish troops which is at
> Sok-el Djama.[35]

The war between Turkey and Italy in Tripoli and Cyrenaica lasted from

1911 to 1916, but the historic contribution to it of aircraft occurred between 21 October 1911 and 25 August 1912. Tripoli was occupied by Italian troops on 5 October, and by 21 October nine aircraft, five 'top-line' pilots, six reserve pilots, and one sergeant and 29 groundcrew had deployed. Reconnaissance flights to establish the location, direction and number of Turkish troops were flown from 23 October. On 25 October one aircraft was hit by ground fire. On 28 October a pilot noted inaccurate artillery fire and subsequently gave corrective directions. On 1 November another pilot dropped bombs on the ground forces. On 15 December an aircraft was hit by anti-aircraft artillery shrapnel. The pilot then swooped low over the gun battery, as if to congratulate the gun crew, and dropped some of his visiting cards as he flew by. This precedent was unlikely to be followed in subsequent conflicts. In December and January flights were halted by bad weather, while the combination of weather, intensive flying and occasional non-fatal accidents began to impose strain on both pilots and aircraft. On 23 February a camera was carried and one photo plate exposed on each flight. On 2 May a night reconnaissance flight was made, with the pilot having secured an electric torch to his helmet so that he could see his controls and instruments. During the period, propaganda leaflets were dropped, aimed at both civilian and armed forces. And finally, on 25 August, air warfare claimed its first fatal casualty, when Cavalry Second Lieutenant Piero Manzini failed to recover from a sideslip soon after take off.[36] All in all, it was a comprehensive initiation into air warfare, except for the absence of airborne opposition.

Two contemporary reports add both colour and perspective to what by any measure was a historic sequence of events. *Flight* received 'some interesting details' from a Mr Quinto Poggioli, who had recently taken his pilot's certificate in England under the Royal Aero Club's regulations and who therefore could be regarded as a trustworthy correspondent: 'On the 25th Oct, Capt. Piazza with his Bleriot, and Capt. Moizo on [*sic*] his Nieuport, observed three advancing columns of Turks and Arabs of about 6,000 men. The Italians, after receiving this information, could successfully calculate distances and arrange for their defence. On the following day, the 26th Oct, the battle of Sciara-Sciat took place, resulting in the loss to the Turkish army of 3,000 men. During the battle, two aeroplanes, Lieut. Gavotti with his Etrich and Capt. Piazza were circling the air. The flights took place above the line of fire, so as to be able to direct the firing of the big guns from the battleship *Carlo Alberton* and also of the mountain artillery. The aeroplanes were often shot at by the guns of the enemy, but with no result. The only difficulty they had was caused by the currents of air from the firing of the big guns. Previously, on 22 October, Capt. Moizo when reconnoitring passed over an oasis and, in order to observe better the movements of the enemy, descended to an altitude of about 200 metres and in consequence the wings of his aircraft were pierced by bullets in six or seven places and also a rib was broken. On November 1st, Lieut. Gavotti (Etrich) flew over the enemy carrying four bombs, carried in a leather bag; the detonator he had in his pocket. When above the Turkish camp, he took a bomb on his knees, prepared it and let it drop. He could observe the disastrous results. He returned and circled over the camp, until he had thrown the remaining three bombs. The length of his flight was altogether about 100 kms.'[37]

Later, as would so often happen in the future, the battle damage report of the most gallant pilots would not be corroborated. Another correspondent described the valuable work done by the aeroplanes attached to General Caneva's army, but observed that as a bomb-dropping device the aeroplane was not successful, nor, in view of the actualities of warfare and what was known about the aeroplane today and tomorrow, was there any surprise in such a lesson. On the other hand, as a gatherer of information it earned the highest praise and on many occasions was indispensable to Italian success.[38]

There was no single concept of air power before 1914. No individual and no one nation could claim a monopoly of vision, or indeed a monopoly of myopia. In several countries there were soldiers, sailors and civilians who lacked the imagination to see beyond the existing limitations of powered flight. There was another minority, largely comprising civilians with no responsibility, but including young soldiers and sailors whose imagination and excitement outran their professional understanding, who foresaw the transformation of war itself. And then there was the majority of intelligent and responsible soldiers, sailors and politicians who identified the continuity, and the extension of continuity in military aviation for their own environments. They were responsible for allocating resource priorities, for recruiting pilots and, with more difficulty, groundcrew who could maintain and repair internal-combustion engines. No matter how far resources were expanded with the lengthening shadows of war, allocation to an unproven, flimsy, restricted and peripheral weapon system could not sensibly be given priority.

As the nations of Europe began to prepare for war, there was little reason for any of them to divert large funds to the infant air forces. Battleships, artillery, lorries, machine guns and, increasingly, submarines dominated defence budgets which therefore were already subject to keen interservice and inter-arms competition. In addition, the three leading European democratic governments had to face opposition to defence expenditure from within their own parties and political exploitation of defence arguments from their opponents. In Britain, the strategic environment was even more complex because the Royal Navy and the British Army were preparing to fight two quite different kinds of war. Indeed, much of the subsequent disagreement over the most effective structure to manage the new form of warfare had its roots not so much in opposition to an independent air force, but in naval disinclination to see air power controlled by the Army.

Failure to Unify

The subsequent evolution of air power in several countries has been strongly influenced by the relationship between the older services and the newcomer. In Britain, the relationship became inextricable from the nature of air power itself. In the USA, the pattern was repeated. With hindsight, the struggles and rancour which marked the relationships had a debilitating effect and impeded the evolution of air power in several countries throughout the first century. It may therefore be salutary to recall that it was inadequacy in war which prompted the creation of an independent air force in Britain in 1918.

C.G. Grey, the outspoken editor of *The Aeroplane* was a consistent critic of government military aviation policy and strongly supported the development of a British aeronautical industry. His encouragement of moves towards a third service originated from frustration at what he perceived as War Office ineptitude and inflexibility over the details of the Air Battalion of the Royal Engineers in April 1911. 'In fact', he observed later in the year, 'there seems to be a deliberate attempt somewhere to retain the Air Battalion as a mere branch of the Royal Engineers instead of helping it to become, as it must some day, a separate service, independent of either the War Office or the Admiralty.'[39]

Certainly, the insistence by the government at the time that any officer who wished to become an Army aviator would have to pay his own flying school expenses, subsequently gaining a refund of £75, did not indicate total commitment to military aviation, especially when compared with government attitudes in other countries.[40] The British School of Aviation at Hendon did offer tuition for £75, 'including all expenses, Third Party insurance and all breakages if any.' And, 'If the pupil obtains his pilot certificate without breakages, a sum of £10 is returned to him.'[41]

A practical penalty of retaining the Air Battalion in its Royal Engineer environment was the need for everyone to undergo his annual month-long course in musketry and drill, thereby stopping flying completely throughout March 1912. This was not quite what theorists had in mind when they stressed continuity in warfare between the ground and the skies. Inevitably, when finances were tight, flying was not given high priority. *The Aeroplane* continued to fulminate against 'imbecility', 'maladministration' and 'fiasco' associated with the Air Battalion, quite happily quoting when necessary from other publications:

> The poverty is revealed by the fact, published in the *Pall Mall Gazette* last Wednesday that officer pilots have been commanded to restrict their cross country flights to the route between Salisbury and Aldershot, a route with which they are all familiar and which therefore offers them no instruction. The reason for this absurd order is that expenses, even in petrol and oil, must be kept down to the finest point, and that there must be no risk of occasional transport by train because of a breakdown. In short, flying is not encouraged. I am able to supplement the information given during the week and to say that expenses entailed in last year's work have not yet been met and that there is no apparent prospect of the current working expenses of the battalion being defrayed. Needless to say practically no equipment exists for taking the field in an emergency and, instead of the fourteen officers of the paper establishment, there are only seven or eight, of whom only six are pilots . . . they labour under the humiliation of the consciousness that the British Air Battalion is the object of the pity of French and German military aviation.[42]

Even allowing for some obvious close liaison between disgruntled airmen and a sympathetic Society correspondent, this picture of neglect was typical of several accounts percolating through the British press and into Parliament. The expectations in early 1911 from the formation of the Air Battalion had simply not been met. Nor were matters any more advanced in the Navy. One extensive, sympathetic and realistic survey in early 1912 referred to Navy undermanning, the impracticality of diverting highly-trained mariners to an 'untried science', and the lack of preparations for the airplane's employment at sea. Problems of weather, recovery at sea and difficulties of airplane storage were also examined, with the conclusion that a specially-designed ship with a flying deck would be preferable. As in land, the primary role would be reconnaissance, but bombing of coastal towns and the locating of weak points in coastal defences could prove valuable, but nothing could be done until sufficient aircraft and a corps of aviators were established.[43]

Within a few weeks of both those pessimistic analyses, a major step forward was apparently taken by the creation of the Royal Flying Corps, announced in Parliament on 4 March and instituted on 13 May 1912. The Corps was to comprise a Military Wing, a Naval Wing, a Central Flying School, a Reserve and the Royal Aircraft Factory at Farnborough.[44] The scheme was the product of a sub-committee of the Committee of Imperial

Defence, comprising soldiers, sailors and civilians. The revolutionary intention, as explained by Under-Secretary of State for War Colonel Seely, was for a unified flying service: 'There is to be one flying corps embracing soldiers, sailors and civilians, who can fly, and who will undertake the obligation to serve their country in time of war in any part of the world . . . The corps will be one corps and as far as possible all the officers will be paid alike and treated alike, because they will run the same risk and have the advantage of doing the same daring thing. In a purely land war the whole flying corps will be available, and in a purely naval war the whole flying corps will be available for naval war . . .'[45] To supervise the new structure a consultative committee known as 'The Air Committee' was to be established as a permanent sub-committee of the Committee of Imperial Defence.

The opportunity to concentrate resources, manpower and air-mindedness was created, but it proved to be a chimera. In retrospect, the surprise is not that unification failed, but that under the circumstances it was proposed at all. There was no unifying Ministry of Defence and, despite the creation of the Imperial Defence Committee, no unified strategy. In a European war, the Army was preparing to deploy an expeditionary force to the continent while the Navy would support quite separate amphibious landings on the German North Sea coast, in addition to waging traditional blue water naval warfare. The Navy had already accepted an airfield at Eastchurch from the Royal Aero Club and was pursuing its own flying training programme. Even aviation enthusiasts with *The Aeroplane* were sceptical about creating some kind of sailor–airman aeronautical marine because of the very different environments in which they would operate. Proposals for the wholesale allocation of the Corps to either environment raised doubts among laymen and specialists alike.

There were perhaps other considerations. Colonel Seely had announced the names of his committee to Parliament, but not the fact that the proposals had actually been drafted by three air-minded soldiers : Brigadier David Henderson, Captain F.H.Sykes and Major D.S.MacInnes. The Corps HQ was to be on Salisbury Plain: in the heart of Army country; the aircraft factory was to grow from the Army aircraft factory. Small as they both were, the infant Air Battalion outnumbered the handful of naval officers and men at Eastchurch.

Nor did the structure of the new Corps induce closer co-operation. The commandant of the Central Flying School would be the senior officer in the Corps, but there was no direct co-ordinating command of the Military and the Naval Wing. A separate Air Department was established at the Admiralty while the Military Wing passed into the Army's Military Training Directorate under Brigadier Henderson himself. The Air

Committee took no action to encourage closer co-ordination. Of more serious, longer-term consequence was that neither Wing was expressly tasked with UK air defence, despite the specific debate on the proposals on 6 March. In theory, the whole Corps would be allocated the task: but who was to direct it?

From 1912 to the outbreak of war two issues forced the two Wings further apart. The Army wished to procure the bulk of the Corps' aircraft through the Royal Aircraft Factory; the Navy, on the other hand, wished to order direct from commercial manufacturers.[46] The former concentrated on an aircraft for reconnaissance, the latter was interested not just in reconnaissance but torpedo dropping and fleet defence. The disagreements reflected the strategic dichotomy, with the Navy looking at a much wider spectrum of operations, including the protection of naval bases and assets in the United Kingdom itself.

Traditionally, the outer defence of Britain was provided by the Royal Navy. If that 'wooden wall' should be breached, the Army was responsible for repelling invaders. As late as December 1913, Lt.Col.Sykes as head of the Military Wing was specifying its duties, which would, he assumed, 'Eventually . . . include the provision of an Air Service for Home Defence, and for the defence of fortresses and defended ports at home and abroad. At present however its functions are limited by the provision of an air service for the Expeditionary Force, and as long as its horizon is thus confined, it would appear necessary to design its war and peace organisations mainly with the idea of these functions.'[47] In other words, the Military Wing would go to France without providing for UK defence despite having consistently over the previous two years claimed responsibility for it.[48]

Not surprisingly, Winston Churchill, as First Lord of the Admiralty, had become increasingly concerned about the German airship threat to his naval shore based establishments and the lack of War Office provision to counter it. In October 1913 he drafted specifications for aircraft for the Naval Wing which included 'a home-service fighting aeroplane, to repel enemy aircraft when they attack the vulnerable points of our island, and to carry out patrol duties along the coast'.[49] In March 1914, in presenting the Naval Estimates to the House of Commons, he commented on naval and military aviation, and the air defence of Great Britain. He outlined the naval air functions of reconnaissance from land or from ships of both enemy fleets and enemy coasts: attacking enemy invasion fleets and defence of 'nerve centres of naval power' at home which would be provided by anti-aircraft guns, searchlights and aircraft – 'you should be master of your own air'. Unfortunately, Churchill the strategist was inseparable from Churchill the politician and he went on, 'With the Military Wing, with which great progress has been made, we are already in a position of effective strength, and any hostile aircraft, airship or aeroplanes which reached our coast during the coming year would be promptly attacked in superior force by a swarm of very formidable hornets. This is the true military protection of vulnerable points.'[50]

It would not be the last time that a defence minister in the UK offered sizeable hostages to fortune, but none would be lost in such dramatic circumstances as the subsequent German airship and *Gotha* raids on London. Even the gesture towards the Military Wing concealed the extent of the rift which now separated what were virtually two separate air services.

Churchill's original strong support for a unified Corps was progressively eroded by disputes over air service funding, flying training costs at Upavon, late or non-existent delivery of aircraft from Farnborough and rivalry between the two aeronautical departments. In June 1914 the Admiralty unilaterally abrogated the RFC relationship, issuing regulations by which the Naval Wing became a distinct branch of the Royal Navy known as the 'Royal Naval Air Service'. The Admiralty decision merely gave formal recognition to the factual position. In July, Churchill complained to the Prime Minister about the extent of the breakdown of co-operation which extended well beyond aeronautical matters: 'There ought to be a full and free interchange of technical information between the Naval and Military Wings. I have given direction that every facility in our power is to be given to the War Office, and that no secret is to be withheld, it being absurd that Departments of the Government should treat each other like foreign powers. It is obviously wasteful and wrong that the Navy and the Army should develop types and design of aeroplanes in strict isolation, and without pooling their knowledge and communicating regularly with each other . . .'[51]

Under the circumstances it was a strange letter. The Minister had just authorised an action which ignored a previous Cabinet decision and which far from seeking to improve relations, had formally endorsed their severance. The letter's content however clearly identified problems which the onset of war was about to exacerbate.

The First Air War
In August 1914 the mobilised strength of the British air services comprised 276 officers and 1,797 other ranks, of whom 130 officers and 700 ratings were in the RNAS and 146 and 1,097, respectively, in the RFC. The RFC possessed 179 aeroplanes while the RNAS had 39 aeroplanes, 52 seaplanes and seven airships. Only 100 of the total were serviceable. 105 officers, 755 other ranks and 63 aeroplanes were despatched to France with four RFC squadrons, while the RNAS unit which deployed to Belgium comprised 20

officers, 80 other ranks and 10 aircraft. On 11 November 1918 there were 27,333 officers and 263,837 other ranks in the Royal Air Force, with a ratio of slightly less than 20 groundcrew (including officers) for every pilot. Those figures may be compared with a total British armed forces strength in 1918 of five million, and losses during the war of one million killed and two million injured for an overall 'attrition' figure of 35.8 per cent.[52]

The RAF in 1918 was three times the size of the French and the Italian Air Force and 50 per cent larger than the last arrival: the United States Air Service.[53] In 1918 the British aircraft industry delivered 30,671 airplanes and 1,865 seaplanes and flying boats, more than double the output of 1917. Between 1 August and 11 November 1918 the RAF lost 2,692 aircraft from all causes, but received 2,647 from industry to replace them.[54] At the end of the war Britain had the largest air force and aircraft industry in the world. That is the statistical framework of the expansion of air power in four years.

By 1918 all subsequent roles of air power had either been established or attempted. A distinction had emerged between 'strategic' and 'tactical' which was to remain until it was blurred after World War II when 'strategic' bombardment came, in American minds at least, to be exclusively synonymous with air attack on the Soviet Union. In the perspective of a century, 'While the role of the air weapon in the Great War was a modest one, the role of the Great War in the rise of air power was anything but modest.'[55]

In August 1914, individual French and British reconnaissance aircraft were credited with early sighting of the German envelopment leading to the Battle of the Marne. By 1918 intensive reconnaissance of German positions and artillery co-operation was an important element in the British series of victories which finally rolled back the Germans to the Armistice. In the battle of the St Mihiel salient in 1918 the US Air Service despatched 200 bombers and 100 fighters in attacks on German ground forces in one day. At the battle of Piave, Italian aircraft interdicted Austro-Hungarian reinforcements and supplies and broke their communications on either side of the Piave river. Germany repeatedly massed aircraft from overall numerical inferiority to achieve superior concentration of force at critical points, both to support ground offensives and to intercept allied bombing raids. Both sides conducted counter-air operations against airfields, frequently with devastating effect on an opponent's ability to mount air operations in the immediate aftermath of the attack. By 1918 surface movement was increasingly conducted at night to avoid hostile aerial reconnaissance and the achievement of surprise became more difficult, although not impossible. In the first months of the war Russia deployed a squadron of four-engined bombers able to carry half a ton of bombs, two machine guns and a crew of three over 300 miles with an endurance of five hours.

At sea, air power progressed from the first intrepid experiments with deck launchers to the entry into service in 1918 of the 'flat top' aircraft carrier HMS *Argus*. Airplanes and airships joined the hunt for U-boats, escorted convoys and attacked submarine bases at Zeebrugge and Ostend. Before the advent of HMS *Argus*, the cruiser HMS *Furious* was able to launch but not safely recover aircraft from a forward abbreviated flight deck and seven Sopwith *Camels* successfully attacked German airship sheds in July 1918. Germany, Italy and Britain all made a limited number of torpedo attacks. There were however relatively few naval engagements in the War, and the considerable surface fleet superiority enjoyed by the allies reduced the requirements of naval reconnaissance. At the battle of Jutland in 1916 aerial reconnaissance made no contribution to either side. Signal intelligence and submarine reports were much more significant information sources on naval traffic. On the other hand, the British RNAS made a significant contribution to the war in Europe by attacking targets on land or behind the north-western flank of the German forces in Flanders.

From the time of the Wright brothers' achievement and the contemporary developments in Europe, the aeroplane had been identified as primarily a military instrument. By 1918 its technology had taken massive steps forward. Aircraft and engine designs would improve very little over the next 20 years. Three 'wireless officers' had accompanied the RFC to France in 1914. One-way communication from the aircraft to the ground evolved into multi-frequency radio transmission and reception leading to both embryonic ground control of formation attacks and the jamming of channels by the opposition. In 1917 at the battle of Messines, both sides intercepted the other's air-to-ground wireless transmission to locate targets. From the outset cameras were used to supplement wireless reports and after the western front became entrenched, photographic reconnaissance was essential for every kind of activity from artillery fire to large-scale offensive and defensive operations. Perhaps the most distinguished historian of the air war considered that by 1917, 'the aeroplane had now become indispensable to the conduct of war'.[56] Marshal Petain asserted the capital importance of the air arm, in the sense that no power could afford to be without it.[57] And yet if one asks, would the outcome of the war have been any different without air power, the answer must be 'no'. In retrospect, compared with the impact of air power on warfare in the Second World War, and subsequently up to the Gulf War of 1990–91, a more appropriate assessment would be progress from peripheral in 1914, to influential in 1918, but never dominant and never determining the outcome of any theatre of war.

That conclusion prompts closer examination of three issues in the war:

the rationale for a unified air force, the relative merits and penalties of offensive operations and, most controversial and because of subsequent events, of disproportionate significance to air power's evolution, strategic bombardment.

The Unified Air Force

The formal recognition in 1914 of the RNAS's independence from the RFC in Britain acknowledged the reality of different strategies, different procurement priorities, different operational environments and different command structures. As the country went to war, the flying services and especially the RFC paid the penalty for inadequate military aircraft procurement in the preceding years. This was partly the result of dependence on one source: the Royal Aircraft Factory, and partly the product of inadequate funding across the entire war *matériel* field.

The first result was the formal handover of responsibility to the Admiralty for Home Defence on 3 September. Churchill anticipated it two days previously with the first of three minutes to his Director of Air Division ordering the stationing of 'the largest possible force of naval aeroplanes' at Calais and Dunkirk in view of the extreme probability of an attack on London by airships. 'The proper defence is a thorough and continual search of the country for 70 to 100 miles inland 'to attack airship bases and airships themselves preparing for their missions'.[58] On 3 September he directed that aerial searchlights must immediately be procured and anti-aircraft guns increased in number. Then, on 5 September he directed that an Admiralty committee meet later that day to construct a 'programme of action' to establish 'a strong force of aeroplanes to deny the French and Belgian coasts to the enemy's aircraft and to attack all Zeppelins and air bases or temporary air bases which it may be sought to establish . . . to maintain an intercepting force of aeroplanes and airships at some convenient point within range of a line drawn from Dover to London and local defence flights at Eastchurch and Calshot . . . a squadron of aeroplanes at Hendon for the purpose of attacking enemy aircraft which may attempt to molest London ... the Hendon flight should be able to fly at night and their machines must be fitted with the necessary lights and instruments . . . the squadrons should be in telegraphic and telephone communication with other stations.' Churchill completed this third directive with a sentence which would become dreadfully familiar to staffs in two wars: 'I expect to receive no later than tomorrow a definite programme of action within the lines of this minute . . .'

The gap between directive and capability was considerable. Moreover, while the 'offensive counter air' strategy made a lot of sense it demanded land-based aircraft in competition with the expanding requirements of the

RFC. Moreover, as the war evolved, RNAS operations on the continent came to overlap those of the RFC. The RFC was the aviation arm of the Army focused on the western front; the RNAS pursued naval interests on the continental coastal flank and the North Sea. But in London, the concern of the politicians was the increasing vulnerability of the country, and especially the capital, first to Zeppelins and later to bombing aircraft. No airship was actually destroyed over Britain until 1916, although many successful raids were made on their hangars and one or two were shot down over the sea.

During 1915 each service accused the other of interfering with its duties and its sources of supply, especially aircraft engines. Among other abortive attempts to resolve the difficulties, a Joint War Air Committee (JWAC) was established in February 1916, 'To ensure that the manufacture and supply and distribution of *matériel* required by aircraft are in accordance with the policy of aerial warfare laid down by His Majesty's Government, to avoid clashing or overlapping demands upon the manufacturing resources available, while securing the full and harmonious use of the same, and to eliminate correspondence between the Departments upon points which effect more than one.'[59]

The significance of this objective for the JWAC was not in the practical success it was to achieve, but in its definition of the extent of the problem. For example, until the end of 1915 the RFC still procured one-third of its engines from France, in competition with the RNAS: a situation popular with French manufacturers. Between August and November, British contracts for aircraft, engines, parts and accessories from France totalled nearly 12 million francs.[60] Later in the war, when the British aviation industry was responding to demands and, more importantly, when funding for all military aviation had been considerably increased, the detrimental impact of competition was not so marked.

Meanwhile the JWAC had no executive authority and even had it been allocated any, there was no 'policy of aerial warfare' against which to determine priorities between the two services. But, as the leading analyst of the moves towards a unified air force has observed, the Committee did at least induce both services to set out what they saw as their responsibilities, in separate minutes to the Committee on 3 March 1916.[61] The RNAS listed five duties 'best carried out by personnel with naval training': attacking enemy fleets, dockyards, arsenals, factories, etc.; coastal patrols against enemy shipping, submarines, aircraft and mines; observation and contribution to bombardment of enemy coastal facilities; fleet reconnaissance; and assisting the Army whenever and wherever required.

The RFC memorandum allocated first priority to support of the military forces in the field: reconnaissance, artillery, observation, fighting in the air, and attacks on ground targets. Thereafter, however, it identified the issues in dispute by arguing that all air forces working in a theatre of land operations should be entirely under the control of the theatre Army commander, which would include long-range offensive operations 'against military or national objectives'. Naval encroachment in this activity induced wasteful competition and weakened its impact. The Army memorandum concluded that the alternative to the division of responsibilities was 'a joint or independent air service which hardly seems to be within the sphere of practical discussion at the present moment.'

The minute emanated from the department of the Directorate of Military Aeronautics, headed now by Major-General David Henderson. Henderson, with Lt.Col.Sykes was to be an influential figure over the next 18 months as an independent force did become an increasingly important element in the discussions. The competition to discharge the role of strategic bombing was generated in London, and as will be explained below, was strongly opposed by most of the RFC leadership which was deployed across the Channel. This was the first well-documented air power conflict over the interaction of roles, resources and service allocations. It was to be replayed incessantly, internationally to everyone's detriment and was still playing to a packed audience in 1994 in Washington between the USAF and USN, over the identical question: long-range air attack. The major difference was that in 1916 controversy was stimulated by disagreements during a period of expanding resources, while in 1994 they were dwindling.

In 1916 neither service would compromise and after six weeks the JWAC collapsed. It was replaced by an Air Board in May which was still only an advisory body and largely perpetuated the entrenched positions set out in March, without providing any solutions to the problems. Then in December, David Lloyd George replaced Asquith as Prime Minister and the political change was swiftly reflected in a strengthening of the Air Board's authority. Control of aircraft design and supply was allocated to the Ministry of Munitions and the Air Board given authority to mediate between the Army and Navy under a new president, Lord Cowdray.

Certainly there was a need for reform, both between and within the aeronautical services. In December 1916 the Army and Navy had on order 9,483 aircraft of 76 varieties and 20,000 engines of 57 kinds.[62] British industry had produced 5,716 aircraft and 5,363 engines in 1916, importing a further 917 planes and 1964 engines, largely from France. In March 1916, 41 companies formed the Society of British Aircraft Construction (later the Society of British Aerospace Companies) (SBAC) to identify common interests and facilitate wartime expansion. There was, however, a long way still to go before the aviation industry would fully meet the nation's military aviation requirements.[63]

Moreover, the Cowdray Board remained dependent on the War Office and the Admiralty for items such as airfields, armaments and non-technical stores. Its advice was given by soldiers and sailors back to their own services and it had no authority to allocate men or aircraft and none to provide for home defence. As with the earlier committees and the Curzon Board, co-operation was constantly bedevilled by rivalries and jealousies among senior commanders, politicians, industrialists and press lords; so much so that its location, the Hotel Cecil, became known as the 'Hotel Bolo' after a well-known enemy agent who had harmed rather than assisted the allied cause.

Meanwhile, a number of other factors were combining to compel yet another examination of the way the air war was being waged. In February 1917, a squadron of *Gotha* G1V bombers began to form in Flanders. No.3 squadron was tasked with attacks on England designed 'to "provide a basis for peace" by intimidating "the morale of the English people" and crushing their "will to fight". Materially, the raids were to disrupt the British war industry, disorganise the communications between coastal ports and London, attack the supply dumps of the coastal ports, and hinder the transport of war materials across the channel.'[64] The crews reflected at the time that this was quite a responsibility for 30 aircraft, each carrying 660 lb of explosives, but to British civilians and politicians with an eye to publicity and advancement, it was to be taken very seriously.

As has been noted, bombing attacks on Britain had been widely forecast before the war, but the breaching of 900 years of impregnability first by Zeppelins and then by the *Gothas* induced a psychological impact which was dramatised in the press and exploited in politics. It may perhaps be compared with the impact of terrorist bombing in New York in 1993 on a population which had grown accustomed to the idea that attacks on national resources, territory and civilians were something that happened elsewhere but not in the USA.

In June 1915 the MP for Hull wrote to Mr Balfour, First Lord of the Admiralty, after one airship raid, 'Citizens of all classes are in a state of great alarm, the night after the raid a further warning was given and tens of thousands of people trooped out of the city. The screams of the women were distressing to hear. Could you let us have half a dozen aeroplanes?'[65] The impact was probably greater because devastating raids had been expected immediately after the outbreak of war, but none materialised until 9 January 1915. By late 1916, however, air defences had begun to inflict unacceptable losses on the Zeppelins, and more seriously, on their trained crews with the result that operations against Britain were suspended for six months.

On 25 May, after two months of work-up training involving navigation and formation flying, No.3 *Gotha* Squadron made its first attack on England, but thick clouds restricted the raid to targets in Kent. On 13 June, 18 aircraft achieved complete surprise over London. Liverpool Street Station, the main target, the Royal Mint and a school in east London were severely damaged, contributing to 162 deaths and 432 injuries. Ninety-two British aircraft sought to intercept them, but achieved nothing and lost two observers to German gunfire. Historians have subsequently related this attack, and a further successful raid on London on 7 July, with the subsequent establishment of the Smuts Committee. It is therefore interesting to note the contemporary assessments made in Berlin. On 25 June, Bethman Hollweg, the Imperial Chancellor, wrote to Hindenburg: 'We could help peace by avoiding irritating the chauvinistic and fanatical instincts of the English people without cause. There is no doubt that the last air attack on L [*sic*] has had a disastrous effect in this respect. According to reliable reports, the anger of the British public has reached such a pitch that English statesmen who were not averse to making peace, have declared that no English government which was willing to treat with Germany after such an occurrence would be able to withstand the indignation of the nation for a day. As I am unable to believe that such air attacks are absolutely necessary from the military point of view, may I be allowed to suggest that they be given up, in view of their disastrous political effect.'[66]

On 7 July, while the *Gothas* were actually en route again, Hindenburg replied: 'Your Excellency deprecates the air attack upon London. I do not think the English nature is such that anything can be done with them by conciliation or by revealing a desire to spare them. The military advantages are great. They keep a large amount of war material away from the French Front and destroy important enemy establishments of various kinds.'[67] Hindenburg went on to ask Bethman Hollweg for the source and facts on which the Chancellor had formed his judgement but received no reply: Bethman Hollweg had already resigned.

Both comments could be substantiated and foreshadowed similar future disagreements over the impact of strategic bombardment. The initial objectives given to Hauptman Brandenburg for No.3 Squadron were explicit and strategic, including the Admiralty, War Office, Bank of England, General Post Office, the City generally, Woolwich Arsenal and the docks, although he was given complete discretion as to dates, attack size and specific targets. The Squadron was subsequently diverted in March and April to attack targets on the western front in support of the German offensive. In May 1918, after suffering increasingly heavy losses, even at night, from British AA fire and interceptors, the strategic offensive was halted and thereafter the heavy bombers were allocated to army support.

Justifying Hindenburg's argument, British aircraft had been diverted from the western front to the defence of London, much to the delight of their crews, but only temporarily. Haig remained determined to concentrate resources on the western front and Trenchard's response was to call for increased offensive counter-air attacks on the bomber airfields. There was undoubtedly panic in London, and it fed across into reduced output in factories in the area. Workers failed to turn up for night work and the following day shift suffered from the consequent disorganisation. Output from the Woolwich Arsenal was estimated to fall to 20 per cent of normal as a result of a severe night attack.[68]

But Hollweg was also correct: the panic and disruption did not prompt calls for peace, but angry demands for the government to improve defences and retaliate. On 14 June the War Cabinet agreed to call back two squadrons of fighters from France 'for a week or two'. Haig agreed, provided that they were back in France by 5 July. On 2 July a series of War Cabinet meetings concluded with the decisions to double the size of the RFC from 108 to 200 squadrons, increase the size of the RNAS, expand aircraft production accordingly and launch reprisal attacks on Mannheim.[69] If there was a lesson for the future it was that civilian morale could be brittle and production could be disrupted, but the impact of anger and determination on the outcome of the campaign could well be much greater. It was an indicator, if not a lesson, which was to be missed completely by many subsequent air force commanders and air power theorists.

Four days after the *Gotha* raid of 7 July, Lloyd George tasked the South African member of the Imperial War Cabinet, General Smuts, 'To examine the defence arrangements for Home Defence against air raids and the existing general organisation of the study and higher direction of aerial operations.'[70] During the next five weeks Smuts took advice from several sources. General Henderson argued strongly for an end to divided responsibility for aeronautics and the creation of 'a complete united service dealing with all operations in the air, and with all the accessory services that expression implies . . .' He also alluded to a 'considerable force of bombing machines' which could become available in 1918.[71]

Cowdray relayed the optimistic view of the Munitions Ministry that aircraft production would treble by March 1918 and quadruple by June. Cowdray himself advised against the creation of an independent force, arguing that all that was needed was an extension of his Board's powers to co-ordinate air policy. Thereby he illustrated that he still failed to understand the need for a comprehensive restructuring of policy making, procurement and an organisation to implement the whole.

Smuts responded to his mandate with two reports. The first was submitted on 19 July and dealt with provision for home defence, largely reflecting measures and proposals already in hand for a unified command and co-ordinated strengthening of the salient components: fighters, guns, searchlights and observation posts. On 17 August however, the second report became the most important single document in the history of air power.

It reviewed the weaknesses of previous committees and boards, observing that 'Under the present constitution and powers of the Air Board, the real directors of war policy are the Army and Navy, and to the Air Board is really allotted the minor role of fulfilling their requirements according to their ideas of war policy.' The Air Service, he argued, was as subordinated to military and naval control as was artillery, and therefore the Air Board could neither originate nor execute a policy of its own. Thereafter followed the central passage of the Report:

> The time is however rapidly approaching when that subordination of the Air Board and the Air Service can no longer be justified. Essentially the position of an air service is quite different from that of the artillery arm. To pursue our comparison: artillery could never be used in war except as a weapon in military or naval operations. It is a weapon, an instrument ancillary to a service, but could not be an independent service itself. Air Service on the contrary, can be used as an independent means of war operations far from and independently of, both Army and Navy. As far as can presently be foreseen there is absolutely no limit to the scale of its future independent war use. And the day may not be far off when aerial operations with their devastation of enemy lands and destruction of industrial and populous centres on a vast scale may become the principal operations of war to which the older forms of military and naval operation may become secondary and subordinate . . . In our opinion there is no reason why the Air Board should any longer continue in its present form and there is every reason why it should be raised to the status of an independent Ministry in control of its own war service . . .

Smuts went on to recommend the creation of an Air Ministry, an Air Staff of the highest calibre, the amalgamation of the RFC and the RNAS, transfer of personnel by consent, closest liaison with Army and Navy, attachment of Air Service units with command and control by Navy and Army and seconding of Army and Navy officers to Army and Naval contingents of the Air Service. He concluded with a familiar sentiment: that 'air predominance' was important for the winning of the war and 'in the long run, Air Supremacy may become as important a factor in the defence of the Empire as sea supremacy.'[72]

Like all good texts, this also left room for selective interpretation. RFC commanders either ignored it or disagreed with it. The Admiralty accepted it with little demur. First attempts to establish the new system fell apart amid a welter of personal and professional disagreements between press Lords Northcliffe and Rothermere over the position of the Minister, Trenchard as Chief of the Air Staff, Sykes as his replacement and General Henderson as Vice-President of the Air Council. The Royal Air Force came into being on 1 April 1918. On the 13th, Trenchard resigned after failing to establish a working relationship with Air Minister Rothermere. The promised surplus of combat aircraft failed to materialise and the feared German bomber offensive, as has been noted, dwindled away. Meanwhile ex-RFC and RNAS squadrons continued operations largely unaffected by events in London.

Because of the content of his first report, Smuts did not specifically refer to air defence in his second. As a result, his proposal for an independent air force became synonymous with his forecasts of 'independent', strategic bombardment. His practical proposals for close liaison between all three services, including the placing of air force units under Navy and Army control when circumstances warranted it, were submerged below his one sentence reflection about the possibility of 'older' forms of warfare becoming 'secondary and subordinate'. In reaffirming the waste of duplication and the novel character of 'air service', Smuts gave a resounding, permanent justification for the creation of a third service to master the third dimension. Unfortunately, at the same time he offered a text to the air power zealot and a threat to independent seapower and landpower, ensuring that the real cost of independent air power would be recurring internecine war between the three services. Seventy-five years later it was still necessary to argue that air power was a complement to sea and land power; more valuable in some circumstances than others; sometimes dominant, sometimes supporting other activities; sometimes, indeed, capable of independent decision; and that duplication and unnecessary competition for resources and roles were detrimental to the national interest and to the application of air power itself.

Offensive Operations

It is a truism that defensive operations may defer defeat, but will leave the options and initiative with the opponent. To enforce one's own will, to wield a military instrument in international relations, will almost invariably require offensive action. Those Army and Navy officers who disagreed with Smuts's vision of a direct strategic attack on an enemy's heartland were nonetheless imbued with the spirit of the offensive. Indeed, perhaps the greatest irony of the trench war stalemate was that it was the product of generals schooled in the principles of offensive action. Without exception they continued to look to the offense to secure victory, either by smashing through the defences on the western front, or by outflanking them via the Dardanelles and Salonika, or by novel technology under the water or in the skies.

Trenchard was a soldier of that generation. Neither he nor any other general or admiral in any country had any training or preparation for air warfare. In 1914 everyone went to war. There were no pilots to spare to set up air warfare courses, even if there had been anything to study. Learning about tactics, concentration of force, logistics, airfield construction, maintenance, staff and command structures: all had to be by experience and trial and error in warfare of unprecedented scale, mechanisation and complexity. Trenchard, and the RFC, have been widely criticised for sustaining an unrelenting offensive despite heavy casualties, in similar fashion to his superior General Haig on the ground. The topic is especially pertinent in a later age when the concept of 'optional' warfare has sharpened public sensitivity to casualties to an extent far removed from that of 1914–18.

The RFC, as has been noted, served almost exclusively as the aviation arm of the ground forces, as did every other major army air service. Bearing in mind however that the contribution of air power to the armies largely comprised reconnaissance and only much later direct, larger scale offensive air support, the allocation of effort within the British air services in August 1918 was unique: 55 per cent to pursuit, which included ground attack by then, 22 per cent to bombardment, which included attacks in support of ground forces and offensive counter air, and only 23 per cent to observation.' Germany and France on the other hand both allocated approximately 50 per cent of their strength to observation and 8 and 15 per cent respectively to bombardment.[73]

Trenchard explained his rationale in 1916 in a memorandum to his Commander in Chief:

> It is sometimes argued that our aeroplanes should be able to prevent hostile aeroplanes from crossing the line, and this idea leads to a demand for defensive measures and a defensive policy. Now is the time to consider whether such a policy would be possible, desirable and successful.
>
> It is the deliberate opinion of all those most competent to judge, that this is not the case, and that an aeroplane is an offensive and not a defensive weapon. Owing to the unlimited space in the air, the difficulty one machine has in seeing another, the accidents of wind and cloud, it is impossible for aeroplanes, however skilful and vigilant their pilots, however numerous their formations, to prevent hostile

aircraft from crossing the line if they have the initiative and determination to do so . . .

From the accounts of prisoners, we gather that the enemy's aeroplanes received orders not to cross the lines over the French or British
front unless the day is cloudy and a surprise attack can be made, presumably in order to avoid unnecessary casualties. On the other hand,
British aviation has been guided by a policy of relentless and incessant
offensive. Our machines have continually attacked the enemy on his
side of the line, bombed his aerodromes, besides carrying out attacks
on places of importance far behind the lines. It would seem probable
that this has had the effect so far on the enemy of compelling him to
keep back or to detail portions of his forces in the air for defensive
purposes . . . The sound policy, then, which should guide all warfare
in the air would seem to be this: to exploit the moral effect of the aeroplane on the enemy, but not let him exploit it on ourselves. Now this
can only be done by attacking and by continuing to attack.[74]

By 1918 there was a general agreement among commanders on both
sides that the most effective way of destroying enemy aircraft in numbers
was by offensive counter-air attacks on airfields. Moreover, the attrition
rates of the RFC should be placed in the context of the time. For example,
in July 1916, 210 aircraft were lost, 97 of them from enemy action. One
hundred and eleven aircrew were lost in four weeks. No.70 squadron during nine weeks in the autumn lost 27 of 36 original aircrew and 20
replacements. Emotively, their ages were recorded as 17 to 22.[75] Trenchard,
at his Army headquarters, would have been aware that the British Army
had suffered 57,470 casualties on the Somme on 1 July alone, of whom
19,240 had been killed. Many of those also would have been too young to
vote. He would have expected little sympathy for an RFC casualty rate
measured in tens, rather than thousands.

Late in the war losses among the 'Corps' aircraft, i.e., those discharging
reconnaissance and observation tasks either over or close to the lines
diminished considerably as the RFC/RAF fighters began to dominate a
numerically-inferior opponent. One statistic however was to recur with
depressing regularity. Nearly 50 per cent of RFC losses on the western
front in 1918 were not due to combat. Added to the fragmentary evidence
of losses during training, the figures suggest a roughly even division of
casualties during the war between combat and non-combat causes.[76] But
two criticisms must be levelled against Trenchard: the first in that his
acceptance of high attrition rates frequently outran the ability of the training organisations to replace them, and second that, unlike the Germans, he
does not seem to have appreciated the importance of concentration of

force. On several occasions a numerically-inferior German air force concentrated sufficient aircraft in space and time to achieve local air
superiority. Ironically, Trenchard frequently read combat reports which
clearly explained what the German were doing and achieving. The RFC
had discovered the inherent paradox of offensive air power. Attacks on
enemy targets, either tactical or strategic, will undoubtedly force him to
divert more resources to air defence. But the more successful the policy in
forcing the enemy on to the defensive, the more difficult and costly it
becomes to inflict proportional damage on the original targets.

Two further observations on air combat are pertinent. Dominance in the
air by one side or the other usually accompanied technological superiority.
Victory by numerical superiority was occasionally achieved when over-val-
orous fighter pilots sought engagements in which they were heavily
outnumbered; but with superior aircraft that was at least their own choice.
Awareness or perception by either side that the opponent was better
equipped led to poor morale and reduced effectiveness. That would
become a recurring and unwelcome feature in air power, where man and
machine were inextricable.

Closely associated with technological superiority was the art of the
fighter pilot. Legend surrounded the 'knights of the skies', like George
Guynemer who shot down 28 aircraft in 1917 and who broke off a duel
with Ernst Udet when he saw that his opponent's gun had jammed. Udet
went on to shoot down 52 more allied aircraft and survived the war.
Guynemer disappeared over the battlefield in Flanders in October 1917.
The reality and requirements for aerial combat were spelled out for future
generations by Oswald Boelcke in 1916: seek the advantage before attacking, attack from the rear if possible with the sun at one's back, follow the
attack through, keep the opponent in sight and fire only at close range.[77]
Chivalry in combat, in the air as on the ground, is the prerogative of the
victor. It may follow, but never precede, an ambush.

The calculation of the interaction of attrition and residual combat effectiveness against the desired outcome of operations calls for a very clear
understanding of objectives and careful monitoring of effort. RFC losses
were meticulously recorded, but there seems to be no evidence of the other
calculations. When casualties outran replacements, activities simply
reduced or ceased altogether. No modern air force could fight a war in that
way; at least, not for long.

Strategic Bombardment

The most controversial feature of RAF development between the wars and
in operations in World War II was the precedence given to strategic bombing. Yet not only was there little evidence to give it sound foundations in

World War I, there was little support for it among senior commanders, including Trenchard. In seeking to extract the hero from mythology some historians have criticised Trenchard either for unthinking acceptance of the efficacy of strategic bombing in the later stages of the war, or of hypocrisy, or of moving politically with a changing tide. In fact not only his integrity, but his professional contemporary judgement can be fully substantiated.

The RNAS had conducted long-range attacks on airship sheds and subsequently against industrial targets in Alsace, Lorraine and the Rhineland. They were curtailed during the winter of 1916–17 by bad weather and the diversion of effort to assist the RFC. Nonetheless, increasing German opposition had led to plans for long-range escort fighters and modified fighter bombers.[78] Experiments were carried out with bomb sights, ballistic trajectories and long-range aerial navigation. By November 1917 industrial targets in Germany were being examined for their significance to the German war effort and their relative vulnerability. Bombload requirements were assessed and the need for concentrated and repeated attacks identified.[79] At that time, as a result of the promises from the Munitions Ministry, a strategic bombing force of 2,000 aircraft was expected, each capable of delivering almost 1,000 lb in 1918.

In anticipation, and in response to sustained German bombing during the autumn of 1917, on 15 October the War Cabinet directed that 'immediate arrangements should be made for the conduct of long-range offensive operations against German towns where factories existed for the production of munitions of all kinds.'[80] Meanwhile, Trenchard had already been directed to attack industrial targets and established No.41 Wing at Ochey on 11 October, comprising two RFC and one RNAS bomber squadron. In early 1918 plans were laid for the expansion of the Ochey Wing to discharge the envisaged, large-scale strategic bomber offensive on Germany. Trenchard, very much against his will,[81] was persuaded to take command of the 'Independent Force', reporting direct to the new Minister for Air, Sir William Weir, bypassing Haig and Foch in France and Sykes, the new Chief of the Air Staff, in London.

Despite his personal inclinations, Trenchard determined to do the best he could with the resources at his disposal, noting in his diary 'I have stood firm for $3^1/2$ years now, first against one lot and then against another, and I have guided the development of the Air Service in battle and in this bombing, and I have not diverged right or left from my principles, so I shall try to carry this out to the end if they will only allow me to do so . . .'[82] In the cynical world of memoirs by royalty in the 1990s, it is worth noting that Trenchard kept copies of papers related to the Independent Force in folders which somehow got separated from his main collection of papers and were deposited with other personal effects at the RAF Staff College.

In May 1918 the Ochey Wing was reinforced by two more squadrons and on 6 June Trenchard took over the Wing, now renamed the Independent Force. On 23 June Trenchard explained his views on the bombing of Germany in a memorandum to Weir. He began by asking 'When is it more important to concentrate all the aeroplanes on the battle front and when can a proportion of them be diverted from the Battle Front to the work of bombing the industrial centres of Germany?' His answer was, 'When the aviation of each of the Allies is strong enough to hold and to beat the German Aviation.' Once that point was reached, all additional machines would be of greater value attacking Germany than bombing on the battle front. 'It is', he argued, 'an accepted fact that Germany and German troops is [sic] the only enemy that counts. It seems to me unanswerable that if it is possible to hit the German armies in France and at the same time hit Germany in Germany, this is a better concentration of effort than if we only hit one part of Germany.'

Trenchard then reminded the Minister that 'This has always been my view from the beginning of the war against Germany . . . I said that the first necessity was to provide those machines which were necessary for fighting and bombing the Germans in France and that the others were a luxury until sufficient machines were provided, but when sufficient machines were provided, I said it was a necessity to have long-distance bombing machines for fighting Germans in Germany. This is still my opinion and nothing has happened to change this view . . . In my opinion the British Aviation is now strong enough both to beat the German aviation in France and to attack the industrial centres in Germany.' Then however, the GOC hedged his bets, 'It therefore appears that for the future we ought to expand that force which is fighting the German aviation in France so as to keep the same proportions on the battle front we have now got relatively to the enemy, and at the same time to add ever increasingly to the forces that are bombing Germany.'[83]

In other words, Trenchard's position so far was consistent. He supported strategic bombardment, but only after the defeat of German aviation on the battle front; now he was prepared to pursue it, providing that the effort came from extra formations and was not diverted from the armies in the field.

In August four other bomber squadrons were added to the Independent Force (IF) and in September a fighter squadron for escort duties. Trenchard's plan 'was to attack a large number of objectives in Germany so as to force the enemy, if possible, to disperse his defensive forces at various points, and then to concentrate for two or three days and nights on the same objective.'[84] The impact of weather on his plan was soon evident: from 13 to 23 June no flying was possible because of rain, high winds and thunder; during the remainder of the month partial cloud or rain impeded attacks on three further occasions. In July, no flying was possible on 15 days and 18 nights and on several others cloud and high wind frustrated attempts to bomb in the Rhine Valley.

On 20 July the third session of the Inter-Allied Aviation Committee took place at Versailles. The Committee had met twice before, in November and May, and was now to address an agenda which included anti-submarine warfare, aircraft reinforcements between the western front and the Mediterranean, future aircraft construction, the current air situation and future programmes, 'Aerial Bombardment' and an 'American Proposal for a Generalissimo of the Air'.[85]

In his autobiography, *From Many Angles*, Sir Frederick Sykes makes no mention of this meeting, and hence no mention of the supporting papers prepared for him, as British representative, by Trenchard. Several questions had been submitted beforehand by France and Italy, and copies were sent direct to Trenchard as GOC IF. He in turn sent his answers direct to Weir for passing over to Sykes. They subsequently re-emerged as appendices to the procès-verbal to the Committee meeting. They comprise the clearest possible evidence that in 1918 Trenchard had no illusions whatever about the theory and reality of strategic bombardment.

The French representative asked what tonnage of 'projectiles' each of the Allied Aviation Services could drop in 24 hours during the months July-December 1918; how far could the tonnage be carried; should intermittent bombing be replaced by a 'definite plan', with the objective of 'obtaining greater results by the massed use of bombing squadrons . . .'

In response, Trenchard sent two tables to Weir, with a covering memorandum. The tables were accompanied by a footnote which read, 'These figure are purely theoretical and can in no way expect to be borne out by fact', because of unpredictable weather and aircraft availability. The covering memorandum amplified the tables in unambiguous language. 'The tonnage . . . could be arrived at with some trouble. The figures however would be of no value that I can see as the amount must depend on the weather more than the machines. Nor would the information be any guide as to the amount of bombs which could be dropped on any particular objective, as many factors offset work which can be accomplished by aeroplanes, such as state of aerodromes, pilots available, serviceability of machines, etc.'

Answers, he continued, 'would be misleading, and would give a totally false impression to the man who knew nothing of aviation . . . [while] to the expert who really understands aviation the figures would be of no value as he would realise how little they signify.'

As for plans, he bridled, 'There are two kinds of plans:

(a) A plan which when drawn up looks very nice on paper, such as the obliteration of one town after another and

(b) A plan based on the practical possibilities of bombing Germany which takes into account the weather, distance and also the other difficulties with which aviation has to contend . . .

The first plan has never been seriously attempted because it is useless. The second plan is that upon which the British Aviation is now working and carrying out, thoroughly and satisfactorily.'[86] So much for French suggestions that the Independent Force did not have a plan. And indeed Trenchard was being a little economical with the truth. Only seven days previously he had advised Weir that he had been unable to carry out his plan in its entirety because of range limitation, engine failures, the need to train new pilots and crews on 'easy objectives' and the limited numbers of aircraft at his disposal.[87]

Sykes's answers to the French questions made no reference to any of the practical difficulties set out by Trenchard. Instead he enunciated a bombing strategy which 'to be effective must be neither intermittent nor ineffective, but conducted in pursuance of a carefully conceived policy and with a thorough elaboration of detail.' Attacks on aerodromes and railway communications to support allied ground and naval forces would be made in emergency, but such attacks should be relegated to the allotted task, 'the dislocation of the enemy's key industries'. An inter-allied bombing plan was required without delay; success in dislocating the key munition industries would contribute to the submarine war and the western front while attacks on the German aircraft industry should 'entirely cripple production'. The attacks would force diversion of resources away from attack to defence and therefore 'may be not unfairly be regarded as a measure of Home Defence by anticipation on the part of the allies.' If such diversion of resources were not made, 'the German government would be forced to face very considerable and constantly increasing civil pressure which might result in political disintegration.' Astonishingly, this launch into strategic unreality was accompanied as annexes by the attachment of Trenchard's bombing tables, complete with factual disclaimers, and Trenchard's accompanying critical memoranda. There were agreements in the papers on the need for an independent allied C-in-C and on some other items, but the stark contrast in the central topic with the practicalities in 1918 of strategic bombing could not have been greater. In the event, the nearest the Independent Force got to the 'theoretical' bombing estimate was in October 1918 when it achieved 3.5 per cent of the projected tonnage.[88] Between 1 July and 30 October, 71 days and 74 nights were lost completely because of weather, or approximately 60 per cent of the available hours, while many other attacks were impaired or diverted because of poor weather in the target area. The Force responded to requests from Marshal Foche for attacks on railways behind the front line and launched repeated attacks on airfields, the latter increasingly important as enemy air defences increased. By 11 November the original five squadrons, plus the five added in August and September, had lost 352 aircraft or almost three times their basic aircraft strength. Trenchard's monthly reports did not list casualties.[89]

Needless to say, the public despatch from Trenchard issued as the Tenth Supplement to *The London Gazette* of 31 December 1918 concentrated on the achievements of the Independent Force, selecting the successful mission reports from the unexpurgated monthly series sent to Weir. Not publicised was a plan prepared by Trenchard's staff for implementation by the allied bombing force agreed by the Supreme War Council in October. Its preamble included a caveat about weather, but the paragraph defining the plan itself was to cast a long shadow over the RAF during the following 25 years:

There are two factors – moral effect and material effect – the object being to obtain the maximum of each. The best means to this end is to attack the industrial centre where you
(a) do military and vital damage by striking at the centres of supply or war materials
(b) achieve the maximum of effect on the moral by striking at the most sensitive part of the whole of the German population – namely the working class.

In the 'Execution' of the plan, Trenchard's earlier concept of widespread attacks to disperse defences, followed by numerous concentrated attacks on one or two objectives, was repeated. 'The moral factor in bombing attacks must not be overlooked, and in all cases where Factories or Works are attacked, the workmen's dwelling-quarters should form part of the objective.'[90]

Beyond this point there is no need to look for the influence of this or that theorist on the evolution of RAF strategy between 1919 and 1939. The practical experience of the Independent Bomber Force was submerged in the selective presentation in the *London Gazette*: down to the easy acceptance in it of the assertion that, 'At present the moral effect of bombing stands undoubtedly to the material effect in a proportion of 20 to 1, and therefore it was necessary to create the greatest moral effect possible.'[91]

As several historians have recognised, the adoption by the RAF of a bomber strategy after World War I had much to do with resource limitations, with a public desire to avoid a repetition of the slaughter of the western front, with an underestimation of the impact of air defences, with an overestimation of bombing accuracy and destructive power, and with a misunderstanding of civilian response to bombing. And yet in every item the evidence was there in World War I, except the desire somehow to break free of the trench deadlock.

The greatest irony is that Trenchard himself had no illusions whatever either about the achievements of his Independent Force, nor about the requirements for the future. To his diary on 11 November he confided, 'Thus the Independent Force comes to an end. A more gigantic waste of effort and personnel there has never been in any war . . . It has undoubtedly caused unrest in Germany, but it would have undoubtedly caused the same unrest had it not been "Independent".'[92] Sixteen years later he observed, 'Concentration, so-called, and bombing offensive depends [sic] on many things besides numbers. It depends on morale and equipment. What you can do is dependent upon that you have to do it with. I could not afford to have losses which morale would not stand . . . Furthermore it was no good talking about bombing Berlin or any other objective immediately you got a few machines which had the performance to do it. You have to prepare. It is a matter of organisation. You have to study meteorological conditions, a hundred and one questions of navigation, etc. You might do it as a stunt, but wars are not won on stunts. If you undertake a bombing offensive, it must be one which you can keep going.'[93]

Appearances sometimes to the contrary, this was the Trenchard who would loyally carry out his orders even when deeply opposed to them; who did care about his own troop's morale but had a ground force commander's evaluation of casualties against the wider objectives of the war; who was essentially a commander in the field, and above all who had an unusually realistic appreciation of air power's potential.

Another memorandum was written late in the war by another far-sighted air power enthusiast. Its message is still relevant, but it passed from the Ministry of Munitions to the War Cabinet and thence to an appendix in memoirs and histories without, apparently, any notice or consideration by the Air Staff. On 21 October 1917 Winston Churchill, in a paper addressing 'Munitions Possibilities of 1918', allocated Section IV to considerations about the 'Air Offensive'. As with the Smuts report, one sentiment is often quoted, but there is much more to consider. Churchill had no doubts about the ineffectiveness of 'terrorisation of the civil population' to compel a great nation to surrender. With considerable foresight he observed, 'Familiarity with bombardment, a good system of dugout or shelters, a strong control by police and military authorities, should be sufficient to preserve the national fighting power unimpaired. In our own case we have seen the combative spirit of the people roused, and not quelled, by the German air raids . . .'

Many other observations swept across the spectrum of air power: the importance of combining air interdiction of a battle front with ground force pressure on the enemy to make him even more dependent on resupply; the impact of ground force manoeuvre against an enemy whose own movement is constrained by air attack; the need for an independent 'general' staff studying the possibilities of air warfare; the need for 'systematised' staff study to clarify disputed points which hitherto had been overlaid by 'the dominating and immediate interests of the Army and the Navy', such as the vulnerability of aerodromes, the significance of railway interdiction, comparison of air and artillery bombardment. the science of bombing and the need to achieve accuracy comparable to that of naval guns. On casualties he pointed out that an air offensive had never been 'considered on the same scale or with the same ruthlessness in regard to losses for adequate objects as prevail in the operation of armies', i.e., not used like infantry with repeated attacks regardless of losses until the objective was achieved. The primary objective of such sanguine offensives would be the air bases of the enemy and the destruction of his air fighting forces. He speculated that losses of 2,000–3,000 aircraft, with their pilots, might be taken to ensure that 'his air forces might be definitely beaten and, once beaten, could be kept beaten.' And the objective worthy of such casualties? 'Real mastery of the air', after which 'all sorts of enterprises which are now not possible would become easy', including air mobility for ground forces, the destruction of specific factories, attacks on all his camps, depots, etc. Churchill was talking about command of the air, and he placed it precisely into the setting of military history: 'the indispensable preliminary to all results in the air, as in every other sphere of war, is to defeat the armed forces of the enemy.'[94]

Clausewitz would have understood. Command of the air was indispensable for the success of all other air activities: that made the enemy's air force his centre of gravity. Trenchard had instinctively attacked that centre of gravity throughout the war. When the post-war RAF, with Trenchard at its head, identified the enemy's industrial heart as that centre, without first preparing to secure command of the air, the disastrous roads to Wilhelmshaven and Berlin lay open.

CHAPTER 2

FROM PERIPHERAL TO PERVASIVE TO DOMINANT

The Inter-War Years

For contemporary air power analysts there was at once too much evidence and too little in the First World War. Trenchard kept a personal record of the impact on German morale of his bombing by recording items of correspondence taken from prisoners of war and from their oral testimony after capture.[1] Paradoxically, it was because the physical damage effected by bombing was so slight, compared with the psychological impact, that Trenchard and others anticipated far greater results from an increase in scale of air attack. In retrospect, it had not been possible to distinguish between the impact of shock, which obviously declines with experience, and a deeper, more permanent effect. Churchill was much closer to the mark with his anticipation of resilience.

After the war, air power evolved in two different directions, epitomised by developments in Germany, which were in salient respects similar to those in the Soviet Union, and in Britain, which were more similar to those in the USA. In Britain, the infant RAF had to fight to preserve its independence in the absence of any obvious residual threat and in the face of swingeing defence cuts and a war-weary public. Germany was emasculated militarily by the Treaty of Versailles, was embittered, quickly revanchist and saw potential enemies, or objectives, just across her frontiers. The evolution of both air forces has been comprehensively portrayed, but significant features in both have particular relevance to air power's second century. They concern the relationship between doctrine: the theory, and practice: the application of air power in terms explored in the previous chapter.

In Britain, the influence of doctrine became so pervasive that alternative interpretation of facts, or facts which did not fit the doctrine, were either seriously undervalued or overlooked. Yet the doctrine was enunciated by intelligent senior officers, most of whom had been competent combat pilots and commanders. There is no doubt that its roots lay at least as much in the need to preserve the third service as in the strategic requirements and capabilities of the period.

Immediately after the war, Sykes, the Chief of Air Staff, drew up a blueprint for the peacetime RAF. It was one of the most comprehensive and imaginative documents written on the potential of air power. Sykes reproduced the text of his 'Air Power Requirements for the Empire' in his autobiography *From Many Angles*, but not the appendices, which are preserved with a copy of the original typescript among the Bracknell papers.[2] In one critical respect, the absence of the appendices leaves in the text a misleading impression about Sykes's priorities. His first section, on 'General Considerations and Recommendations', continued the thinking which had characterised his presentations to the Inter Allied Aviation Committee of the Supreme War Council the previous July and which had underlaid the proposals for an allied 'Independent' Bomber Force. His objective now was to secure 'a really efficient Air Service and a sound basis for commercial expansion.'[3] His panorama was not just British and Empire military aviation, but one which envisaged a close interdependence between the military and the civil sector.

He emphasised that 'aviation provides a distinct and separate striking force of tremendous potentiality. Before a formal declaration of war it may be possible to deal a paralysing blow at some nerve centre: the Air Force must be the first line of defence for the Empire.'[4] Consequently, the separate territories of the Empire should be prepared to protect themselves and assist each other. In section two, Sykes examined the strategic considerations of offense and defence. In one paragraph, he encapsulated the significance of air power in an age of total war, and, in an analysis which was to gather momentum over the next 20 years, England's particular vulnerability:

Future wars between civilised nations will be struggles for life in which entire populations, together with their industrial resources, will be thrown into the scale. Evolution has brought about the creation of air fleets to meet the demands of such warfare. These will consist of home defence units and striking forces. The objectives of striking forces will be nerve centres, the armies and navies of the opponent , the population as a whole, his national moral and the industries without which he cannot wage war. In compiling the strength necessary for our air fleets it must be remembered that England is still more vulnerable to attack by air than her neighbours owing to the geographical position of London and the fact that our population and industries although dispersed within our island, are necessarily crowded together in a comparatively small area. The immunity of our industries from air attack is henceforward as vital to our existence as the security of our sea communications.[5]

Thereafter followed logical conclusions about the need to provide both offensive and defensive aircraft, with a basic requirement of 15 squadrons to be extended to 20 because longer-range bombers would shortly make the west of England and Ireland also vulnerable to attack. The strike force would also total 20 squadrons, employed in peacetime on 'civil duties'. Naval co-operation would be provided by 23 squadrons, but any gratitude the Royal Navy might have felt about such apparent jointery was sharply tempered by the accompanying assertions that, 'in the near future much of the work done by surface vessels will be performed by the Air Force . . . It is within vision that certain types of aircraft will be able to carry out cruises of long duration and perform the functions of a surface craft with greater speed and radius of action.'[6] 'Air force' would be concentrated over even further distances by aircraft carriers deploying '40 to 50 torpedo planes and bombers'.

Provision for Army co-operation, or 'Expeditionary and Reserve Forces' was to comprise 57 squadrons, and together with those for overseas theatres such as Egypt, Mesopotamia, the Mediterranean and India, the total RAF strength would be 154 squadrons, of which 62 would be 'War Establishment', or fully combat-capable, and 92 would be 'cadre' or skeleton to be expanded to war establishment when required. Total manpower would be 7,125 officers and 75,722 other ranks. The squadrons would be supported by training wings, schools of aerial fighting and gunnery, photography and bombing, signals, navigation and meteorology, Army and Navy Co-operation Schools, repair depots and a larger number of overseas bases.[7] Sykes estimated the total cost of the programme as £21 million, 'or about the cost of two battleships',[8] but he did not include any costings in his memorandum.

However, the actual shape of his Air Force would have been very different from the outline in the Memorandum. No combat-ready 'war establishment' fighters were provided for Home Defence. All 20 were to be 'cadre'. Conversely, all 20 'strike' squadrons were to be War Establishment, while of the total number of 62 'War Establishment' squadrons 32 were to be bomber and six fighter. Of the remainder, six were reconnaissance and 18 naval co-operation.[9] In other words, Sykes's Royal Air Force would have been prepared to implement an immediate bomber offensive, but not to withstand one.

It was never proven. His proposals were 'turned down by the Cabinet on the score of expense' [10] and within two months the new minister for War and Air, Churchill, had engineered his removal to become Controller of a new Civil Aviation Department, replacing him as Chief of the Air Staff with Trenchard.

Hereafter, Trenchard was rightly to earn the sobriquet of 'Father of the Royal Air Force' and quite wrongly to be credited with the origination of the bomber doctrine. In the preceding chapter Trenchard's serious misgivings about the effectiveness of strategic bombardment have been illustrated. Indeed, even his aphorism about the relative, moral and material impact of bombing reflected the ineffectiveness of the latter rather than the success of the former. He never was an intellectual airman: he was a practical, shrewd, far-sighted identifier of what was feasible and what was not. His activities in the first year of his tenure as CAS clearly illustrated his priorities, but left his doctrinal ideas inextricable in practice from those of Sykes. As a result, the RAF began the inter-war years with a hopeless mismatch between intentions and capabilities.

In October 1919 Trenchard prepared three 'Schemes' of proposals for the future Royal Air Force for Churchill to submit to the Cabinet.[11] In his covering minute, Churchill wrote, 'Air Marshal Trenchard attaches the greatest importance to Scheme B . . .' which envisaged 34 full-strength squadrons and 21 training (cadre/squadrons), for a total of 3,400 officers and 35,000 other ranks, plus supporting bases, training schools, etc. for annual costs of approximately £18 million. As the estimates were broken down into itemised Votes, for a service approximately one-third the size of that proposed by Sykes, either Trenchard's costs were inflated or Sykes's were very inaccurate. In the event, Trenchard's views were disregarded and a modified Scheme C was adopted, providing for 50 squadrons [12] of which slightly more than half would be at full strength, with a total establishment of approximately 28,000 other ranks and 2,800 officers. In other words, the post-war RAF was to be approximately one-tenth of its size at the end of the war, and would cost about £15 million, or the equivalent of one-and-a-half battleships.

In Trenchard's original paper prepared for Churchill in October 1919, he had proposed to establish one squadron at full strength and five 'training' squadrons for Home Defence out of 83.[13] In his 'preferred' Scheme B there was none, but Bristol Fighters were to equip an undetermined number of 'training' squadrons, along with Avro-504s and DH-9As. The two Army Co-operation squadrons were also to be equipped with Bristols. In the adapted Scheme C there remained no front line provision for UK air defence, and the 'strike' force was reduced to the squadrons of Handley Page and De Havilland bombers. In effect, the RAF at home was reduced to 11 squadrons, including five for naval co-operation.

Churchill had advised the Cabinet in his Secret Memorandum, 'Scheme C . . . does not provide any machinery for mobilisation, or any system of Territorials, or for the training of a Reserve. It has additional defects in that it makes no provision for meeting any sudden call of war wastage, even for a small war, and reduces the number of squadrons for work with the Navy, including those for overseas bases, to a dangerously low figure.'[14] The Cabinet elected to disregard the cautions and the RAF was committed to a doctrine of strategic bombardment without the resources to support it and an awareness of home-base vulnerability with no provision to defend it. There were other casualties in the reduction from Scheme B to Scheme C: the 'Intelligence' part of the School of Photography and Intelligence' was dropped, as was a proposed Bombing School to be established at Frieston. In sum, the operational decisions of 1919 laid the basis for a great deal of trouble, and subsequent weaknesses over the inter-war years.

Sykes's vision was flawed by his failure to acknowledge the limitations of contemporary air power. Aircraft could not replace surface ships. And, if British industrial concentration made her more vulnerable than her potential opponents, what were the implications for a British bomber offensive? Sykes's own comments in 1942: 'The harvest of neglect is inexorable. It is not possible to catch up in two years of war the years that the locust has eaten', were literally accurate but hardly appropriate for the man who had left the RAF with an impossible doctrinal legacy.

It was a doctrine to which Trenchard was to become irrevocably committed. His natural inclination was to adopt the offensive; his appreciation of the practical difficulties of interception led him to attach low priority to defensive counter-air operations; and when the RAF faced the threat of dismemberment by the Army and Navy in the 1920s, the 'independent' responsibility of strategic bombardment, with 'Imperial Policing', became the doctrinal bulwark of an independent RAF. In 1921 Arthur Balfour, Chairman of the Standing Defence Sub-Committee of the Committee for Imperial Defence, investigated the relationship between the three services and concluded, 'Are there or are there not military operations of first class importance in which the main burden of responsibility is thrown upon the air force, while the other services play either an insignificant part or no part at all? The Air Force claim that there are, and it seems to me their opinion must be allowed.'[15] Balfour was persuaded by Trenchard's arguments, with Sykes's roots, that the primary task of the RAF would be the defence of the British Isles, to be achieved largely by a counter-offensive, and that, in addition, more use could be made of the RAF as a substitute for naval and military forces.

Fortunately for the RAF, Trenchard's vision was to lay down the infrastructure on which British air power could be built. Whereas Sykes's memorandum had ranged loftily over concepts, Empire and broad intentions, Trenchard wrote of a force which could be expanded in the future; concentrating on the training of officers and men. An apprentice school and a Cadet College would provide the long-term pilots and technical groundcrew. Short-service commissions would be introduced and officer entry encouraged from the ranks and the universities as well as the Cadet College. The science of aeronautics had to be expanded, and the RAF must have its own Staff College. It was insufficient for the Air Force officer to be a 'chauffeur' and nothing else. Above all, 'to make an Air Force worthy of the name, we must create an Air Force spirit, or rather foster this spirit which undoubtedly existed in a high degree during the war, by every means in our power'.[16]

Some of the features of the post-war period are familiar to air staffs and politicians at the beginning of air power's second century. In the 1990s a major confrontation, albeit virtually bloodless, has just ended. There is no other major potential threat on the horizon. In several countries defence budgets have sharply dwindled, interservice rivalries re-emerged, and difficult choices been made within and between armed forces over role and resource allocation.

Trenchard's principle of preserving the foundations at the expense of the size of the front line proved invaluable. But its success was jeopardised initially by the depth of the cuts imposed and thereafter by failure to identify the disparity between doctrinal aspiration and technical and strategic reality. In 1929, shortly before he retired as Chief of the Air Staff, Trenchard addressed the Imperial Defence College in London on 'The War Aim of the Royal Air Force'. The lecture script was subsequently circulated confidentially in the Air Force 'so that officers shall understand these reasons.'[17] It succinctly identifies the legacy of RAF policy and doctrine left by Trenchard to his successors.

He began by observing that there was some divergence of views between the three services about what the RAF's 'war aim' should be. In particular, 'that the *main efforts* [italics in the original] should be directed to attack the opposite air forces, a view with which the Air Staff strongly disagree.' He explained that he had recently agreed with his Army and Navy counterparts that the aim of the Air Force with the Navy and Army was 'to break down the enemy's resistance'. That was not best done by attacking airfields, because aircraft could be widely dispersed, use improvised landing grounds, craters could be filled in and personnel sheltered.

Instead, he continued, the mobility of aircraft over long ranges would be exploited. Thereafter followed a classic definition of air power flexibility. The objectives of air attack could change frequently as a campaign progressed. It could be enemy fleets, it could be ground force mobilisation, communications or transportation, or munitions factories, or the armies direct. 'The air forces will be turned against the objective which is the best at the time'. The Air Force would not be fighting a war by itself but it might not always 'operate from the same zone or theatre of war' as the Army or the Navy. Nor were the 'Air Staff desirous of carrying out indiscriminate bombing attacks on the civilian population as such', but 'air attacks will be directed against military objectives in the broadest sense'. Trenchard had previously made no secret of the fact that 'munition workers' and 'steve-dores' were justifiable targets,[18] and the qualifying 'as such' after 'civilian population' implied that.

But, he continued, we will inevitably have intense air fighting, because air superiority is gained by attacking the enemy's 'vital centres' so power-fully that they must defend themselves rather than counterattack. Defence demands 'altogether disproportionate strength' and so, as the offensive grows, the opponent is forced to divert more and more of his resources to defence until finally they are all concentrated on the defence. 'The issue to be fought out is which side by maintaining its bombing attacks in the face of losses can continue to lead and keep the other on the defensive. It is a lead which has constantly and continually to be maintained.' Meanwhile, he argued, any clamour on one's own side to divert resources to defence should be resisted, because that would result in our being placed on the defensive. 'When one side has in this way thrown the other on to the defen-sive, it has gained air superiority.' In summing up, Trenchard re-emphasised that the main offensive would not be concentrated against the enemy air bases and air forces, objectives would vary, they would 'in the broadest sense be military', and 'air superiority will be gained in the course of these attacks on vital centres by whichever side can continue to lead and can maintain its offensive in spite of the losses and impose on the other a defensive role.'[19]

That was, to say the least, an unusual definition of 'air superiority', far away from that enunciated by Churchill in 1917 and unaccountably divorced from Trenchard's own experience as Commander of the Independent Force in the closing months of the war and his awareness then of the need for, and difficulties in achieving, a sustained concentrated bombing effort. It was a flawed concept in 1929, irrespective of the short-comings of bomber aviation. With the advent of radar and the next generation of monoplane fighters it would lead to disaster until an alter-native definition of 'air superiority' was offered and achieved. The misconception was doubly unfortunate when it was accompanied by such a comprehensive exposition of air power's fundamental characteristic of flexibility. In passing, it may be noted that this thinking owed nothing to Douhet. There is no record that Trenchard ever referred to him or was aware of him. In 1977 Air Marshals Harris and Slessor individually and categorically assured this writer that they had never read nor heard of Douhet's ideas before the Second World War.[20]

For its success, the theory depended on heavy and sustained air attack plus a willingness greater than that of the opponent to endure losses. It implied a capacity to mount such an offensive in the first place. Ten years after Trenchard so clearly identified the RAF's war aim, its capacity to achieve it was analysed in a presentation to the RAF Staff College which was to remain unremarked by historians for a further 40 years. Wing Commander F.J.W. Mellersh, AFC, addressed No.17 Course on 11 May 1939 on 'Air Armament, Training and Development'.

In a lengthy and comprehensively detailed account, Mellersh described the services' residual armament problems – both air-to-ground and air-to-air – their aggravation by the rapid expansion of the service, and the progress already made. An Armament Group had been established in 1934 responsible for training and development: five years after Trenchard's explanation of the RAF's war aim to the Imperial Defence College. By 1937 training was being supervised, but bombing development largely consisted of trying to find out what other people were doing, with not much success.

Another innovation was a 'Bombing Analysis Section', intended to analyse the results of bombing at Armament Training Stations. This 'innovation' took place in early 1939 and was intended to examine the impact of weather and varying conditions of flight. An Air Ministry decision to use full-time observers had prompted a rapid expansion in training facilities but a considerable shortage of recruits. In addition there was a shortfall of 2,000 air gunners and no Central Air Gunners' School. As a result most observers were really unfit to go on to squadrons, while air gunners were being trained during firing exercises. No Air Fighting Schools like those in World War I had been created. Target-towing aircraft were obsolete and useless for the gunners of the new generation of fighters and bombers. Most pilots were still training on biplanes and transferring direct to squadrons without any experience on their new aircraft. Weapon-training detachments required a minimum of four weeks, with good weather. In the previous year most squadrons did not complete the course and the majority of operational squadrons were not being assessed. Those results which were monitored were considerably inferior to those achieved in the earlier generation *Hart* biplane. The formation of bombing and gunnery schools by the Air Ministry was still being awaited, so that pilots could attend them between flying training and joining their squadrons. Meanwhile, insufficient long-distance formation practices, unfamiliar characteristics in new aircraft and lack of trained and experienced crews were combining to obscure an evaluation of exactly how far 'the modern high speed bomber is inferior [*sic*] to its predecessor of the *Hart* type'. It was hoped that increases in squadron salvo attacks, on a larger scale and under more realistic operational conditions would provide better results.

The Wing Commander described the development of improved bombsights and made another far-sighted observation, '. . . there are so many errors in high-altitude bombing which are inevitable . . . which make it very doubtful whether precision results will be achieved.' The PGM was still 30 years away. The establishment of a Bombing Development Unit, where research into bombing problems and bombing tactics could take place, was still awaited. It could not satisfactorily be done by the front-line squadrons themselves.

One most serious concern remained: 'There can be no doubt that the defence now provided in most of the bombers in service is totally inadequate. The solution to this problem, like most of the others, seems to lie in the provision of larger, more powerful and better equipped aircraft.'[21]

There were many specific reasons why the RAF, just four months before the outbreak of the Second World War was so ill-equipped to carry out a doctrine which had been formulated 20 years previously and expressed as a war aim 10 years before. With 50 years of hindsight they are easy to identify and residual argument is primarily about how much weight to allocate to each. Of greater concern is the need to identify the nature of several which have in various guises recurred since 1939 in different countries and became either visible, or possible, again as air power moved towards its second century. They are generally familiar, but a summary of them may stimulate slight unease among air staffs world-wide in the 1990s.

There was an assumption that all future wars would, in their totality, resemble World War I. 'Lessons' were selected to fit existing theories and not vice versa. Military evolution would be linear, rather than unpredictable and influenced haphazardly by other kinds of technology, current resource availability and geopolitics. Technology would produce only an increase in effectiveness in offense, regardless of the lesson of military history that novelty in offense would always stimulate a defensive response. There was a failure to examine the practical requirements of policy, from resource allocation on the appropriate scale, down to the operational implications of target location, identification, acquisition and destruction. The interaction of potential objectives, possible attrition and the requirement for combat reserves was not addressed. Resource constraints impelled aggressive interservice role definition, aggravated by inflexibility in the thinking of all three services. The time taken to expand the supporting infrastructure in crisis was underestimated, especially as regards training units and training time. Provision for, and successful completion of, small-scale operations in conditions far removed from large-scale warfare in Europe obscured fundamental operational weaknesses across the RAF as a whole. If Trenchard had not laid the foundation at the same time as he was compelled to reduce the front line the subsequent expansion and reconstitution could not have reached the point where the *Luftwaffe* was defeated in 1940 and the war returned to Germany in 1941. The specific points refer to the RAF between the wars; the generalities may be projected forward, possibly indefinitely.

Wing Commander Mellersh's concluding observation to the students of No.17 Course at Andover was both a tragic prologue for the RAF in the early days of the imminent war and a perennial cautionary word for those to whom most wars will be unexpected: 'There seems to be a tendency to hitch our waggon to a very distant star, and for many of the important problems nearer at hand to be neglected. The equipment in our Squadrons is by no means as efficient as it should be, and I feel sure that if part of the time now spent on long-range problems were devoted to the perfecting of our existing equipment, we should be very much better off. Many of our aircraft may be obsolescent, but, if we go to war, they are the ones we shall have to fight with, and it is of vital importance to us to ensure that our weapons really *do* work efficiently.'[22]

The *Luftwaffe*

Meanwhile the *Luftwaffe* had moved in a different direction. While the Royal Air Force struggled to survive after 1919, the Treaty of Versailles and its extensions eliminated the German Air Force and its supporting aviation industry. But a national army was allowed and its commander General Hans von Seeckt was in no doubt about the future importance of air power. He recruited 180 pilots into the army to preserve military aviation awareness and in 1923 secretly proposed the creation of an independent air force. Meanwhile Germany signed a secret agreement in 1922 with Russia to train German aircrew at Lipetsk, an airfield about 310 km south-east of Moscow. From 1924 to 1933 fighter, reconnaissance and bomber training took place clandestinely as Germany established the nucleus of a new air force. German officers participated in Soviet exercises which already emphasised the use of aircraft in combined arms ground offensives. Within the terms of the Versailles Treaty Germany also developed an extensive civilian aviation structure, including the national airline *Lufthansa* and numerous gliding and 'civilian' flying schools. The prominence of Goering in Hitler's Nazi party encouraged resource allocation to aviation and when the latter became Chancellor in 1933 preparations for the creation of the *Luftwaffe* accelerated. An Air Ministry was created in 1933 and in 1935 the creation of the *Luftwaffe* was announced.

The thinking which underlay the tactical and strategic employment of the *Luftwaffe* was set out in Service Manual No.16, issued in 1936, but was the product of preparatory work at Lipetsk. In several respects the ideas differed markedly from those held in the RAF in the same period.[23]

The three primary missions of the *Luftwaffe* were to combat enemy air forces, intervene in ground or naval actions and combat the sources of the enemy's strength and disrupt his logistic supplies to the front line. There was little evidence of Douhet's theories of strategic bombardment. While a concept of air supremacy was lacking, as in British policy, a major point of difference was the explicit targeting of an enemy's air forces, bases and production, over and in his own territory. The *Luftwaffe* was an independent service, but not an end in itself and was therefore to be concerned with the task of 'subduing the enemy's armed forces.'[24] But, as in all other air forces at the time, attack was the principle which had to be 'dominant over all others.'[25] Germany and its armed forces could not be adequately protected by defensive measures alone, although fighters and AA guns were acquired. Already, in a war game played in 1934 in a scenario in which Germany had been attacked by France, the Air Force Commander General Wever had despatched his bomber squadrons deep into French territory. When he was advised that his aircraft had suffered 'losses' of 80 per cent he replied, 'That would deprive me of my confidence in strategic air operations', and promptly changed the game rules to reduce his 'attrition' rates.[26]

While Manual No. 16 was never amended, there is clear evidence that strategic bombardment was not overlooked in *Luftwaffe* planning. In terms very similar to those of Trenchard in 1929, German doctrine stated that 'The nature of the enemy, the time of year, the structure of his land, the character of his people as well as one's own military capabilities' would determine how air power would be applied.[27] Taken together, the doctrinal guidelines realistically reflected the strategic environment in which the *Luftwaffe* could expect to operate: in the neighbouring territories of France, Czechoslovakia and Poland. As late as 1939, General der Fleiger Helmut Felmy, then Commander of *Luftflotte* 2 observed to his subordinates that the *Luftwaffe* did not yet possess the resources for a successful strategic bombing offensive against Britain.[28] This at a time when the British air staff had been concerned for several years by the threat of a swift 'knockout blow' from the Luftwaffe.[29]

Germany abandoned two four-engined bomber designs in 1936 shortly after General Wever's death in a flying accident. Whether his influence would have sustained the projects, which were to specifications akin to those of the RAF *Halifax* and *Lancaster* but which were slowed down by engine development problems, remains hypothetical.

It was believed that twin-engined bombers such as the Dornier 17,

Junkers 88 and Heinkel III could be used either tactically or strategically in neighbouring countries. But when Hitler did decide to take the war westwards over the North Sea and eastwards into the Soviet heartland, he had no weapon to match his political objectives. He lacked a bomber force which could sustain an offensive against the United Kingdom or reach the redeployed Soviet factories in the Urals. Indeed, it may be argued that the greatest strategic success enjoyed by the *Luftwaffe* occurred before the outbreak of war. In 1935 Hitler alarmed the British government by claiming parity with the RAF in size, and imminent parity with the French Air Force. In 1938 the French Chief of Air Staff, in the company of the French Ambassador, was shown round the Heinkel works in Orienberg where he saw three test models of an HE-100 fighter. In fact the fighter never went into production but Milch and Udet conducted an elaborate charade giving the impression that the aircraft was already in mass production. After the visit the General commented to the Ambassador 'If war breaks out at the end of September, as you think it will, there won't be a single French aircraft left after fourteen days.'[30] Such sentiments were not conducive to high morale either in the French Air Force or in the French government.

Despite the strategic shortcomings, the matching of tactical doctrine and aircraft was exact. The air power component of blitzkrieg was summarised in June 1939 by the new Chief of *Luftwaffe* General Staff Jeschonnek: 'The largest possible force, including the squadrons' reserves, must be committed to the first, sudden attack. The fact that the enemy anti-aircraft defences have not yet acquired an effective operating routine must be exploited to the utmost and the assigned area bombarded as intensely as possible.'[31]

Thus by 1939, of the two air forces which were to dominate the first two years of the Second World War, one had a doctrine which was beyond the capacity of its equipment while the other was equipped to discharge a doctrine which was designed for a short war in a restricted geographical area. Both believed that maximum priority should be given to the offensive; both underestimated the volume of resources it required and the attrition likely to be incurred.

General Wever had believed that air superiority would be an elusive goal, affected, as in World War I, by the introduction of new aircraft, improved technologies and the capacity to replace losses. Events in World War II would illustrate the accuracy of his forecast, especially in the first decisive air battle over Britain in 1940.

Air power in World War Two
Air power had been peripheral between 1914 and 1918. In the Second World War it dominated most theatres and in at least two was decisive. In

the era of blitzkrieg Jeschonnek's tactical squadrons swept ahead of the armoured divisions into Poland, France and Russia. Within 24 hours the *Luftwaffe* destroyed 1,811 Soviet aircraft and by the beginning of October 1941 the USSR conceded the loss of 5,316.[32] The Soviet air force, like the Polish and the French before it, was swept from the sky and ground forces exposed to the full weight of the *Luftwaffe's* close air support and interdiction attacks. In the later stages of the war the roles were reversed as the German commanders were faced by allied air superiority and tactical air power in North Africa and western Europe.

The interdiction of the German forces preparing to withstand the allied invasion of 1944 was comprehensive and contributed massively to the success of the June landings. In the Atlantic, the ring was closed on the U-boats when land-based aircraft from east and west could destroy them at any point. In the Pacific air power changed the face of US seapower at Pearl Harbor, destroyed the battleships assigned to the defence of Singapore, decided the command of both sea and skies at Midway and accelerated Japanese capitulation at Hiroshima and Nagasaki. All these campaigns were fought alongside navies or armies or both. Only in the battles between Germany and the USSR was air power less than strategically decisive after blitzkrieg gave way to attrition. In all these theatres, defeat of the enemy's armed forces was regarded as the prerequisite for victory, although in the Pacific combat between the armed forces was complemented by naval blockade and direct air bombardment of the Japanese mainland. In Europe, however, the air war assumed a dimension of its own, first over Britain, and then over Germany. Both have been comprehensively and repeatedly analysed since 1945, but, in addition to the many contrasting features of the Battle of Britain and the allied bomber offensive against Germany, there were others which were common. One or two may be uneasily familiar 50 years later.

The Battle of Britain

In the Battle of Britain it is generally and justifiably argued that the decision by Goering to switch the German bomber attacks away from Fighter Command to London on 7 September 1940 was a turning point. As the Battle itself was the first decisive point in the war, the German error had exceptional significance. By that date Fighter Command, even with two months respite after Dunkirk, had lost approximately one-third of its flight commanders and one-fifth of its squadron commanders. In two weeks the Command had lost the equivalent of a month's output from the Operational Training Units. The survivors were flying up to four sorties a day and there were no reserve squadrons fit to replace the battered ones. The switch of the attacks to London relieved the direct pressure on the airfields and allowed the fighter squadrons to concentrate on attacks in one major region, with well-documented results. Hitler's anger at the British raid on Berlin the previous week, Goering's humiliation, the belief among some *Luftwaffe* commanders that attacks on London would stimulate the final defeat of Fighter Command, plus residual ideas of brittle civilian morale and political vulnerability: all were factors contributing to the fateful decision, but underlying them all was one pervasive weakness: faulty intelligence.

The Fifth (Foreign Air Forces) Department of the Ic (Intelligence) Division of the *Luftwaffe* General Staff was headed from 1938 to 1942 by Major, later Oberst G. ('Beppo') Schmid.[33] Seldom can one department have produced so many misleading reports in such a short space of time with such disastrous consequences. Some of the weaknesses in the *Luftwaffe* system were peculiar to the time and the place, but others might be recognised, in modern form, by some air staffs in the 1990s.

Schmid himself had, until 1935, been an army officer with no knowledge of air operations. Before his appointment as Head of D5 he had worked for Goebels and in Goering's outer office. At that time D5 was also responsible for press relations, propaganda censorship and armed forces morale. Schmid's appointment owed more to his political and ideological affiliation to the Nazi party than to any air force expertise. His personal relationship with Goering would ensure that his influence considerably exceeded that usually associated with his military rank. His appointment typified the lack of importance attached to intelligence by the German High Command. Goering had no time for military attachés, and appointments in Ic tended to be filled by second rate or rusticated officers with few promotion prospects. At the *Luftwaffe* Air War College, intelligence was not regarded as a prestigious area of study.

Schmid therefore had a well-tuned ear to the requirements of Goering and his empathic Chief of Staff Jeschonnek (who in 1938 had opined that the *Luftwaffe* could defeat Britain on its own). Schmid confidently assured them in early 1939 of the *Luftwaffe's* superiority over any other European air force in numbers, quality, armament, organisation, and 'especially the tactical and operations side of the preparation for war in the air'.[34] This theme was expressed publicly by Goering on 3 September 1939 in a speech in Berlin, with the assertion that the British could not deny 'that our superiority is overwhelming'.[35] Schmid also emphasised the particular vulnerability of Britain to air attack because of her geographical position and industrial sensitivity. Ironically, that particular assessment was also believed in Britain.

In May 1939 however, an exercise carried out by *Luftflotte* 2, under General Felmy's command, had led to the conclusions that British

commerce through West of England ports was out of bomber range, that
terror attacks on London were likely to be unproductive and that direct
attacks on the RAF were likely to result in unacceptable losses for the
Luftwaffe. This was not what Jeschonnek and Goering wished to hear and
Felmy was quickly relieved of his command.[36] His successor,
Generalleutnant Giesler was asked to study further the problem of an air
war across the sea and offered an unequivocal conclusion, '. . . an air war
against Britain in 1940 can only result in partially important success, which
could not have an effect and threaten the British conduct of the war until
the second year of the war'.[37] Goering preferred to listen to his
'Intelligence' officer rather than to the operations staff and by 1940 Giesler
had also been replaced.

The speed and effectiveness of the victories in Poland, Norway and the
Low Countries in 1939 and 1940 induced euphoria, seemed to vindicate
Schmid and certainly reinforced the general view in the *Wehrmacht* High
Command that intelligence was not essential for their military successes.
Further weaknesses, however, were about to be disclosed. As the British
government had suspected, there was no shortage of reconnaissance data
about British military and industrial targets available to the German
General Staff. There was, however, no organisation to analyse this material for target selection. There were no technical specialists of any sort in
D5. There were insufficient targeteers and those who were there were held
to be incompetent. Assessments of British industrial capacity still depended
on a study in 1937, *Study Blue*, which informed the subsequent offensive
but by 1940 was completely out of date.

The *Luftwaffe* High Command was particularly vulnerable to erroneous
intelligence data because many of the air commanders, including
Kesselring, Sperrle and Stumpf had no air warfare experience before 1939,
and Jeschonnek had fought in the infantry in World War I. There was no
industrial expertise in the targeting staffs, a fact reflected by the target
options considered in the summer of 1940, which included the residential
area of London to stimulate panic and choke the approach roads to the
planned invasion area; the working class areas to stimulate revolution and
peace talks; London's traffic system; the 'newspaper district', and the
armament centres in the Midlands 'where the war can be won'. Some of the
D5 staff argued for destruction of the aircraft industry 'by indirect methods
with attacks on individual places of concentration on the subcontractor's
works.'[38] There was no fundamental analysis of target importance, despite
the specific guideline in Service Manual No. 16 that a 'centre of importance' should be identified and concentrated on. The identification of a
British centre of gravity was beyond the capabilities of D5.

The most visible example of D5's incompetence is Schmid's widely publicised intelligence assessment of 16 July 1940.[39] In it he underestimated RAF fighter strength in general and *Spitfire* performance in particular; he critically overestimated the RAF's aircrew availability; he assessed the RAF's command structure as inflexible and failed to mention radar at all. Three weeks later he did refer to British radar, alleging that it impeded flexibility by tying fighters to the vicinity of their own bases and preventing the rapid concentration of fighters at crucial points.[40] This inaccurate assessment was not helped by the fact that there was no regular communication between the *Luftwaffe's* Signals Directorate Listening Services and D5. There was no systematic analysis of Sigint by the air staffs. Indeed, in 1944 the Signals Director still had to be ordered to share Sigint with the air staffs. In 1940 there was no central co-ordination and analysis of multi-sensor intelligence.

That combination either induced, or at the very least failed to modify a targeting policy which in early 1940 did not identify Fighter Command as the RAF's, and indeed Britain's centre of gravity; then was slow to identify the critical contribution of the radar and sector bases; then underestimated the vulnerability of the radar units; failed to appreciate the strategic significance of shifting the attack to London and even then failed to identify a strategic target array on which to concentrate.

The *Luftwaffe* had been preoccupied with the fact that its operational capabilities were usually employed against targets which were highly visible and directly related to a ground force front. By 1940 its failure to develop similar levels of professional competence in its intelligence staff had a direct and critical impact on perhaps the most decisive single battle of the war.

With overwhelming superiority, intelligence shortcomings can be subsumed, but not when the margin is narrow, and certainly not when front-line resources are constrained. The problem was to recur later in the war; but in a very different form.

The Bomber Offensive
The allied bomber offensive against Germany still stimulates controversy about the efficacy of Bomber Command's attacks on industrial centres, the failure of the USAAF to attack unescorted by day without prohibitive losses, and the morality or otherwise of large-scale area attacks which by their nature would fail to discriminate between industrial workers and their families.

By 1994 much of the debate was academic, although still provoking strong emotions, but in the aftermath of the Gulf War and in the uncertain international environment of the late 1990s, four topics were of great importance. They were the persistent influence of 'operational'

considerations on strategic bombardment policy, the reliability of targeting intelligence, the higher direction of the bombing campaign, and the
priority to be afforded to neutralising enemy air defences.

Between November 1944 and January 1945 disagreements between
Commander in Chief Harris and RAF Chief of Air Staff Portal over bombing priorities were extensively aired in top-secret personal letters. Their
content, in echoing the arguments of World War I, and in reminding a
later generation in the 1990s both how much progress had been and how
much remained to be done, gave them an historical significance in the evolution of air power which far transcends the detail of what became an
increasingly frank exchange of views.

In September 1944 the allied Combined Chiefs of Staff resumed control
of the three strategic bomber forces: USAAF 8th and 15th, and RAF
Bomber Command. On 25 September Bomber Command was given a
Directive setting out its new priorities: 'First Priority: Petroleum Industry,
with special emphasis on petrol (gasoline) including storage'. Second priorities were to be the German rail and waterborne transportation systems,
tank production plants and ordnance depots and MT production plants
and depots.[41] The Directive was amplified by Eisenhower's Deputy, Air
Marshal Tedder, in a note to Portal which was copied to Harris. To the dis-
interested reader 50 years later it seems a coolly logical appraisal but Harris
interpreted it very differently. Tedder wrote, 'As I see it, there are two
methods of ending this war, one is by land invasion and the other is by
breaking the enemy's power and control behind the lines. I myself do not
believe that these two courses are alternative or conflicting, I believe they
are complementary.' That was a view taken about Kuwait and Iraq 46
years later, and with which all but the most single-minded strategic bom-
bardiers could have agreed. Tedder however went a stage further: 'I do not
believe that by concentrating our whole Air effort on the ground battle area
we shall shorten the war. Nor do I believe that we would shorten the war
by putting our whole Bomber effort against industrial and political targets
against Germany . . . The various operations should fit into one comprehensive pattern, whereas I feel that they are more like a patchwork quilt.'[42]

On 1 November Harris wrote to Portal disagreeing with Tedder's observation and explaining the practical constraints under which his Command
was operating.[43] He claimed that, in fact, the war had already been 'vastly
shortened by concentrating the bomber effort in the last three years against
war potential industrial targets inside Germany.' It had made a major
contribution to Russian successes in the east, to the allied success in the
Mediterranean and 'to the walkover which the armies experienced in
France.' Conversely, he argued, when heavy attacks on Italian cities ceased,
the Italian campaign 'bogged down progressively'; in subsequent

correspondence, Portal was to ask Harris for evidence to support his claims, but the Commander in Chief's rationale was sustained more by the hardening of 20 years of RAF doctrine than by systematic bomb-damage assessment and strategic evaluation.

Harris also pointed out that a great deal of targeting variation had been prompted by 'diversions' such as tactical bombing for the British Army in France, the bombing of coastal guns, and attacking the *Tirpitz* and submarine bases. But even when he was attacking the targets listed in the Directive, several other factors intervened. In bad weather sky markers had to be used, 'and we necessarily in those conditions paint with a large brush'. Other targets were selected to test 'special equipment'. But above all was the 'decisive effect of weather and tactical factors on what can be done at any given moment', for example, cloud with high icing indices and the need 'to make [the enemy] spread his defences out and keep them spread', so that the defence provision was not unnecessarily simplified. Specialist attacks required diversionary, non-specialist raids which might not seem to fully fit the desired pattern. 'The bomber offensive cannot be run as a programme merely by ticking off items as accomplished one by one from a list.' That assertion was weakened slightly by a later comment that, 'In the last 18 months Bomber Command has virtually destroyed 45 out of the leading 60 German cities. In spite of invasion diversions we have so far managed to keep up and even to exceed our average of $2^1/_2$ such cities devastated a month.' He concluded by asserting that completion of 'this vast plan', which the Germans themselves believed to be 'their worst headache', would do 'more towards accelerating the defeat of Germany than the armies have yet done, or will do.'

Portal countered by emphasising the importance of the oil plan and questioning some of Harris's arguments about specific target selection. In correspondence extending for 14 letters the two men's positions became intractable. Harris explained that oil targets were small and usually outlying, demanding visual identification by day or visible ground markers by night.[44] But during the winter months only about eight clear days and nights could be expected and of those, 20 per cent would be unpredictable. It would therefore be impossible to sustain an oil campaign against oil targets beyond those located in western Germany.[45] Instead, he continued to argue, area bombing would include not only oil but the other target sets also.

Had Harris rested his argument there, Portal could have pointed out that adherence to the area campaign, by Harris's own admission, demanded repeated attacks to deny Germany the opportunity for reconstruction. Like Trenchard before him, Harris had to vary his targets consistently to deny the *Luftwaffe* the opportunity to concentrate defences against the

bomber streams. Not until the attacks on Iraq in 1991 would a bomber
force be able to strike simultaneously and heavily enough against strategic
targets to bring decisive force to bear. Even then, as explained below in
Chapter 8, the desired effects were not always achieved, against target
arrays far smaller than those faced in 1944. But Harris also chose to attack
the targeting intelligence upon which the 'panacea' target had been identified. His particular irritation was directed against the recommendations
emanating from the 'Ministry of Economic Warfare' (MEW) who 'in the
past have never failed to overstate their case on "panaceas", e.g., ball bear-
ings, molybdenum, locomotives, etc., in so far as, after the battle has been
joined and the original targets attacked, more and more sources of supply
or other factors unpredicted by MEW have become revealed.'[46] And later,
'I throw doubt on the oil policy because as I say I put no reliance whatever
on *any* estimate by the Ministry of Economic Warfare . . . because of their
past record (their amateurish ignorance, irresponsibility and mendacity is
[*sic*] perhaps most flagrantly exampled on the specialised side of their SOE
activities).'[47]

In vain did Portal explain how targeting did not emanate from MEW,
but the Combined Strategic Targets Committee, drawing on specialist
advice from British and American oil engineers, on photographic interpretation, repair probabilities and analyses plus ground intelligence
wherever possible. 'Documentary' evidence on the raids on Ploesti and
Bucharest earlier in 1944 had at first been inaccurate by up to 63 per cent,
but 'for the last two months they coincided exactly . . .' although, he continued, 'there were some substantial but compensating errors.'[48]

The ultimate, cumulative impact of the oil targeting on German military
capability, and especially on aircraft availability, is now well documented.
It is also clear that allied technical and industrial intelligence was far better founded than its German equivalent. Nonetheless, it had made mistakes
and even at this stage of the oil campaign was still capable of widely inaccurate analysis. As a result, many thousands of tons of bombs were wasted,
and many scores of aircrew lost to little purpose, quite apart from any disputes about area bombing. *Desert Storm* would illustrate that there was
still some way to go to secure reliable and relevant target intelligence for
strategic bombardment.

By mid January 1945, the responsibility for deciding bombing priorities
itself had become an issue. On 18 January Harris ranged one last time over
his objections to the oil plan, and his fears that its pursuit would negate all
that had been achieved already by Bomber Command. He bitterly attacked
a procedure whereby he was 'merely sent lists of targets by the Air
Ministry, made out in priority in committee presided over . . . by an ex-sta-
tion commander of my command who has always been persona non

grata . . . I am therefore left only with the power of selecting from those lists, within their dictated priorities, as the tactical and meteorological circumstances permit. It may perhaps be that the powers of a Bomber Commander in Chief should be limited to the tactical and technical running and the administration of a force, while others directly or indirectly control the strategic policy and the *ad hoc* overall application of the force, virtually without prior consultation with the Commander in Chief while the responsibility for what results is in the outcome his. It is, to say the least of it, a peculiar position, even if it is an unavoidable one, which I doubt.'[49]

This was the letter which culminated with the Commander in Chief's affirming that he had no faith in the oil policy but that he had implemented it to the best of his ability and was not prepared to lay himself open to the charge that a policy doomed to failure had failed because he had not really tried to make it work. That placed him in 'an intolerable situation'. It was for the CAS to consider whether he should remain in it.

Portal's reply is well known for its temporising both on Harris's personal position and on the C-in-C's opposition to allied policy. An earlier paragraph however illustrates how far dogged pursuit of one objective could threaten that flexibility which is air power's most valuable asset. Portal wrote: 'I think it is fairly evident that where a force is concerned that is capable of striking at an infinite variety of targets in an area stretching from Northern Norway to Austria, and when the choice of the policy for its employment has a direct bearing on operations of the other Services and the Allies on every front, then this policy must be laid down by those responsible for the higher direction of the war. The commander of an army or fleet has a relatively constricted area which he can influence. His enemy is in front of him and all he has to do is to destroy the forces in contact with his own. Even for that he gets a directive from higher authority.'[50]

The corollary to the ubiquity and flexibility of air power is that it must not become synonymous with one role, which is where it was heading in Bomber Command. In the nuclear age it would move off again in a similar direction in both the RAF and the infant USAF. Acrimony over the emergence of 'independent air power' had been aggravated by fears by the army and the navy of subordination and exclusion in the face of air force assertions of superior effectiveness in their traditional environments. There was more than a little irony therefore in a situation in which air force commanders subsequently objected to a diversion of effort requested by those same army and navy colleagues. The issue would have considerable relevance in a later age when the roles of a total weapon system, such as a B2, tended to be debated only within the context of USAF's strategic commitments. 'Ubiquity' in practice means that air power contributes to environments in which the priorities of the other services may dominate.

In subsequent conflicts in Korea and south-east Asia, friction would develop between air power policy makers and the commanders responsible for its application. Happily in the Gulf Conflict of 1990–91 the clear-cut allocation of and harmonious acceptance of responsibilities between policy staff and executive commanders was a model for the future. The same, however, still could not be said about relations between air forces and navies. One other issue simmered below the surface of the Portal-Harris confrontation until abruptly spelled out by Portal on 8 January 1945. Stung by Harris's allusion to the futility of allied attacks on German fighter production, he reminded the Commander in Chief that 'Had the American air forces joined with Bomber Command in bombing cities instead of fighter production, there is every possibility that the whole combined offensive might have been brought to a standstill. It was only by a narrow margin that they gained the ascendancy which virtually cleared the skies for *Overlord*, the prerequisite condition for its launching, and obtaining freedom to proceed to the attack of oil. The situation was clearly appreciated by the Air Staffs at the time . . .' Portal then quoted from the Combined Bomber Offensive Plan of 12 April 1943 which stipulated the checking of the growth of German fighter strength for combined services action on the continent. Then the CAS drove not only to the heart of Harris's campaign but also to the 20 years of too easily accepted doctrine which had preceded it: 'Thus, while area bombing, if it could have been continued long enough and in sufficient weight, might in the end have forced the enemy to capitulate, his countermeasures would have prevented us from maintaining such a policy to the decisive point. We would have been forced to precision attack to maintain the air situation needed to continue the offensive at all.'[51]

This epitaph on area bombing was written by a previous Commander in Chief of Bomber Command, himself also a product of the RAF's bomber schooling of the inter-war years. By January 1945 Harris was a national hero. He believed deeply in his policy and he had infused that belief into his crews, whose loyalty and affection he retained long after the considerable post-war criticism and despite the heavy losses they endured at the time. Had that not been the case, Portal would surely have relieved him of his command. The correspondence between them reminds us that wars are fought by men, and men who have risen to the top of their chosen professions are likely to be strong characters who have usually been proved correct in their decisions and successful in their actions most of the time. They are not easily convinced when they are wrong. There is, however, no room in war either for this kind of policy disagreement or the well-documented personal animosities which disfigured other senior relationships.

Fortunately, allied superiority in the air and on the ground was so great in 1945 that the corrosion induced by personal disagreements among commanders mattered little to the war's outcome. It may not always be thus. Somehow an air commander, along with his navy and army colleagues, must be able to distinguish between determination and stubbornness as well as between co-operation and concession. The fewer the resources available, the stronger the opposition, the more complex the problems, the greater the need for both determination and co-operation. In air power's first century, armies and navies have not had a monopoly of professional and intellectual thrombosis in responding to unforeseen problems.

In 1944 the problem facing both British and American bombers had been the *Luftwaffe:* the opposing enemy force. Early attempts to apply pre-war USAAF doctrine, of large-scale air bombardment by self-defending bombers had ended with disaster over Schweinfurt. The advent of the long-range escort fighter, plus the critical decision on 21 January by General Doolittle to encourage the escorts 'to meet the enemy and destroy him rather than be content to keep him away'[52] initiated a war of attrition, producing the results referred to by Portal. It was not just the concentrated attack on German fighter production in February 1944, but the ensuing, increasingly one-sided combat between USAAF and *Luftwaffe* fighters, which prepared the way for allied air superiority over Normandy and ultimately everywhere else. In the week of 19 February the USAAF lost 227 bombers and the RAF 157. But in the same period the *Luftwaffe* lost 282 fighters,[53] which amounted to over one-third of its operational strength, and over 100 irreplaceable veteran pilots and commanders. More than 5,000 allied aircrew died or became prisoners of war in Operation *Argument*, but the USAAF's VIII Fighter Command ended the week with 90 per cent more *Mustang* P-51s than it had at the start. The huge number of aircraft lost by the allies were speedily replaced, but the *Luftwaffe* could not do the same. After three weeks of nearly continuous combat, General Spaatz sent an exclusive message to General Arnold, 'The operations during the past week had the major purpose of forcing the German fighter force into battle. Three attacks were made without any attempt at deception . . . it is too early to gauge the full effect of destruction of fighter production plus their heavy air wastage, we of course are all confident that the air battle is in our hands.'[54]

Throughout warfare it has been a most desirable objective to inflict damage on the enemy without having to become involved in a fight. In air warfare a temporary technical advantage has occasionally made it possible. The *Gothas* achieved it for a while in 1917, the *Mosquito* achieved it in the later stages of the Second World War. In the Gulf War the F-117 would achieve it and stealth technology offered the prospect of a longer period of offensive advantage. Set against a century of air warfare, however, the periods of immunity were fleeting. Whatever the strategic objective, if it is important enough, the enemy will seek to defend it, and sooner or later the offensive immunity will be lost, combat will recommence and attrition between the opponents will become a decisive factor. In the Second World War, the arm which had promised to reach into the enemy heartland and make trench warfare unnecessary became itself committed to a prolonged battle of attrition. A total of 55,573 Bomber Command aircrew lost their lives, out of a Royal Air Force total of 70,253. The USAAF lost 35,000 in the combined offensive. The British Army lost 147,000 in the entire war. Of great significance is the fact that in the First World War the officer losses of the British Empire totalled 38,834 and, as one distinguished historian has observed, 'this slaughter of the nation's elite was widely regarded as the most tragic and damaging aspect of that war'. Yet the cost to Britain of the alternative in 1939-45 proved to be very much higher.[55]

There the comparison with the First World War ended. Whereas air power was only peripheral to that first major conflict, not only was it dominant throughout the second, but without the strategic bomber offensive the outcome would have been very different. The Battle of Britain had ensured that Britain would not make peace, but for four more years the only way to take the war back to Germany was by air. As a result, at no time could, or did, Germany concentrate all its air power on the Soviet front. On the contrary, at the end of June 1944 – at the time of the Soviet offensive in Belorussia, only one-third of the German fighter force was deployed against Soviet forces, while two-thirds faced the allies in the west.[56] But more significantly it was a fighter force which, despite being afforded priority in production and increased in size, was worn down after four years of incessant combat. In June 1944 the *Luftwaffe* lost 1,441 fighters over France and Germany, while below them the allied armada landed without interruption from the air: a situation which may be contrasted with the events across the Channel four years previously.

Without the bomber offensive, German priorities could have focused on the eastern front and other theatres; there would have been no diversion of resources to homeland air defence and no pressure to allocate other resources to retaliatory terrorist weapons such as the V1 and the V2. The war on the continent would have been decided without British and American participation and the subsequent face of Europe would have looked very different – either way. The theorists were correct in forecasting a capacity to strike at the heart of an opponent; they erred in assuming that such a blow would in itself be decisive and in not foreseeing that the enemy would marshal his defences in the air just as he had always done on land and at sea.

After Hiroshima, there were those who argued that Douhet had finally been vindicated. But one penetrating and objective analysis of Douhet's theories said all that was to be said: 'Atomic weapons seemed to grant a new relevance to Douhet because a few bombs could now devastate a country . . . If the only circumstances that make Douhet relevant is nuclear holocaust, then he is totally irrelevant.'[57]

By 1945, several well-founded conclusions about air power had replaced earlier forecasts. For example, by General Omar Bradley: 'Granting the axiomatic and supreme importance of air superiority . . . A proper conception of the term regards it as securing control of the air in order to insure the unrestricted use of that element in carrying out offensive operations against the enemy not only in the air but on land and sea.'[58] Or, by the United States post-war American Strategic Bombing Survey, 'The German experience suggests that even a first class military power - rugged and resilient as Germany was – cannot live long under full scale and free exploitation of air weapons over the heart of its territory.'[59]

General Spaatz believed that strategic air power was the 'most powerful instrument of war thus far known, because of its ability to concentrate force from widely dispersed points on to specific targets, because it could penetrate deeply to destroy vital targets beyond the reach of armies and navies and because it could be economical in the force required to concentrate on a limited number of vital target systems; in sum, strategic bombing was the first war instrument of history capable of stopping the heart mechanism of a great industrialised country.'[60] Up to that point General Spaatz had simply confirmed the forecasts of the pre-war enthusiasts, but he went further: 'The first and absolute requirement of strategic air power in this war was control of the air in order to carry out sustained operations without prohibitive losses.' One would have thought that this also would have been a final word: air superiority allowed strategic bombardment to take place; it was not and could not be the product of strategic bombardment.

In July 1945 the theory and practice of air power seemed for the first time to be at one. But the explosion in August of the atomic weapons at Nagasaki and Hiroshima began a second divergence which was to last as long as the first one, albeit for different reasons. Now, however, the theory was to dominate the confrontation between East and West, while the application of air power elsewhere in the world would largely proceed subject to more practical influences. The confrontation is traced below in Chapter 3.

Variable Contributions

The jet engine, ballistic surface-to-surface missiles, surface-to-air missiles, radar and the atomic bomb were the most dramatic inventions of the Second World War. With other evolutionary processes they would have a synergistic impact on air warfare. For example, the construction of much larger aircraft with pressurised cabin and powerful engines directly facilitated air transport, but also provided the volume for in-flight refuelling tankers and the installation of command, communication and control systems hitherto confined to ground operations. Electronic warfare was reinforced by mobility and large power sources. Speed and endurance were no longer incompatible if the airframe was big enough to support both powerful engines and their required fuel load. Between 1945 and 1995 there were only two further innovations affecting air power. The impact of the exploitation of space would, initially at least, be largely restricted to improved communications. The second innovation, however, the microprocessor, would considerably accelerate the existing synergies in air power. It offered increased control, increased speeds of decision-making, increased power and increased precision by order of magnitude, while at the same time reducing weight, volume and power-generating requirements. In other words, more than any other single invention the microprocessor would enhance the attributes of air power and reduce the penalties of heavier-than-air operations.

The synergism would explode over Iraq in January 1991 and generate euphoria among air force commanders. Two quotations capture the spirit of *Desert Storm:* 'I am utterly convinced that the outstanding and vital lesson of the last war is that air power is the dominant factor in this modern world and that, though the methods of exercising it will change, it will remain the dominant factor as long as power determines the fate of the nations.'[61] Another: 'For good or ill, air mastery is today the supreme expression of military power. And fleets and armies, however necessary and important, must accept subordinate rank. This is a memorable milestone in the march of man.'[62]

The quotations were appropriate to 1991, but in fact the first was said by Marshal of the Royal Air Force Lord Tedder in a lecture at Cambridge in 1947 and the second by Winston Churchill at the Massachusetts Institute of Technology in 1949. They were both referring to World War II. A cursory survey of warfare between 1945 and 1991 should induce caution about making similar statements in the aftermath of *Desert Storm*.

By the time the next major international conflict broke out in Korea in 1950 a number of wars were under way in several parts of the world. They were mainly located in the territories of the British and French empires. They were not usually dignified with the name 'war'; rather they were 'emergencies' or 'insurgencies'.[63] Reference to some of these conflicts is made in Chapter 6 below. With one exception, Algeria, air power was not 'dominant' anywhere and seldom aspired to a level above peripheral. Its impact was largely restricted to tactical mobility and harassment. There was no opportunity for strategic bombardment, while topography and climate were frequently not conducive to sustained operations of any kind. At Dien Bien Phu air power overreached itself in the face of carefully sited anti-aircraft artillery. In Indo China and in every other colonial conflict, the imperial power enjoyed complete air superiority but with no impact on the political outcome. Consequently, an assertion that, since 1939, 'no state has lost a war while it maintained air superority'[64] defines warfare in the context of air power rather than the other way about. In Algeria, on the other hand, the French achieved a military victory over their opponents by extensive and imaginative use of helicopters and fixed-wing aircraft for tactical mobility, reconnaissance, harassment and sanctuary denial. A generation later in south-western Oman, in not dissimilar territory, a handful of RAF aircraft would reduce rebel activity. But the military situation was resolved on the ground and 'the limited part that air support was playing had little influence on the course of events.'[65]

In Korea itself, air power statistics were formidable. Over a million sorties were flown by the allied air forces; 476,000 tons of ordnance were dropped and over 2,000 aircraft lost in four years. In the early weeks of the war US aircraft intervened decisively in the battle around Pusan, establishing complete air superiority and inflicting such heavy losses on North Korean ground forces that they lacked the strength to break through. Thereafter, interdiction of North Korean roads and railway logistics isolated the Inchon landing area and prepared the way for the allied invasion of North Korea itself.

Yet the confident forecasts about the implications of air power's dominance were wide of the mark in Korea. Nuclear weapons were politically unacceptable, quite apart from a scarcity of targets. Chinese fighters enjoyed sanctuary in their airbases across the Yalu. Interdiction slowed down North Korean supplies but never halted them, as the traffic was dispersed, concealed by day and moved forward under cover of darkness. Air power could not halt the Chinese onslaught of November 1950 and air reconnaissance failed to detect its preparation or arrival across the Yalu. The subsequent manpower-intensive supply lines of the Chinese proved resilient to interdiction while 'strategic' bombing was frittered away without any identification of the enemy's centre of gravity. Further north, along the Yalu, a continuous battle for air superiority to reduce losses in the UN bomber force was finally won, but with little significance for the fighting on the ground or the final political outcome of the war. The war was, however, regarded as an aberration and therefore could not invalidate theories of 'dominant' air power.

Meanwhile conflicts erupted elsewhere with or without the presence of air power. Rapid reinforcement defused an Iraqi threat to Kuwait in 1961.

Ostentatious deployment of RAF nuclear-capable 'V' bombers to
Butterworth, Malaya, in 1965 might have deterred an over-enthusiastic
Indonesian government, but 'Confrontation' was actually settled along the
jungle borders of Borneo. In the war between India and Pakistan in 1965
air superiority was never contested, air power was largely restricted to
ground support and the air war came to an early halt as a result of shortage of spares and weapons imposed by international embargo. Air power
has been similarly peripheral in subsequent scuffles in south Asia.

Meanwhile, controversy continues to surround the contribution of air
power in the war in south-east Asia. One argument alleges that political
constraints and interference from Washington inhibited air power so much
that only when it was fully applied by the *Linebacker II* campaign in
December 1972 was the political objective achieved and the Hanoi regime
forced to the conference table. The other side points to the lack of a clear-
cut political objective; the failure to identify the enemy centre of gravity;
confused tactical priorities; duplicated and competitive command and control; inappropriate targeting; prohibition of offensive counter-air on North
Vietnamese airfields; failure to build up in-theatre expertise; repetitive and
inflexible routing; unfavourable topography; and unfavourable climate: a
list of factors combining to reduce the impact of air power in the theatre no
matter what political constraints had been imposed.

In the Vietnam War, one million fixed-wing and 37 million helicopter
sorties were flown. Seven hundred aircrew were lost over North Vietnam
and altogether 3,700 fixed-wing aircraft and 4,900 helicopters were lost.
Good close air support by helicopters and fixed-wing aircraft was developed and the disasters endured by the French a decade earlier were avoided.
The SAM threat was countered by ECM and *Wild Weasel* defence suppression. Precision guided munitions were introduced with devastating
effect, especially on bridges. Despite being unable to attack North
Vietnamese aircraft on their bases, air supremacy was established.

But whether air power was not allowed to 'dominate' the war in Vietnam
or whether circumstances combined to reduce its effectiveness, the result
was the same. It did not determine the outcome and even the reasons for
the Hanoi government's going back to the conference table in 1973 may
ultimately be found to be more complex than simply submission to the
B-52 attacks on Haiphong.

An alternative interpretation of the air campaign was offered by one
scholarly and brave USAF analyst which is likely to set a bench mark for his
successors. He sought to relate air power to changing political requirements and concluded: 'Difficult to fathom is the airchiefs' lingering
conviction that their doctrine was right throughout Vietnam - and that is
it right for the future . . . For the Air Force, the guerrilla struggle during

most of the Vietnam war was an unacknowledged anomaly that may well reappear... Bombing doctrine remains geared to a fast paced conventional war, and the conviction that such doctrine is appropriate for any kind of war permeates the service . . .'[66]

The contribution of air power to conflict in Afghanistan is also examined in detail in Chapter 6. Here, Soviet air superiority was challenged from the ground and many factors other than air power induced Soviet withdrawal.

During the 1980s, Iraq and Iran fought each other to a stalemate. Iran had a technological advantage in the air at the outset, with F-14s, F-4s and the legacy of the Shah's well-provided, USA-sourced air force. It attacked oil facilities in Mosul and Kirkuk, dams, petrochemical plants and Baghdad city on several occasions. Neither side however possessed sufficient offensive support aircraft to make much impact on a war primarily fought by ground forces. In due course, cut off from US sources of weapons, aircraft and spare parts, the Iranian Air Force withered on the vine. The Iraqi Air Force showed no inclination to launch large-scale attacks against either tactical or strategic targets until in 1983 Iraq bought a handful of *Super Etendard* long-range attack aircraft from France, together with AM-39 stand-off air-to-surface missiles. They were used against Iranian oil installations and shipping in the Gulf, supported by air-to-air refuelling. In May 1987 they hit the USS *Stark* by mistake, killing 37 sailors and injuring many more. A year later USN vessels in the Gulf were at a much higher state of alert, and the USS *Vincennes*, equipped with the most modern *Aegis* air-defence system, fired missiles at an intruder identified by the crew as hostile. The intruder was an Iranian civilian Airbus, with over 200 passengers on board. All died. Consequently this particular war had wide-ranging unexpected ramifications, but although it brought two of the most powerful Third World countries into conflict, air power had no influence on its outcome.

Meanwhile, deep in the southern hemisphere, Britain had reacted unexpectedly and decisively against the Argentinian invasion of the Falkland Islands.[67] Here air power on both sides influenced the strategy and tactics employed by the participants. Argentinian land-based air power savaged Royal Navy vessels and forced British aircraft carriers to stand off the Islands at maximum operating range. Had Argentinian bombs been correctly fused the losses suffered by the Royal Navy would have been even greater. A single *Vulcan* attack on Port Stanley airfield prompted a defensive redeployment by *Mirages* on the mainland. Conversely, however, the deployment of an Argentinian aircraft carrier was inhibited not by air power but by the threat from British submarines. In the short and very small-scale Falklands operation air power undoubtedly exercised a strong influence on the outcome, but it was essentially and, in view of the geographical circumstances, inevitably seapower which was the dominant arm.

In sum, in a number of conflicts, ranging in scale from Korea and Vietnam, through Iran-Iraq to the brief but decisive conflict in the Falklands, the forecasts of Tedder and Churchill, not to mention those of countless other air power enthusiasts, were simply not borne out. As Mark Clodfelter so eloquently illustrated in his Vietnam study, if air power is to be applied effectively, it must be relevant to the desired political objective and appropriate to the strategic environment. The ability of air power to dominate a conflict and determine its outcome would be the product of many other factors as well as the political objective. They would include possession in the first place of a potentially influential air force and the resources to sustain it in combat, the political will to use it, the extent of the defences arraigned against it, the topographical and meteorological environment, technological advantage, and the levels of destruction and casualties either side is prepared to accept. The list could be extended considerably and it could be applied with equal relevance, albeit with variations in individual factors, to either seapower or land power. The exception, between 1945 and 1991, was the incessant conflict between Israel and her neighbours.

Air Power as a National Instrument

When Israel became independent in May 1948 the infant state was only nine miles wide to the east of Tel Aviv, 70 from the coast to the Dead Sea and 400 miles long from the Lebanon border to Eilat on the Gulf of Aqaba. Its population was two and a half million. It was surrounded by hostile states : Egypt, Jordan, Lebanon and Syria, with a total population of approximately 50 million. Beyond them were several other states which either opposed the establishment of the State of Israel from the outset or joined the opposition during the next 45 years. For the greater part of this period Israel was either involved in open war with her neighbours or in hostile confrontation. The state was the product of armed struggle and has depended on military strength for its subsequent evolution. For 40 years the cornerstone of that military strength has been the Israeli Air Force (IAF).

The chronology of the modern state of Israel is punctuated by significant events in the history of air power: the June War of 1967, the War of Attrition, the October War, the Entebbe raid, the Osirak raid, the Beka'a Valley, Tunis and finally, part of 'The Patriot War' of 1991. Israel's strategic environment is unusual and therefore 'lessons' read across to the future of air power, or indeed to contemporary air power elsewhere, need to drawn with particular caution. Moreover, until Israel regards her political position as secure and no longer feels dependent on her armed forces, any military information released 'officially' is unlikely to be neutral, and a similar caveat is required for Arab sources. That said, there is much to be learned about air power from its contribution to Israeli security; most, but not all, is positive.

Most other air forces originated in peacetime and entered combat in either World War I or World War II with at least an embryonic structure, concepts of operations and a combat force. In May 1948, however, Israel possessed a handful of unarmed aircraft and 22 registered pilots. Its combat strength was increased during the War of Independence by four ME-109s, three B-17s and then by a trickle of assorted relics from World War II. The aircraft made one or two spectacular contributions to the war but scarcely affected its outcome. For a while, the cameos of struggles played out in Whitehall and the Pentagon were repeated in Israel before the 'independence' or otherwise of the IAF was determined. There does not appear to have been any appeal to theorists by either side. The first leaders of the IAF had served in one or other of the allied air forces, all in junior ranks and none had any experience of bureaucratic in-fighting. Their common-sense was based on experience and perception. So was that of the Israeli Defence Force (IDF) high command, personified by Yigael Yadin, ex-Haganah commander who subsequently commented, 'When I took on the post of IDF Chief of Staff [in October 1949] I knew that our problem of problems . . . [was] this: were we going to make the same mistake as other nations that established independent air, sea and land forces? Or were we going to establish one general staff for all the forces . . . as befitted a small country, a small force, and short, internal communication routes. It was clear to me that the second way was correct, and that if I could not solve the problem that way I had better resign my post.'[68] The issue at stake, however, was not the 'independence' or otherwise of the IAF, but the nature of its contribution to Israeli security and its subordination not to 'the IDF' but to the Israeli army.

There was a curious reprise in Israel in 1948 of circumstances in Britain in 1917. David Ben-Gurion, like David Lloyd George before him, called upon a South African to advise him about his air force. In less than a week Wing Commander Cecil Margo constructed the blueprint for the IAF. He observed that the IDF command had failed to include senior IAF officers in operational planning, dissipated already minuscule assets and failed to provide adequate support. The IAF's primary role, said Margo, was to defend Israel and its ground forces from enemy aircraft: that required air superiority. Because Israel was outnumbered by its opponents, victory in the air war had to be given resource priority. Once the air war was won, the IAF could help the ground forces. At the time, army demands were draining the IAF's limited resources and weakening Israeli security rather than

enhancing it. Margo fleshed out his comments with recommendations for
new mission planning, control and targeting procedures and finally urged
Ben-Gurion to place the IAF supreme commander on an equal footing
with the heads of the other armed services, answerable to the IDF Chief of
Staff.[69] Ben-Gurion listened, and on 26 July 1948 declared the air force to
be an independent branch answerable only to the IDF Chief of Staff and
appointed Aharon Remez to be its commander. But there was still a long
way to go before Margo's recommendations were to be completely carried
out.

David Ben-Gurion wished to base the nation's defence on a small regular army expanded in crisis by reserves. Remez argued that such a
mobilisation would be threatened by air attack, and therefore air superiority was essential from the outset. Consequently, the air force had to be
the exact opposite of the army. He repeated Margo's position: it had to be
a powerful, full-time force capable of seizing an initiative and establishing
air superiority. It had to have control of its own supplies, training, manpower, intelligence and operations. It also had to take priority in defence
resource allocation.[70] In December 1950 Remez resigned after failing to
persuade Ben-Gurion or Yadin and a large number of IAF officers followed him.

The debate rumbled on into 1953 until changes in leadership slowly
began to modify entrenched positions. Dan Tolkowsky, air force commander in 1953, subsequently and astutely reflected that part of the
problem had been that the airmen had translated their experience from
World War II into an Israeli environment where the air force simply lacked
the capacity to apply any kind of doctrine. No wonder the indigenous IDF
leadership had no grasp of operations. Ezer Weizman recalled that in the
War of Independence the ground forces lost 6,000 killed, while the air
force lost 10 pilots, and some of these by accident. 'None of the battles
were decided by the Air Force.'[71]

Instead of perpetuating the debate, Tolkowsky took two practical initiatives: first he preached and practised combat readiness so that
commando and other army operations could be supported without notice;
and second, he began to train his crews to attack the opposition on the
ground. He also crystallised the significance of air power to Israel. 'From
the ground forces point of view, we were unfortunate. We were surrounded
by enemies on all sides. But from the Air Force point of view it was a ter-
rific advantage. We could offer three hundred and sixty degrees of
protection, and Cairo, Amman, Damascus were only minutes way.' And
since to attack Israel the Egyptians or the Iraqis had first to move their
forces across large expanses of open desert, it should have been 'obvious for
any fool that this was an ideal situation for the use of air power.'[72]

This evaluation came to dominate Israeli defence policy, but the trans-lation of the concept into combat success took time. In the nine days of the Sinai conflict in 1956, more usually referred to in the west as 'the Suez con-frontation', Tolkowsky's air force made a significant contribution - fighting for air superiority and providing close air support - but did not exercise any decisive influence in a strategically indecisive campaign. Of greater signif-icance was the subsequent reconstruction of national war-fighting doctrine which was virtually an adaptation of blitzkrieg. IDF commanders had studied the theories of Basil Liddell Hart and his advocacy of fluid mobile warfare in conjunction with heavy air attack. They added to them the ingredient of pre-emptive attack.[73]

In the nine years between Sinai and the Six-Day War of June 1967 the concepts identified by Remez, Margo and Tolkowsky were related to the ground strategy and given substance by re-equipment, expansion and above all, by training. In 1957 only 17 cadets applied for flying training, and the primary ambition of a young Israeli was still to be a commando in the Palmach tradition. The IAF Flight School had been a low priority both for resources and instruction, suffering in part from the exclusively elitist image of the fighter pilot inherited from the first generation of IAF aircrew. The problems were solved within 12 months by a barbary fighter pilot, who at first resigned when assigned to the position of commander of the Flight School in July 1957. In 12 months Shaya Gazit increased the intake to 80. He organised a personal letter from Tolkowsky to every qualified high school graduate; he insisted on all new instructors being fighter pilots and on two of his instructors going into a newly-formed *Super Mystere* squadron. Subsequently he reorganised the flying training syllabus to accel-erate conversion to jet aircraft. It was a combination of strong leadership, personal example, personal contact, the removal of the chasm between training and operations and, above all, insistence on unalloyed standards of excellence. After several frank exchanges of view with the IAF Commander, Ezer Weizman, Gazit became head of Training Command where he imposed his standards on front-line as well as training squadrons, using computerised records to monitor both unit and individual perfor-mance.

The allocation of front-line aircrew to flying training posts can be a source of additional turbulence and it can increase costs. If, however, front-line experience is not considered necessary, or if flying instruction comes to be perceived as a dead end, one has to ask why does it remain a uniformed commitment at all. The cheapest approach of all is a civilian flying school, and the hope that 'operational conversion' will produce both the military officer and the combat pilot. The interaction in the IAF between training and operational flying had been further developed by 1994, when flying instructors continued to 'belong' and train with their front-line squadrons during their training tour.

The preparation of the pilot for combat received an increasingly sharp focus from 1963. Commander in Chief Weizman instructed his chief of operations, Yak Nevo to prepare a plan for 'achieving air superiority through massive deployment of the IAF', a euphemism for Offensive Counter Air (OCA). The plan was to become the blueprint for the annihilation of the Arab air forces in the June War of 1967.[74]

Never was the aphorism 'train as you intend to fight' so comprehensively addressed. Nevo and Colonel Raphael Sivron, later to be Air Attaché in London, requested and received detailed intelligence on almost every Arab airfield in the region, collating runway data, aircraft and associated personnel. From those data, minutely detailed over-the-target requirements of bomb weight and aircraft were compiled to close runways long enough for the trapped aircraft around them to be destroyed. All the IAF aircraft types likely to be involved in such an attack, which was virtually the whole of the air force, carried weapon loads within Israeli airspace at the heights, speeds and distances necessary to ensure that mission performance data were exact. Precision bombing and ground-attack gunnery became a squadron's first priority, concentrating on low-level navigation, precise timing and complete radio silence from start up to touch down. Finally, the entire plan, known as *Moked*, for 'focus', or 'sacrificial fire'[75] was drawn up in outline and completed with operational appendices which would be kept up to date by the appropriate staffs. It would be kept until a threat to Israel was perceived to require a pre-emptive response. The plan took four years to construct, refine and practise. It was to be executed in four hours on 5 June 1967.

Subsequent analysis of the June War has naturally concentrated on the factors which produced the devastating IAF victory, its impact on the ground campaign in Sinai and the subsequent revision world-wide of airfield protection and defences. It is therefore worth noting that the outcome was by no means a foregone conclusion.

Nasser, like Saddam Hussein a generation later, pursued a provocative political and military policy without the detailed strategic planning and military preparation to support it. Nonetheless, at a meeting on 2 June with his senior commanders he warned them that Israel might attack between 3 and 5 June.[76] The air force commander, General Sodki, argued for a pre-emptive strike against Israeli airfields, radars and troop concentrations, even though no detailed Egyptian Air Force (EAF) plans for such an offensive existed. He was refused by Nasser who explained that for political reasons Egypt must absorb a first blow before retaliating. In those circumstances the EAF was expecting to lose less than 20 per cent of its strength. Despite that meeting and those assumptions no action was taken to raise alert states or disperse aircraft, to the extent that Sodki did not cancel a proposed inspection of air bases in Sinai on 5 June. As a result, most air defence guns in the region were at 'guns tight' when the IAF attacks began at 0845.

Meanwhile, a pre-war IAF internal analysis of the *Moked* plan had concluded that to achieve a 90 per cent probability of closing the runways required many more planes than the 200 which the IAF possessed.[77] Rapid turnarounds and repeated attacks were therefore essential. Even if Sodki had managed to launch a small number or pre-emptive attacks, he would have hit an IAF which had considerably reduced its air superiority training and would have undoubtedly disrupted a complex plan which depended on absolute synchronisation for its success. Thereafter the sanctuary which the IAF enjoyed to turn round its aircraft for repeated waves of attack would have been jeopardised. The perennial lesson is that even a modest OCA effort can disturb an opponent's offensive equilibrium, and the more detailed the plan the more sensitive to disruption it becomes.

The opportunity was comprehensively missed later in the day by Syrian and Jordanian aircraft which, faced by only 12 *Mirages* retained by the IAF to protect the homeland, attacked scattered targets across Israel. There was no apparent co-ordination or concentration even though Iraqi *Hunters* did reach the *Mirage* base at Ramat David. After the EAF had been eliminated, the Syrian and the Jordanian air force, together with a number of Iraqi aircraft, received similar treatment. It is generally agreed that the Arab air forces lost approximately 400 aircraft, the great majority on the ground, to almost 1,000 IAF sorties which cost the lives of 20 pilots. Thereafter, the Egyptian Army was decimated by ground attack in the Sinai desert.

After 1956 Nasser had been preoccupied by the attacks from the British and the French and had consequently underrated the potential of the IAF. In the aftermath of the June War, the Egyptian government moved completely the other way, ultimately basing its military strategy and deployments on the assumption that the IAF was invincible The war of Yom Kippur in 1973 sparked a great deal of controversy about the impact of surface-to-air defences on tactical air operations. Just as in the 1967 conflict, the outcome was greatly influenced by the pre-war attitudes and preparations of the two main combatants, so the events of the October War had their roots in the 'War of Attrition' after 1967.

The decision by Egypt to rely heavily on surface-to-air defences (SAD) rather than aircraft originated in the ignominy of the EAF as a result of its annihilation in 1967, but there were other factors which will continue to recur elsewhere.[78] At the time, the EAF also commanded the SAD but their equally inept performance was overlooked. In the subsequent reorganisation of the Egyptian armed forces, the SAD were taken away from the EAF and a new Air Defence Command was subordinated to the Army. Nonetheless, plans in 1967 to rebuild the Egyptian armed forces proposed an 800-strong EAF by 1971.

The target was not achieved. It was estimated that only one in 1,000 candidates could pass the medical and aptitude tests. Another estimate was that only one candidate in a million could become a fighter pilot. Egypt's population at the time was 35 million and already in 1967 was producing 50 pilots a year. There were insufficient flying instructors, even with infusions from India and the USSR, while language difficulties slowed down the process still further. Maintenance could not keep pace with the increased flying load and flight safety suffered. Between 1967 and 1970 more pilots were lost in training accidents – 83 – than in combat with the IAF. It was subsequently asserted that these generic problems were not unique to Egypt. Not only did the EAF fail to reach a 1:1 pilot:aircraft ratio but the problem was common to most of the Arab world.

Conversely, SAD offered many advantages. While Soviet systems were manpower intensive – a SA-2 battalion for example required 280 people – the required skill levels, even for the comparatively advanced SA-3, were far less than for combat aircraft and there was no shortage of Egyptian conscripts. Training to operational level took only 12–15 weeks compared with three years for aircrew. Medical standards also were lower. Egyptian estimates of the cost of a SA-2 battalion were $8,000 in 1969, compared with $250,000 for a MiG-21.[79] Although there is no evidence to suggest that comparative costs were a significant factor in the preference for SAD then, it was undoubtedly a significant factor in Third World considerations in the 1990s.

The final factor in the Egyptian defensive decision was the influence of the USSR. It was quick to rearm the EAF after 1967 but was loth to supply offensive aircraft and actively encouraged both the separation of the air defence system from the EAF and the former's expansion. In the 1990s, the original political motivation inspiring Soviet support for Egypt may have disappeared, but the economic stimulus of hard currency exports, the possession of a marketable range of SAM systems and a receptive Third World fully aware of the implications of vulnerability to modern air power could combine to reconstruct several of the Egyptian circumstances of 30 years previously.

The War of Attrition presented the IAF with several problems. Egyptian policy was to maintain pressure on the Bar-Lev defensive line on the east bank of the Suez Canal by artillery and nuisance raids until international pressure could be brought to bear on Israel to withdraw from Sinai.

Spasmodic air combat took place with disputed claims being made by either side. But the accumulative impact on the IAF began to impose a strain. The IAF had lost 10 per cent of its aircrew in the June War. Peacetime aircrew strength of the Israeli combat squadrons was roughly one-third active and two-thirds reserve in an establishment of 30. Of those, six would be squadron executives and senior pilots, the other three or four would be 'ab initios' from flying training. Consequently, the bulk of the fighting was borne by a small number of veterans. Ironically, their consistent superiority over the EAF contributed to the EAF's sense of inferiority as Egyptian Intelligence failed to distinguish between the limited number of veterans and the rest of the reservist/ab initio IAF.

A longer-term problem was disclosed: a cadre-reserve combat force designed for a national emergency was not best suited to continuous, smaller-scale engagements. It was this potential weakness in an otherwise impressive IAF that prompted the Israeli government to escalate the war in an attempt to stop Nasser's corrosive campaign. In July 1969 the SA-2 batteries in the northern area of the Suez Canal were destroyed. Six months later the IAF launched a bombing campaign against military and industrial targets in Egypt which began to threaten Nasser's political survival. In January 1970 he turned to the USSR for help, arguing that his fight was not really with Israel, but the USA. The Soviet government responded by despatching 32 battalions of SA-3 missiles, two squadrons of SU-15 and six squadrons of MiG-21 interceptors, together with aircrew, groundcrew, maintenance and electronic workshops. By late 1970 there were between 15,000 and 20,000 Soviet military in Egypt.[80]

In the same period two bombing errors by the IAF killed a large number of civilians, including school children and prompted a temporary suspension of US shipments of *Phantoms* and *Skyhawks*, reinforcing a neutral viewpoint that by 1970 Israeli air power was no longer quite the dominant factor it had been previously. Indeed, IAF operations had been counterproductive: stimulating a massive enhancement of Egyptian air defences and the public commitment of Soviet forces to Egyptian defence at a time when Israel's patron was heavily tied down in Vietnam and in no mood to risk further direct confrontations with the USSR.

On 7 August 1970 a cease-fire was agreed, but it failed to stop the completion of the SAD belt along the west bank of the Canal. Israeli air power had been stymied in the War of Attrition by a combination of political and military factors, and some at least of the IAF crews were pleased to be out of it. Squadrons' attrition-exchange ratios had changed from 1:40 in the air to 2:4 against missiles. One professional and gallant *Mirage* squadron commander subsequently observed: 'When the cease-fire was declared we thanked God'. One night at the forward base of Bir Gafgafa he had actually declined a directive to scramble, saying, 'We have no strength left.' Another reflected: 'We were fighting a centipede – you hit it here and two more legs grow in its place. You hit it there and it keeps growing. We were fighting an enemy that seemed not only irrational but with unlimited resources. It was like trying to empty an ocean with a bucket.'[81] One Arab military scholar summarised the cause and effect of the War of Attrition in terms which could have been applied equally accurately to the *Intifada* on the West Bank and in Gaza 20 years later: 'The War of Attrition aimed both at imposing a higher price on Israel for keeping the occupied territories and bringing the Middle East crisis to the attention of world opinion.'[82] It also marked the switch of Egypt's political objective from the total 'liberation' of Palestine to one of confining Israel to her pre-1967 borders.

Three years later on 6 October 1973, Nasser's successor Anwar Sadat launched operation *Badr*, named after a battle won by the prophet Mohammed in the holy month of Ramadan in 624. The political objective was to give impetus to the peace process by initiating a limited war to place Israel in a less advantageous position. Inability to confront the IAF in the sky compelled a strategy of limited ground operation under cover of the SAD. On this occasion the Egyptian and Syrian attacks were well synchronised.[83] Both allies achieved tactical surprise, even though the IAF had been on fully mobilised alert for several hours. The problem was that the IAF had prepared to repeat the 1967 pre-emption, this time against Syrian and Egyptian missiles. Defence Minister Dayan however persuaded Prime Minister Meir to let the IDF accept a first blow for international political reasons and as a result the IAF's first task was to deal with the EAF strike across Sinai which accompanied the ground force crossing of the Canal. There was therefore an immediate mismatch between the political objective, the IAF's operational posture and, in the event, the weapons fit as IAF aircraft which had been bombed up for the anti-missile strike were scrambled for air-interception sorties.

Further confusion followed. The IAF established air-to-air superiority over Sinai and began its delayed attack on the Canal missile batteries early the following morning. Then that attack was abruptly checked when the Syrian attack over the Golan Heights began to threaten northern Galilee and the IAF squadrons were switched to the northern frontier.

At this point, in retrospect, the priority allocation of resources to the IAF probably saved Israel from extinction. Certainly the IAF checked the Syrian armoured advance for long enough to allow the ground force reservists to reach the front line and incidentally ensure that their arrival was not interrupted by hostile air attack. In due course the Syrian armour was turned and thrown back to Damascus. In the subsequent post-war analysis, however, IAF satisfaction was tempered by a great deal of critical reappraisal.

There had been only one plan for the IAF in the north, a variation of the pre-emptive, anti-missile attack across Sinai, itself very similar in concept to *Moked* in 1967. But in October 1973 the Syrian missiles were on the move; they included SA-6 on which initially the IAF had no intelligence. In the first anti-missile attack only two Syrian batteries were destroyed. There was no system for forward air control to focus close air support; initially all requests from ground force commanders had to go up to the General Staff for approval. This was the penalty for the centralised control which had facilitated the strategic switch from south to north but had failed to incorporate any tactical flexibility into the structure. Ironically, the same Raphael Sivron who had been one of the architects of *Moked* now appeared on the northern front co-ordinating swiftly delegated tactical air control. His problems were aggravated by Syrian missiles inhibiting battlefield reconnaissance. Even the hardened professionalism of the IAF pilots was frayed by what appeared to be inconsistent orders, inaccurate target intelligence and mounting losses with not a lot to show for them.

These factors are of longer-term significance than the straightforward statistics of the SAD versus aircraft argument. The IAF plan was inflexible and based on assumptions which had been appropriate for 1967 but not for the political and technological circumstances of 1973. Initiative, aggression and bravery by individual pilots were an inadequate substitute for a carefully co-ordinated attack on the layered, in-depth air defence lines either on the Canal or over the Golan Heights.

Meanwhile heavy fighting continued in Sinai as the Egyptians consolidated their positions on the east bank under the umbrella of the SAD. IAF frustrations increased as lack of intelligence concealed the exact location of Egyptian bridges over the Canal. Any time spent looking for targets, as opposed to their swift acquisition during a pre-planned, tactical-defensive approach, was dangerous over the missile-protected area. In 1971 the IAF had abandoned high-level reconnaissance over Egypt and had subsequently lost a *Globemaster* over Sinai to slant range SA-2 while on a photo-reconnaissance sortie. Only after Yom Kippur was it discovered that there had been photographs of the Canal bridges but they were not considered relevant to the IAF because they were not airfields nor SAD sites. The IDF still controlled all intelligence sources, including IAF photographic interpreters.[84] The error did not affect the outcome of this war, but in *Desert Storm* in 1991 the acquisition, interpretation and timely and appropriate distribution of tactical intelligence was still a weakness impeding the flexibility and success of air operations.

On October 14 the Egyptian ground forces made the fateful decisions to move out into Sinai beyond their SAD umbrella and to move their strategic reserve across the Canal. Whether the moves were made in response to

Syrian requests to divert Israeli pressure from the north, or whether in ignorance of the real Israeli ground force strength is uncertain. There are, however, no doubts about the resulting impact of unrestricted IAF ground attack. Air-ground synergy was restored and Israeli troops crossed the Canal, fanned out and overran or destroyed a significant number of SAM batteries. The exact number remains in dispute because of the widespread use of dummies and decoys by the Egyptians. Egyptian sources stated that most of the damage to SAM batteries came from ground fire, including five out of nine moved across to the east bank. Such a loss would certainly account for the Egyptian failure to co-ordinate the movement of offensive ground forces and their air defences.

The significant feature in this phase which should recur in the future application of air power, is the suppression of SAD by ground forces, in their own interest. If air power can deliver more firepower in support of either offence or defence, and if that contribution is being constrained by enemy SAD, then AAA and SAM batteries become a high priority target for counter-battery fire. A soldier will need a lot of persuasion to give hostile SAD target precedence over hostile artillery, but to achieve the greatest air-ground synergism it will frequently be necessary.

In the next major encounter between the Syrian and the Israeli air force, in the Beka'a region in 1982, the synergism worked again even though IDF ground forces did not enter the Beka'a Valley. The annihilation of the Syrian air force took place while the British and Argentinian forces were contesting the Falkland Islands. In terms of the evolution of air power, the battle in the Middle East was a generation ahead.

On 6 June 1982 the IDF launched Operation *Peace for Galilee*, designed to destroy the PLO in southern Lebanon. The contribution of the IAF was constrained by the presence of the SAM batteries to the east in the Beka'a Valley. Syria had deployed SA-6 units there in April 1981. By 1982 the position of every one was known, as were the missile acquisition and guidance frequencies. On this occasion there were no diversions from a carefully co-ordinated strike plan. On 9 October the 19 missile batteries were engaged first by long-range artillery and surface-to-surface missiles which were to destroy the majority of them.[85] Subsequent attacks were delivered by a variety of IAF aircraft dropping free-fall bombs and anti-radiation missiles. In a peculiar operational sequence, the Syrian Air Force then rose to defend the air defence batteries and massacre ensued.

This was indeed a copybook air operation. Target intelligence was comprehensive and precise. Battle damage assessment was provided by battlefield drones. Ground and air fire were completely co-ordinated. Thorough Sigint and Elint guaranteed electronic victory also as ground control, fire control, acquisition and every other ground-based and airborne Syrian radar was either jammed or destroyed. On the Golan Heights in 1973 the electronic-support aircraft had become separated from the *Phantoms* and *Skyhawks* seeking to engage the SA-6s. In 1982 they were in position and contributed greatly to the F-15s' and F-16s' one-sided victory. This was a combined arms victory on the ground and in the air.

It marked a complete recovery by the IAF to the levels of effectiveness traditionally associated with it. The period between 1973 and 1982 had been punctuated by two single spectacular operations: the hostage rescue from Entebbe in 1976 and the attack on the Osirak nuclear installation in 1981.

In 1975 IAF Commander in Chief Peled had laid out IAF mission priorities as: (1) air superiority, (2) strategic, (3) deep interdiction, and (4) close support.[86] In the Yom Kippur War the IAF retaliated heavily against Syrian military, industrial and economic targets after *Scud* attacks against Galilee. As already noted, one response to Nasser's War of Attrition comprised free-ranging attacks deep into Egypt. If the original meaning of 'strategic' and 'tactical' are adhered to, where the former relates to the war as a whole and the latter to a specific combat area, General Peled's priorities are not only logical, they also illustrate the fact that to a country the size of Israel they are very often one and the same.

In 1994 the IAF was still superior to its neighbouring air forces, and to most of those in the rest of the world, for that matter. Its continued success over 35 years can be traced to a number of specific ingredients. No single one is unique to the IAF, but the combination is, and therefore when the IAF is held up as a role model to emulate, the interaction between the ingredients should also be noted. There are several.

Not only is there conscription in Israel for everyone over 18, there is ample motivation for them. One distinguished retired IAF officer observed: 'Our success, our high motivation and quality are based on the special situation of our nation, the Zionist movement and the high priorities that the government has given us for a long time.'[87] The IAF recruits from among the best of the conscripts. Promotion depends solely on merit, with competence in the air a primary requirement, although 'somebody who is just a good "stick and throttle" jockey will not get too high.'[88] Character, leadership and intellect have consistently been distinguishing features of IAF commanders. Perhaps significantly, IAF promotion is based on a 'mutual-valuation system' in which every officer has to answer questions not just about his subordinates but about his commanders.

Aircrew are selected for technical skills and the ability to make difficult decisions quickly in high-stress situations. They complete an initial eight-year engagement, followed by periods of three years with apparently an unlimited reserve commitment thereafter. It is difficult to imagine any other air force despatching a previous commander-in-chief as a reservist to a regional subordinate position, as happened to General Hod in 1973. In the event, his presence and ability to implement delegated tasking authority on the Golan Heights proved critical. Nevertheless, in recent years the fighter squadrons have been fully manned by regulars,[89] while all reservists fly once a week and in crisis, no distinction is made, in theory at least.

The product has obviously succeeded in blending strong individuality with corporate responsibility, reinforced by habits of constructive self-criticism. Doctrinal guidelines, for example, are re-evaluated annually and after the major conflicts special research studies were undertaken.

For the greater part of its history, the IAF has been better equipped than its opponents. The *Super Mystere*, the *Mirage*, the *Phantom*, the F-15 and the F-16 have all been superior to their Soviet-produced contemporaries. In later years aircraft superiority has been matched by missiles and electronic warfare systems. As a consequence, the IAF has not yet flown against an enemy similarly equipped.

Such superiority is not bought cheaply. Ezer Weizman's request for 100 *Mirages* in 1959 was costed at 200 million dollars.[90] In 1973 the 130-aircraft F-4 force had cost approximately 600 million dollars.[91] Israel is not economically self-sufficient and relies on foreign assistance and borrowing to maintain its economy. Fifteen per cent of the total population (46,500) were employed in defence industries in 1988, compared with 10 per cent in the UK, 11 per cent in the USA, three per cent in (West) Germany and six per cent in France.[92] Israel has been fortunate in receiving financial assistance from the US government since 1949. In 1974, when the armed forces' losses the previous years were made good, military assistance jumped from 307.5 million dollars in the previous year to 2.482 billion dollars after President Nixon had asked Congress for emergency aid, including loans for which payment would be waived. Coincidentally, a modest military loan programme began in 1959, the year of Ezer Weizman's search for *Mirages*. From 1971 to 1994 US aid to Israel averaged 2 billion dollars per year, of which two-thirds has been military assistance. After 1987, military assistance levelled off at 1.8 billion dollars per year.[93]

In the Arab-Israeli conflict, air power really did dominate, because it was in complete harmony with the strategic environment. For 35 years air power was Israel's chosen security instrument. It was suited to the topography and climate. It capitalised on a literate and technologically-advanced population. It offered defence and attack against all manner of external threats. It derived the maximum effectiveness from superior technology wielded by highly-motivated professionals who remained professionals when they became reservists. Funding was not unlimited, as the *Lavi* project illustrated, but in Israel's case, without provision for security, there could be no provision for anything else.

But even for Israel, air power could not provide absolute security, especially against enemies within her own frontiers. In air power's second century, the IAF will face three emerging challenges, none of them in the air. They will be the new generations of mobile SAM, mobile surface-to-surface missiles and targets concealed in a civilian population. If any air force has the skill, determination and imagination to meet such challenges, it will be the IAF.

CHAPTER 3

THE DOMINATION OF CONFRONTATION

The most visible influence on the evolution of air power between 1945 and the collapse of the Soviet empire in the early 1990s was the armed confrontation between East and West. It became formalised in the North Atlantic Treaty Organisation (NATO) and the Warsaw Treaty Organisation (WTO). The confrontation became focused on central Europe but it seeped across the globe to influence regional conflicts worldwide and, with strategic bombers, intercontinental missiles, sea-based aircraft and missiles it bought the two superpowers within direct, mortal range of each other.

In fact, it was air power which strongly influenced the nature of East-West confrontation, rather than the converse. The evidence lies in the origins of NATO doctrine, strategy and force structures and in the Soviet military response.

Air Power and the Creation of NATO

After August 1945, Britain and the USA were quick to demobilise. Twelve months later US forces in Europe had been reduced from 31 million to 391,000; British forces from 1,321,000 to 488,000. Meanwhile, it was estimated that the USSR's armed forces strength was about 6 million.[1] Nevertheless in Europe, British and French concerns were initially not with a Soviet threat, but with ensuring that German military power should remain constrained. The celebrated 'Iron Curtain' speech by Winston Churchill in Fulton, Missouri in March 1946 was an embarrassment to the British government, which, at the time, had not ruled out post-war co-operation with the USSR. During 1947, however, the European scene began to darken with the progressive installation of Communist or

Communist-sympathising regimes in eastern Europe. The salient events are well documented. Britain was unable to sustain the burden of assistance to Greece and Turkey and the responsibility was picked up by President Truman in the enunciation of the Truman Doctrine on 12 March 1947. Marshall Aid was proposed on 5 June but rejected by the USSR and the east European states. In September 1947, the USSR created the Cominform to oppose the implementation of the Marshall Man and to co-ordinate the activities of the Communist movement internationally, including the armed struggle in Greece. In February 1948 a Communist *coup d'état* took place in Czechoslovakia. In March 1948 Belgium, France, Luxembourg, the Netherlands and Britain signed the Brussels Treaty to strengthen their economic and cultural ties and to build up a common defence system known as the Western Union Defence Organisation. In June 1948 the USSR imposed the Berlin blockade. Discussions began in July between the USA, Canada and the Western Union powers about Atlantic security and on 4 April 1949 the North Atlantic Treaty was signed by those seven countries plus Norway, Denmark, Italy, Iceland and Portugal.

In theory, the new alliance would collectively identify the threat, determine strategic priorities, devise a structure and procure the necessary forces. In fact, the strategy and force structure would be determined by existing capabilities, or, in the case of the European partners, by their lack of them. American national air strategy was projected and translated into a NATO setting, with considerable long-term implications for the Alliance.

In the United States, the drive by the United States Army Air Force to become independent, emulating the example of the Royal Air Force, had been considerably stimulated by the detonation of the atomic bombs over Hiroshima and Nagasaki. At last it seemed as if the prophecies of Douhet and Mitchell were to be substantiated.

'If we disregard the overall vision and consider only specific assertions,' wrote the strategic analyst Bernard Brodie, 'it is clear that in World War II Douhet was proved wrong on almost every important point he made . . . But it is also true that he was able to create a framework of strategic thought which is considered by many responsible airmen to fit the atomic age astonishingly well.'[2] A decade later Brodie reinforced his conclusion: 'Because of a revolution in weapons which Douhet could never have dreamed of, his philosophy is less challenged today than ever before. People may still reject strategic bombing but not because they doubt its efficacy. Quite the contrary. It is probably true that without the nuclear bomb Douhet's theses would by now have succumbed to those other technological developments since World War II which have made strategic bombing far too costly and uncertain for ordinary bombs. It is also true however, that the framework of strategic thought he created is peculiarly pertinent to any general war in the nuclear age.'[3]

General Arnold, Commanding General of the US Army Air Forces drew together three influential threads in November 1945:

> Future attacks on the United States may well be without warning . . .
> In any future war the Air Force, being unique among armed services
> in its ability to reach any possible enemy without long delay, will
> undoubtedly be the first to reach the enemy and, if this is done early
> enough, it may remove the necessity for extended surface conflict . . .
> It is entirely possible that the progressive development of the air arm,
> especially with the concurrent development of the atomic explosive,
> guided missiles and other modern devices will reduce the require-
> ment for, or employment of, mass armies and navies.[4]

At this time the Air Force was still constitutionally a part of the US Army. General Arnold's assertion of an air threat to the USA, of the primacy of the air arm and of a declining requirement for armies and navies promised to take the light blue embryo beyond independence to interservice supremacy. At the same time, President Truman was seeking what a later age would describe as a 'peace dividend': imposing drastic reductions in armed service funding while fostering 'a sound economy . . . prosperous agricultures', and proposing to 'share our great bounty with war-stricken people over the world.'[5] But he also conceded that, 'This is an age when unforeseen attack could come with unprecedented speed.'[6]

While planning for the post-war period, USAAF staff had not postulated any specific enemy.[7] Even in 1946 threat perception was not unanimous. A view from the newly designated Strategic Air Command was that 'No major threat or requirement now exists nor, in the opinion of our country's best strategists, will such a requirement exist for the next three or five years.'[8] General Arnold's successor as Commanding General of the USAAF, General Carl Spaatz was less certain, and not inclined to share some of his colleagues' enthusiasm for the potential effectiveness of the United Nations: 'In modern war,' he emphasised, 'any nation losing com-mand of the air approaches to its vital areas is in serious peril . . . The surest defence will be our ability to strike back quickly with a counterof-fensive, to neutralise the hostile attack at source, or to discourage its continuance by striking at the vitals of the aggressors.'[9]

In the aftermath of World War II, such sentiments were well-founded in the USA. The only conceivable threat to the country could come from the USSR. The Soviet Union had no blue water navy and the several million soldiers of the Red Army were unable to reach the USA either across the ocean or across the northern ice cap. The USSR was, however, developing long-range bombers and atomic weapons and was known to have shared in the allied inheritance of V2 technology and scientific expertise. Discreet military contingency planning against a longer-term Soviet threat would therefore be a prudent defence policy.

General Spaatz did not restrict himself to comments on direct threats to the USA mainland. In October 1945 he had expressed 'unease' at the haste of demobilisation in a letter to General Arnold. 'With the rapid weakening of our forces in Europe and Asia, the USSR is able to project moves on the continent of Europe and Asia [sic] which will be just as hard for us to accept and just as much an incentive to war as were those occasioned by German policies . . . I believe we should proceed rather slowly toward demobilising our armed forces, particularly units of our Strategic Air Command.'[10] The implication was clear: the long arm of SAC could protect US interests abroad as well as deter or retaliate against attacks on the USA itself.

That capacity still lay in the future. In August 1946 the State Department proposed an air attack on Yugoslavia in response to the shooting down of two USAAF C-47s over that country. General Norstadt, on behalf of the USAAF, had to explain that the Air Force was too weak to risk war. Only three months later did the Air Force despatch six B-29s to fly along the borders of Soviet-held territory in Europe and to survey ' airfields to determine their suitability for B-29 operations'.[11] Most crews would no doubt have preferred their potential airfields to be selected by the more traditional methods of ground survey, measurement and facility evaluation, but nonetheless this was the first dispatch of B-29s to Europe in response to 'Communist' provocation and as a harbinger of future events.

Indeed, the identification of suitable European airfields for use by B-29s had already taken place. In January 1946 General Spaatz and Air Chief Marshal Tedder, RAF Chief of Air Staff, personally surveyed several British airbases to determine which could be improved to handle B-29s. Four were identified without publicity.[12] For several years the atomic bomb would be moved in sections by transport aircraft, together with its assembly team. At the forward operating base the weapon would be assembled and loaded on to a bomber. Hence the need for specific atomic weapons-handling facilities.

Meanwhile, internecine warfare between the US armed services over resource allocation was being aggravated by the lack of a clearly defined security policy in the immediate post-war years. During the hearings of the President's Air Policy Commission held in late 1947, charged with 'making an objective inquiry into national aviation policies and problems', General Eisenhower observed to his joint service colleagues, 'Gentlemen, those five civilian gentlemen [the five members of the Commission] are just patriotic American citizens trying to do something they've been asked to do by the President. I think we really owe it to them to tell them that there is no war plan.'[13]

On 26 July 1947 the USAAF achieved its goal of independence, as the United States Air Force. Air Force commanders were confident about their doctrine of strategic bombardment, but the newly-appointed Secretary of the Air Force Symington had to be asked by General Vandenberg, General Spaatz's successor: 'In a war with the USSR, is our purpose to destroy the Russian people, industry, the Communist Party, the Communist hierarchy or a combination of these? Will there be a requirement to occupy, possibly reconstruct, Russia after victory, or can we seal off the country, letting it work out its own salvation?'[14] No guidelines were available.

There was a confluence of interests in the USAF's concentration on a primary role of strategic bombardment. It obviously provided the service with a role inaccessible to the Army and Navy, although the United States Navy would persist with developing its own nuclear weapon carriers. But it was also politically attractive, offering the possibility of fighting an adversary at long range, well away from American territory, with the maximum emphasis on technology and a minimum commitment of manpower. In the post-war years the USA was not as sensitive to manpower casualties - as opposed to manpower costs - as it was later to become with the legacy of Vietnam.

Few people were aware in 1946 and 1947 that the USAF would have had great difficulty in implementing its strategy. Not only was there a very small number of atomic weapons available, but in January 1947 SAC had only six weapons technicians available to arm such bombs, only 10 modified B-29 aircraft operational and 20 trained crews. No Air Force bomb-assembly teams would be available in SAC until the end of 1947 to replace civilian teams disbanded in 1946. Air Force commanders were exhorted to emphasise in public addresses 'the rate of rebuilding the Air Forces and not our deplorable condition'.[15] Against such a background, a US Joint Chiefs of Staff (JCS) assessment of the relative strengths of East and West, produced in May 1947, lacked a certain amount of credibility:

The Allies [sic] do not have the capability of mobilising or transporting, in the early stages of a war, ground and tactical air forces of sufficient strength to destroy the Soviet Armed Forces which would have to be encountered in depth along any of the avenues of approach which lead to the heart of Russia . . .

On the other hand . . . the United Nations has a capability of undertaking soon after the beginning of the war an offensive strategic effort against vital Russian industrial complexes and against Russian population centers. If this effort, adequately expanded, did not achieve victory it would destroy elements of Soviet industrial and military power to such an extent that the application of this and other forms of military force should accomplish the desired end . . .

Approximately 80 per cent of the entire industry is within the radius of B-29s operating from bases in the British Isles or the Cairo-Suez area.[16]

In May 1947 there were no Western 'Allies'. There was no definition of US political or military objectives in a war with the Soviet Union. There were insufficient bombers or atomic weapons with which to attack the 70 or so 'strategic' targets identified in the USSR. The JCS was also a little ambiguous about the actions of the 'Allied' forces; it was presumably a counterattack along 'the avenues of approach' leading to the heart of Russia? The reference to 'population centres' illustrated the strong Air Force influence on the document. Implicit in the analysis was the impact of strategic bombardment on civilian morale, despite the reported evidence in World War II that at the very least such a result was uncertain. Indeed, a belief in the vulnerability of civilian morale in the face of air attack was to persist in the minds of USAF planning staffs for another 45 years. Nonetheless, the assessment illustrated the JCS identification of the problems of waging traditional ground warfare against the USSR compared with the attraction of long-range air bombardment. One US commentator drily explained the attraction to the USA of a strategy based on long-range atomic bombardment as:

> . . . the perfect fulfilment of all wishful thinking on military matters; here is war that requires no national effort, no draft, no training, no discipline, but only money and engineering know-how of which we have plenty. Here is the panacea which enables us to be the greatest military power on earth without investing time, energy, sweat, blood and tears – as compared with the cost of a great Army, Navy and Air Force – not even much money.[17]

In sum, there was by mid-1947 a strategy for the defence of the United States based primarily on long-range strategic air bombardment and the threat was identified in the USSR. Over the next two years, controversies over unification, the procurement of naval super-carriers and the USAF's B-36, all against a background of a strong presidential desire to drive down the US defence budget, would inhibit the construction of a USAF fully capable of discharging its allocated strategic roles.[18] The USAF position was, however, perfectly in tune with the convergence of international interests associated with the formation of the North Atlantic Alliance.

The British Foreign Secretary Ernest Bevin had led the European initiative to create a North Atlantic defence organisation in which US military strength would be enlisted in the defence of western Europe against a militarily-superior Soviet Union. From July 1948, US and Canadian representatives had attended meetings of the Brussels Treaty planning staffs and learned at first hand the considerable economic and military problems faced by the Alliance members. A participant subsequently recalled, 'Western ground forces numbered only ten divisions. In-theatre combat aircraft probably numbered no more than 400'[19] against some 15,000 in the Soviet Air Force. In that same month the JCS had moved on from the previous year's assessment to draw upon a war plan, *Half Moon*, which specified early and sustained atomic air attacks on the Soviet war-making capacity launched from bases in Britain, Iceland, the Middle East and Okinawa.

Over the next 12 months, informal allied meetings were succeeded by NATO staff planning, culminating in the first North Atlantic Strategic Concept of 1 December 1949. One of six 'Principles' underlying military planning was that 'each nation should undertake the task, or tasks, for which it is best suited. Certain nations, because of their geographical location or because of their capabilities, will be prepared to undertake appropriate specific missions.'[20] The first 'Basic Undertaking' was to 'Ensure the ability to carry out strategic bombing promptly by all means possible with all types of weapons, without exception. This is primarily a US responsibility assisted as practical by other nations . . .'[21]

This policy would come as no surprise to the United States Congress. The North Atlantic Treaty had been accepted by the Senate on 21 July 1949 and later that month General Bradley, representing the Joint Chiefs of Staff, explained the new 'collective' strategy to the House Committee on Foreign Affairs and the assumptions made by the Joint Chiefs: 'First, the United States will be charged with the strategic bombing . . . We have repeatedly emphasised in this country that the first priority of the joint defense is our ability to deliver the atomic bomb . . .' Other assumptions also to be reflected in NATO's 'Basic Undertakings' were that the USA and other Western Union countries would conduct naval operations, that 'the hard core' of ground forces would be provided by the European countries and that the UK, France and other 'closer' countries would provide the bulk of short-range attack and air-defence aircraft while the USAF's tactical aircraft would be maintained for support of 'our own' ground and naval forces.[22]

This was a strategic marriage of convenience. It formally and dramatically raised the stakes in any military adventure against western Europe which the USSR might have been contemplating. In early 1994 it was still not possible to establish for certain the offensive intentions towards western Europe of the Soviet government under Stalin. There was, however, nothing discreet about the US debate over defence spending and strategic priorities. The USSR may or may not have been aware of the JCS's detailed war plans but it could not have missed their unambiguous general drift. Hiroshima and Nagasaki had demonstrated a US willingness to use atomic weapons. Stalin, captive to his own ideology, but a cautious and unemotional analyst of power, may have had little inclination to test US determination. He may also have considered that the formal defensive relationship now established between the USA and the Western Union had changed considerably the ambivalence of the previous strategic environment.

The Berlin Diversion

Meanwhile, on 24 June 1948 the surface blockade on Berlin had been imposed. British response was swift, with an airlift to feed and supply the British garrisons begun within 24 hours. The following day USAF transport aircraft in Europe followed suit. On 15 October a Combined Airlift Task Force was established. By the time that the USSR lifted all surface restrictions on links with Berlin 12 months later more than 2,325,000 tons of food, coal and other supplies had been airlifted into the beleaguered city. Throughout the period RAF and USAF fighters frequently patrolled the air corridors and despite several instances of harassment or 'buzzing' of transports by Soviet aircraft, no measures were taken by the USSR to interrupt the continuous stream.

The USA had, however, responded to the crisis with more than just a protected airlift. In June 1948 one squadron of B-29 bombers from 301st Bombardment Group was already deployed on rotation to the then USAF Airbase at Furstenfeldbruck in Germany. Two other squadrons were despatched to join it on 2 July. On the 17th and 18th that deployment was followed by the movement of two further Groups of 30 bombers each, Nos. 307 and 28, to England, with the intention to deploy an additional Group later, all to be stationed in England for the duration of the Berlin crisis.[23] It was widely believed at the time that the B-29s were able to drop atomic weapons and that a clear signal was being given to the USSR not to interfere with the airlift, although no diplomatic statement to that effect appears to have been made.

In fact none of the bombers was equipped to deliver atomic bombs, and even if they had been there were few weapons available and even fewer ground crews to prepare them.[24] General Kenny, Commander in Chief of

SAC at the time was concerned both about the lack of capability and the diplomatic vacuum:

> The Russians may of course be worried about our 90 B-29s now in Europe but we don't seem to be using them as a club. Perhaps in time the Russians will figure that as long as we don't mention them around the green table, that they are no good anyway.[25]

Whatever the Russian perceptions, they never did interfere with the airlift. But at least of equal significance, the well-publicised strategic posture of the USA did not deter them from imposing the blockade in the first place, and the ostentatious B-29 deployments did not foreshorten it. The impact of air power was in the airlift itself and even that was effected despite the disinclination of the USAF Commander in Chief General Vandenburg to 'divert' his long-range transport aircraft from supporting the SAC to mounting the airlift. He believed that the only way the airlift could be mounted was to denude SAC of the transports necessary for the implementation of JCS war plans should the Berlin crisis erupt into war.[26] It did not, and it was unglamorous airlift which allowed air power to resolve the post-war world's first critical confrontation, not the threat or application of strategic bombardment.

That particular moral got lost in the contemporary struggle for resources raging in Washington. Provisions for a transport fleet greater than that required to support the SAC would have entailed a concession to the possibility that strategic bombardment would not, in fact, determine the outcome of all future wars and would have forced deeper reductions in numbers of heavy or medium bomber squadrons.

As has been noted, NATO's first declaratory policy was collaborative defence, but in practice the incorporation of USAF doctrine and squadrons into the Alliance framework resulted in a dependence on deterrence or strategic retaliation to prevent further Soviet expansion in Europe. In the circumstances it is difficult to identify any other possible outcome, but, with hindsight, the Berlin crisis did indicate that the threat of strategic bombardment might be inappropriate to the scale of incursion or provocation. At the time, such doubts as were expressed were rather more about the efficacy or even morality of the strategic option, rather than its relevance to national or Alliance policies.

In April 1949 a Joint Services Committee in Washington expressed reservations about a strategic air offensive against the USSR. Atomic and conventional air attack against the 70 target areas designated by SAC might inflict a 30–40 per cent loss in Soviet industrial capacity, but it would not be permanent: it would not *per se* bring about capitulation, destroy the roots of Communism or critically weaken the power of Soviet leadership to dominate the people; indeed it might actually 'validate Soviet propaganda . . . unify the people . . . and increase their will to fight'. Nevertheless the Committee unreservedly endorsed SAC plans, stating that 'every reasonable effort should be devoted to providing the means to be prepared for prompt and effective delivery of the maximum numbers of atomic bombs to appropriate target systems.'[27]

Other commentators were less ambivalent: 'It would be ingenuous to assume that the Russians would abandon the type of warfare in which they would be the strongest in favor of one which would leave their finest weapon, the Red Army, on the sidelines. There can be no question, therefore, that a war with Russia would be a land war from first to last . . . At H-hour of Russian D-day, Soviet armies would strike westward in an effort to overrun western Europe and reach the Channel in the shortest possible time . . . Strategic bombing could not take one single Russian infantry man out of the western front . . .'[28] These are some of the more moderate observations by the Military Editor of the *Washington Post* who argued instead for a balanced force response in Europe to the Soviet threat.

President Truman himself had reservations about such concentration on atomic bombardment: 'I don't think we ought to use this thing unless we absolutely have to. It is a terrible thing to order the use of something that is so terribly destructive beyond anything we have ever had. You have got to understand that this isn't a military weapon. It is used to wipe out women, children and unarmed people, and not for military use. So we have to treat this different from rifles and cannon and ordinary things like that.'[29] Fortunately, it was never necessary for the Alliance to decide whether nuclear weapons should be used pre-emptively, or in swift retaliation, or as a last resort.

Division of Labour

Although the choice of strategic bombardment to defeat the USSR and its allies never had to be validated, it dealt an extensive injury to the development of tactical air power within NATO. The success of combined-service, ground-air operations in World War II was not forgotten by the USAF; it was simply considered as overtaken by events. The perceived logic was summarised in early 1949 in the 'house journal' of the USAF :

An Air Force Combat Command should be so organised and constituted as to make it readily feasible to employ maximum strength in the performance of the mission at hand be it strategic, tactical or defensive . . . the tactical employment of air power, being anchored to surface action, is unlikely to assume a place of importance in any major conflict of the future before the decisive action has neared completion. Since an Air Force properly organised and equipped to achieve success in the decisive phase will be capable of performing the necessary tactical operations in the exploitation phase, the peacetime maintenance of a specialised tactical air arm at the expense of the strength and effectiveness of the decisive air echelons is unwarranted. The soundness of this concept is already recognised in the Air Force . . .'[30]

Decoded, the message read: 'The decisive action in any future war will be taken by strategic bombardment; only then will tactical aviation be required; aircraft capable of the former will also be able to discharge the latter; therefore we do not need to allocate resources to specialist tactical aviation . . .' The sentiment was substantiated by the contemporary USAF decision to reduce planned provision for ground-support light bomber groups from five to two and provide for just three squadrons of tactical reconnaissance aircraft.[31]

Such an approach was politically convenient for the USAF, strengthening as it did the young service's independent posture, while the strategic and operational rationale appeared sound. But its value to NATO was to be challenged by the inability of the European allies to fulfill their complementary role, and by the acquisition of the USSR of atomic weapons, in a strategic environment further complicated by the eruption of the Korean War.

Despite formal acquiescence in the 'division of labour' summarised in the NATO Strategic Concept, Britain had already decided that the USA could not be left with a Western nuclear monopoly. The debate was not made public at the time, and it was not associated with any interservice squabbles over resource allocation, but RAF commanders were as adept as their USAF contemporaries – albeit a little more subtle – in presenting the case for strategic bombardment in terms of national necessity. After his retirement, Marshal of the RAF Sir John Slessor observed:

> The RAF today, without a long-range bomber force, would be like the Royal Navy of Nelson's day without its line of battle. If we were to provide as our contribution to the Pax Atlantica only ground-support and maritime aircraft and fighters to defend ourselves - the gunboats and frigates and seaward defences of the modern air fleet - then we should sink to the level of a third-class Power.[32]

This public rejection of the burden sharing specified in the NATO Strategic Concept passed without comment. It was a view shared by the military and by all three major British political parties. The British Chiefs of Staff had stated their own requirement in January 1946 for an atomic bomb to be delivered by the RAF. They included in their arguments the position that 'Britain, as a great power, could not leave her security in the hands of the Americans who, however friendly, could veer so unpredictably from generous international collaboration to self-centred isolationism, as their precipitate cancellation of Lend Lease had shown so recently.'[33] In 1947 specifications for four-engined jet bombers capable of delivering the atomic bomb were given to British industry, although the decision to begin production was not made until 1952.

At the time the RAF was the second largest air force in NATO. Inevitably, a decision to fund a nuclear-capable bomber force would constrain resources available for the British contribution to the European 'balanced forces' specified in the NATO Strategic Doctrine. The government, however, continued to provide for both atomic and conventional force capabilities. Jet conversion of RAF fighters continued, the procurement of a twin-engined jet bomber went ahead, and plans were laid to expand the 2nd Tactical Air Force in Germany.

But no partner, not even the USA, could meet the military requirements specified by the Alliance after the invasion of South Korea in June 1950. The impact of that event on the West was likened by one eminent participant to 'the terror of the year 1000' and it stimulated the rapid consolidation of NATO's organisations and senior command, together with such increased cost requirements that in the words of the same commentator, 'The military authorities called for contributions which the economic conditions of the allies could not sustain. There was a risk that the warrior would be crushed by his own armour. The effort involved in surviving threatened to destroy the survivors.'[34]

It was therefore hardly surprising that the Alliance force goals announced in Lisbon 18 months later in February 1952 of 9,000 combat aircraft and 96 ground force divisions by 1954 would prove unattainable. Before the end of the year British defence expenditure was cut, rather than increased. France expressed inability to increase her forces in accordance with the Lisbon directive and even the USAF, authorised to expand to 95 Wings was considered insufficient 'to win a major war by defeating superior strength in the air and on the ground. A force of this size is intended to be primarily a deterrent . . .'[35] In April 1953 the Lisbon force goals were officially deferred despite the strong dissatisfaction of SACEUR, General Ridgway, who considered his forces in Central Europe too weak to accomplish their mission.

The Lisbon goals never were achieved. NATO staff in 1952 began to study the use of small 'tactical' nuclear weapons against enemy airfields and ground forces. By December 1953 the Chairman of the US Joint Chiefs of Staff could announce 'Today, atomic weapons have virtually achieved conventional status within our armed forces.'[36] In December 1954 the NATO Council approved a Military Committee paper assuming the use of nuclear weapons to counter the 'massive preponderance' of Soviet conventional strength.[37]

The substitution of nuclear weapons for the conventional forces stipulated at Lisbon was politically attractive. It not only avoided the increasing of defence expenditure, it actually facilitated reductions. Fewer servicemen, fewer conventional weapons, less maintenance, smaller staffs, less complicated exercises: the strategic environment became much simpler. It also meant that USAF tactical air forces also developed a nuclear capability, thereby avoiding sensitive issues such as priorities to be afforded to army co-operation. More insidiously for air power, an emphasis on nuclear weaponry reduced the need for air-to-air combat training, or low-level accurate navigation, or precise target identification and acquisition. Instead, a 'fighter' needed to be a bomber 'interceptor' while in the USAF's jargon a 'tactical fighter' became a nuclear-capable fighter bomber, typified by the F-100, F-104 and F-105. Consequently, there was little need to give priority in procurement to air-to-ground weapon accuracy. When the USAF is criticised for having to relearn in the Vietnam War old skills forgotten from Korea and World War II, it has to be remembered that the policymakers believed that nuclear weapons had made such skills redundant.

Of longer-term significance, dependence on nuclear weapons destroyed the semblance of equality between the USA and her European partners envisaged in the original 'job sharing' at NATO's formation. Now, with the imminent exception of the nuclear forces of France and Britain, the protection afforded direct to Europe by 'tactical' nuclear weapons would also be the responsibility of the USA. The strategic subordination of western Europe was complete. The timing of the strategic modification, however, was less than perfect, following the Soviet detonation of a thermonuclear device in 1953 and the subsequent introduction by the USSR of nuclear weapons into Europe. The first medium-range Soviet ballistic missiles were deployed in 1956, and the first *Scuds* a year later. By 1960 the threat of nuclear retaliation in Europe to conventional attack was not altogether credible.

Flexible Response

For seven years the USA and her NATO partners grappled with the need to revise NATO strategy, to seek a politically acceptable, and militarily operable, compromise between two preferred solutions. The USA preferred to confine any conflict with the USSR to Europe. The European preference was to protect territory at its eastern frontiers and invoke intercontinental escalation as the overarching deterrent. The compromise was the revised NATO doctrine of 1967, known colloquially as 'Flexible Response'.

It was explained in the Communiqué issued by the NATO Council of Ministers on 14 December 1967, that the concept 'which adapts NATO current political, military and technological developments, is based on a flexible and balanced range of appropriate responses, conventional and nuclear, to all levels of aggression or threats of aggression . . .'[38]

There was probably never a good time for this decision to be taken. The only significant 'development' was the Soviet acquisition and deployment of nuclear weapons with an intercontinental reach. It would, however, be difficult to identify a less favourable time for the Alliance to seek an expansion of conventional strength necessary to implement the lowest requirement in a posture ranging from forward defence, through controlled tactical nuclear weapons, up to intercontinental nuclear exchange.

For example, this Council meeting was held in Brussels, and paragraph 16 of the Communiqué noted that France had not taken part in the discussion on the new strategic posture 'and did not associate herself with the corresponding decisions'. This anodyne statement concealed the serious impact on NATO of France's withdrawal from the Alliance's integrated military structure in July of the previous year. French air force squadrons and air defence ground units were withdrawn from Germany, USAF units were expelled from France, Alliance logistic and reinforcement routes and rear bases generally were compressed into the Low Countries thereby greatly easing Warsaw Pact air and missile targetting. Contemporary politicians and commanders sought to minimise the impact on NATO's vulnerability to surprise attack, but the move by President De Gaulle could have proved disastrous for the Alliance's defensive posture. In the event, it simply aggravated the problems of moving to a strategy now to include a conventional base which required a strengthening of conventional forces at a time when the USA was preoccupied with Vietnam, the UK was implementing a defence review and reduction, the Soviet Air Force was embarking on a major re-equipment programme and the Arab-Israeli June War had reminded everyone of the vulnerability of unprotected airfields to surprise attack.

Every year thereafter, NATO exercises of various kinds were held to work out the new concept. The scenarios were all variations on a theme: a large-scale offensive by the Warsaw Pact with different durations of warning time available to the West. The 'attacks' were met by conventional forces and after very few days recourse to nuclear weapons was usually necessary. The Alliance was no more capable of waging a protracted conventional war in central Europe after 1967 than it had been before the Lisbon force goals of 1952 were announced. Now, however, a much greater responsibility was allocated to NATO air power.

The revised strategy was still extant in 1985, when the British Defence White Paper identified its three essential ingredients, 'Conventional forces to deter any Soviet non-nuclear attack, to counter it as far forward as possible, and to allow time for reinforcements to arrive . . . Theatre nuclear forces to enhance deterrence by providing a link between conventional and strategic nuclear forces, providing flexibility for options short of a strategic nuclear exchange, and deterring use of theatre nuclear forces by the other side [and] . . . complicating any plans an aggressor might have for massing [conventional] forces for such an attack . . . Strategic forces to provide the ultimate deterrent.'[39]

By 1985, air power had come to permeate every facet of NATO's strategy and, not without coincidence, it was a critical component in the WTO's combined arms offensive doctrine also.

Dependence on Air Power

The Warsaw Treaty Organisation enjoyed many geopolitical and military advantages. They included contiguous territories from east to west and north to south, conferring depth and breadth for deployment, reinforcement and resupply; comparative proximity to the main power base in the USSR; considerable numerical superiority in in-position ground forces in the central region; and in all foreseeable circumstances the initiative of timing, location, extent and method of aggression against the western Alliance.

Conversely, NATO was committed to forward defence, which, by definition, had to be responsive. The central region was separated by geography from the northern and the southern flanks. Rear areas were either shallow, as in the case of the centre, or remote as in the south-west, in the United Kingdom and across the Atlantic. The political nature of the Alliance commitment complicated a rapid, unanimous military response. But only a proportion of national front-line ground forces were in, or readily transportable to, positions appropriate to forward defence. As a result, the warfighting contribution from NATO's air power was expected to be extensive.

Airborne early warning aircraft (AWACs) contributed to surveillance in peacetime and would have given warning at the outset of hostilities to allow allied aircraft to concentrate defensive strength in airspace penetrated by WTO formations. Air-defence aircraft, together with surface-to-air defences, would have been called upon to protect home bases, reinforcement concentrations and routes and win local air supremacy over the battlefields. The inevitable imbalance of firepower on the ground in the early hours could only have been redressed by air-to-ground support, complemented by deeper attack on second-echelon and other reinforcements to reduce or check the opposing ground force momentum.

The contribution of WTO air to the conflict would have been attenuated by air-to-air engagements and by NATO counter-air operations against air-fields. Early strategic reinforcement, and the provision of continuous in-theatre mobility would have been the responsibility of air transport forces, supplemented only much later by large-scale land and sea transport. Tactical reconnaissance, although increasingly complemented by unmanned systems, would also have required the allocation of manned air-craft. The contribution of NATO 'dual capable', in-theatre aircraft, primarily USAF F-111 and British *Tornado* GR-1, would have been par-ticularly significant. They could have attacked airfields and ground force-related targets deeply beyond the battle area by night and day in all weathers with conventional weapons. In extremis, SACEUR could have been authorised to use some of them to deliver nuclear weapons over a sim-ilar combat radius, should NATO's conventionally-armed, ground-force defences have been collapsing in the face of sustained WTO momentum. Moreover, the nuclear capability was perceived to be a significant link in NATO policy, which deliberately refrained from identifying specific points in a possible escalatory process, running from conventional defence, through theatre nuclear capability to the strategic involvement of nuclear-equipped forces.

Therefore the perceived ability of NATO's air forces to make both a strong conventional contribution, and if necessary a nuclear introduction, to warfighting strategy was a very important element in the Alliance's peacetime deterrent posture. There was no comprehensive, formally pro-mulgated NATO doctrine covering all these aspects of air power. All major commands were closely integrated and the chain of command itself, from SACEUR down through the major subordinate commanders, was clearly delineated.

A major problem facing SACEUR, however, was that in the first 48 hours he would be largely dependent on the same aircraft to provide air defence, air superiority and offensive air support. For several years NATO countries had, because of economic pressure, procured multi-role rather than specialist air-defence or offensive air-support aircraft. The most widely deployed example of the former was the F-16 fighter bomber. Specialist interceptors were restricted to the *Tornado* F-3s of the RAF and a handful of British and German F-4s. Specialist offensive support aircraft included USAF A-10s, British *Harriers* and British and German *Tornado*

GR-1s. The *Tornado*, together with the USAF F-111s also had a counter-air, anti-airfield responsibility. Other aircraft which in peacetime trained largely for the air defence role, such as the USAF F-15s or the French *Mirage* 2000s, could also be employed against targets on the ground. To complicate matters still further for SACEUR, several of his most effective combat aircraft, among them the *Tornado* GR-1s, the F-111s and some of the F-16s were also 'dual-capable', that is able to deliver either conventional or nuclear munitions.

SACEUR's dilemma at the outbreak of hostilities would therefore be twofold. First, what proportion of air power to allocate to air defence, and how much to offensive air support? Second, how many of his dual-capable aircraft should he withhold from the early days of combat, for subsequent allocation to theatre nuclear weapon delivery?

Air Power in the Warsaw Treaty Organisation

These questions were to remain rhetorical, but their potential resolution was especially acute because of the increasing prominence the WTO itself came to allocate to air power within the framework of its strategic concepts. Even in 1994 disagreements among Western analysts continued about the role for nuclear weapons envisaged by the Soviet General Staff in the decades of confrontation. The consensus, however, was that if the USSR in its WTO guise could have avoided nuclear escalation it would have sought to do so. Between 1970 and 1978 Soviet defence expenditure rose by 4 per cent a year in real terms, and was believed at the time to account for something like 11–13 per cent of the USSR's gross national product.[40] Between 1967 and 1977 spending for the Soviet Air Force increased more rapidly than spending for any other military service and over three times the rate for defence spending as a whole from 1969 to 1973. Soviet tactical aviation increased in size by about 50 per cent in the same period.[41]

The new generation of MiG-23, MiG-27, SU-17, SU-24 and SU-25 aircraft conferred a much greater offensive capability and, as was customary with the advent of new Soviet weapon systems, their operational rationale was widely and openly described in Soviet and east European military publications. There was no disagreement between NATO and Warsaw Pact sources on the requirements which were placed on the Pact's air forces in the 1980s. Their first task was to establish air superiority in the theatre of operations (TVD).

In December 1981, Colonel Alexander Musial, of the Polish Air Force, described it as follows:

> The experience of the most recent wars has shown that the air forces
> have always substantively affected the course of the combat action of

their own troops. Consequently the problems of combating air forces have been given much attention, and deserve still more, because a breaking up or serious weakening of the enemy's air force and nuclear missile groupings leads to a fast decline of his capabilities. By ensuring supremacy in the air, it creates favourable conditions for the action of troops taking part in the operations of the TVD . . .

Enemy air force and missile groupings should first be routed in those areas where the principal tasks of the war are being implemented, i.e., in the main TVDs, where the strongest groupings of ground forces and air forces are deployed. The west European TVD is one of them. Therefore it can be stated that in no other theatre will the course of the operation depend so much on the situation in the air as on the skilful use of our air force and on the break up of enemy air forces. This is so because he who seizes the initiative in the air will dictate his own conditions.[42]

Meanwhile, at the Voroshilov General Staff Academy in Moscow, attended by senior army, navy and air force officers from the USSR and allied nations, the concepts were fleshed out with details on aircraft allocation, sortie rates and timing. 'Sixty per cent of Frontal Aviation aircraft and 75 per cent of the medium and heavy bomber regiments'[43] were to be assigned to the first 'strike' echelon, tasked 'to destroy enemy aircraft runways, command posts etc, in a duration of 24–36 hours.'[44] SACEUR was aware of the General Staff's summary of the air power which could be made available to discharge the air operation:

> . . . aviation groupings organised for conducting air operations can be as follows:
> – in the Western Theatre of Military Action: three to four front air armies, one or two Long Range Aviation Corps and separate divisions, and Naval Aviation, as well as the Air Forces of Warsaw Pact countries, forces and means organic to the front, and operational formations and large PVO (Air Defence) units.[45]

A later note on the conduct of the air operation emphasised:

> The main forces during the attack on enemy main aviation groupings must be protected continuously from the actions of fighter aircraft. To achieve this purpose, enemy fighters can be destroyed on the airfields and in air engagements . . .[46]

The 'air operation' was not however an independent air undertaking, but an essential precursor to a combined arms offensive. Soviet official military aviation journals, such as *Aviation and Cosmonautics*, included in virtually every issue articles on combined-arms offensive operations. The air supremacy established at the outset by the air operation would have been sustained by tactical fighters sweeping ahead of and over the advancing armoured forces. All other forms of air support would then have taken advantage of a benign air environment. Ground-attack aircraft would have dislodged NATO ground-defensive positions, destroyed reinforcements, protected WTO flanks and prepared the ground for breakthrough. Helicopters would have complemented fixed-wing and ground-force firepower, placed troops behind enemy formations and with fixed-wing transports reinforced and resupplied fast-moving ground forces. All air activity would have been supported by mobile surface-to-air defences.

Follow On Forces Attack (FOFA)

In the late 1970s however, the United States Army introduced a new concept, known initially as the 'air land battle', which was to intrude on the air-orientated Alliance strategies, have far-reaching repercussions in Moscow, influence the coalition approach to *Desert Storm* and ultimately appear in modernised form in the mid-1990s. In several respects it resembled the USSR's own concept of combined operations but its roots lay in a well-founded concern about the weakness of NATO's linear and maldeployed ground defences and a perceived opportunity offered by emerging technology (ET) to resolve it.

The concept of 'AirLand Battle' originated in the US Army's Field Manual 100-5 (FM 100-5), 'Operations', as revised in 1982. It sought to disrupt and defeat superior Warsaw Pact ground forces by simultaneously holding the leading echelons in an attack and then disrupting the momentum of succeeding reinforcing or exploiting echelons by striking around and over the forward troops. It was, however, also intended to be applicable beyond NATO areas.

The expression 'the extended battlefield' was used to denote a threefold expansion of the defence. First, in depth, 'with engagement of enemy units not yet in contact to disrupt the enemy timetable, complicate command and control and frustrate his plans, thus weakening his grasp on the initiative'. Second, 'the battle is extended forward in time to the point that current actions such as attack on follow-on echelons, logistical preparation and manoeuvre plans are interrelated to maximise the likelihood of winning the close-in battle as time goes on.' Third, the 'range of assets figuring in the battle is extended towards more emphasis on higher level army and sister service acquisition means and attack resources.'[47]

General Bernard Rogers subsequently averred that the US Army's thinking was independent of the contemporary NATO doctrinal revision which produced the concept of Follow On Forces Attack (FOFA). The latter was 'a multinational product', and, 'Although both incorporate some ideas which are similar, AirLand Battle is designed to have world-wide application and carries some features that do not apply to the deterrent and defensive missions assigned to Allied Command Europe.'[48] The differences included army stress on short-term battle influence while FOFA looked much deeper and AirLand Battle laid greater overt emphasis on counteroffensive than the more defensively orientated FOFA.

In a slightly later seminal article General Rogers, in his capacity as Supreme Allied Commander Europe, set out the rationale, substance and requirements of the FOFA concept.[49] He referred to the ever-growing gap 'between the conventional force capabilities of the Warsaw Pact and NATO [which] is a cause for serious concern,' and the need to strengthen the conventional leg of Flexible Response. Thereby the Alliance's entire deterrence posture would be reinforced. The key lay in 'The increased range, accuracy and mobility of modern weapons systems [which] have added depth to the battlefield.'

For its implementation, FOFA required existing forces to be brought up to 'established standards for manning, equipping, training, sustaining and reinforcing; to continue with essential modernisation, and ensure that we fully exploit our superior western technology to develop and procure the conventional means to attack effectively the Warsaw Pact follow on forces and to jam their communications and blind their radars.' He went on to itemise the 'architecture' to implement the concept. It included real time surveillance, target acquisition and precise intelligence, a responsive C^3I structure and 'accurate and decisive' weapon systems for targets well to the rear of the FEBA (Forward Edge of the Battlefield).

The 'new' concept was essentially the harnessing of emerging technology (ET) to the traditional warfare concept of interdiction. And there was some impressive technology becoming available at either end of the 'requirements' list, including the Joint Surveillance Target Attack Radar System (JSTARS) which could locate moving and some fixed targets on the ground 100 miles behind the FEBA, the MRLS artillery rocket system, the *Apache* attack helicopter, the NAVSTAR Global Positioning System and a number of PGMs designed to counter specific targets such as armour, bridges, radars and C^3 links.

The enunciation of the doctrine coincided with the advent of the Reagan administration and a major surge in US defence funding, begun by President Carter after the Soviet invasion of Afghanistan. Calculated in constant 1985 dollars, the US defence budget increased by 53 per cent between 1980 and

1985.[50] Technological competition between the USA and USSR was intense, while the detrimental impact of Soviet defence expenditure and resource allocation on the Soviet economy was not recognised in the West at the time. It was usually possible to identify technological advances in the USSR but not their full extent or implications. The West was also concerned that for a number of bureaucratic and industrial reasons weapon gestation could take far longer than in the USSR, allowing the opposition constantly to erode US technological advantages.[51] Consequently, while those advantages were still enjoyed in 1985 in computers, electronics, smart weapons, specialist weapons, optics, robotics and aircraft engines, the USSR was believed to be narrowing the gaps in many of them.[52]

That was not the perception in Moscow. Soviet political and military leaders were aware of deep economic problems (see Chapter 7) and foresaw their military advantages being overtaken by a determined US government increasing resource allocation in superior technology which would be employed in a new dynamic NATO concept of operations. The political and military response was predictably well co-ordinated: a propaganda attack targeted at the West which accused FOFA of being provocative, destabilising, of accelerating the arms race, dangerous and another product of US manipulation and exploitation of its NATO allies.[53]

One interesting, and typical, Soviet response was from a young academic at the USA-Canada Institute in Moscow: 'The implementation of the Rogers Plan can undermine all chances for success of the negotiations on the reduction of armed forces and arms in central Europe and seriously hinder a constructive solution to the problem of confidence-building measures . . .'[54] As explained in Chapter 7 this particular commentator was to play a major role in seeking to reconstitute Russian military strength in the 1990s.

After two years of careful examination of FOFA, the Soviet General Staff began to comment publicly upon its implications for warfare in general and Soviet operations in particular. In May 1984 Marshal Ogarkov observed that, 'Such a qualitative leap in the development of conventional weapons inevitably entails a change in the nature of preparing and conducting operations.'[55] The following month a member of the General Staff Academy staff wrote that high-precision weapons 'were changing the face of modern combat by constantly raising the intensity of the fire struggle' with a significance which now extended from the traditional 'close exchange of fire' to 'simultaneous fire against practically the entire depth of the enemy's combat formation'. The same observer later spelled out a further serious implication for the Soviet military: 'The general speeding-up of the battlefield has sharply curtailed the time available to commanders and staff for making and implementing decisions. This has made it most important to speed up the collection of intelligence, its analysis, making a decision, giving orders, organising co-operation, and so on. The guidelines of the past are no longer appropriate. In the Great Patriotic War, a regiment and a battalion often had up to three or four days to prepare for an offensive – now it is much less.'[56]

In sum, FOFA was perceived to be rendering Soviet force structure, doctrine and procedure obsolescent. Even allowing for inherent military pessimism and the lobbying potential for even more resource allocation, there is strong evidence to suggest that the Soviet General Staff were deeply concerned about an imminent turn of the conventional warfare tide to the advantage of the USA and her allies. How far their analysis was justified by contemporary NATO capabilities as opposed to theoretical projection was constantly debated in the West.

For example, as late as 1990, before the arms limitation agreements agreed that year had been signed and before confrontation between NATO and the Warsaw Pact had 'officially' ended the Deputy Commander of Allied Forces in Central Europe observed that 'three critical elements' still needed to be improved 'to enhance our capability' to attack follow on forces. They were surveillance systems to locate and identify moving targets, a responsive data function and command system and better anti-armour weapons for all weather, day and night use.[57] In 1984 General Rogers had estimated that FOFA could have been implemented with a one per cent increase in the collective budget for alliance members over 10 years.[58] By 1990 that figure had not been raised.

The concept had nonetheless stimulated considerable debate between analysts and, more ominously for its reincarnation in the 1990s, between armed services. Some critics questioned such excessive reliance on interactive technology. Typical were two succinct comments by Stephen Canby in 1984: 'Throughout the ages, the introduction of a qualitatively new weapon has been heralded by the prognosis that war will never again be the same. To date, these predictions have always proved false. There is no reason to believe that tactics will not adjust to precision weaponry'[59], and 'automated techniques are extremely flexible within the set of the predictable, and are totally inflexible outside that set', therefore, 'Automaticity implies extreme inflexibility whenever the enemy can discover – and operate outside of – the bounds of the predictable.'[60]

Others questioned the operational rationale behind the concept, pointing out that if NATO's linear defences were broached by the first WTO attack, FOFA would be irrelevant. Alternatively, because of the flexibility associated with the Soviet principle of exploiting penetrations, the location and direction of operational manoeuvre groups or successive echelons would be very difficult to identify.

Air force criticism remained muted in Europe, but in the USAF the point was strongly made that the AirLand Battle doctrine had emerged from the US Army without consultation until after its promulgation in 1982. Earlier editions had been staffed between units of the 'Air-Land Forces Application Agency' located, typically, at two locations: Langley Air Force Base and Fort Monroe. An explanatory 'Primer' published in 1978 identified the needs for tactical air force contribution to the battle, and, perhaps reflecting Israeli experience in 1973, for 'divesting the enemy of his air defence umbrella' by the friendly ground-covering forces.[61]

Nonetheless the doctrine was a unilateral production by the US Army and a Memorandum of Understanding signed in April 1983 by Generals Meyer and Gabriel committed the Air Force and Army to co-operate in tactical training based on the AirLand Battle doctrine, but did not replace any existing air force doctrine or priorities.[62] Moreover, the AirLand Battle was to be implemented at corps level, while USAF assets were, for maximum flexibility and activity commensurate with their radii of action, co-ordinated at Army level. In the NATO theatre the existing command structure was flexible enough to make the system viable, but it was no coincidence that in the Gulf War US corps commanders criticised the lack of air support when in fact General Schwarzkopf had directed air priorities elsewhere. Not far below this particular surface was the perennial struggle by the US Army to control its own air support assets: the armed helicopter, with the USAF seeing a potential erosion of its tactical air responsibilities.

Before 1991, however, the major contribution of the FOFA concept to NATO's security was not in reinforcing the conventional rung of the flexible response ladder. It was in its domino impact on the Soviet Union. As is explained more fully in Chapter 7, the Soviet general staff first recognised the significance of emerging technology and FOFA for their own military capabilities. They realised that the Soviet economy and industrial base were too weak in their present form to produce such technology or the counters to it. Therefore a combined programme of arms control and economic reconstruction which would slow down Western military growth and lay the basis for a re-energised and modernised Soviet defence industrial base was one which they could support. In 1985 they could not foresee that there would be no speedy economic restructuring, that arms control would be accompanied by the collapse of their alliance bastion and followed by the disintegration of the entire Soviet military structure.

The Legacy
Thus air power had shaped the formulation of the first NATO strategic concept with contemporary Western technological advantage in nuclear

weaponry, it had sustained flexible response for 23 years, and finally it brought the period to a close by threatening to exploit conventional technology to the manifest discomfiture of the Soviet Union. If the demolition of the Berlin Wall was the symbol of the collapse of the Soviet-Communist domination of eastern Europe and threat to the West, it may be credibly argued that the first crack in the military cement was made by pressure from NATO's air power, enhanced by emerging technology and presented in a coherent doctrine.

If so, the pen which scripted the doctrine was probably mightier than the contemporary air power sword. By far the most comprehensive and objective analysis of FOFA was produced in 1987, two years after Gorbachev had begun to enlist the support of the General Staff for his economic reforms, and before he had launched his arms-reduction initiatives, by the Office of Technology Assessment of the US Congress. In assessing NATO's 'current capabilities to attack follow on forces' it stated, *inter alia*, 'NATO's current reconnaissance and C^3 systems and procedures are not designed to provide timely information on the precise location of mobile targets . . . most existing air-delivered weapons cannot destroy armoured vehicles in significant numbers . . . few NATO aircraft can reach more than 150 km beyond the East German border . . . few NATO aircraft are able to operate well at night or in bad weather, and all face competing demands from other missions . . . ground-launched weapons have little to offer at present . . .'[63] Once again doctrine had far outrun the capability to implement it. Happily, on this occasion the potential opposition believed it, and contributed to their own defeat.

A postscript to this episode appeared in June 1993 with a further revision to FM 100-5 in the light of the experience in the Gulf War. The emphasis remained on multi-dimensional, non-linear combat marked by firepower and manoeuvre over extended distances which could both expand and contract. Simultaneous attack on direct contact and behind the FEBA would be enhanced by surface-to-surface weaponry guided by systems, such as JSTARS, to envelop units separated by time and distance.

As in the case of its predecessors, the revised FM 100-5 was in a strong military tradition in seeking to take and exploit offensive or counteroffensive initiative by superior speed in thought, action and response. It sought to capitalise on technological and manpower superiority. But whenever an opponent might have air power, it would depend totally on friendly air superiority to be won. The JSTARS aircraft and its ground-receiver units, plus all the logistic, maintenance and personnel 'tail' of the mobile combat forces would require protection, while helicopters would still require a benign air environment. Hostile reconnaissance and reciprocal surveillance and control would need to be removed, otherwise an opponent would himself have an opportunity to locate and intercept the friendly enveloping forces. In a fluid battle with either no definable forward line of own troops, or a rapidly changing one, friendly-force identification would become critical for any form of direct or indirect fire support.

Despite some Army claims to the contrary, AirLand Battle III was still an unproven doctrine in the mid-1990s. FOFA had not been needed in the central region of Europe. Khafji in the Gulf in January 1991 was a minor skirmish. The 100-hour ground war at the end of February was fought against a largely static, exposed, decimated, demoralised, dislocated and blinded Iraqi army, which had already begun preparing to retreat. The land campaign in the Gulf War is examined in Chapter 5, but it seems far too small and unrepresentative a base from which to develop an all-embracing concept of warfare.

Moreover there was a danger that the doctrine presumed that air superiority would be achieved, and air assets applied, in priorities dictated by Army requirements in a corps area of interest. Only if the corps area of interest was the only area of interest, would such presumptions be credible. It was hoped that the accumulated lessons accruing from successful army-air force co-operation over 80 years would ensure that a broader perspective would prevail when circumstances required it. The extension into areas not originally within the Alliance's remit could become a strong safeguard against regression into single-service parochialism. If so, it would be a legacy of great benefit to the joint-service exploitation of air power.

Even though the Cold War mercifully subsided rather than exploded, its domination by air power for 45 years added considerably to the store of 'lessons' for the future.

CHAPTER 4

AIR POWER IN ARMS CONTROL

The military confrontation in Europe between East and West seemed in 1985 likely to continue indefinitely. Yet within six years the Warsaw Pact had been dissolved, a conventional arms reduction treaty had been signed, Soviet Air Force units had largely been withdrawn from eastern Europe and the Soviet Air Force itself began to disintegrate as a result of the break-up of the Soviet Union.

The ending of confrontation had two major roots. One was the product of arms control negotiations begun almost a decade earlier. The second, more difficult to quantify but much more important, was the drive by Mr Gorbachev to reduce the burden of defence expenditure on the Soviet economy. The arms control negotiations culminated in the Conventional Forces in Europe (CFE) Treaty of November 1990. The quest for economic reconstruction had repercussions on Soviet and later, Russian military security which were still reverberating in 1994.

Periodically since the 1960s each side introduced arms control proposals which usually sought to enhance the military position of the proposer and, wherever possible, achieve a propaganda coup. At least, that was how most gestures were regarded.[1] In 1972, however, the two sides agreed to hold a Conference on Security and Co-operation in Europe (CSCE) which would be attended by both confrontational and neutral/non-aligned states, and to hold talks on Mutual and Balanced Force Reductions (MBFR) in which the participants would comprise the members of the opposing alliances with the exception of France. Both series of negotiations were to be marked by strong disagreements over the inclusion of air forces: disagreements which reflected the different strategic perceptions of air power of each side.

The initial WTO position in the MBFR talks, which began in Vienna in October 1973 called for reductions in nuclear and conventional air and ground forces, and proposed that foreign forces should be withdrawn from the central region. The NATO response excluded nuclear weapons and specified ground forces only.

The sides could not agree on the size of WTO forces on the central front: NATO having no doubts about WTO numerical superiority, while the WTO insisted that the forces were in mutual balance. Nor could they find common ground in procedures for the verification of compliance with reduction proposals. Because of NATO's position, no air-related measures were discussed with the exception of 54 nuclear-capable US *Phantom* F-4s in abortive discussions in 1975. The WTO reciprocal offer to withdraw an equal number of Sukhoi *Fitter* fighter bombers was disdained by NATO in the belief that they were being withdrawn anyway on grounds of obsolescence. This short-lived stage was overtaken by new missile deployments in 1979 and the subsequent transfer of nuclear topics from MBFR to the Intermediate Nuclear Forces (INF) talks. The inclusion of the F-4s in NATO proposals, which also sought the withdrawal of a Soviet tank army, did, however, establish a precedent which was to complicate negotiations a decade later and threaten a major NATO miscalculation.

The MBFR talks sputtered inconclusively in Vienna for 15 years, providing a highly-coveted quality of life for military and civilian participants alike, but with little or no contribution to European security. NATO perceptions of asymmetries in numbers, weapons and strategic deployments continued to preclude acceptance of WTO proposals for 'balanced' reductions by each side. Final failure to agree on a verification regime ensured that no progress had been made by the end of 1988, when a new series of negotiations was about to begin in Vienna.

Meanwhile the second strand of European security negotiations had begun in Helsinki in July 1973 with the first of the CSCE meetings. Membership included all members of the two alliances plus the neutral and non-aligned (NNA) nations. Participants agreed that they would consider 'appropriate proposals on confidence building measures such as the prior notification of major military manoeuvres on a basis to be specified by the Conference and the exchange of observers by invitation at military manoeuvres under mutually accepted conditions. The Committee/Sub Committee will also study the question of prior notification of major military movements and submit its conclusions.'[2]

As in the MBFR talks, the concentration at Helsinki was on land forces with the quantification by numbers of ground troops. The only mandatory clause in the final *Document on confidence-building measures and certain aspects of security and disarmament* agreed by the foreign ministers of the participants in August 1975 required that notification should be given 'of major military manoeuvres exceeding a total of 25,000 troops, independently or combined with any possible air or naval components.'[3] In a formal statement on 19 July 1975, the USA removed any ambiguity from the Western position by confirming the exclusion of 'independent naval and/or air manoeuvres as well as air and naval manoeuvres' from the Helsinki regime.[4]

The Western position on air forces therefore remained constant: non-negotiable, with, at this time (1975), the concurrence of the USSR. For the next 10 years, the mandatory notification requirement of the Helsinki agreement was observed by both sides, together with optional agreements to notify smaller-scale military manoeuvres, to exchange observers and to notify major military movements'.[5] One hundred and thirty manoeuvres were notified and 72 invitations sent to observers; none of them involved independent air or naval exercises.

One other aspect of the Helsinki process would have greater long-term significance than the more restricted, specific CBM agreements. Whereas the MBFR talks were concentrating on the central front, CSCE's context was 'Europe' which specifically included the territory of the USSR up to a depth of 250 km from its frontier 'facing or shared with any other European participating State . . .'[6] The definition was a compromise between the inclusion of all 'European' USSR and excluding it altogether. It acknowledged the relevance to Western security of military deployments within Soviet territory and thereby prepared the way for future progress.

Despite the deterioration of East–West relations as a result of the USSR's Afghanistan adventure and tensions provoked by the deployment of new generations of intermediate-range missiles in Europe, follow-up CSCE meetings took place in Belgrade in 1977–78 and Madrid in 1980–83. In Madrid a number of proposals were made for a further CSCE meeting at Stockholm which was to cover both Confidence- and Security-Building Measures (CSBM) and Conventional Disarmament in Europe (CDE). A French proposal defined the relevant geographical area as 'from the Atlantic to the Urals': the first definition of the area subsequently to be covered by the CFE Treaty of 1990.[7] The West resisted Soviet attempts to extend coverage westwards to an area of the Atlantic comparable to that of the European Soviet Union and insisted on the continued exclusion of independent air and sea activities. Only air and sea activities 'affecting security in Europe' and 'directly connected with notifiable activities taking place on land' were to be notifiable under the proposed agreements.[8] Again therefore, the Western position remained consistent and, in so far as military activities in the whole of the Soviet Union west of the Urals were now to be included in the next round of negotiations, increasingly advantageous. So far, the emphasis remained on ground forces in these areas, but if air forces were ever to be included, bases in Belorussia, Ukraine and Russia itself would fall within negotiating range, while SAC bases in North America would be exempt. There is no evidence of such an awareness in Western contemporary analyses of the Madrid/Stockholm process. Indeed, there is no evidence that these negotiations had any impact upon Western air strategy or future policy.

Nevertheless, a minor formal concession was made by the West at Stockholm with the acceptance of a sub-threshold for notification of participation by air forces in combined activities:

> The participation of air forces of the participating States will be included in the notification if it is foreseen that in the course of the activity 200 or more sorties by aircraft, excluding helicopters, will be flown.[9]

Again, a WTO demand to include independent air activities was rejected by the West. The NATO members continued to argue that the source of instability and insecurity was on the ground, and that in any event, notification of air activities presented too many difficulties for verification. Conversely, the WTO continued to emphasise the particularly dangerous nature of military activities undertaken by naval forces 'heavily equipped with modern strike weapons' and air forces endowed with 'high mobility and highly effective strike weapons.'[10]

In early 1986, under the influence of Mikhail Gorbachev and Eduard Shevardnadze, the Soviet Union's position softened to an agreement to defer the question of the notification of air activities to a subsequent phase of the negotiations, expressed as a firm intention in the concluding session of the Stockholm Conference: '. . . the Soviet Union intends in the future to raise at the Conference on Confidence- and Security-Building Measures and Disarmament in Europe questions regarding notification of independent manoeuvres of air and naval forces . . .'[11]

Further mandatory multilateral agreements were reached on on-site and aerial inspections in an observation and verification regime. In addition to invitations to attend manoeuvres, provision was made for up to three verification inspections per year on the territory of each participating state to monitor compliance with agreed CSBMs.

The Stockholm agreements would have been a major landmark in progress towards greater European stability and security had they not begun to be overshadowed and overtaken by unilateral initiatives from Gorbachev. Mandatory notifications, observer exchanges and on-site inspections did begin to penetrate the military confrontation and illuminated some of the operational realities obscured by the comprehensive WTO shroud of secrecy and deception. Indeed, while the USSR had undoubtedly derived some political advantages from the CSCE process, the military advantage lay with the West. The Western concentration on ground forces as the source of instability had predominated; air forces had been excluded or marginalised, and the Western perception of WTO geopolitical strategic depth had been enshrined in definitions of the territorial region subject to the Stockholm agreements: 'From the Atlantic to the Urals' which quickly became identified by its acronym ATTU.

During 1987 and 1988 the provisions of the Stockholm Document were implemented with comparatively little disagreement. Seventy-three military activities were notified, triggering 31 observations. Only one Soviet exercise involved notifiable air activity. European on-site inspections were carried out. These statistics were encouraging, but of much greater significance were contemporary proposals for a new and revolutionary approach to the whole question of conventional force confrontation in Europe.

The Gorbachev Initiatives

From the earliest days of his assumption of authority in the USSR in March 1985, Mikhail Gorbachev had proffered a more conciliatory attitude towards the West. Interchanges between diplomats, summit meetings and progress towards agreements on nuclear weapons reduction were accompanied, as noted above, by a more flexible stance at Stockholm. In Paris in October 1985, Gorbachev referred to principles of 'reasonable sufficiency' and 'non-provocative' or 'defensive' defence. The language was suitably Delphic but from a Soviet source, the concepts were novel.[12]

The ideas were repeated at the 27th Party Congress in Moscow in February 1986 and expanded in a speech in East Berlin in April. Much of the content of the proposals (reductions in European land and air forces and reductions in Canadian and US forces in Europe) was akin to that associated with the MBFR talks, but he also injected two concepts from Stockholm : the possibility of on-site inspection and the designation of the area to be covered as 'from the Atlantic to the Urals'.[13]

In July in Moscow he tackled a particular Western concern head on: 'Let us look at it this way. For those types of weapons of which the West has more, let it make the corresponding reductions and for those of which we have more, we will unhesitatingly eliminate this surplus.'[14] The acknowledgement that the WTO did in fact enjoy numerical superiority in some areas was a major concession to the West. It was, however, tempered by the consistent assertion that NATO had a numerical superiority in 'strike' aircraft. In February 1987 at an International Forum for a Nuclear Weapon Free World in Moscow he further refined the proposal for asymmetric reductions: 'If there is any imbalance, we must restore it by letting the one with more of them scale them down. It is important . . . to carry through such measures as would make it possible to lessen, or better still, altogether exclude the possibility of surprise attack. The most dangerous kinds of offensive weapon must be removed from the zones of contact.'[15]

This statement continued the more flexible and conciliatory movement in Soviet arms control policy, but it also sharpened the focus of the deep disagreement in strategic perceptions between the two sides. To NATO, the destabilising factor was the numerical superiority, proximity, structure and doctrine of WTO ground forces in the central region. The threat was a territorial invasion achieved with surprise by a high-speed combined arms offensive supported in depth by an unbroken reinforcement train stretching back to the Soviet Union itself.

The USSR, on the other hand, was equally adamant that the threat to stability came from NATO air power. Consistently through 1987 and 1988 Soviet spokesmen emphasised what they alleged to be Western numerical and qualitative superiority in 'strike' or 'attack' aircraft, seeking to distinguish between 'offensive' aircraft and 'purely defensive' fighters/interceptors. The perceptions and potential negotiating position of the USSR on the contemporary correlation of air force strengths was explained in September 1988 by Marshal Sergei Akhromeyev, then Chief of the Soviet General Staff, in an internationally-publicised address in Stockholm. He identified three contentious issues: strike aircraft, carrier-borne forces and fighter aviation:

> NATO countries outnumber Warsaw Pact countries in tactical strike aviation – approximately by 1,500 aircraft. Almost 70 per cent of the total number of all NATO combat aircraft based in Europe and on aircraft carriers are strike aircraft. A question arises: are air force operations less dangerous than those of ground forces? It is obvious that by the scale of employment, speed, manoeuvrability and strike capabilities air forces excel ground forces. Strike aviation can ensure strategic surprise attack, engage targets within one-and-a-half to two hours on D-1 to a depth of 1,000 km, that is throughout the entire depth of the theatre of operations. Neither tanks nor artillery would succeed in reaching the border within this period of time.
>
> Multi-purpose aircraft-carrier task forces possess a great strike power. Each aircraft carrier is a floating airfield which is a base for up to 100 aircraft (80 of which are nuclear capable). Seven out of 15 US Navy multi-purpose aircraft carriers are assigned to the Western Atlantic Fleet . . .[16]

Later in his address he observed:

> As for tactical strike aviation, we insist on including it in the subject
> matter of the talks strictly following the agreed goals of the talks,
> that is, the elimination of a surprise-attack potential. In doing so,
> meeting NATO halfway, we have agreed to exclude from the talks the
> naval aviation issue. It goes without saying that fighter aviation that is
> purely defensive should also be excluded.[17]

Ten weeks later, during a speech before the General Assembly of the United
Nations on 7 December 1988, Gorbachev announced unilateral reductions
of 800 aircraft in 'the European part of the USSR . . . and in the territories
of our European allies . . .'[18] in a broad ranging survey of the Soviet Union's
foreign and defence policies.

Finally, in January 1989, the Committee of the Ministers of Defence of
the Warsaw Treaty Member States issued a lengthy statement 'On the
Relative Strength of the Armed Forces and Armaments of the Warsaw
Treaty Organisation and the North Atlantic Treaty Organisation in
Europe and Adjacent Water Areas' including detailed tables and charts
illustrating the 'Correlation of Forces in Europe'.[19] In it, the Pact acknowledged an overall numerical superiority in 'Tactical combat aircraft of the
air forces, air defence forces and navies' of 7,876 to 7,130, or 1.1:1, but
with a superiority in 'AD interceptors which cannot be employed against
ground targets' of 1,829 to 50, or 36:1. Conversely, in 'naval combat aircraft' the figures were 692 to 1,630, or an adverse ratio of 1:2.4. Overall, in
the 'total number of attack aircraft (bombers, fighter bombers, ground
attack aircraft) in the air force [sic] and tactical naval aviation', there were
2,793 to 4,075, or 1:1.5.' For combat helicopters, 'including those in the
navies', the totals were 2,785 compared with 5,270, or 1:1.9 against the
Warsaw Pact.[20]

This Soviet position was based on a compound of shrewd strategic
analysis, a misunderstanding of one NATO concept, concern about possible weaknesses in Soviet decision making in crisis, and the distorted
perceptions bred from decades of belief in the USSR's own anti-Western
propaganda.

The Soviet General Staff was in no doubt about the quality and potential
war fighting contribution of the NATO air forces, and especially of the
United States Air Force. As we have seen, the critical contribution of air
power to NATO strategy was well publicised in the West and well known in
Moscow. The first activity in a WTO combined arms offensive would have
been the attempt to neutralise NATO air power by the 'Air Operation'.
Therefore any prior reduction in NATO air forces, and especially

asymmetric reductions which left the bulk of WTO air-superiority fighters untouched, would be a major negotiating coup which could only strengthen the WTO's own strategic posture.

Moreover, the potential threat from NATO air power was perceived in Moscow to be growing rapidly in the early 1980s. Several authoritative writers had commented on the impact of modern technology in warfare. Marshal Ogarkov, Chief of the General Staff in 1984, was particularly associated with such views. In May 1984 he described a 'qualitative leap in the development of conventional means of destruction which will inevitably entail a change in the nature of the preparation and conduct of operations . . .automated search and destroy complexes, long-range, high-accuracy terminally-guided combat systems . . . and qualitatively new electronic control systems . . . [made it possible] . . . immediately to extend actual combat operations not just to the border regions, but to the whole country's territory, which was not possible in recent wars. [All this greatly enhanced] the initial period of war and its first operations.'[21]

Such thinking was accompanied by a reappraisal of earlier Soviet views that nuclear escalation would be unavoidable in an East-West conflict. Instead a protracted conventional war was now feasible and, to complicate matters still further, the new military technologies gave the defender an opportunity to seize the initiative from an attacker, if not pre-empt him altogether.[22] Such analyses encouraged a more confident if ambivalent assertion of the growing importance of a 'defensive' doctrine, but also heightened fears of NATO air power, which was perceived to be re-equipping with new families of PGMs and US cruise missiles, which manifested the multiple threat of long-range, relative invulnerability and terminal precision.

This analysis, which seems to have been a unanimous view in the Soviet General Staff, explains the early military support for Mikhail Gorbachev's economic and political reforms and for the conventional arms control initiatives. The technological advantages which the West appeared to enjoy had to be matched. But the economy of the USSR was stagnating and its industrial base corroding into obsolescence. With economic reconstruction would come modernised technology, from which in turn modern weapons could be generated. Time to catch up could be bought by arms control negotiations which could slow down the Western competition. One comment in 1985 epitomised General Staff thinking on the relationship between a modern industrial base and modern weaponry:

What is demanded today for series production of modern weaponry, the newest combat technologies, is not common or ordinary but the most modern, often unique equipment; fundamentally new instru-

ments, numerically-controlled machine tools, robotics, the latest generation of computers and flexible production systems.[23]

The strategic coherence in the Soviet position on NATO air power was
given a sharper, polemical edge by the General Staff's interpretation of
NATO's AirLand Battle and Follow On Forces Attack concepts. Nine
months before his appearance in Stockholm on the arms control stage,
Marshal Akhromeyev set out the General Staff's perception of NATO
activities:

> With each passing year, the US and NATO armed forces become
> increasingly attack and strike orientated . . . At the same time, increas-
> ing attention is being paid to preparing for actions in a protracted
> conventional war using new weapon systems. A decisive role in this
> process is assigned to preparing for a sudden attack and subsequent
> large-scale military actions, simultaneously spreading them through-
> out the entire depth of the USSR and its allies. This is precisely the
> aim of the latest US and NATO operational-strategic concepts of
> AirLand battle, Air Sea battle and Follow On Forces Attack.[24]

Even the most cursory military intelligence survey of NATO peacetime
deployment disclosed that the alliances' forces were in no geographical or
numerical position to launch any kind of attack, least of all on a scale postulated by the Marshal. Similarly, the widely promulgated AirLand battle
and FOFA doctrine were palpably designed as counteroffensives within
the depth of WTO, attacking formations in eastern Europe, and without
any capacity to reach deeply into the USSR. Moreover, Akhromeyev was
clearly unaware of the USAF's ambiguous partnership in what were essentially US Army concepts of operations.

It is, of course, politically convenient to maximise a threat : a tendency
not monopolised by the Soviet General Staff. In this case it was part of a
carefully co-ordinated campaign to characterise NATO air power, rather
than WTO armour, as the major threat to European security and stability.
There may have been another factor motivating Akhromeyev. He and his
colleagues had observed the inertia which had characterised previous
Soviet governments in the face of serious problems, ranging from the failure to check economic and industrial decay, to the ignominious responses
to the intrusion of two Korean airliners and Matthias Rust's arrival in Red
Square in May 1987. If they did believe in the possibility of a NATO attack,
they must have had serious misgivings about the prospects for a speedy
political decision in Moscow to either counter or pre-empt it. It became
even more important to reduce the opposition's capability to take

advantage by a paralysing air attack akin to that planned by the General Staff itself.

Thus by the end of 1988 the Soviet Union expressed on behalf of an apparently monolithic WTO a plausible and persuasive case for the essential inclusion of aircraft in future conventional arms reduction negotiations which could be supported by the General Staff. It had begun tentatively 16 years earlier at the outset of the MBFR and the CSCE talks. It had been sustained, albeit with flexibility, during the Stockholm CSCE phase. It was now a strongly held position ready to be tabled in the CFE negotiations scheduled to begin in Vienna on March 1989.

The Western Response

Since 1973, Western opposition to the inclusion of air forces in arms control negotiations had been equally consistent, for several reasons. One, in common with ground forces assessments, was the failure by both sides to agree on the existing sizes of the opposing air forces and the WTO's insistence on mutual reductions from an alleged position of equilibrium. Another arose from the comparative distances between the central region and North America on the one hand and the unbroken series of airbases stretching back from the inner German border to the USSR on the other. 'Mutual' withdrawals would confer considerable geographical advantages on the WTO for a rapid reinsertion of air force units to the central region. Because of NATO's existing requirement for heavy and rapid reinforcement over the Atlantic in times of crisis, the Alliance had no wish to inhibit such movements by arms control agreements or even CBMs. And finally, the potential wartime demands on NATO land- and sea-based air forces were so complex and far-reaching that no limitations on their activities could be contemplated.

Nonetheless, from 1986 onwards the Gorbachev arms control initiatives were threatening to take the high international moral ground and preparation of a co-ordinated Western response was allocated to a NATO High Level Task Force. The stance on air forces remained unchanged.[25]

Initially, NATO military staffs were cautious, and suspicious about the underlying motivation below Gorbachev's entire collection of proposals, recalling previous exhortations from Moscow to peaceful co-existence and defence restructuring. As early as January 1977, Brezhnev had stated that the military doctrine of the USSR lacked any offensive content and was solely defensive in character.[26] The theme was repeated regularly by Soviet spokesmen in a period when Soviet ground force modernisation and expansion continued apace, with the additional refinement of the creation of the Operation Manoeuvre Groups designed for high-speed exploitation of an offensive breakthrough. Western observers and analysts could discern no slowing down in Soviet military procurement programmes and production, nor was any visible during Gorbachev's first three years of office. After 40 years of confrontation, Western military staffs who were fully aware of Warsaw Pact strategy, from its exposition at the Voroshilov Academy down to readiness states of armoured divisions in East Germany, were not to be easily convinced that Gorbachev's speeches were any different from declarations of peaceful intent by previous Soviet leaders: declarations more relevant to the war of propaganda than to force structures. Nor were suspicions reduced by satisfied comments from Moscow such as, 'Already the very fact of proclamation of the [defensive conventional] doctrine is having a salutary effect on the climate and the situation in the world.'[27]

Despite such concerns there was a generally held military view that the Gorbachev initiatives should be probed because the three potential, novel concessions of asymmetric negotiations, on-site inspection and the inclusion of Soviet territory did hold out the promise of Western security enhancement. The military formations responsible for constructing the Western response were dominated by soldiers, reflecting both the numerical balance within NATO armed forces and the unanimous NATO perception that the major threat to the West was of ground-force invasion. That domination was undisturbed by the traditionally independent United States Navy whose spokesmen saw no advantages whatever to be gained from the inclusion of seapower in the talks, a view strongly endorsed by its NATO partners.

No soldier, sailor or airman joins the armed forces to become an arms control specialist. Not surprisingly, therefore, military duties in Helsinki, Madrid, Stockholm and Vienna had seldom been seen as career-enhancing, however conducive to a superior quality of life. Moreover, there had frequently been an unfortunate association in Western military perceptions between Western peace movements and manipulation from the Kremlin. On occasions little distinction was made between ill-informed or avowedly left-wing critics of the Western military establishment and those whose moral and academic stature could in different circumstances have enhanced their credibility in the arms control debate.

In addition to sharing the general suspicion and caution of their army and navy colleagues, NATO air staffs had their own professional reasons for scepticism. Soviet spokesmen consistently sought to distinguish between 'offensive' and 'defensive' aircraft, seeking to exclude from negotiations not only all the fighter/interceptors deployed by USSR Air Defence Forces (PVO) and by the other national air forces of the WTO but also the MiG-23, MiG-29 and older fighter/interceptors deployed forward with the Group of Forces in Central Europe.

The distinction was both technologically and operationally spurious.

Many WTO fighters did in fact have a multi-role capability and trained for both air-to-ground and air-to-air roles. But of much greater significance was the likely operational environment of their activities when deployed as fighter interceptors. Soviet expectations about their environment were explained in great detail to senior WTO and friendly nations' officers at the Voroshilov General Staff Academy.

'Contemporary operations in Theatres of Strategic Military Action (TSMA) are characteristically initiated with massive actions of the Air Forces. This fact has been proven by the experiences of World War II, the wars in the Near East, and the local war in Vietnam',[28] was the opening sentence of the study at the Voroshilov on 'Air Defence in a Strategic Operation'. The study went on to explain in detail how national air-defence forces would move forward to link up with Front fighter aviation troops of the Front air army to provide unbroken cover from 'the direction of the main strike', i.e., of the combined arms offensive – or 'counteroffensive', back to a depth of 1,000 km. 'Therefore in the period when staging areas are being occupied by Front forces and fleets for an offensive operation in a TSMA, a deep and echeloned air defence is established.'[29] The defensive fighters were, in fact, charged with providing air cover for the WTO ground offensive from deep forward penetration to the transit of reinforcing echelons and accompanying logistic support. In sum, not only were fighter interceptors an integral element in the WTO combined arms offensive, but their role in clearing the skies above it, denying defensive and counteroffensive opportunities to NATO aircraft, was essential for its success. It was therefore understandable that NATO air staffs regarded the WTO proposals as yet one more attempt to emasculate NATO air power.

There was also a further complication. The NATO strategy of 'flexible and appropriate response' implied a strategic web of deterrence ranging without specified thresholds from conventional weaponry through theatre nuclear weapons to the final array of the US strategic nuclear arsenal capable of reaching deep into the USSR. The bombers of Strategic Air Command were an essential ingredient in the Western alliance's layered deterrence posture. The fighter interceptors of the USSR's PVO were deployed primarily to counter them. The unanimous Western position was therefore that no exceptions could be made for PVO, quite apart from considerations of their potential to deploy forward.

The Soviet position was in one sense rather puzzling, suggesting a disconnection between the doctrine and plans expounded at the Voroshilov Academy and the realities of the Western threat. If the USSR was genuinely concerned about the penetration potential of SAC, it did not make much sense to denude the motherland of interceptors in order to protect a combined arms offensive in the central region of Europe, unless the

General Staff was assuming that the objectives of an offensive in central Europe could be achieved before a decision to launch SAC was reached.[30]

Western concerns expressed during the MBFR and the CSCE negotiations were reiterated. In crisis, NATO would depend heavily on rapid reinforcement by squadrons from across the Atlantic. No limitation on either their movement or their numbers could be negotiated. Nor could any proposals to restrict aircraft by specific geographical zones be accepted. Quite apart from the fact that the range and speed of modern combat aircraft rendered territorial limitations unworkable, the asymmetry of reinforcement time and distance in central Europe from North America on the one hand and from the USSR on the other led to further unanimous rejection by the West.

Finally, the United Kingdom and France had additional reasons for opposing the Soviet proposals. Deductions by any percentage in the ATTU would affect only a proportion of the air forces of the USA and the USSR, but would impose reductions on the whole of their own. In theory, this was a position shared by the other continental members of both alliances, but there were three factors which set Britain and France apart. First, both had interests beyond Europe, and had frequently deployed to support them. Second, reductions on 'strike' aircraft would have a disproportionate effect on the substrategic nuclear components of the forces of both countries. And third were the concerns about the implications of numerical ceilings for the production programmes of national aerospace companies competing in the international markets, when no such limitations would apply to production in the USA and in the USSR beyond the Urals.

Consequently, Western airmen were only too happy to leave initiatives in the CFE talks to their army colleagues who, in turn, were quite prepared to keep their eyes down on the ground without having to worry about the awkward, complicating and negotiation-threatening issues of air power. Had this position been sustained either the CFE negotiations would have followed the MBFR sequence into deadlock or a serious Western strategic miscalculation would have taken place. In the event, the US government was to instigate a dramatic change in the Western stance.

During 1988 a small number of Western airmen and defence analysts began to question, privately and quietly, a position which refused to entertain any negotiation on air forces. No Western uniformed air power specialist had hitherto begun to think seriously about air-related CBMs, let alone arms control. The string of Moscow-sourced initiatives, however, began to prove impossible to ignore in meetings of civilian and military analysts convened to discuss the whole spectrum of arms control and CBM negotiations. Gradually an 'alternative' Western position began to be constructed. Exponents who were still serving members of NATO armed forces were generally unwilling to express their reservations publicly because of the propaganda value of such dissension to the WTO and to anti-military factions in the West. Moreover, part of the argument for the alternative position could not have been made public in any event because of its security classification at the time.

For many years Western military intelligence had tracked the numbers and location of WTO aircraft with objective accuracy. The advent of satellite-derived information had extended that awareness to airbases across the length and breadth of the USSR. On no occasion between at least 1967 and 1989 was the Royal Air Force, for example, taken by surprise by the advent of a new Soviet aircraft or major weapon system, even if its precise quality and capabilities took longer to establish.[31] Consequently, the numerical assessment of WTO air forces published by NATO in November 1988, which gave the WTO a total of 8,250 combat aircraft was, not surprisingly, similar to the comparable figure of 7,876 used by the WTO three months later.[32] The WTO numerical superiority of in-position, land-based aircraft was assessed at nearly 2:1 for fixed-wing aircraft and 1.5:1 for helicopters.

This numerical imbalance had been viewed with equanimity by NATO staffs until the mid-1980s. Frequent net assessments of WTO capabilities had always concluded that NATO air forces had qualitative advantages which would redress their quantitative inferiority. Chief among them were aircrew and groundcrew quality, technological superiority in aircraft and weapons, and superior training and leadership. By the end of 1988, however, several developments were beginning to cast a shadow over such NATO advantages in the longer term.

Most widely publicised, although not its operational impact, was the rapid and continuing expansion of Western commercial airlines which was inducing unusually high exit rates among pilots from several NATO air forces: in particular those of the United States, West Germany, Norway and the United Kingdom. Meanwhile, expanding civilian economies and increasing opportunities for highly-qualified engineers and technicians were attracting groundcrew ranks from air force careers.[33] Groundcrew problems remained manageable, but NATO air commanders were in regular contact with personnel staffs as aircrew experience levels, especially among squadron pilots and flight commanders began to diminish. Some nations were unable to sustain NATO-agreed crew-to-aircraft ratios while many were compelled to fill staff and support appointments with officers from non-operational backgrounds or leave them vacant, reducing the traditional sources of aircrew reserves available in a crisis to bring front-line squadrons up to wartime manning levels. NATO front-line combat squadrons usually had between 25 and 50 per cent more aircrew allocated to them than the number of aircraft on the squadron. This manning ratio provided for normal peacetime flying, including exercises, and included an element for leave, ground-training courses and other temporary absences. In a crisis, the squadrons would have been augmented by aircrew familiar with the aircraft and role but employed elsewhere in the training or support areas. As a result of the manpower crisis, not only were front-line experience and manning levels dropping alarmingly in some roles but the ability of the air forces to redress the weakness in a crisis was also being undermined. The situation was further exacerbated when resource restrictions began to force a reduction in flying hours by some NATO air forces to levels disturbingly close to those of the WTO, but without long undisturbed tours of duty on the front line to compensate.

Meanwhile, other factors, including changing family expectations, an increased burden of combat training and reduced expenditure on support amenities were impinging upon retention rates and beginning to inhibit recruiting. Retention measures such as bounty schemes were tried to enhance pilot retention, for example in the US Navy and in the Royal Norwegian Air Force. They had only a temporary impact. Problems in the USAF were highlighted by the frequent superiority of National Guard and Reserve Squadrons in USAF-wide competitions: a reflection of the fact that they often had more experienced aircrew flying more hours per month than the regulars. Bearing in mind the fact that at this time NATO was still concerned about the aggressive intentions of the WTO, it is not surprising that the potential gravity of Western air force manning and experience levels remained a source of in-house, rather than public concern.

Conversely, there were disturbing signs that Soviet aircrew quality and training were improving. Lessons learned in Afghanistan were being translated to regiments in Europe, especially in helicopter operations. The new long-range fighter-interceptors were inducing the Soviet Air Force to experiment with looser ground control, more free-ranging fighter sweeps and larger formations of bombers and fighter escorts. The impact of *perestroika* and the reduction of the influence of the political officers on the regiments were encouraging greater pilot initiative, more professional leadership and greater flexibility in training. By no means all Soviet regiments were demonstrating such advances, but the trend was unmistakable. It was not known at the time in the West that, in fact, the Soviet Air Force was becoming equally concerned about recruiting, retention and resources and, in addition, was beginning to suffer acute maintenance problems.[34]

The second traditional Western advantage, of superior aircraft and associated equipment and weapons, was still present, but there too the gap was narrowing. A new generation of Soviet aircraft and weapons were entering service: MiG-29, MiG-31, SU-27, TU-160, TU-95 *Bear* H, and new heli-copters, together with new families of air-to-air and air-to-ground weapons which heralded the ending of the West's technological advantage. At the same time the funding of 'next generation' aircraft in the United States was receiving increasingly adverse scrutiny in Congress, while the expansion of western European defence budgets associated with the late 1970s and early 1980s had been reversed. The combination of techniques collectively known as 'stealth technology' would sustain a measure of Western advantage but it was restricted to a handful of USAF aircraft and, in any event, would sooner or later be emulated by the USSR and become vulnerable to countermeasures.

If the Gorbachev policies of restructuring and openness were to be applied to the whole of the Soviet Air Force a progressive increase in oper-ational effectiveness could be expected to enhance the existing numerical advantage enjoyed by the WTO. Further, the MiG-29 *Fulcrum* and SU-27 *Flanker* were ideally suited to the tactical and longer-range escort require-ments of the Air Operation and combined arms offensive. Nor were there any modifications to WTO air force deployments, training, doctrine or strategy consistent with declarations of 'defensive defence'.

Ironically, all these improvements in the Soviet Air Forces were widely publicised in the West, but used as arguments for increasing Western capa-bilities, not for using arms control negotiations as a means of constraining them.

It was obvious to some military specialists that if air forces were to be excluded from negotiations, their residual impact on a conflict in Europe after ground forces had been reduced would be proportionately greater. The two Western viewpoints disagreed over who would benefit from the residue. In the immediate future, NATO; but the longer term was very uncertain. Air staffs, with some justification, saw the more immediate risks of operational restriction rather than long-term advantage from the inclusion of aircraft in negotiations.

Finally, the minority argued that because the Soviet Air Force proposals were so obviously unrealistic, the West should accept the principle but offer counterproposals which would embrace all combat aircraft in the ATTU region, thereby eliminating the numerical imbalance, denying the USSR sanctuary in her western districts and forestalling the prospect of a post-CFE correlation which would become less favourable to NATO. This view, still militarily unpopular in the West, was publicly expressed for the first time in London in early 1989. After examining the issues set out in this chapter, the author concluded:

In sum, there are good grounds for the NATO alliance to move very cautiously in CST (Conventional Stability Talks) on air power issues. Aircraft cannot occupy territory and it is difficult to envisage a scenario in which Western Europe would be the victim of a surprise air attack unaccompanied by invasion. On the other hand an invasion preceded by a large-scale, disarming air attack and accompanied by unopposed close support aircraft is not a prospect to be viewed with equanimity by generals or air marshals. And, the greater the reductions in ground forces, the greater the influence of combat aircraft upon them. In the longer term therefore, NATO cannot afford to ignore Soviet numerical air superiority any more than the disparity on the ground especially as current generation Soviet aircraft and weapons have either narrowed or actually ended the traditional technology lead enjoyed by the West to offset numerical inferiority.

Underlying all considerations will remain the nagging doubts shared by many military men and others less cautiously inclined in the West. Will Secretary Gorbachev's United Nations initiatives be translated into practical military reductions, redeployments and redefinitions? Will his many internal problems weaken his influence, or inclinations, over a massive, unwieldy, entrenched, privileged and heavily committed military machine? And even if he does impose his will on the Generals, what of the long term ambitions of an economically restored, militarily slimlined USSR?

About some things however, the West can be certain. The USSR will continue to seek the moral high ground in debate over arms control and reductions; will continue to seek the fracture of the European-Atlantic relationship; will continue to encourage discord among the European partners of the alliance and will continue to depend solely on military power to substantiate her superpower status. Under those certainties CST negotiations must proceed positively but cautiously. To fail to consider the place of air power in them could be to hand the USSR a certain diplomatic trick and more permanently, a long term military advantage. Perhaps the examination question is not "Should air power be included?', but, 'When?'[35]

The CFE Negotiations

Meanwhile, on 10 January 1989 the 23 members of NATO and the WTO signed an agreement to begin negotiations on conventional armed forces in Europe in Vienna 'no later than in the seventh week following the closure of the Vienna CSCE meeting.'[36] Among the objectives were 'the elimination of disparities prejudicial to stability and security; and the elimination, as a matter of priority, of the capability of launching a surprise attack and for initiating large-scale offensive action.'[37] The objectives were to be achieved by, among other measures, 'reductions, limitation, redeployment provisions, equal ceilings . . .'[38] The subject of the negotiations was to be 'the conventional armed forces . . . of the participants based on land within the territory of the participants in Europe from the Atlantic to the Urals . . . Naval forces and chemical weapons will not be addressed.'[39]

In the initial position paper presented by NATO's CFE negotiators at Vienna on 6 March 1989 there was no mention of aircraft. Instead, proposals concentrated on 'overall levels of forces, particularly those relevant to surprise attack and offensive action such as tanks, artillery and armoured troop carriers . . [whose] substantial disparity in numbers . . . most threatens stability in Europe. These systems are also central to the seizing and holding of territory, the prime aim of any aggressor.'[40] In addition to proposing overall ceilings for each category, NATO introduced a 'sufficiency' rule, whereby no country should retain more than 30 per cent of the overall total in each category, and 'stationed forces' sub-limits restricting permissible levels to be stationed outside national territory.

In response, the WTO delegations proposed that in a 'first Stage (no later than 1991–1994), all the Participating States will eliminate imbalances and asymmetries between NATO and the Warsaw Treaty . . . and will take steps to eliminate the capability to launch surprise attack or initiate large-scale offensive action. For this purpose attention will be focused on reducing the most destabilising types and categories of armaments . . .'[41] As expected, the Warsaw Pact placed first on its list of 'destabilising' armaments 'attack combat aircraft of short-range/tactical aviation', with 'combat helicopters' third after tanks.[42] The alternative 'tactical' reflected the distinction in the Soviet Air Force between the centrally-controlled medium and long-range bomber regiments and the tactical air forces distributed geographically in central and eastern Europe and among the Military Districts of the USSR. It also introduced the artificial distinction between 'defensive' and 'attack' to the negotiating table and by implication excluded all Warsaw Pact air superiority fighters and air-defence interceptors. A further proposal was to reduce the categorised forces to equal collective ceilings which 'would be 10–15 per cent lower than the lowest levels possessed by the military political alliances.'[43]

During the first round of the negotiations, which continued until 23 March, no discussions of aircraft took place as the NATO delegates maintained their established position. The second round began on 5 May and initial exchanges on the aircraft problem were not promising. On that day, in a generally conciliatory opening plenary address, Ambassador Grinevskiy of the USSR reminded the delegates that, while there was an understanding that the negotiations should concentrate on 'those systems having the most significant capabilities for carrying out a surprise attack . . . our partners exclude from the list such systems of strike tactical aviation whose attacks have begun all contemporary wars.'[44]

Four days later the senior Soviet military delegate, General Tatarnikov, made a lengthy intervention in which he compared the destructive range and capabilities of a strike aircraft to that of an armoured personnel carrier. 'Logic', he argued, 'and the mandate of the negotiations require, with regard to this comparison, that priority be unconditionally given to reducing in the first importance tactical strike aviation. Without reducing this type of offensive armament, we will not achieve stability and security in Europe.'[45]

Two days later the US delegation sustained the Western position that the distinctions made were artificial, that aircraft were a low priority, that their inherent mobility posed far more complex problems of verification than was recognised by General Tatarnikov, and that the WTO enjoyed such numerical superiority in aircraft which would be employed in any campaign in Europe that the proposal not to deal with them in the current phase of negotiations would not pose any danger to the East.[46]

On 23 May the Warsaw Pact delegations presented their first detailed numerical proposals for reduction. The exclusive fixed-wing focus on 'strike' was maintained. Each alliance ceiling was to be 1,500 fixed-wing aircraft and 1,700 helicopters. No country should hold more than 1,200 of each, and no signatory should base more than 350 aircraft and 600 helicopters outside its own national boundaries. Each category was further subdivided by numerical limits in each of four zones within ATTU: zone of contact, central, forward and rear. No further aircraft definitions were offered, but by implication the proposal excluded interceptors, maritime land-based training, medium and heavy bomber aircraft.

At that point there seemed no way to reconcile the positions of the two sides. Meanwhile, NATO staffs were preparing in Brussels for the scheduled annual meeting of Heads of State and Government in the North Atlantic Council on 29 and 30 May. The air staffs were not expecting to be called upon for a contribution and were preparing to take an extended weekend leave.

In the space of seven days, however, a dramatic change in the Western position began to take shape, instigated by President Bush and his closest advisers. US representatives visited NATO staffs in Brussels and on 25 May three senior British Ministry of Defence officials flew at a few hours' notice to Washington to meet their opposite numbers in the Pentagon, where they were made aware of the US intention to include combat aircraft in the negotiations.

On 30 May a decision by NATO on a proposed follow-on system to the *Lance* short-range surface-to-surface missile was awaited. In a press communiqué issued in Brussels on 30 May,[47] the deferral of a decision on *Lance* until 1992, together with the reiteration of NATO's original CFE position at Vienna, at first overshadowed a statement by President Bush during the meeting that combat aircraft would be included in the negotiations. 'We will expand our current proposal to include reductions by each side to equal ceilings at the level 15 per cent below current Alliance holdings of helicopters and of all land-based combat aircraft in the Atlantic-to-the-Urals zone, with all the withdrawn equipment to be destroyed.'[48] At a stroke, the nature and extent of the CFE negotiations were completely changed. There would be a bumpy ride ahead, but now at least both sides were on the same road.

There appear to have been several reasons for President Bush's unexpected initiative. Soviet willingness in the second round of talks to reduce ground forces and move towards the Western framework for negotiations may have induced a more conciliatory response.[49] The inclusion of aircraft had been raised at an international conference in England in early May attended by SACEUR and staff members of both the Senate and the House of Representatives Defense Committees. This was probably the first occasion when the 'alternative' position was examined in depth by NATO policy makers and advisers.[50] The President was under pressure in the West to respond more positively to what was then seen as a successful propaganda offensive in Moscow. The introduction of aircraft reinforced the emphasis on conventional, as opposed to nuclear forces. In Congress, the initiative would lay a strategic basis for a subsequent reappraisal of defence procurement. Perhaps most significantly, Admiral William J. Crowe, Chairman of the US Joint Chiefs of Staff, observed that the implementation of the initiative should redress the Soviet Union's and the Warsaw Pact's major advantage in conventional forces.[51] That was the first official statement by any senior US military spokesman which acknowledged that hitherto the Eastern bloc had held 'a major advantage' in air power. It also reflected the success of those who had quietly argued that it was in the best longer-term interests of NATO to seek a reduction in Warsaw Pact conventional air strength.

The initiative was, however, a statement of intent, expressing broad principles only. There was no attendant definition of combat aircraft and no indication of how cuts would be shared between members of the opposing alliances. At the time it was assumed that the revised ceilings would be based on the figures already issued by the respective alliances.[52] On the NATO figures, a reduction of 15 per cent would have required the destruction of 600 fixed wing and 375 rotary wing aircraft by the West and approximately 4,800 and 1,575 by the Warsaw Pact.

Military staffs on both sides were thrown into disarray. The initiative put the Soviet General Staff back on to the defensive. Their wish to include aircraft had been met, but on terms which were politically difficult to avoid and which militarily would not only eliminate their capability to mount an Air Operation as hitherto envisaged, but would present them with very difficult choices in selecting which aircraft to withdraw from which role - including air defence. The initiative took Soviet decision makers completely by surprise, which is hardly surprising as NATO air staff were equally unprepared. In July there was evidence of considerable debate still taking place in Moscow about how best to respond. There was a strongly held view in the Soviet Air Force that the NATO proposals to include PVO aircraft were so unacceptable that air forces should be removed from the negotiations altogether. This view was quickly overruled by the Foreign Ministry, but it was clear that the issue of Soviet national air defence would become serious and potentially threatening to the negotiations.[53]

In Brussels, there was no formal staff structure in existence to drive forward and amplify the aircraft measures and fears were expressed of unilateral national positions emerging in an Alliance vacuum. Nonetheless, NATO air staffs were instructed to convert the 'initiative' into detailed proposals in little over four weeks. It soon became obvious that the aircraft numbers published by NATO the previous November were inadequate as a negotiating base because they did not include training aircraft nor those in storage. In reassessing the totals for both sides, NATO staffs had to take two factors into account. The figures published previously were based on national declarations within NATO and intelligence assessments of Warsaw Pact front-line strength. In fact, both sides possessed training aircraft which could be modified to deliver weapons and in some cases, as the RAF had demonstrated in the Falklands war, aircraft designed for one role could be swiftly adapted to carry completely different weapons. Second, both sides had undisclosed aircraft in storage: some modern, bought as attrition replacements, others obsolescent but still capable of contributing to an air war in which primary defences had been degraded. The potential impact of even small numbers of combat aircraft in comparison with similar numbers of tanks or artillery made it necessary to seek far more precise figures as a basis for both reductions and subsequent verification. Consequently, all NATO member nations revised their national declarations of aircraft stocks and intelligence staffs reappraised the Warsaw Pact's combat potential.

At the same time, the independent national relationships within NATO provided further complications for the air staffs. All the European negotiators were sensitive to the fact that 15 per cent cuts shared equally between the Alliance's air forces would entail a cut in the totality of their combat strength, while the USA, Canada and the USSR would be called upon to destroy only a percentage of their aircraft deployed in the ATTU area. The USA was loth to destroy any front-line aircraft of the calibre of the F-15, F-16 and F-111.

Definitions of 'combat aircraft' and 'combat helicopters' also proved difficult to conclude. NATO staffs were faced with the problem of reaching agreement on a definition which would retain as much operational flexibility as possible without leaving loopholes which a future WTO could exploit to greater advantage. As a result, a considerable amount of midnight oil was burned in national defence ministries and NATO headquarters throughout June 1989.

Its product was presented to Vienna by the United Kingdom delegate on 13 July. The revised NATO fixed-wing combat strength, including trainers and in storage, was declared to be 6,700. The Warsaw Pact total was 12,000. The proposed new ceilings, 15 per cent below NATO strength, were to be 5,700 fixed-wing, ground-based combat aircraft and 1,900 helicopters for each group of countries belonging to the same treaty alliance. No one country could retain in ATTU more than 30 per cent of the overall limits in these two categories, i.e., 3,420 combat aircraft and 1,140 combat helicopters. Helicopters and aircraft withdrawn from service to achieve compliance with the new ceilings were to be destroyed.[54]

Combat aircraft were defined as 'fixed wing or swing wing aircraft permanently land-based of a type initially constructed or later converted to drop bombs, deliver air-to-air or air-to-surface missiles, fire guns/cannons, or employ any other weapons of destruction. Any permanently land-based version or variant of these aircraft which has been modified to perform another military function is also included.'[55] The definition of combat helicopters was similarly worded.

The NATO proposal had been tabled on the last day of the second round of the talks, precluding any response by the Eastern bloc even had one been prepared. Later that month however on 21 July, Marshal Akhromeyev addressed the United States House Armed Services Committee, giving a *tour d'horizon* of the USSR's position on matters of national security. *Inter alia* he sustained the distinction within 'tactical aviation' between 'attack aviation' and 'fighter aviation'. 'The latter is designed, unlike air defence fighter aircraft, to protect the battlefield against air strikes of a potential enemy.'[56] This bland disregard of the comprehensive and critical role of the air-superiority fighter did not convince his audience and did not reflect more realistic reappraisals already taking place in Moscow. His explanation of the rationale behind the existence of a separate home-defence air organisation was, however, more persuasive. He reminded his

audience that 'the territory of the Soviet Union is 21 million square kilo-
metres. In general, the geostrategic situation for our country is not
favourable. Air strikes can be delivered on its territory practically from any
direction. That is why we have to maintain a dedicated armed service - the
national air defence forces . . . They are not equipped with any offensive
weapons systems and the Soviet Union is not going to deploy them unless
it is forced to do so by the actions of other countries.'[57]

The reason why all 'tactical aviation' had to be included in the negotiations was explained by a prominent Soviet analyst at the same time as
Marshal Akhromeyev was arguing to the contrary, although that was not
his intention. 'A frequent objection in the West to the inclusion of tactical
aviation in the category of offensive weapons is that aircraft cannot seize
and hold territory which, it is claimed, is the normal goal of aggression.
This is an obvious fact; however, it should be noted that, with the proper
use of tactical aviation, it is possible to seize and hold territory using substantially less tanks and motorised rifle units.'[58] Quite so.

Meanwhile, the debate in Moscow was to produce the first move
towards compromise on aircraft in the third CFE round, which began in
Vienna on 7 September. After three weeks of sessions which concentrated
on land force issues, on 28 September the East German ambassador tabled
a new proposal on aircraft. The previous concentration on 'attack' aircraft
was abandoned. Instead, a definition of a 'combat aircraft' was offered
which resembled that of the West: 'a fixed or moveable wing aircraft constructed and equipped with weaponry and equipment for fulfilling the
tasks of engaging objects on the ground or on the ground and in the air
through the employment of guided and unguided rockets, bombs, munitions and other combat means, as well as for reconnaissance and ECM
[electronic countermeasures]'.[59] The step towards realistic categorisation
was reinforced by specification: 'strike aircraft, fighter bombers, ground
attack aircraft, tactical fighters, reconnaissance aircraft and ECM aircraft.'[60] The definitions however were for 'combat aircraft of frontal
aviation forces (tactical air forces)'.[61] The definition of 'combat helicopters'
was similarly worded.

In line with the broader definition, previous ceiling proposals were also
revised: 'In the zone of application, the collective common ceiling for each
group of states belonging to the same alliance will be 4,700 combat aircraft
and 1,900 combat helicopters. The ceiling for each individual nation will be
3,400 combat aircraft and 1,500 combat helicopters. The ceiling for units
stationed outside national territory for each alliance will be 1,200 combat
aircraft.'[62]

Superficially, the gap between the two sides' proposals was close: within
1,000 (4,700–5,700) in fixed-wing numbers and identical in helicopters.

While welcoming the moves, Western analysts pointed out the breadth of the residual divide. The proposal explicitly excluded 'air defence interceptors of the air defence forces, which are assigned to protect the territory of a state . . . from strategic and carrier based aircraft, as well as air and sea-based cruise missiles . . .'[63] but suggested the construction of a separate ceiling for interceptors 'on condition that the systems against which they are intended to defend are not built up'.[64]

By Western counts this excluded not only 1,500 PVO interceptors in the USSR but also another 1,200 fighters possessed by the non-Soviet Warsaw Pact allies, which could contribute both to national defence and a conflict on land in central Europe. Moreover, by specifically referring to combat aircraft in 'tactical aviation' the proposal excluded training and land-based maritime aircraft, while leaving the position of the SU-24 *Fencer* and the TU-22 *Backfire* medium bombers ambiguous. In addition, WTO attitudes towards US carrier-borne aircraft were explicitly reflected in the rationale for a separate air-defence interceptor category. In other words, the new proposal would leave the Pact with a large residual numerical advantage of aircraft capable of contributing to any future conflict in the ATTU area.

During the remainder of the talks in the third round, agreements were reached on the principles of information exchanges and verification; but WTO proposals for specific intrusive inspections of aircraft and weaponry as well as by overflights and satellite were not discussed in detail. By the end of the round, on 19 October, the two sides were still far apart on the issue of both the total numbers to be included in an agreement and their categorisation, despite conciliatory statements.

The opening of the fourth round of talks on 9 November was overshadowed by the accelerating collapse of Communist regimes in eastern Europe and the breaching on the same day of the Berlin Wall. Discussions during the round concentrated on land forces, although NATO air staffs had began to reappraise the air situation in the light of the apparent disintegration of WTO military cohesion, with its attendant implications for co-ordinated operations, including air defence. On 14 December, however both sides tabled draft treaties which enshrined the positions taken on 13 July and 23 September.

Despite the lack of formal progress after 14 December, the consensus view among Western staffs was that the unexpected rate and extent of political upheaval in eastern Europe made a CFE treaty in 1990 more not less essential. In the fifth round momentum was regained on 8 February by a new NATO proposal which included aircraft and helicopters as well as tanks and armoured fighting vehicles. The proposal was for a reduced alliance ceiling of 4,700, equalling that proposed by the WTO in September, with a further sub-ceiling of 500 for air-defence interceptors, while unarmed training aircraft would be excluded altogether. Helicopters could be subdivided into those considered attack or attack-capable, and 'combat support' which did not employ anti-armour or air-to-air guided weapons with an integrated fire-control and arming system. A CFE ceiling would only be imposed on the former of 1,900 for each. The latter would be subject to information exchange and on-site inspection. A further gesture towards Soviet interests was made by permitting recategorisation of attack helicopters if their weapon systems were removed. This last proposal would allow conversion by the USSR of multi-role helicopters, such as the Mi-8, for use in the civilian economy.[65]

The continued application of a 30 per cent sufficiency rule in the NATO proposal imposed a maximum holding by any one country of 2,820 aircraft plus 500 interceptors for the USSR, and 1,140 combat helicopters. It would have involved cuts of approximately 800 aircraft and 400 helicopters by NATO, and of 4,900 and 3,000 by the WTO.[66]

Four days later the WTO made a counterproposal agreeing an alliance ceiling of 4,700, but with a further interceptor sub-ceiling of 1,500 and a similar figure for combat-capable trainers. The combined total of 7,700, which still excluded land-based aviation was 1,000 higher than NATO's own pre-CFE total of declared combat aircraft holdings. Not surprisingly therefore, while civilian analysts saw the gap closing, NATO military staffs saw a sustained WTO numerical superiority plus opportunities for treaty circumvention by the transfer of aircraft from limited tactical aviation to unrestricted naval aviation.

At the same time the USSR was becoming even more concerned about the implications of the disintegration of the WTO. At the outset of the CFE negotiations in March 1989, it had been logical to view the aircraft possessed by the WTO as an extension of the USSR's own ruling military capability. Just 12 months later, Hungary, Poland, Bulgaria, Romania and Czechoslovakia were no longer governed by sympathetic governments and the future relationship with the German Democratic Republic was at best uncertain. Under the NATO proposal of 8 February, the USSR would have been restricted to 3,320 combat aircraft, her erstwhile allies to 1,880 and NATO to 5,200. To Moscow, such a prospect was unacceptable, hence the USSR's adamant position over the 'additional' sub-ceilings and exclusion of land-based naval aviation.

As the process towards German unification within NATO gathered speed during the summer of 1990, the USSR became even more beleaguered at Vienna. At the same time her internal political problems multiplied and deepened. NATO staffs became increasingly concerned about possible military instability within the USSR itself. How should further conciliatory compromise on aircraft in CFE be measured against the impact of a WTO collapse on the one hand, and the risks of politically-irresponsible future Soviet military adventures, spearheaded by an air force which had been protected from CFE reductions and fostered by defence procurement priorities, on the other?

Nonetheless, the gap between the two sides narrowed a little further on 4 July by a WTO proposal. The aggregate limit of 7,700 proposed on 12 February, was reduced to 6,950: comprising 4,700 'tactical combat aircraft', 1,500 air-defence interceptors and 750 combat trainers. The proposal included the option of converting the excess of combat trainers to 'trainers' already excluded from the treaty – by removing armaments and weapon-aiming systems.[67]

The proposal excluded land-based naval aircraft and made no mention of any single nation limits. The proposal to allow 'conversion' of combat trainers was incompatible with the Western position that any combat aircraft modified to fulfil any other function must still be classified as 'combat' and treaty-limited. Thus, while the WTO step was acknowledged, Western concerns about opportunities for circumvention remained. In emergencies, weapon systems could rapidly be introduced into compatible aircraft, as British experience in the Falklands had demonstrated. Already reports were circulating in NATO about the transfer of some Soviet combat squadrons from Tactical to Naval Aviation, and such a loophole could readily be exploited if it were not closed.

During the following two months, while negotiations on ground forces reduced one obstacle after another, little or no progress was made on aircraft or helicopters. Indeed, agreement on the latter seemed to be receding. The Soviet Union sought to exclude two variants of the Mi-24 helicopter – the Mi-24R reconnaissance and Mi-24K artillery/fire control models – from the 'attack' category. It was also argued that the heavy lift Mi-26 should also be excluded altogether, because it was unarmed and used in many civilian functions. In addition, it was reported that the Soviet Union wished to increase its own national allocation of helicopters to 40 per cent.[68]

On the other hand, the political environment surrounding the talks began to brighten. The NATO London Declaration of 6 July was favourably acknowledged by Mr Gorbachev on 16 July, together with his acceptance of German unification. Bilateral negotiations between the USSR and its WTO allies indicated that, whatever the outcome of the CFE agreement, Soviet forces would be extensively reduced in eastern Europe and the capacity for a large-scale, co-ordinated, surprise attack by the WTO in western Europe was rapidly becoming operationally impracticable.[69]

Paradoxically, these developments were accompanied by rumours, not of converging positions on aircraft, but of concern lest the issue should thwart the signing of a CFE treaty. It was suggested that an agreement on aircraft could be postponed to a 'second stage' of negotiations. Despite official denials, the rumours were sufficiently strong in Washington, in some European capitals and at NATO headquarters to cause concern among those who believed that the exclusion of aircraft from a treaty would be a serious military and political weakness. However difficult the aircraft negotiations, the circumstances in a future, putative 'CFE Two', were unlikely to be any more favourable.[70]

At the beginning of October, however, the unification of Germany transformed the entire military position in the central 'region' and, at a stroke, removed the USSR's strongest ally. The West was prepared to make further concessions. After meetings in New York on 3 October, Secretary of State James Baker and Foreign Minister Shevardnadze announced the outlines of an agreement which would form the basis of a CFE Treaty. Baker announced that the USSR would be limited to a combat aircraft total of 5,150, plus a politically-binding, but non-verifiable limit of 400 land-based naval aircraft.[71] In addition, the minister agreed that the USSR should be allowed to retain 37 per cent of a total helicopter holding of 2,000 for each side. This represented an increase of 1,000 over the previous NATO proposed aggregate and a 7 per cent increase in the 'sufficiency' rule. Finally, the USSR dropped its attempts to include NATO's carrier-based aircraft.

The ground was now prepared for a final stage of negotiations which would translate the agreements in principle into detailed numbers.

The Treaty
Combat Aircraft
Not surprisingly, the air-related clauses in the CFE Treaty signed in Paris on 19 November reflected compromises on all sides from the original positions held before the first negotiations began in Vienna 18 months previously. The definition of 'combat aircraft' made no distinction between offence and defence and included the 'look-alike' concept as far as 'an aircraft which performs military functions such as reconnaissance or electronic warfare'.[72] 'Combat trainer' versions were, however, dealt with separately under the second Protocol to the Treaty. 'Each State Party shall have the right to remove from the numerical limitations on combat aircraft in Articles IV and VI of the Treaty no more than 550 such aircraft [combat trainers] of which no more than 130 shall be of the MiG-25U model or version.'[73] A concession was made towards the Soviet argument that training variants of front-line aircraft should not be counted as combat aircraft by 'permitting up to 550 to be disarmed or certified as disarmed within a period of 40 months from the entry into force of the Treaty.'[74]

Agreement on total numbers of combat aircraft marked a gradual movement by NATO towards the higher figures consistently requested by the
USSR. Each side was to be limited to a total of 6,800 combat aircraft, with
a national limit for each state party of 5,150.[75] No zonal limits were
imposed on aircraft or helicopters.

The provisional agreement reached in New York the previous month on
land-based naval aviation was not included within the treaty. Instead, a
simultaneous declaration was made of a 'politically-binding' ceiling of 430
aircraft for each side and of 400 for any one country, which would not be
subject to verification. While the numbers involved on either side were not
large, approximately 150 in NATO and 510 in the WTO, the agreement
marked a major concession by the West. Several types of Soviet treaty limited aircraft, for example the SU-20 and the TU-16, were already in service
with Soviet Naval Aviation, and without verification there would be no formal method of either detecting redeployments or substantiating denials of
such authority. Such Western concerns, muted during the acclaim of the
signing of the treaty, were slightly increased when the USSR subsequently
declared only 6,445 treaty-limited aircraft; well below the expected total,[76]
and calling for reductions of only 1,295. Assertions that previous unilateral
reductions, destruction and withdrawals beyond the Urals accounted for
apparent discrepancies were regarded with a Western suspicion not entirely
grounded in 40 years of mutual distrust.[77] All parties were to be allowed to
revise their declarations within 90 days, and before 18 February 1991 the
USSR raised its total by 166 to 6,611, reportedly after reassessing a number
of MiG-25 and SU-15 operational conversion fighters.[78] In March 1991, a
US Navy official alleged that 670 aircraft had been reassigned from the
Soviet Air Force to Naval Aviation since 1988.[79] If so, at least a similar
number of naval aviation aircraft would need to be withdrawn from service
to conform to the 'political agreement' of November 1990.

NATO, meanwhile, after identifying every machine which could be
remotely classified as combat-capable, including cannibalised 'hangar
queens',[80] could only declare 5,531, including 704 USAF aircraft. As a
result, of all the CFE treaty-limited items, only in fixed-wing, land-based
combat aircraft did the USSR, taking into account the excluded aircraft of
Soviet Naval Aviation, retain numerical advantage over NATO.

Combat Helicopters

The definition and regulation of combat helicopters prompted a complex
series of compromises. Each side would retain 2,000 attack helicopters,
with maximum individual state holdings in-theatre of 1,500.[81] 'Combat
helicopters' were to be categorised as 'specialised attack', 'multi-purpose
attack', or 'combat support'.[82] The USSR was to be allowed to retain 100

Mi-24R and Mi-24K helicopters, subject to information exchange and internal inspection, above the 'sufficiency' total for the 'specialist attack' category.[83]

'Multipurpose attack' helicopters could be excluded from the agreement provided they were converted to the category of 'combat support' by the removal or incapacitating of hardpoints and launching devices, and by the removal of all integrated fire control and aiming systems.[84] Such conversion was to be accompanied by photographic evidence of component removal and by certification of all conversions.[85] Finally, all combat helicopters were to fall within information exchange, verification and inspection regimes.[86]

Before the expiry of the extended data-declaration date, the USSR also raised its total of attack helicopters by 150 to 1,480. In the original 'Correlation of Forces' publication in February 1989, the USSR had published a total of 2,200 'combat helicopters', but without any categorisation or definition.

Air power in Co-operative Security

The original 22 signatories to the CFE Treaty in November 1990 had expanded to 29 by the time ratification was completed in July 1992. It assumed *de jure* international status in November 1992 after all signatories had deposited their instruments of ratification at The Hague.[87]

The delay had been caused primarily by the disintegration of the USSR during 1991 and subsequent negotiations between members of the Commonwealth of Independent States about the allocation of treaty-limited equipment. The seven new signatories were Georgia, Moldova, Azerbaijan, Ukraine, Armenia, Belarus and Khazakstan. On 15 May the seven, plus Russia signed an agreement at Tashkent apportioning the equipment, including combat aircraft and helicopters. Of the 5,150 aircraft and 1,500 helicopter entitlement for the USSR, Russia was to receive 3,450 and 890, respectively, Ukraine 1,090 and 330, Belarus 260 and 80, with the remainder shared among the smaller states.[88]

This allocation prompted considerable concern in Moscow which is examined in detail in Chapter 7. The Russian figures did not include the proportions of the original Soviet Air Forces deployed beyond the Urals, and therefore the total Russian Air Forces probably numbered 8,000 combat aircraft.[89] But a high proportion of Soviet combat aircraft had been deployed into eastern Europe or based in the western regions of the USSR. Many of the squadrons withdrawn from eastern Europe during 1989 and 1990 were relocated in Belarus, Ukraine and the Caucasus area. Consequently the Russian Air Force lost many of its best aircraft, together with their bases and maintenance and logistic support at a time of widespread political and economic uncertainty. Not only would further aircraft modernisation now be required, but an extensive programme of airbase and infrastructure improvement too to make good the losses to the other republics. Resentment at the combined impact of the treaty and internal disintegration contributed to military disaffection with the Yeltsin regime which was still audible in 1994.

Comparisons between the CFE Treaty and the impact of the Versailles Treaty of 1919 on the German armed forces were however premature. The Russian General Staff were anxious about events in their 'strategic space', or 'near abroad' – both euphemisms for the territory of the old USSR - but resentment, and in some cases possibly residual suspicion against the West was not accompanied by any overt signs of belligerent intent.[90]

Moreover, there were accompanying, permanent elements of stability associated with the CFE Treaty which were lacking at Versailles. For example, within the Treaty itself, Articles 14, 15 and 16 established a comprehensive verification regime which dealt equally with all signatories.[91] In addition, the Vienna Document of 4 March 1992 which concluded the Vienna CSCE meetings from 1989, introduced for the first time an agreement on visits to each other's 'normal peacetime airbases' by all the signatories.[92] The visits were to be to specific bases by invitation of the host country; not a major step in itself but a valuable addition to the CFE process.

The third measure, with the greatest potential significance for international air power, and indeed for all other arms control activities, was the Treaty on Open Skies (OST) signed on 24 March 1992 by former NATO and non-Soviet WTO members, plus Russia, Belarus, Ukraine and Georgia, at the Helsinki CSCE Review Conference. Article 14 of the CFE Treaty committed its signatories to negotiating an aerial inspection regime, but by early 1994 the OST had already been ratified by the USA, Canada, the Czech Republic, Denmark and Slovakia with several other signatories preparing to complete the process.

Although originally proposed by President Eisenhower in 1955, the modern successful sequence was launched by President Bush in May 1989 with a proposal for unarmed reconnaissance flights over the territories of the USA, the USSR and their allies. Negotiations continued during 1990 and 1991, gradually resolving differences on aircraft provision, sensors, information analysis and dissemination, frequency and route restrictions, culminating in the 73-page treaty.[93]

Quotas for observation flights were allocated to each signatory; for example, 42 to the USA and to the Republic of Belarus with the Russian Federation, and four each to Spain, Bulgaria, Greece, Hungary, Iceland and the then-Czechoslovakia. A number of airfields in each signatory country were designated as 'open skies airfields', from which each obser-vation flight would originate and terminate and from which inspection flight distances were specified. Unlike the CFE Treaty, the OST covers all the territory of all the signatories; this is of great mutual advantage to Russia and the USA.

After the Gulf War exposed the practical limitations on satellite-derived intelligence, the OST acquired even more importance. In June 1993 a trial was flown over the UK by a Russian AN-30 transport aircraft to test the management of air-traffic control procedures and technical regulations on camera operations. The OST authorised optical, infra-red and synthetic aperture radar sensors, but this flight was restricted to optical surveillance. The flight plan took the aircraft over two nuclear power stations, a Royal Air Force radar station, a military electronic-warfare training range, two airfields, a ballistic missile early-warning station, a submarine-construc-tion yard, a nuclear submarine base and a dockyard.[94]

While SIGINT was an obvious omission from the sensors authorised, the combination of the other sensors, plus the freedom to route plan every-where except in previously-notified 'hazardous' airspace in accordance with international civil airlines procedures, marked a major confidence-building step.

The three measures taken together: CFE, CSCE airbase visits and OST, were the first successful applications of the concept of 'co-operative' secu-rity, as opposed to 'collective' security in air power's first hundred years. It could be argued that they only came about because confrontational tension between East and West was already relaxing, and that subsequent events rendered them superfluous. Such a conclusion would fail to take into account their symbiotic relationship and the fact that international ceilings for combat aircraft and other weapons had now been agreed in a region which had seen incessant warfare for more than a thousand years. Moreover, the twentieth century innovation of air power had arrived as a further and potentially decisive destabilising element. Now, on the thresh-old of the twenty-first, it also had the potential to induce compliance with existing treaties and to make clandestine preparations for further conflicts much more difficult. While geopolitical conditions varied considerably elsewhere in the world, there could be transferable precedents in this European sequence, either within the broadening framework of the OST or in the manner of CFE/CSCE agreements. But there were undoubtedly solid inducements for both sides to reach these agreements in Europe and in the aftermath of the recently-agreed treaties it is easy to overlook the fact that the characteristics of air power which make it such a formidable instrument are exactly those which make it so difficult to circumscribe in arms control agreements.

As noted above, the CFE negotiations illuminated the problems of defining what was and what was not a combat aircraft when airframes can be modified and weapon systems affixed comparatively easily. Even the most rudimentary weapon carrier becomes influential when more sophisticated aircraft have cleared the defences ahead of it.

The distinction between offensive and defensive, as with most weapons, was fatuous. The well-meaning attempts to classify aircraft by weight, size or combat radius all failed when faced with lightweight combat aircraft carrying smart weapons and sustained by in-flight refuelling. Zoning is irrelevant to an aircraft which can cover several hundred miles in a few minutes from a base well beyond an arms-limited territory. Aircraft attacking airfields from aircraft carriers and vice versa blur the line between sea- and shore-based aviation; a fact well recognised by navies world-wide. The greater the flexibility, the greater the ubiquity of combat aircraft, the more difficult it becomes to define roles, characteristics, locations and any other traditional arms-limitations criteria. Therefore attempts to copy the European successes and transfer them to air forces, say in the Middle East or to the Pacific Rim, should be done with circumspection. Indeed, 'lessons' about air power limitation require the same caveat as 'lessons' about its application: they must be relevant to the political and technological circumstances of the time and place. That said, air power in a concept of co-operative security may become a more powerful instrument in international security than appeared possible before May 1989.

CHAPTER 5

THE GULF WAR: UNIQUE OR A PRECEDENT?

The Victory

The Gulf War between Iraq and a UN Coalition led by the United States actually began with the invasion of Kuwait on 2 August 1990 and ended with a ceasefire on 28 February 1991. But fighting between the two sides took place for only 43 days from 17 January. Until 24 February the war was fought almost exclusively by air. In the ensuing 100-hour period of ground engagements, Iraqi resistance was slight, fragmented and largely absent. The optimism of air force planners appeared completely vindicated; the judgement of those who had forecast thousands of Coalition casualties was discredited and the bombast of Saddam Hussein was ridiculed. The Iraqi army was expelled from Kuwait at a cost of 340 Coalition combat deaths and 776 injuries.[1] Of those, approximately 25 per cent of the deaths and 10 per cent of the injuries were the product of friendly fire.[2]

The fear of the pessimists had not been groundless. The Iraqi air force (IQAF) was the world's sixth largest with more than 700 combat aircraft on its inventory, including a number of MiG-29s, SU-24s, MiG-23s, MiG-25s and French F-1s. In addition, 11,000 missiles and 8,500 AA guns were deployed across Iraq and in the Kuwait Theatre of Operations (KTO). Baghdad itself was protected by an air-defence density exceeding that of Murmansk and twice that of any previous target in eastern Europe.[3] Projections of possible Coalition aircraft attrition rates varied considerably. In 1967 the Israeli Air Force had lost 20 aircraft in 1,000 sorties, or 2 per cent, and a similar figure six years later in the Yom Kippur conflict. In December 1990 USAF General (retired) Charles L.Donnelly advised the House Armed Services Committee that the Coalition would lose 100 aircraft in 20,000 sorties over 10 days. Not known at the time was the fact that

Brigadier General Glosson had advised the President in October that he estimated a Coalition loss of not more than 80, and more probably nearer to 50 aircraft.[4]

The Iraqi ground forces had an assessed total manpower of approximately one million men, with 5,000 main battle tanks, 5,000 armoured infantry vehicles and 3,000 artillery pieces larger than 100 mm.[5] In addition, Iraq was known to possess chemical and possibly biological weapons. The cumulative risks prompted the Coalition to assemble 63 hospitals, two hospital ships and 18,000 beds in the war zone, with a further requirement for 5,500 beds in Europe and 17–22,000 in the United States.[6] In all the explanations for the overwhelming and speedy Coalition success there was a common theme. On 21 February, the Chairman of the Joint Chiefs of Staff, General Colin Powell, observed to the Senate Armed Services Committee, 'Air power has been the decisive arm so far, and I expect it will be the decisive arm through to the end of the campaign, even if ground forces and amphibious forces are added to the equation . . . If anything, I expect air power to be even more decisive in the days and weeks ahead.'[7] Soon after the ceasefire, Secretary of Defense Cheney offered the judgement, 'The reason the . . . Iraqi forces collapsed as rapidly as they did, I think, was because of the campaign we mounted against them. This was a force that was very successful against Iran; a force that had fought an eight-year battle with Iran; it was well equipped with Soviet equipment. It was not a backward force by any means. It was crushed, I think, by the air campaign and the way in which we went about the campaign meant that when we finally did have to move our ground forces in and we sort of kicked in the door, they collapsed very rapidly'.[8]

Not surprisingly, many airmen were euphoric. 'In previous wars, the impact of air power has always been a bone of contention, an article of unresolved and unresolvable debate. In the Gulf War, it was clearly overwhelming and decisive. The clarity of the aerial victory also provided a symbolic beacon of sorts. It symbolised the maturity of air power, the domination of air power and the need for a new paradigm of warfare. . . . a three dimensional paradigm . . . Operation *Desert Storm*, although not large by historical standards, was one of those symbolic events that few people are fortunate to witness. It symbolised both a fundamental shift in the way many wars will be conducted, and the need for a new way of thinking about military operations. Viewed from the Iraqi perspective, *Desert Storm* symbolised the terrible penalty for adhering to the old model. It is time to change, and airmen must lead the way.'[9] The present writer cautioned in early 1991 against hasty conclusions but observed that, 'The Gulf War marked the apothesis of twentieth-century air power.'[10]

It was hardly surprising that analysts of a different coloured cloth were not quite so eulogistic about air power, nor convinced that air power was no longer the subject of 'unresolvable debate'. In the Pentagon, and in Ministries of Defence, the acknowledgement of the primacy of air power would have had threatening implications for procurement programmes, resource allocation, force structures and careers too serious for the other services to concede. Ultimately, diplomatic references were made to joint service success. The final DOD report to Congress allocated 131 pages to the 39-day air campaign, 106 to the 100-hour ground war, and 85 to maritime operations throughout *Desert Shield* and *Desert Storm*.

One United States Army analyst observed in 1993, 'Perhaps the most widespread illusion of the overwhelming impact of advanced technologies is that air power alone could have eventually forced the Iraqis to evacuate Kuwait and succumb to all appropriate UN resolutions. It cannot be overlooked that chronic inferiority in air power is a strategic liability for which it is almost impossible to compensate in normal conventional warfare, and there is no doubt that the air campaign was fundamental to the ultimate victory. Still this analysis is flawed for several reasons.' Those adduced by the writer were that a strategic air campaign might not have persuaded Saddam to withdraw; that the deployment of a smaller land force might have tempted him to extend the war and that, 'Third, it was ultimately the ground campaign that forced the Iraqis to agree to all UN resolutions.'[11] The argument of whether or not air power on its own would have secured the expulsion of Iraqi ground forces from Kuwait is now of less importance than the careful search, with all the benefits of 20–20 hindsight, for circumstances which are likely to recur elsewhere. Nonetheless, one final observation on the argument should be made. It is, ironically, prompted by the research of that US army commentator, Colonel McAusland.

If, as is alleged, Iraqi ground forces 'were destroying the Kuwait City desalination plant' on 24 February, and if General Schwarzkopf's assumption that this action could only suggest that they were about to leave, and that 'Furthermore, if they intended to pull out of the city they obviously intended to leave Kuwait,'[12] was correct, then the date is very important. Orders for the destruction must have been given either earlier that day, or previously. But the ground offensive was only launched on the 24th and, coupled with the accelerated destruction of Kuwaiti oil wells from the 22nd onwards, there is sufficient circumstantial evidence to suggest that Iraqi ground forces were, in fact, preparing to withdraw from Kuwait before the Coalition ground force offensive began. If that is the case, air power did secure the primary Coalition objective of its own and *Desert Sabre* was indeed no more than *Desert Roundup*. USAF Chief of Staff, General Merrill McPeak, was widely criticised in 1991 when he observed that 'this is the first time in history that a field army has been defeated by air power.'[13] He may be proved to be correct. The jury should remain out until Iraqi evidence is comprehensively and unequivocally made available.

A Unique War?

Attempts to identify 'lessons' from previous conflicts for application to future ones are fraught with danger. If they are rigidly applied, the general is accused of preparing to fight the last war all over again. If they are ignored, he has 'learned nothing from history'. Even if the 'correct' lessons are shrewdly and objectively extracted, they may prove quite inappropriate to a future conflict elsewhere. The most difficult task for the analysts is therefore to distinguish those features of a conflict which are transient and unique in time and place from those which are likely to recur elsewhere in the future.

Only the future will confirm which aspects of the Gulf War were unique; but certainly the combination of circumstances and features of this conflict were unusual, they were interactive and to a great extent they had a synergistic impact on the application of air power. Indeed, as the combined impact was so favourable for the application of air power it is necessary to reflect that on many occasions in military history defeat has been snatched from the jaws of victory. The Gulf War fought by the Coalition was distinguished by skilful diplomacy, intelligent planning, clear identification and pursuit of objectives, imaginative and inspiring leadership and executed with comprehensive professionalism and dedication. But even if on this occasion air power did win the war, or at least dominate and determine its outcome, it does not automatically follow that the face of warfare will be changed everywhere else. An examination of this war's circumstances and features, together with the postulation of an alternative scenario, induce caution about such a projection.

The interactive factors on this occasion which facilitated such an overwhelming impact by air power included an unusual degree of international consensus about the justification of Coalition action; favourable geography, topography and climate; massive Coalition technological superiority; considerable numerical superiority; Iraqi strategic ineptitude; and unprecedented Coalition supremacy in the quality of the combatants. From the outset, these features were identified and exploited by Coalition commanders to an extent rarely seen in the history of warfare.

The International Political Environment

There was an unusual degree of international consensus in the political response to the Iraqi invasion of Kuwait. There was a coincidence of perception: of the flouting of international law; of aggression by a large, well-armed state against a much smaller neighbour; of the forcible readjustment of international boundaries; of a threat to oil production and oil supply; and of a singularly vicious and unscrupulous regime. Such perceptions stimulated unanimous condemnation within the UN Security Council and facilitated the construction of the US-led Coalition.

The consensus had extensive operational implications. The immediate problem was to deter, and if necessary, check further Iraqi moves southwards and to provide reassurance and support to Saudi Arabia and neighbouring Gulf states. The ability of air power to be swiftly projected across the globe was exploited.

On 2 August, President Bush ordered the carrier USS *Independence* into the Gulf of Oman from the Arabian Sea and the USS *Eisenhower* into the Red Sea from the Mediterranean. By 8 August they were in position to attack targets in the northern Gulf area and south-west Iraq. On 6 August the President ordered F-15s from Virginia and the 82nd Airborne Division from South Carolina to deploy to Saudi Arabia. Twenty-four F-15s departed on 7 August and arrived in theatre 15 hours later. Within four hours they were flying combat air patrols along the Iraqi-Saudi border. The first troops of the 82nd arrived in Dhahran on the 9th and two brigades were deployed by 21 August. In the first two days of the deployment, Military Airlift Command flew 91 missions into theatre,[14] in support of combat aircraft deployment and transporting the first CENTCOM command elements. By 10 August, 45 F-15Cs, 19 F-15Es, 24 F-16s, 12 RAF *Tornado* F-3s and 112 *Jaguars* were either on combat air patrol or airbase alert. By 23 August over 500 combat aircraft were at readiness in the theatre, including F-117As, F-4G *Wild Weasels*, F-111s and B-52Gs in Diego Garcia, and supplied by E-3 AWACs, EC-135, U-2/TR-1, KC-10, KC-135 and C-130. By then, any opportunity which had existed for Saddam Hussein to move south was, if not tightly closed, rendered extremely precarious.

More than 1,000 aircraft, many loaded with armaments, deployed non-stop from the USA to the theatre, requiring an air bridge sustained by nearly 100 tankers flying from bases in the Azores, the UK, Spain, Germany, Italy, Greece and Egypt.[15] Direct overflights and *en route* facilities were available because of the international consensus. This support may be contrasted with the constraints placed on long-range US air power in support of Israel in 1973 and in attacks on Libya in 1986. Later in the period, several east European countries granted overflight rights, as did Thailand and India for flights from the Pacific region. Without such co-operation neither the speed nor the scale of response in August 1990 could have been achieved. As it was, 90 per cent of all support was transported by sea. Munitions transit time by sea could take as long as 72 days, therefore USAF units were dependent on airlift and prepositioned in-theatre stocks for their combat capability in the early days.[16]

This early insertion of Coalition air power provided the air cover for all subsequent deployments by air and surface into the theatre. The two major airheads Riyadh and Dhahran, and the major ports of entry at Al Jubayl and Damman were all within range of the IQAF. Thereafter the combination of AWACs, combat air patrols and air-to-air refuelling would reduce considerably the risk of pre-emptive attack by the IQAF during the Coalition ground-force build-up. Command of the air was established over northern Saudi Arabia from the outset.

The second and greatest operational advantage gained from international co-operation was access to, and support from, airbases in the region: in Saudi Arabia, Bahrain, Oman, the United Arab Emirates, Turkey and Egypt. Twenty-one principal airfields and several secondary bases were used by the Coalition. Some, like Khamis Mushait, the home of the F-117s, were modern bases with hardened shelters and modern living and working conditions. Others, like Al Kharj or Tabuk provided little more than a runway and hard standings. Consequently, British airlift priorities in the early days of deployment were ammunition and beds. The main theatre arrival bases at Dhahran and Riyadh had long, modern runways, extensive operational facilities and more ramp space than most commercial airports, but still space was restricted and other bases had to be used for arrivals.

Both the US and the British air forces benefited from existing military contact with Saudi Arabia. British Aerospace had 300 civilian and military personnel servicing the Al Yamamah contract for *Tornado* GR1 and F-3 aircraft at Dhahran. Of these, approximately 200 remained during the conflict to provide valuable co-operation with the RAF maintenance effort. The USAF association with Saudi Arabia had continued since World War II, when Dhahran had served as a staging resupply post for US forces in Asia. Since then US engineers had rebuilt Dhahran airfield and constructed several more bases including Taif, King Khalid Military City and Khamis Mushait. In addition the sale of F-15s and E-3 AWACs to Saudi Arabia, with associated training programmes, facilitated USAF-RSAF co-ordination. Without such an infrastructure a deployment of the size and speed of *Desert Shield* could not have been mounted.[17]

In the north of the theatre, the Turkish base of Incerlik was made available for the *Proven Force* operations, providing facilities for 95 combat and 31 support aircraft, including F-15/16/111s and EF-111s, E-3Bs and KC-135As.[18] From 18 January onwards, Iraq had to face air attack from both north and south, constraining any inclination or opportunity the government may have had to reinforce air defences south of Baghdad by redeployment from the north.

Host-nation support, however, extended far beyond making air bases available. Of the utmost significance was in-theatre availability of fuels. All surface fuels and most jet fuel, except for thermally-stable jet fuel and JP5, were provided by Saudi Arabia, Oman and the UAE. Fuel delivery to air bases was considerably assisted by host-nation support: Saudi Arabia provided 800 general purpose trucks and 5,000 tankers and trucks to distribute Saudi fuel to the Coalition. Elsewhere, the British Royal Engineers constructed a 100-km fuel pipeline with six pumping stations from Al Jubayl to RAF deployment bases.[19] In addition, the USAF deployed 92 per cent of its ground-refuelling assets to the theatre. USAF aircraft alone consumed 15 million gallons of jet fuel a day at the height of the war.[20] Detailed fuel allocations by type and user remained classified in early 1994, but a high peak of total Coalition air and surface consumption probably reached in excess of 20 million gallons of fuel per day.[21] In the air, USAF KC-135 tankers alone transferred 136 million gallons of fuel to more than 69,000 receivers.[22] Total Coalition tanker fuel transfer probably totalled more than 200 million gallons between August 1990 and February 1991. Of that, perhaps two-thirds would have been loaded in-theatre, almost entirely from in-house support.[23]

Inevitably it took a little while for fuel provision to be smoothly co-ordinated. At the beginning, deploying squadrons could find themselves competing with each other for local supply as existing base reserves were literally drained. On 11 August, one reinforcing fighter squadron was deployed for six hours before it could be refuelled and mount a combat alert.[24] Similar competition existed for the acquisition of liquid oxygen and liquid nitrogen, as well as for items such as telephones, camp beds and fork-lift trucks. On at least one occasion a fork-lift truck was 'transferred' from the custody of one nation to another without formal negotiations but barter, rather than 'appropriation' was a more customary method of Coalition support-equalisation. The benefits of host-nation support were not entirely one sided: in three months the local cost of an ISO container for multiple office and storage space rose from 550 to 25,000 dollars. The full significance, however, of Saudi Arabian in-house support to US forces is reflected in the total evaluation by 1 August 1991 of 13.4 billion dollars.[25]

US access to prepositioned stocks in Saudi Arabia, Oman, Diego Garcia and elsewhere could in different circumstances have been denied. Access to such facilities depended on its reaffirmation by each country.[26] The USAF had 1 billion dollars' worth of fuel, ammunition and equipment on the Arabian peninsula and aboard three maritime prepositioned ships. Prepositioned munitions accounted for approximately half the tonnage eventually dropped in the war, but largely comprised general-purpose and cluster weapons. Nonetheless, this volume was equivalent to 3,500 airlift mission loads and facilitated an airlift concentration on weapons incorporating the latest technology, including PGMs.[27]

The converse of the international consensus for the Coalition was the international isolation for Iraq. Again, historical parallels are enlightening. In earlier days clients of the USSR had been resupplied in crisis and in combat: Egypt in 1973, Syria after the Beka'a Valley fiasco of 1982, and North Vietnam continuously. In 1990, however, although an undisclosed number of Soviet technicians remained in Iraq, no spares, reinforcement or resupply would be forthcoming to the largely Soviet-equipped IQAF. It is highly probable that the awareness of stock limitations constrained any inclinations the IQAF may have entertained to increase its preparedness for war. While the Coalition air forces consistently flew campaign rehearsals beyond the view of Iraqi and Jordani radars, complete with large packages of up to 80 aircraft supported by tankers, AWACs and fighter CAPs,[28] IQAF training gradually diminished. Air Marshal Wratten, the RAF commander in-theatre subsequently observed: 'During the two months or so before hostilities began . . . [He] normally flew fewer than two hundred sorties per 24-hour period and this included all roles. Occasionally he dropped to less than one hundred and in the period immediately preceding 15 January 1991, he hardly flew at all.'[29] Air Marshal Wratten made further deductions about IQAF capabilities and it came as little surprise to the Coalition air commanders when the IQAF launched only 25 interceptors on the first night of hostilities and only an average of 30 strikes a day over the next few days. Indeed, Iraq's position may have been worse than isolated. It was widely reported in January that the Soviet Union had passed to the Coalition technical information on Soviet-supplied air-defence electronics, communication systems and construction and other data which would have contributed to the Coalition's neutralisation of Iraqi air defence.[30]

Similarly, information on 300 HAS (Hardened Aircraft Shelters) built by European contractors to higher than NATO specifications for Iraq was also made available to the Coalition.[31] Co-ordinated air attacks by PGM on them began on 26 January, stimulating both a rapid exit of IQAF aircraft and a swift response from their destination, Iran. Isolation also deprived the IQAF of sanctuary. In the early stages of the Iraq-Iran war, IQAF aircraft had been deployed out of the country to avoid the then superior Iranian Air Force. Ironically, one bolthole was reportedly at Riyadh airbase, where a number of TU-16 bombers sought refuge.[32]

Reports of IQAF aircraft flying to Iran in 1991 began to circulate by 20 January, but an unequivocal statement confirming a large-scale exodus was made on 26 January by the Iranian Security Council refusing Iraqi requests for their return: '. . . if a plane from either party makes an emergency landing in Iranian territory it will be seized until the end of the war.'[33] After the war the Iranian government stated that 148 IQAF aircraft landed in Iran and that they would be retained as partial payment for Iraqi war reparations.[34]

No Iraqi source ever confirmed that the exodus had been ordered by the Iraqi government, and there was contemporary doubt about whether it was part of a calculated plot or a desperate measure by individual squadrons or aircrew who literally saw their cover being blown away HAS by HAS. The present writer received strong circumstantial evidence in April 1992 from an authoritative Iranian government official who asserted that approximately half the aircrew had wished to return to Iraq and had been allowed to do so; the others had been granted political asylum. It is highly unlikely that so many would have opted to return -probably 80 to 90 - if they had deserted during the conflict. In either case, the kind of sanctuary ultimately offered by the Iranian government was not much help to the beleaguered IQAF in 1991. The direct consequence of Iraq's isolation was that every airbase was vulnerable to attack and no recovery, no resuscitation, no reinforcement was coming from across a friendly 'Yalu'. Conversely, almost all the Coalition airfields were beyond the reach of the IQAF, even if it had launched a desperate attempt to disrupt the Coalition air campaign at source.

In sum, the significance of 'international' support for the application of air power in the conflict did not lie in the operational contribution of Coalition partners. With the possible exception of the RAF's airfield attack and tactical reconnaissance, the USAF, the USMC and the USN could have waged the air campaign on their own. The scale and speed of the land-based air contribution depended, however, on unprecedented international co-operation while the intensity of the air preparation and campaign depended almost entirely on local fuel availability. In future scenarios, those two considerations are likely to be at least as significant to the application of air power as airbase availability.

A Carrier Alternative?

Such conclusions prompt reflection, in the light of the Gulf experience, on the future utility of carrier-based air power as a substitute for, or complement to the deployment of land-based aircraft. At the outset of the air campaign, six carriers were in position: three in the Red Sea and three in the Gulf, embarking 398 fixed-wing aircraft of which 202 were strike/attack or multi-role. Of a total of 110,837 Coalition sorties, carrier aircraft flew 18,120, of which 4,855 were strike attack, and 3,805 combat air defence.[35]

Many of the advantages of and limitations on carrier availability were demonstrated in the war. Two arrived in theatre by 8 August after moving to the Red Sea from the Mediterranean and to the lower Gulf from the Indian Ocean in four and six days, respectively. On the other hand, sailing time from the USA and Japan for the remainder took the better part of a month. Most importantly, none of them was dependent on the international consensus to reach the theatre. For the foreseeable future that advantage over land-based aircraft is likely to remain.

Once on station, they were not as susceptible to *Scud* or conventional air attack when Iraq lacked the capacity to locate or track them. Those circumstances might not be repeated elsewhere should a potential opponent possess a land-based strike attack/reconnaissance aircraft and not be prepared to concede the strategic and tactical initiative to an encroaching task force.

In the Gulf, it is possible that Iraqi use of CBW weapons was constrained by the threat of considerable Coalition retaliation by escalation, widely understood to be by nuclear weapons. If so, the source would have been USN vessels such as the cruiser *San Jacinto*, designated with a 'special weapons platform',[36] or other *Tomahawk* TLAM (Tomahawk Land Attack Missile) carriers in the task forces. Indeed, on the first night of the air campaign the US Navy launched more than one-third of the total of 282 *Tomahawks* fired against Iraq during the campaign. They made a major contribution to the neutralisation of links in the Iraqi C^3 and air-defence systems which were above ground and vulnerable to the TLAM's 1,000-lb warhead. Others, with warheads containing spools of carbon-fibre wire were directed against electrical power plants causing generator short circuits and further degrading the air defences.[37]

The *Tomahawks* were not, however, fired from aircraft carriers, but from surface vessels, including a small number from submarines. The unrefuelled strike-attack range of carrier-borne aircraft was some 200 nautical miles; far less than the circuitously routed *Tomahawks*. Moreover, to exceed 200 nautical miles, the Navy depended on Air Force land-based tanking. Had Air Force tankers not been available, two-thirds of the Navy's strike sorties could not have been launched.[38] Many land-based aircraft were equally dependent on air-to-air refuelling but carrier-borne dependence on AAR (Air to Air Refuelling) would call into question their function in power projection in the first place. Large-volume tankers could not be launched from carriers, while to increase the number of smaller tankers or 'buddy-buddy' refuellers could only be at the expense of other carrier-borne aircraft. Quite apart from take-off weight and landing constraints, there is seldom if ever any spare deck/storage space on a carrier for augmentation in a crisis. All six carriers in the Gulf sailed with their maximum aircraft complement.

The USN was criticised after the war for lacking any system to integrate the simultaneous employment of aircraft from more than one carrier. 'After the initial preplanned strikes, multiple carrier strikes were not attempted because they were too hard to organise given the pace of the war . . .'[39] Some senior naval officers were concerned about the impact on naval 'independence' of subordination to the Air Force Tasking Order (ATO). Others were unhappy that the ATO was insufficiently time responsive. Such concern was not alleviated by communications incompatibility between CENTCOM and USN systems, requiring the USN's copies of the daily ATO to be delivered manually to the USN for transcription by discrete USN channels.

Some UN complaints about the inflexibility of the ATO are more convincing than others. Many units on land and at sea received essential information from the ATO direct by telephone. Both the Marine Corps and the USN were able to reserve large numbers of sorties for their own use[40] but that did not help the USN locate the Iraqi minelayer *Aka*, which repeatedly laid mines and slipped back unscathed into hiding in the waterways of the Shatt-al-Arab.[41] No fixed-wing carriers were disabled by mines, but their combat radius was further constrained by operating beyond Iraqi mine-laying range.[42] For carriers to operate elsewhere in future, they will require mine countermeasures protection. That will entail either adding mine countermeasures vessels to the composite task force, whose function is to support the carrier, or a capability to the carrier's aircraft/helicopter complement with the risk of reducing its combat potential.

Even with such limitations, carrier-borne attack and support aircraft made a significant contribution to the air war. The carrier group in the Red Sea was nearer to IQAF bases in western Iraq than its land-based colleagues in Saudi Arabia. Similarly, the Gulf carriers could finally attack the eastern Kuwaiti salient and south-eastern Iraq from closer range, thereby maximising sortie rates. On 17 January, USN and USMC aircraft launched 'a significant number' of Tactical Air Launched Decoys (TALD) to deceive and saturate hostile radar-controlled air defences. In addition to drawing missile fire, and thereby probably explaining some of the Iraqi claims to have shot down many Coalition aircraft, they exposed SAM acquisition and guidance radars to HARM (High Speed Antiradiation Missile) missiles carried by accompanying strike-attack aircraft.[43]

Future carrier strike/attack firepower could be increased relatively easily by the greater provision of PGMs. In the Gulf the USN lacked sufficient weapons to mount large-scale PGM attacks. The Red Sea Group for example, had only 594 LGB kits for Mk 80 family series dumb bombs.[44] Only seven of the Navy's newest stand-off land attack missile, the AGM-84E SLAM were launched and these had only a 500lb warhead. The USN lacked a deep-penetrating PGM similar to the USAF GBU-28 or BLU-109E.[45]

However, even if such resources were made available, more than one carrier would be required to launch any attack of 40 aircraft or more. In the Gulf, air power was used to attack several different kinds of target array in parallel, rather than in sequence. Hitherto, air defences had to be rolled back, air superiority won, and both strategic and tactical targets attacked repeatedly and subsequently. Now, as a result of greatly increased bombing accuracy, and with the weight and scale available, simultaneous attacks were possible on 17 January on air defences, C^3, nuclear- and chemical-production facilities, electric power sources, oil installations, airfields, *Scud* sites, and ground forces.

It is possible that such simultaneous, parallel operations will remain beyond the scope of carrier task forces. That was a view held by several senior USN officers in 1991 'who pointed out that *Desert Storm* was not well suited to carrier operations. In their view the CVs [carriers] are suited to one-time raids similar to the Libyan action of 1986, but not to sustained campaigning. This opinion is widely held in the service. It ignores the use of the carriers in both Korea and Vietnam and the fact that our huge investment in carriers cannot be justified by such limited usefulness. In fact, the implication of this attitude is that carriers are little more than political instruments, not real war fighters.'[46]

Ignoring in that judgement the interesting implication that 'real war fighters' are something different from 'political instruments', concern about longer-term carrier prospects is self-evident. Indeed, even the reference to Korea and Vietnam may be unintentionally debilitating. Both Korea and Vietnam have long coastlines and narrow interiors. In both theatres the USN enjoyed unchallenged freedom of operation. There is no doubt that force projection by carrier task force will remain a very desirable option. Hitherto, procurement debates have tended to concentrate on its costs, compared with those incurred by composite land-based, deployable air forces. On the one hand the carrier, its aircraft, its self-defence requirements, its supporting ships, its in-dock refurbishment time, its transit time and its dependence on some overseas foreign facilities; on the other, the land-based aircraft, its airbase, its deployment *en route* and in-theatre overflying and basing requirements, and its dependence on sealift for sustained operations. When looking to the future, productivity should become a more realistic measure of effectiveness. Carrier-borne aircraft share surface-to-air and air-to-air threats with land-based aircraft, but the vulnerability of the floating airbase to mines, air attack and shore-to-ship missiles, coupled with foreseeable constraints on range, payload and scale of its offensive capabilities, suggest that the conclusion of 'the senior [naval] officers', that the carrier is now primarily a 'small-war' instrument, may be uncomfortably near the truth.

In future conflicts, long-range deployment of land-based air power may be constrained by restricted international support while a carrier task force may not. If, as in the Falklands conflict, the opposition can marshal only limited air power in opposition, the carrier may indeed be a 'real war fighter' and a 'political instrument'. With the sustained expansion of high-technology weaponry and increased professional awareness in the developing world, however, such opportunities are likely to decrease.

The Weather

Having reached the Gulf theatre of operations, both sea- and land-based air power were affected by the weather. Between August and January, Coalition aircraft took advantage of almost unbroken blue skies and clear nights to hone their collective skills preparing for the air campaign. Records taken by the USAF in the region over the previous 14 years suggested that cloud cover would be approximately '13 per cent' during January and February, and a planning/targeting contingency margin, including an element for weather, of 20 per cent was included.[47]

In the event, the weather was much worse. The US Air Weather Service determined that the Coalition encountered cloud ceilings below 10,000 feet over Baghdad and Kuwait roughly twice as frequently as historical records would have indicated.[48] The land war was planned to begin after 30 days of aerial preparation; it was delayed by nine days, largely as a result of interruption by the weather.[49] Cloud cover exceeded 25 per cent at 10,000 feet over central Iraq on 31 days of the 43-days' war. Of those it exceeded 50 per cent on 21 and 75 per cent on nine. All offensive air operations, except those of the radar aiming B-52s and the unmanned TLAMs, were affected. On the second and the third day of the war, more than half the F-117 flights were unsuccessful or cancelled because of low clouds over Baghdad. On the two following days, A-10s could only fly a total of 75 sorties instead of the usual 200 a day. An F-16 attack on day two against a rocket-production plant north of Baghdad had to be diverted to an alternate target because of solid undercast. After 10 days, 15 per cent of scheduled attacks had been cancelled because of poor visibility or low overcast skies. After three weeks 50 per cent of attacks into Iraq had been diverted or cancelled because of weather-related problems. On 25 February all F-117 flights were cancelled.

In the four days of the ground war the weather was consistently bad. Conditions varied from solid cloud cover with severe icing from the ground up to 35,000 feet, to clear skies over ground fog which totally obscured targets. Conditions were further aggravated by swirling clouds of greasy smoke from the burning oil wells. In several instances, because of the ensuing low ceilings, only helicopters could operate successfully and their close support operations were restricted when the ground-force offensives outran the helicopters' logistic and planning support capabilities.[50]

The impact of bad weather on operations was aggravated by low-level Iraq surface-to-air defences (LLAD) of missiles, AAA and small-arms fire. Despite the presence in-theatre of 11,000 missiles and 8,500 guns only 13 Coalition aircraft are believed to have been shot down by radar-guided weapons. This very low loss rate was due at medium level in part to active suppression by weapons such as HARM and ALARM, and to ECM and tactical evasions. Such neutralisation, coupled with the extinction of the IQAF as a fighting force in the early days of the war, led General Glosson and Air Marshal Wratten to direct their squadrons to shift to medium altitude for ingress, egress and weapons release. Thereby they avoided the sheer volume of barrage AAA and the threat of IR SAMs up to 12–15,000 feet.[51] The decision was well founded; when low-level sorties were reintro- duced over the battlefield, four aircraft were lost to ground fire on the first day of the ground offensive.

The combination of enforced medium-level activity and bad weather imposed two operational constraints which together delayed the begin- ning of the ground campaign. The first, implied above, was the reduction in offensive firepower. All crews were under rigid rules of engagement to avoid civilian casualties and collateral damage. The risk of damage to civilian targets was raised at every briefing.[52] Indeed, never in the history of warfare can such effort have been dedicated to ensuring that civilians should be safeguarded in air attacks.

But to fly at medium level was to reduce the accuracy of 'dumb' ord- nance, even when delivered by sophisticated weapons carriers such as the F-16. Crews bombed from higher altitudes than those they had trained at. The effectiveness of cluster weapons and minelets was reduced and aiming errors were magnified. PGMs were all affected, depending on their guid- ance systems. Cloud or fog could interfere with a laser designator, causing an LGB to lose guidance. IR seekers were degraded by rain and any other factor which reduced a temperature signature. Any kind of bad visibility inhibited electro-optical acquisition and identification. Undoubtedly some Coalition aircrew lost their lives at low level while seeking to achieve max- imum accuracy. Without such efforts, the rare cases of losses to 'friendly' air-to-surface fire would undoubtedly have been greater.

The second impact of the weather was on battle damage assessment (BDA). BDA was to plague the Coalition commanders throughout the air campaign. A planning objective of *Desert Storm* was to reduce the Iraqi ground force by 50 per cent attrition before the Coalition ground offensive began: an unprecedented demand on air power. Targets included tanks, armoured personnel carriers and artillery.[53] As the air campaign progressed, differing estimates of the effects of the bombing campaign provoked irritation in the command chain and inconsistencies in media reporting. General Schwarzkopf subsequently told Congress that 'BDA . . . was one of the major areas of confusion . . . It led to some disagreements. As a matter of fact it led to some distancing on the part of some agencies from the position of CENTCOM at the time, as to what the bomb damage really was.'[54] On 6 February, while the Pentagon was reporting battle damage to Iraqi ground forces as 'insignificant', French spokesmen were confidently claiming 'a reduction in effectiveness by 30 per cent'.[55] By the eve of the ground war, General Schwarzkopf had abandoned attempts to relate Iraqi ground-force degradation solely to equipment attrition, substituting instead a more subjective assessment which included a wider number of variables. Then, CENTCOM assessed frontline Iraqi division effectiveness at below 50 per cent and rear formations at 75 per cent.[56]

The weather was not the cause of poor BDA, but it considerably aggravated the problem. For example, heavy overcast in the early days of the war prevented adequate reconnaissance of many strategic targets until 21 January, putting assessments behind from the outset and derailing pre-war planning, which assumed that BDA would be available within two days.[57] BDA relied on information from satellites, specialist reconnaissance aircraft including U-2/TR-1, F 4s, *Tornado* GR-1As and *Mirage* F-1s, as well as pilot reports and weapon-targeting systems. It is generally agreed that reconnaissance assets were too few, lacked coordination and left room for conflicting interpretation. As a result, dissemination of both pre- and post-attack intelligence was frequently unreliable and untimely. Pilot reports were suspect because of traditional exaggeration while DIA (Defense Intelligence Agency) analysts in Washington tended to be overcautious; PGM damage extent was not always apparent; Iraqi deception and decoys frequently led to miscalculations. The whole task was exacerbated by a Coalition failure to assess accurately the strength of the Iraqi ground forces at the outset of *Desert Storm*. An original estimate of 540,000 troops in the Kuwait theatre was subsequently revised to 336,000.[58]

Only repeated, low-level or unobscured medium-level optical imagery could have resolved the doubts and reduced the disagreements. Whether the ground offensive could have begun earlier without increased Coalition casualty risks will never be known. Fortunately, the Coalition air forces possessed a sufficient excess of firepower to render BDA weaknesses ultimately irrelevant. Such may not be the case elsewhere in the future.

One weather forecast may, however, be confidently made. Poor as the conditions were in the Gulf by Middle East standards, they were still highly favourable to air operations compared with meteorological conditions elsewhere in the world. In a European winter or a south-east Asian monsoon, cloud ceilings at or below 10,000 feet occur 80 or 90 per cent of the time.[59] Aircrew would encounter low ceilings twice as frequently as those met in the Gulf, rendering visual, medium-altitude bombing and many kinds of PGM delivery very difficult and a sustained 'round-the-clock' offensive impossible. Carrier operations would be additionally restricted by sea states and wind vectors.

Topography

If, in addition, the topography in the Gulf area was to be compared with that elsewhere in the world, further constraints would be considered. Southern Iraq and the Kuwait region are largely arid or semi-arid desert on low undulating terrain. Major cities and conurbations are few, major roads and rail links limited and Iraqi ground forces were mainly deployed away from civilian populations. Consequently, radar returns from ground targets were usually sharp and free of clutter, epitomised by the widely illustrated JSTARS 'picture' of barbed wire twisting in the wind. When acquisition systems were in range, moving targets, such as convoys or armoured columns, could be readily detected. In the air, the lowest flying aircraft and helicopters were visible to AWACs. There were no radar shadows in which to seek concealment, unlike, for example, in Bosnia. Iraqi artillery and armour, even when dug in, presented sharp IR images to 'tank plinking' aircraft, especially in the evening when sand and metal cooled at different rates.

Behind the Kuwait theatre the Tigris and Euphrates rivers and the Hawr al Hammar marshes were crossed by a number of bridges essential for the resupply and potential withdrawal of Iraqi ground forces. They were visible, vulnerable and valuable interdiction targets. Although the dug-in Iraqi forces were consuming little ammunition and requiring little maintenance resupply, day-to-day supplies were gradually choked, despite the adept construction of pontoon bridges and by-passes. By the ceasefire, 37 road bridges and nine rail bridges had been destroyed and another nine road bridges severely damaged.[60] While some units, especially among the Republican Guards were subsequently found to have ample food and water supplies, a general pattern emerged of malnutrition and poor health among front-line troops and those captured at Al Khafji. It appears that the deep interdiction attacks reduced the flow of supplies below the level necessary for the entire army, and that they were monopolised by the politically-elite formations in the Iraqi 'mobile' reserve.

This regional geography may be contrasted with that of jungle-canopied Malaysia or Vietnam, or mountainous Afghanistan, or forest-covered, mountainous Bosnia. Warfare on any scale in such regions would offer different challenges to air power planners from those faced by the Gulf Coalition.

The Technology Gap

Those political and environmental advantages were exploited by superior Coalition technology. It is, however, not so much technology which conveys an advantage in warfare, but its intellectual mastery. This was demonstrated to a remarkable extent and, subject to the qualifications induced by the examination of other, interactive characteristics of this conflict, several technological factors are likely to have a significant impact on future conflicts elsewhere. Three aspects, among many, merit more detailed analysis.

The first is Stealth, epitomised by the F-117: the product of at least 20 years of R & D.[61] It is probable that in due course defensive countermeasures will be developed to deprive the F-117 of its relative immunity. It will, however, require the resources of a superpower to develop, produce and deploy the counter-technology on such a scale as to impose major constraints on F-117 operations.

The F-117 undoubtedly has shortcomings. It is not supersonic; it does not carry defensive weapons; it is not an agile aircraft by F-15 or SU-27 standards; it requires several hours to programme its offensive systems; it does not possess a particularly long range and it cannot operate in bad weather. Yet no previous aircraft, or any other conventional weapon or weapon-carrier has had such a dramatic impact on the course of a conflict, nor has one embodied a concept with such far-reaching implications for future combat.

The statistics of its performance in the Gulf War have been well publicised. Forty-two F-117 bombers were deployed to the theatre, all stationed at King Khalid Airbase near Khamis Mushait in south-west Saudi Arabia, in deep sanctuary from either prying eyes or hostile activity. They flew 1,271 sorties, approximately 2 per cent of all Coalition attacks but struck nearly 40 per cent of strategic targets without loss or damage.

F-117 has adapted two ancient military attributes, concealment and surprise, to a third dimension enshrouded in electronic warfare. At the USAF Electronics Security Command and Electronics Warfare Centre at Kelly Air Force Base in Texas, digital maps of the theatre were overlaced with US signals intelligence data which showed the locations, frequencies and effective radius of Iraqi air defence radars. For good measure, this achievement was announced to the world two months before *Desert Storm* was launched.[62]

The F-117 was never invisible, but the combination of intrinsic technologies considerably reduced its radar, IR and optical signature and hence its detection range. The information from Kelly AFB was fed into its navigational computers before each attack and it flew with impunity, and without any support, to achieve complete surprise over Baghdad. It is this attribute, rather than its much-publicised bombing accuracy shared with several other PGM carriers, which is of longer-term significance. In previous air campaigns it had been necessary to roll air defences back, or fight one's way to the target. It was the F-117 more than any other aircraft, in conjunction with cruise missiles, which enabled the simultaneous attacks to be made on the first night. On a later occasion, a composite force of 75 aircraft, including 32 fighter-bombers carrying PGMs, tankers, defence-suppression and fighter cover, attacked a nuclear construction plant. The force reached the target without loss, but the Iraqi defenders had been warned of its approach and fired smoke pots which completely obscured the target and thwarted the attack. The following night eight F-117s reached the same target undetected, and placed 16 2,000-lb bombs across it.

Several comparisons of bombing criteria from World War II, Vietnam and the Gulf have been made. General Michael Dugan's was of 4,500 B-17, 95 F-105 and one F-117 sortie to achieve an equivalent target destruction.[63] A US DOD summary compared the accuracy probability figures of the B-17: 3,300 ft, the F-105: 400 ft, the F-16 : 200 ft, and the F-117: less than 10 ft.[64] Again, it is not just the reduced CEP, but how many aircraft are going to be required to ensure that at least one gets over the target?

The reduced aircraft requirement and increased effectiveness drive cost savings beyond aircraft and weapon numbers back into procurement, training, personnel, maintenance, fuel, logistics, married quarters, and even pensions: all aspects of air force structure and support. The F-117 will not always enjoy the combat invulnerability which has marked its progress so far, but it is likely to remain ahead of its opposition for a long time yet. With the addition of an all-weather navigation and attack capability it will become an even more formidable weapon system. Sustained by air-to-air refuelling it will become an international instrument with global reach;. When its 'big brother', the Northrop B-2, achieves full operational capability the implications for regional conflict and direct military pressure will be considerable.[65]

Airborne Early Warning and Control (AWACS)

One intriguing but unanswered question in the air war was, 'Could Coalition AWACs aircraft locate F-117?' supplemented by, 'If so, how?' and, 'If not, how were F-117 missions deconflicted from other, non-stealthy flight profiles?' Perhaps in time the security wrap will be lifted. Clearly deconfliction was achieved, whether by discrete routing/airspace/time allocation or by intermittent 'squawks' or, after the achievement of air supremacy, by direct secure voice communication. Somehow the stealthy F-117 was incorporated in the average of 2,240 sorties co-ordinated daily by the E-3s in-theatre. If any one aircraft may be said to be the linchpin, the centre of gravity, of the Coalition's application of air power, it was the E-3, supported on the flanks by USN E-2C *Hawkeyes*. The E-3s flew 448 sorties, the *Hawkeyes* 1,183. E-3s, however, were airborne for 5,546 hours while the *Hawkeyes*, despite flying many more sorties, had less capacity and endurance, totalling 4,790 hours. The greater technological superiority lay with the E-3.

The first five USAF E-3s arrived in Riyadh on 8 August, alongside USAF and RAF interceptors. Thereafter they monitored IQAF activity, co-ordinated the defensive CAPs along the Saudi Arabian-Iraqi border and ultimately rehearsed the large-scale control which was to be applied from 17 January onwards. Without AWACs there would have been much less confidence in protecting the build up of ground forces in *Desert Storm* and hence no application of the Air Tasking Order.

By 17 January 11 USAF E-3s were available from Riyadh and three others flew from Incerlik in Turkey. For most of *Desert Storm* four USAF E-3s were airborne continuously over Saudi Arabia and one over south-eastern Turkey. In addition, NATO E-3s patrolled the Mediterranean and a RSAF E3 operated in southern Saudi Arabia primarily for communications relay. The achievements of the E3s are quantifiable: possibly just one Coalition aircraft shot down by an IQAF interceptor, no Coalition aircraft lost to friendly fire, no mid-air collisions, no AWACs damage, and no AWACs personnel injured.[66] By the end of the war the Coalition had shot down 33 aircraft, and 16 of those were destroyed by 'beyond visual range' missile kills. This was the highest proportion in air warfare and is directly attributable to AWACs aerospace surveillance and control which allowed Coalition aircraft to exploit their longer-range missiles to hit an opponent without having to close within visual identification range.

The IQAF had three 'AWACs' aircraft of their own: Soviet IL-76 airframe with French radar, known as *Adnan*. There was little similarity with E-3. *Adnan* lacked computers and data links. It could control only a handful of fighters, by voice and does not appear to have been integrated with the ground-defence system.[67] It made no contribution to the air war except to the Coalition's target list.

The massive contribution of the E-3 to *Desert Storm* should have come as no surprise. It had been identified as the most important single air power innovation by Western analysts since its development had revolutionised air warfare two decades previously. It had consistently exceeded its specific performance requirement, despite operations in widely differing climatic conditions. By 1991 its contribution was enhanced still further by secure voice communications, the Joint Tactical Information Display System (J-TIDS), which linked it with many other air defence and C³ structures, IFF radar and the NAVSTAR Global Positioning System (GPS).

The Coalition E-3s, like other high-value assets such as JSTARS, were constantly protected by a defensive interceptor screen. Their pivotal contribution to air warfare had already been noted by the Soviet Air Force and there were reports in western Europe before 1990 that counter-AWACs tactics were being developed by the Soviet Air Force using MiG-25s equipped with anti-radiation missiles. E-3 will, however, remain a difficult target, able to see and identify its own attacker well beyond missile-launch range. It has the space and capacity to carry its own ECM defensive screen. Its relative vulnerability, compared with static, ground-based air defence and control systems, is likely to remain slight for the foreseeable future.

Electronic Warfare

In a complementary manner, F-117 and E-3 illustrate the Coalition's domination of the electromagnetic spectrum in *Desert Storm*. F-117 exposed the limitations of relevant Iraqi technology. E-3's uninterrupted activities illustrated the Coalition's mastery of what one neutral commentator has labelled 'the fourth dimension' of warfare.[68] In the first hours of *Desert Storm*, Iraqi air defences were blinded, paralysed and decimated by an electronic and firepower offensive unparalleled for scale and intensity in the history of warfare, while Baghdad's attempts at counter-EW were totally ineffectual. There were about 100 specialist Coalition EW aircraft in-theatre, together with defence suppression F-4G *Wild Weasels* and USN EA-6B jammers and weapon carriers. During *Desert Storm*, Iraqi communications and radars were monitored by USAF, USN, USMC, RAF and French signals-intelligence gatherers. Alert to, but powerless to avoid the dangers of conceding SIGINT, the IQAF switched off several of its air-defence radars, but to no avail. Indeed, Coalition surprise was so complete on 17 January that several of the radars were still switched off.

The overwhelming electronic combat achievement laid the basis for all subsequent Coalition military success. Stand-off, barrage and escort jamming of Iraqi radar and fighter control communications by EF-111A, EA-6Bs and EC-130s blinded and paralysed Iraq's air defence system. When US Army and Navy unmanned decoys stimulated SAM radars, they were attacked by F-4Gs and EA-6Bs carrying HARM anti-radiation missiles. Subsequently, RAF *Tornados* contributed to defence suppression with the parachute-loitering ALARM missiles. The destruction or jamming of long-range surveillance and early-warning radar allowed the attackers to approach undetected. Ground intercept and control radars, together with missile-guidance and acquisition radars were jammed simultaneously or subsequently. IQAF interceptors could not hear their ground controller and could not see their opponents. SAMs and AAA either fired autonomously or without guidance, or both. Meanwhile continuous Coalition monitoring of the remaining Iraqi frequencies provided target information for defence-suppression aircraft within 10 minutes.

Supremacy in electronic combat permitted the swift seizure of command of the air. That in turn made possible the systematic destruction of strategic and tactical targets, the isolation, destruction and demoralisation of the Iraqi ground forces, the denial of any Iraqi aerial reconnaissance and the uninterrupted, undetected deployment, build up and redeployment of Coalition ground forces.

Like stealth and AWACs, electronic combat was not an innovation in the Gulf War. Steady evolution since World War II had erupted dramatically over the Beka'a Valley in 1982, inducing the destruction of 84 Syrian aircraft without any Israeli loss. Then, one or two Israeli ELINT aircraft, a handful of jammers and superior fighters and weapons were confronted by brave, but obviously uncomprehending Syrian aircrew. In 1991 the scene was repeated, but on many times the scale, and the IQAF was much quicker to recognise the inevitable, seeking refuge first in its HAS and then across the border of Iran.

The Spectrum of Supremacy and the Exception

Superior Coalition technology dominated all aspects of the air and air-to-ground war except one: the *Scud* battle. Satellite reconnaissance was patchy, but satellite communications and especially the NAVSTAR-derived GPS system was of inestimable benefit to some aircraft and many ground units. The guarantee of navigational accuracy and positional exactitude to within a few feet has yet to be fully exploited in air power. When GPS is fitted to stealth aircraft, bombs and missiles, the cost effectiveness in economic terms of strategic offensive air power will increase still further.

Coalition superiority in aircraft technology was not quite so complete, at least in theory. The IQAF MiG-29 and SU-24 were close enough to the F-16 and *Tornado* to have presented a more substantial counter. Both sides flew the *Mirage* F-1. The only considerably superior combat aircraft was the F-15E *Strike Eagle*. No other possessed the all-weather, day or night, multi-role capabilities of the F-15E.[69] The two squadrons deployed to the Gulf were employed in attacks against airfields, ground forces, air defences, strategic targets, reinforcement routes and bridges, delivering a variety of PGMs. The F-15E is the most recent example of an aircraft developed as an air-to-air fighter being successfully adapted to the air-to-ground role and is a powerful example for future multi-role development, conferring tactical flexibility and cost savings by weapons and systems interoperability.

One other major contributor in the air to the conflict had not yet reached full operational status: the E-8 Joint Surveillance and Target Attack Radar System (JSTARS), a joint USAF-US Army project. Two aircraft were deployed to the theatre and provided radar surveillance of Iraqi ground force movements and positions in the Kuwait theatre. Neither Iraq nor any other country possessed, nor could develop in the foreseeable future, such a complex reconnaissance and targeting system. JSTARS was able to monitor and target Iraqi ground force movements during the Khafji engagement and pierce the low cloud and smoke of the 100-hour battlefield to provide most valuable information to the fast-moving Coalition divisions.[70]

The success of JSTARS in the Gulf justified its high acclaim and sustained a procurement programme of 20 aircraft, plus associated ground station modules and support systems.[71] With in-flight refuelling the E8 could play its part in strategic deployments and extended patrols in other regions of the world, where its all-weather effectiveness could be equally valuable. It remains to be seen how far its radar-dependent sensors would be degraded by mountainous territory or any other topographical feature which created radar shadow, cover or clutter. Its air-to-ground effective range will remain a line-of-sight equation involving height and horizon and would seem to be considerably less than that of its air-to-air counterpart, AWACs. If so, it may well be more vulnerable than AWACs as a more accessible high-value target.

Patriot versus Scud

The most visible technological star in the Coalition's constellation was the Patriot Air Defence System, usually associated with its Gulf War target, the Soviet designed SS-1B/C Scud. The final DOD report to Congress makes no attempt to quantify Patriot's success. The weapon itself did not have any digital data retention, and even with analysis of data from 'diverse sources and agencies . . . a finite, quantitative scoring of Patriot effectiveness may not be possible.'[72] Before the war the Scud threat had been disparaged as barely insignificant: inaccurate, unwieldy and delivering ballistic missiles (even with chemical warheads) chiefly as nuisance weapons that might cause political difficulties for the alliance (particularly if Israel were to retaliate against the Iraqis), but one that posed little tactical or operational threat to the Coalition. It was intended to reduce the missile's offensive threat by attacking its fixed sites, support bases and production facilities, potential hide sites and support facilities for mobile launchers, but not the launchers themselves.[73]

The full extent of that political misjudgement is graphically described by General Schwarzkopf in his account of Israel's reaction to the *Scud* bombardment and of Washington's considerable concern that Israeli armed forces were about to enter the war with potentially disastrous political impact on the Coalition.[74] In the event, *Patriot* emerged as the symbol of US hypertechnology defeating the blundering obsolescence of Iraq. Designed as a point defence against aircraft, modified hastily to be a point defence against ballistic missiles, its kill rate within its specified envelope was astonishingly high. The one major tragedy of the *Scud* strike on the US barracks at Khobar City apparently occurred when a defensive segment was left unprotected because of computer maintenance. Overall, 42 *Scuds* were fired at Israel, 43 at Saudi Arabia and three at Bahrain. One hundred and fifty-eight *Patriots* were fired, prompting early claims of a 96 per cent kill rate but one which later proved difficult to substantiate.

In the Gulf, *Patriot* and *Scud* cancelled themselves out. Neither affected the course of the battle. The destabilising political potential of *Scud* was neutralised by the confidence-building *Patriot*. Until tomorrow's *Scuds* are fitted with integral ECM and become much more accurate and while US guidance technology continues to improve *Patriot*, the balance of conventional military advantage is likely to remain with the latter. That, however, may not be the future issue.

Had *Scud* carried a chemical, nuclear or biological warhead, the outcome may have been very different. Then, even a 95 per cent interception rate might have been inadequate to restrain Israel's desire for revenge. On the other hand, in conflicts elsewhere the threat of massive retaliation by or on behalf of the target nation may be sufficient to deter such use. But the *Scud* battle raises a far more important and indeed pervasive problem for the future application of air power: how to deal with the highly-mobile, easily-concealable unit.

US pre-war reconnaissance failed to provide accurate data on the number and location of *Scud* launchers. Thirty-six mobile launchers and 28 fixed sites were known. The latter were attacked and all but two destroyed or damaged.[75] But even had the total of both been known at the outset, the location and destruction of the mobile launchers would have proved equally difficult. For a period after 18 January, when anger in Tel Aviv, jubilation in Baghdad and panic in Washington were at their height, one-third of all Coalition aircraft sorties were allocated to the anti-*Scud* campaign, some 600–700 sorties per day.[76] Even in the worst weather, anti-*Scud* alert was maintained. Frequent contemporary and subsequent claims for mobile *Scud* destruction were made, by both air attack and Special Forces action. The Gulf War Air Power Study team scoured the evidence, drawing also upon post-war UN and other visiting teams to Iraq, and its conclusions on the anti-*Scud* campaign were thought-provoking for those responsible for the locating, targeting and destroying of highly-mobile targets in future conflicts elsewhere.

Most, if not all the reports of mobile launcher destruction were found to be of decoys, or vehicles presenting a similar shape or signature to weapon sensors, or other objects which were unfortunate enough to possess 'Scud-like' characteristics. With hindsight, DIA reports in late 1990 of the disappearance of *Scud* vehicles from central bases suggested their operational dispersal. They also highlighted the risks of relying on satellite and periodic strategic reconnaissance to keep track of mobile targets, as well as concealed targets such as those associated with nuclear weapon development.

Over 80 per cent of *Scuds* were launched at night. They took place without pre-launch electronic emission and within six minutes had departed, perhaps leaving very lifelike decoys in their place or in the vicinity while the launchers themselves scuttled back into concealment. Forty-two launches were actually observed by *Scud* air-combat patrols; on only eight occasions did the aircraft get close enough to deliver weapons.

The frequency and intensity of *Scud* attacks declined markedly after the first seven days of the war (from 4.7 a day to 1.5 a day), almost certainly as a result of the constraints induced by the concentrated anti-*Scud* air campaign. Whether that effect was achieved by harassment or destruction remains uncertain. 'Given the level of effort, a few may have been destroyed, but nowhere near the numbers reported during the war . . . it remains impossible to confirm the actual destruction of any Iraqi mobile launchers by fixed-wing Coalition aircraft.'[77]

In the Coalition's technological superiority in the Gulf there is a less obvious lesson for the application of air power elsewhere. Concentration on high technology should not lead to the disparagement of simpler or even 'obsolescent' equipment. The ultimate measure of a weapon or a system's effectiveness is its value as a political instrument, which may or may not equate to its operational impact.

Numerical superiority

If NATO had ever gone to war with the Warsaw Pact, the Alliance would have relied heavily on technological superiority to offset Soviet advantage in numbers. Not so with the Coalition in the Gulf, where technological superiority was reinforced by overwhelming numbers in all kinds of aircraft and weapons except for AAR and SAM. The IQAF faced a Coalition of 3,380 aircraft, or odds of 5:1 against. Dedicated Coalition EW aircraft alone totalled 160. The IQAF flew an average of 30 sorties a day for the first week before dwindling to zero.[78] The Coalition averaged 2,500 sorties a day, ranging from 2,388 on the first night to 3,159 on 26 February, with the lowest total of 932 on 1 March.[79] These figures may be compared to the two epoch making thousand bomber raids launched by the RAF in World War II. Such was the scale of Coalition air power that planners were able to extend the central target list from 80 to 400. Two hundred and ten thousand unguided bombs were dropped, 9,342 LGBs, and 5,448 surface-to-air missiles, 2,039 anti-radiation missiles and 333 cruise missiles launched.[80] Of the total of approximately 110,000 coalition sorties flown in *Desert Storm*, 60 per cent were by weapon carriers and 40 per cent in 'support' missions.

The relevance of such statistics to air power in a future environment elsewhere is problematical, not least because of the artificial distinctions between weapon carriers and 'support', when without ECM and AAR the weapon carrier would either have been incapable of reaching its target or far more vulnerable or both. Changing the mix of packages, reducing their size and reducing their frequency would all, even with sustained technological superiority, ease the task of an air defence. In the Gulf it was the synergy of quality and quantity, spearheaded by stealth, EW and PGMs and extended by AAR which allowed air power to achieve simultaneous and sustained neutralisation and destruction on such a scale. The ability of air power to repeat such an achievement elsewhere will be influenced, among the other factors already examined, by the balance of forces in quantity and quality in-theatre. What air power can do in any circumstances will be influenced by what someone else's air power can do to stop it.

The Human Factor

Some IQAF pilots attempted to fight, and no doubt among the 100 or so aircrew who flew in the early days of the war there were individual acts of heroism, some determination and a lot of frustration. But generally, from the highest levels of command down to average standards of airmanship, the IQAF's performance was inept. The ingenuity displayed on the ground in deception, decoy and concealment associated with *Scud* operations, for example, was not repeated in the air. In the absence of authoritative IQAF sources – no IQAF aircrew were taken prisoner – analysis has to be based on external observation and deduction from earlier activities.

At the top, Saddam Hussein himself was strategically illiterate and his generals were either unwilling or unable to enlighten him. He marshalled his ground forces into an exposed salient where they were vulnerable to envelopment by land, sea and from the air. He apparently expected the Coalition to fight on his terms and disparaged or ignored the overwhelming and well-publicised air power being amassed against him.

Soviet advisers were not much help either. Subsequent comments in Moscow tended, naturally, to disassociate Soviet influence in Iraq and the presence of Soviet Air Force advisers from the 1991 debacle.[81] Nonetheless, IQAF air defences were modelled on those of the USSR and the principles of close ground control resembled those of the SAF. At the strategic level, Soviet advice may even have been counterproductive. In 1990 the Soviet General Staff were known to have a poor opinion of the Western capacity to co-ordinate combined arms operations.[82] There was nothing in Western doctrine or experience to prepare either Soviet advisers or the IQAF for the overwhelming air onslaught of 17 January. A long drawn out land-air campaign inflicting heavy Coalition casualties could have been consistent with a Soviet perspective from Baghdad.

Most analysts have agreed internationally that the IQAF's failure to mount any counteroffensive, or indeed any pre-emption during the Coalition force build up, was a strategic blunder. It was probably the product of an inflexible position prepared originally not against a vengeful superpower, but against Israel, and especially against Israeli air power. Investment in hardened shelters, redundant runways and taxiways, extensive runway-repair equipment, deep C^3 bunkers, and multi-layered air defences, together with well-rehearsed concealment and deployments were all defensive measures designed not to destroy the usually invincible Israeli Air Force, but to neutralise its offensive impact. Air Marshal Wratten summarised the result of this posture and investment, 'He [Hussein] seemed to make no effort to capitalise on and develop the potential of his more advanced aircraft, and his pilots hardly ever flew unlike types in the same formation. In-flight refuelling was infrequently practised and night-flying operations were virtually ignored . . . Thus his assets in all their enormity . . . were not about to be used to assist one of the fundamental principles of war: offensive action. Iraq appeared to have learned nothing from its experiences against Iran, but had continued in its largely defensive, unaggressive and mechanical attitude towards modern air warfare.'[83] As a result, high-value assets such as AWACs, JSTARS and the in-flight refuellers flew unchallenged. Aerospace management devolved primarily to deconfliction of friendly forces. There was no hostile pressure on resource allocation except from the *Scuds*. And above all, the Coalition was allowed to seize the strategic and the tactical initiative. Once grasped, even the most resourceful opponent would have found them extremely difficult to dislodge. It was far too much for Iraq.

The human contrasts with the Coalition could not have been greater. US air commanders were the products of an education and training system which was the envy of the Western world: schooled in the history of air warfare, classical strategy and international politics. In Britain, the USA, and other air power centres such as Australia, air operations in the Middle East and Asia were scoured and modern technology examined to devise doctrinal concepts appropriate to air power in the 1990s.[84] The air commanders brought hard lessons, some personal, from Vietnam to their decision making. The aircrews and groundcrews whom they led were highly motivated and well trained. NATO crews had frequently rehearsed large-formation defensive and offensive operations in an EW environment in the USA and Canada. Their skills were honed over Saudi Arabia in the months preceding *Desert Storm*. 'Just consider', said one expert observer, 'the immensely difficult balancing act of getting 400 fighters refuelled by 160 tankers at night, without communications, and working under tight time lines, without a missed tanker or a mid-air collision, let alone a disorganised attack, and one can begin to understand how operator skill and the ability to adapt under stress were crucially important.'[85] For the first time in a major air campaign no aircraft fell to friendly fire. There were a small number of personal tragedies when nine British and 11 American ground troops were killed by American aircraft. That figure should be placed in the context of the several thousand sorties flown over Khafji and in the 100-hour ground war. By comparison, seven of 10 US tanks lost and 20 of 25 US armoured personnel carriers were destroyed by 'friendly' ground fire.[86] The Coalition lost 39 fixed-wing and seven helicopters in combat, and eight and 14 to other causes. The incidence of probable aircrew error in the fixed-wing losses was far below that of any previous campaign, as indeed was the ratio of fixed-wing combat and non-combat losses, which in World War II, Korea, Vietnam and probably Afghanistan was nearer 50:50.

One associated and frequently repeated misconception regarding British losses should finally be dispelled. In 1,500 RAF *Tornado* GR-1 sorties, six aircraft were lost. Of these only one was lost while on a low-level JP-233 anti-airfield attack and that flew into the ground after leaving the target. Of the other five, three were lost to SAMs: two of them on loft bomb attacks and one at medium level when failing to receive a SAM-threat warning. One other was seen to fly into the ground and one was destroyed by premature ordnance fusing.[87] It has not been possible to establish the causes of the two ground incidents, The British experience reinforces the view that for air power to be effectively applied elsewhere, peacetime training should continue to approximate as closely as possible to the conditions and demands likely to be faced in actual conflict. As in warfare down the ages, in all three dimensions, the quality of the man, or woman, will continue to exert a powerful influence on the outcome, whatever the levels of technology applied.

Lessons for All

It seems that while Iraq prepared for a war with Israel, it ignored the air power implications of the Beka'a fiasco of 1982. The 'lessons' of *Desert Storm*, on the other hand, are being examined minutely in military establishments worldwide. Among Coalition members the aim is to identify shortcomings and to plan to put them right. There are, however, other studies in progress: by those countries who in the foreseeable future, if ever, could not hope to marshal the resources necessary to mount a campaign on the scale, intensity and sophistication of *Desert Storm*; and by those who might risk becoming victims of future such operations, either at the hands of a predatory neighbour or, as predatory countries themselves, provoking international displeasure and the threat of great power/coalition retribution.

One shrewd Indian analyst of *Desert Storm* reflected on the implications of similar procurement for Third World countries. On AWACs: 'Even if we were to discount the initial costs of equipment, the sheer cost of sustaining such an effort would create a substantial problem for developing countries . . . possession of modern sophisticated equipment does not guarantee its effectiveness and employability . . . To operate AWACs meaningfully, a complex infrastructure has to be created at great cost and expertise developed in human resources and doctrines . . . The capital investment in the system, including C^{3}I support, and operating costs to induct and (co-ordinate) such assets into air forces of developing countries would be prohibitive. The limitation of fiscal resources would impinge on other modernisation imperatives.'[88] Nor, he argued, could the combat training of the Coalition air forces be easily replicated: 'Realistic training costs a considerable amount, which a developed nation has difficulty in absorbing. A Third World country in financial straits, as Iraq was, would be hard pressed to maintain the levels of training required by the fast deteriorating politico-military situation . . . Training adversely affects equipment life and is dependent on the economic capacity to replace worn-out and damaged components . . .' Which in turn, argued General Nair, could be influenced by the availability of foreign exchange reserves and the good will of a foreign supplier.[89]

It is possible that a more astute political leader than Saddam Hussein, perhaps one trained at a Western military staff college, will conclude that if he is to risk a confrontation with a superpower he will, like the Coalition itself against Iraq, seek to exploit favourable circumstances and take advantage of the opponent's comparative weaknesses. The following hypothetical scenario illustrates how far such exploitation could be taken. Each step in itself is plausible, however unlikely the entire sequence.[90]

The aggressor wishes to annex a neighbouring territory against the wishes of its government. He begins an international diplomatic offensive justifying his objectives, disparaging the target government and encouraging regional suspicions of Western neo-imperialism. He foments disturbances in the target territory and seeks to cloud issues by accusations of ethnic suppression and of unjustifiable, ex-colonial territorial boundaries. Meanwhile he takes advantage of US, European and Russian arms sales competition to strengthen his armed forces, concentrating on mobile rocket launchers, mobile SAMs and AAA, together with mobile C^3 systems. He purchases large quantities of commercial GPS receivers and imports ex-Soviet chemical warfare experts, together with a number of third-generation, ex-Soviet surface-to-surface missiles (SSMs). He buys large quantities of ex-Soviet naval mines and hires unemployed ex-Soviet and Western special forces as military advisers. International reaction is ineffective and international consensus is fragmentary, but the threat of superpower opposition increases. The international aggressor elects to take the final gamble of military action, and applies the lessons he learned from *Desert Storm*.

His special forces, in commercial vessels, mine the approaches to the harbour used for movement of the superpower's prepositioned military stocks and the harbours of the target state. He deploys mobile SSMs to previously surveyed, concealed sites. He deploys and conceals his small numbers of combat aircraft, taking advantage of civilian locations. His aircrew have been trained by Western contract pilots and, inspired by religious or nationalist fanaticism, are known to be prepared if necessary to fly kamikaze missions against AWACs, JSTARS, tankers and any other high-value targets. He deploys mobile SAM/AAA up to his frontier with the target state, wherever possible locating them in villages or small towns. All deployments take place at night, in electronic silence and using natural cover, camouflage and, where necessary, smoke for additional concealment. Decoys are moved into original equipment locations. Within 24 hours simultaneous attacks are made on airbases in the target country by special forces and surface-to-surface missiles, while ground forces cross the international boundary. The whole invasion is planned to take place in monsoon or poor weather conditions. If a superpower, with or without a coalition, does wish to intervene, it faces the prospect of having to fight its way into the region.

Such a scenario could arise at a time when Western countries, especially the USA, Britain and France, were less inclined to be the world's law enforcers, and were even more concerned about sustaining casualties where national security interests were not obviously at stake. It could arise when a considerable reduction in forces in Europe or the Pacific had eliminated the launching pad of the Gulf operation and when defence cuts had constrained even further the prospects for amassing the forces available in

1991. If the aggressor promised to hold democratic elections in the target country in due course, and skilfully continued his regional diplomatic offensive he would, to say the least, present a problem.

Indeed, as General Nair has succinctly summarised, a novel representation of deterrence would have made its international debut: 'While a Third World country cannot possibly contemplate winning a war against a super-power, it can and must raise the penalties to an unmanageable level, thus deterring offensive designs at their inception.'[91] General Nair was obviously not referring to a scenario where a regional aggressor was seeking to deter retribution, but the concept of inverse deterrence is equally applicable. It has interesting implications for the future application of air power, which will be addressed in the last chapter.

Conclusions?

The coalescence of so many circumstances which occurred in the Gulf War may be repeated elsewhere, but history suggests it is unlikely. Air power determined the outcome, but that is not to say that it will do so elsewhere next time. Technology came closer than ever before to matching the dreams and forecasts of the air power theorists, but may not do so in different environments nor, in the longer term, against the swing of the technological pendulum from the offence to defensive countermeasures.

Air power proved that it could substitute for land power. It proved that even if it could not hold ground it could deny it to hostile ground forces. It demonstrated that it could now reach into the strategic heart of a country to threaten any known static political, economic or military target with the maximum precision and the minimum collateral damage and casualties. Ominously, it demonstrated that strategic surprise could be achieved and be most advantageous. It confirmed the fatal consequences of conceding command of the air to an enemy. That conclusion alone suggests that wherever air power can be applied, it is likely to dominate, or strongly influence the outcome of conflict on the surface.

Whether, and how far it may be applied is itself likely to be influenced by the presence or absence of the features discussed above. There is indeed, 'a strong presumption in favour of air power as the instrument of choice for shaping the complexion of war in most circumstances,'[92] by those countries able to apply it. The world, however, has not yet seen a conflict in which air power was opposed by well-marshalled forces trained and motivated to exploit its comparative weaknesses, nor since World War II a war in which one well-equipped, high-quality air force faced another. In view of the dominance of air power by the USA in the foreseeable future, the former is much more likely than the latter. Meanwhile, the remaining sceptics among ground and naval forces should reappraise the implications of hostile command of the air for their activities, while air power ideologues should reflect at length on all the circumstances which contributed to its apotheosis in 1991.

CHAPTER 6

PEACEKEEPING: CONSTRAINTS, POSSIBILITIES AND IMPLICATIONS

The Bosnian Morass

Within six months of the overwhelming impact of air power in the Gulf War, a new and very different combat arena had emerged: this time in the heart of Europe itself. In June 1991 Croatia and Slovenia seceded from the Federal Republic of Yugoslavia, sparking hostilities with the Yugoslav army. Their example was followed in October by Bosnia-Hercegovina. Increasingly bitter warfare ensued between Croats, Bosnians and Serbs. Several ceasefires brokered by the European Community collapsed, and in December 1991 the UN Security Council voted to send a peacekeeping force and a mediation mission led by Cyrus Vance. In 1992 the pattern of ceasefires, pious platitudes and increasingly brutal conflict continued, despite the presence by July of 14,000 UN 'peacekeeping' forces. Television brought unprecedented scenes of horror into millions of homes as ethnic loyalties and hatreds consumed Bosnia-Hercegovina and threatened to engulf other regions of the former Yugoslavia. The Serbs were generally perceived to be the most intransigent of the combatants but with no monopoly of atrocities.

In due course historians may ponder the failure of the European Community, the CSCE, NATO and the UN to co-ordinate sufficient pressure to compel a ceasefire. They may conclude that no amount of external pressure could have checked the explosion of suppressed hatred which was still consuming the area in 1994.

Frequently, the potential contribution of air power to peace enforcement was debated but seldom was the debate extensive or informed. Inevitably it became ensnared in the political considerations of the governments involved. Ironically, its application became strenuously demanded by many civilians who had previously been sceptical or pessimistic about the use of air power in the Gulf. Not surprisingly, when a Muslim Bosnian minority was perceived to be suffering at the hands of a Serbian aggressor, several Islamic countries and organisations demanded UN action to match that taken against Iraq and made bitter comparisons and accusations of religious motivation when their demands went unheeded. A further divide occurred between those countries which had committed ground troops to the UN force and those which had not. The former were naturally concerned about their troops' vulnerability to retaliation should an air attack be made in the name of the UN. Others clouded the issue still further by making largely spurious comparisons between the contemporary conflict and the highly-motivated, well-organised and strongly-supported campaign of Tito's partisans against many thousands of occupying German forces in World War Two.

There was widespread concern that military action of any sort would impede the flow of humanitarian aid which it had been designed to protect and accelerate. But undoubtedly a factor in the indecision and vacillation displayed by the erstwhile exponents of a 'New World Order' was the uncertain trumpet blown by military staffs in Washington, London, Bonn, Paris and Brussels during 1992 and 1993. Many of their concerns about the efficacy of air power were well founded, both in contemporary events and in several precedents, some almost as old as air power itself.

By July 1992 international frustration at the interruption of humanitarian aid and ethnic atrocities prompted US Defense Secretary Cheney to offer carrier-based or Air Force fighters and close-support aircraft and intelligence-gathering resources 'that others do not have' to pick out targets that threatened or attacked the humanitarian relief effort.'[1] He distinguished clearly, however, between such specific limited objectives and the wider use of force to 'stop the bloodshed and separate the warring factions [in which case] you need to have an understanding of how the application of military force will let you achieve your objective . . . There are a lot of questions that are unanswered when you analyse the situation.'[2]

Calls for air intervention intensified during the following weeks. Mr Paddy Ashdown, leader of Britain's Liberal Democratic Party, an ex-Royal Marine Officer and a politician who enjoyed considerable personal respect, called from Sarajevo for the airspace above the former Yugoslavia to be taken over by the UN with the mandate to bomb any heavy weapons used by either side. 'You cannot stop the conflict, but you can diminish its intensity by suppressing if necessary with force, the use of heavy weapons and tanks. It is nonsense to suggest that we do not have the technology to make these sorts of air strikes. This could freeze the war at a lower level so that the people being attacked would have the chance to defend themselves with small arms. It should end the awful bombardments we are now seeing.'[3]

But for every voice exhorting the introduction of UN air power there were others adamantly opposed. One British government official stressed the difficulties of bombing 'the Serbs into submission', the community being so 'totally intertwined you could not separate refugee from murderer . . . you could not put it past them to start hiding their heavy guns in orphanages, hospitals, refugee centres and schools.'[4] This view was reinforced by a pre-eminent Western analyst: 'Air power is a poor way to try to exert control over such a messy conflict, involving numerous ragged militias as well as an organised army. What would be appropriate targets for punitive strikes? And with how much confidence could they be identified without compounding the tragedy by inflicting accidental attacks on civilians? After the air strikes, who would protect the minority community from retaliatory acts of vengeance?'[5]

In August, the British Prime Minister John Major had cautiously and ambiguously 'not ruled out providing RAF cover for UN missions or forces',[6] but no RAF combat aircraft were deployed to the theatre at the time. Had they been, Major would have been strongly supported by a prominent Anglican churchman, the Right Reverend Roger Sainsbury, Bishop of Barking, who urged the Prime Minister 'to deploy troops and give full support to US planes to get NATO to bomb Serbian targets . . . Only strong Western action is going to get NATO to save the people of Sarajevo . . . I am ashamed to be part of a Church which has given no leadership on this issue and I believe people in the press are ashamed too.'[7]

No action was taken. Peace conferences were organised and ended either in acrimony or with unsubstantiated agreements for ceasefires. Two months later, on 9 October, the UN Security Council established 'a ban on military flights in the air space of Bosnia and Hercegovina', requested the UN Protection Force 'to monitor compliance with the ban', and requested the Secretary General to 'report the further measures necessary to enforce this ban . . .'[8]

The Serbian Republic was believed to possess fewer than 48 fixed-wing aircraft and perhaps 30 helicopters. They had frequently been used to attack Croatian and Bosnian enclaves with light but indiscriminate bombing. In addition, Serbian ground forces had on several occasions been supported by Federal air force jets from the air force still controlled from Belgrade.[9] Serbian disdain for the UN resolution was immediately shown by several bombing raids on Bosnian towns on 10 and 11 October. Between October 1992 and the following April over 500 violations of the UN Resolution occurred, although according to UN sources almost all, if not all, after 12 October were unarmed training or local transport/casualty evacuation flights.

At the time UN Resolution 781 was regarded as a largely ineffective political gesture which would provide no solace to the victims of uninhibited ground forces and present no threat to the 'official' and 'unofficial' units which interrupted humanitarian relief. Indeed, the activities of both Bosnian Serb and Belgrade Serb aircraft were already becoming severely constrained by shortage of fuel, lubricants and spares as a result of UN economic sanctions, Nonetheless, any gesture which reduced the suffering of the civilian population was to be welcomed.

One further positive outcome of the UN Resolution was the opportunity for NATO aircraft to co-operate with those of a former adversary. NATO, British and French AWACs aircraft, supported occasionally by USN E2C *Hawkeyes* discharged the surveillance task for the UN, making two flights per day over the Adriatic, overlapping with two others using Hungarian air space. Communication was facilitated by the location of NATO officers in Budapest and Hungarian MiG-21s were placed on alert on three Hungarian bases to protect the AWACs from any potential Serbian interceptors.[10]

Nevertheless, by December 1992 NATO defence staffs began to examine measures to enforce the air exclusion zone. Once more, however, the signals were ambiguous. In Stockholm, at a CSCE meeting on 14 December US Secretary of State Eagleburger sounded out governments on whether they would support a new UN Resolution to enforce the 'no-fly' zone. In the same period several trenchant criticisms of the 'allies' empty threats' were made by prominent Americans, including Henry Kissinger, George Schultz, Ronald Reagan and Jimmy Carter. President Clinton supported the enforcement of the no-fly zone by military means. In London, however, British military staffs were reported as 'firmly opposed to enforcing the air exclusion zone and issued a warning about the difficulty of mounting an effective operation'.[11] Defence Secretary Rifkind responded to US criticism by stating that it was no use just saying 'something had to be done'. 'Those of us who are responsible for armed forces have to come to a judgement on whether there is a straightforward military solution.'[12]

While this statement begged the question of whether the Serbs were already engaged on a military solution, it did reflect the British assessment that Serbian air activity was negligible and of little consequence, that helicopters were difficult to catch unless spotted by an adjacent combat air patrol, that the risks of the collateral damage of airfields near Banja Luka and Knin were high and therefore the military gains were simply not worth the risks of the retaliatory disruption of the humanitarian aid deliveries or of guerrilla-type attacks on UN ground forces. Allied solidarity was not helped by division within the German government over whether German aircrews were or were not constrained by the Constitution from flying in NATO AWACs aircraft on military action technically outside NATO's area.

While the debate rumbled inconsequentially on into 1993, the USA announced its intention at the end of February to intervene in Bosnia by means of airdrops of humanitarian aid to besieged Muslim enclaves. By mid-April some 30 sorties a day had delivered 2,000 tons of food and 50 of medical supplies. The loads were dropped from 10,000 ft but an unexpectedly high level of accuracy, usually about 40 metres, was achieved by the use of NAVSTAR Global Positioning System data to fix the aircraft's position and by computerised ballistics data on the cargo being dropped.[13]

Measured on the scale of the deprivation and misery in Bosnia, the supplies were minuscule, but starvation is a personal matter and the grateful townspeople of Zepa, Regatica and Gorazde were unconcerned about the political or military motivation of the airdrops. Sadly, the initiative was not received with universal acclaim. The C130 transports were flying within the theoretical range of Serbian AA guns and SAMs, and an Italian transport had been shot down near Sarajevo the previous September. Defence Secretary Rifkind was reported as saying that the airlift was of little value and that if RAF aircraft were to participate, they could also be shot down. 'The Rifkind view is that the Americans are pushing for something that is basically pretty futile but will look telegenic' was one official British defence comment.[14] In the event, USAF C-130s were joined by French and German transports, but the RAF supply effort continued to be made via the airport at Sarajevo amid the ground crossfire and the risk of surface-to-air attack from the surrounding hillsides.

Meanwhile, the sequence on the ground of peace proposals, broken truces and atrocities continued to stimulate anger, grief and frustration until on 31 March 1993 the UN Security Council, in Resolution 816, directed that the flight ban imposed in October should now be enforced. On 8 April the North Atlantic Council decided that NATO would begin to enforce the ruling on 12 April. NATO's action was in accordance with the Alliance's ministerial decisions at Oslo in June 1992 to support, on a case-by-case basis, and in accordance with NATO's own procedures, peacekeeping operations under the authority of the UN.[15] Fighters from the USA, France and the Netherlands were subsequently joined by others from the UK and Turkey. The operation was co-ordinated by NATO staffs from Vicenza in Italy. Meanwhile, a possible constraint on AWACs support was removed by the decision on 8 April of the German constitutional court not to oppose the participation of German aircrew in operations over Bosnia, outside the NATO area.

The political implications of enforcement were again far greater than their impact on events on the ground. Violations of the flying ban dropped markedly after 12 April, but, as has been noted, their military significance had already become negligible. This UN Resolution was, however, the first one to authorise military force in Bosnia in circumstances other than self-defence: a major step across the divide between peacekeeping and peace-enforcing. The second political milestone was the projection of NATO military power beyond the territorial limits and beyond the principle of collective self-defence in the face of 'an armed attack', as specified in the NATO Treaty of 1949.[16]

But by the end of 1993 no enforcement had taken place. Even when violations were spotted by one of the AWACs aircraft, it was not always possible for the fighters on combat air patrol to make visual contact and identification. On 29 April 1993, for example, two USMC F/A-18s, two French *Mirage* 2000s and two RAF *Tornado* F-3s all failed to exploit different AWACs contact reports.[17]

Royal Air Force aircrew privately expressed their frustration at the lack of engagement authority against violators of the ban when the result of ethnic cleansing on the ground was so widely publicised. They were authorised only to warn aircraft that they were in violation of UN Resolution 816, ordering them to land or depart the area immediately otherwise risking being engaged. The violators were usually helicopters: some Muslim, some Serb. As the no-fly zone was imposed to protect the Muslims, and Serb helicopters usually carried Red Cross markings, the RAF crews were acutely aware of the likely 'CNN' factor should either nationality actually be shot down, with the attendant international publicity. Fortunately, their professionalism and political awareness overcame both their emotions and their military inclination to engage targets technically identified as hostile. Consequently the violators frequently landed in their own good time, presumably on completion of their mission, or slipped over a ridge to disappear into radar shadow.

Not surprisingly therefore, the exponents of increased air power activity were dissatisfied with the single step requested by the 'enforcement' of the no-flying zone and continued to press for direct offensive action. Hawks in the USA were encouraged by comments from USAF Chief of Staff General Merrill McPeak. Bombing Serb gun positions would be completely effective and posed 'virtually no risk' to attacking planes. 'Give us time and we will order strikes on every one of those artillery positions and put it out of business,' he said.[18] Mrs Madeleine Albright, US Ambassador to the UN, in a note to President Clinton argued that 'air strikes would reduce the military threat against the relief forces and slow the supply of arms to the front line.'[19]

General Colin Powell, Chairman of the Joint Chiefs of Staff, on the other hand, continued to express strong reservations about the potential impact, and longer-term complications, of military intervention, while his Vice-Chairman, Admiral David Jeremiah, disagreed publicly with General McPeak: 'Hitting tanks spread out in the desert is one thing; hitting artillery near barns, schools and civic centers is another. It is not a simple or easy thing to use air strikes against guerrilla warfare units spread round the country.'[20]

Meanwhile in Brussels on 28 April, NATO's senior national military representatives concluded two days of discussions fearing that air strikes would be inaccurate and would provoke the Serbs into retaliation against UN ground troops, who would either have to be withdrawn or heavily reinforced. Field Marshal Sir Richard Vincent, Chairman of the Alliance's Military Committee said that if air strikes were to be ordered, 'We need to have the clearest guidance on what [the action] is seeking to achieve. It could represent a change in our strategy to former Yugoslavia in a very substantial way . . . The first principle of war is: for God's sake decide what you're trying to achieve before you go out there and start doing it.'[21]

Yet British ministers and officials, while endorsing General Powell's and Field Marshal Vincent's caution, were careful not to rule out the option of air strikes. Mr Rifkind for example, confirmed that bombing Serbian positions remained the most likely form of Western intervention, telling a Parliamentary by-election audience, 'Specific kinds of military action, particularly from the air, can sometimes eliminate sources of aggressors and can deal with particular threats. It has to be looked at extraordinarily carefully to make sure that it would indeed achieve the result that is being advocated.'[22] In this period it is difficult to avoid sympathy for Serbian intelligence sources trying to make some sense of Western air power policy.

Public awareness and political opinion were not helped by the lack of informed public debate on the circumstances likely to inhibit the effectiveness of air strikes at this stage of the conflict. Too often exchanges in the media were tinged with hostile national stereotyping, especially after US forces became involved in another UN operation in Somalia. In December 1992 their mandate was 'to use all measures necessary to establish a secure environment for humanitarian relief operations.'[23] The arrival across the beaches in December 1992 of US Marines in full combat kit to break through massed batteries of press flash bulbs had got Operation *Provide Hope* away to a slightly theatrical start. Farce turned into tragedy in June 1993 when Pakistani troops opened fire on demonstrators in Mogadishu who were protesting against US air strikes a few hours earlier on a weapons compound used by General Aideed, identified by the UN as primarily responsible for obstructing humanitarian activities.

It was easy to read across 'lessons' from Mogadishu into Bosnia and insert one or two prejudices at the same time. A leading article in the London *Daily Telegraph*, not usually tarnished by xenophobia, observed disparagingly, 'The American performance in Somalia has been deplorable . . . The airstrikes at the weekend reflected the worst American military tradition: they sought to do a complex job with minimum casualties, by committing bombs and bullets rather than men . . . It would be incomparably worse in Bosnia . . .'[24] The writer also made many sensible points about needing to spend considerable time and effort in rebuilding institutions and government and to avoid the search for a 'quick fix' and a speedy withdrawal.

Most observers, and certainly all soldiers, would strongly approve of measures which sought to reduce one's own casualties by the application of superior technology. A more appropriate criticism of US tactics in Mogadishu would have been that they were based on 'Military Operations – Urban Terrain', designed to defeat an enemy with well-organised firepower.[25] It has been estimated that 90 per cent of the training for ground forces in peacekeeping is training for general combat capability,[26] but the importance of the remaining 10 per cent is critical. Without that fraction 'Several areas of weakness stand out, including . . . insufficient attention to cultivating civil-military relations and limited understanding of the relationship between military tasks and that of [*sic*] other mission components. In addition, training for UN operations must also emphasise strict standards of discipline and sensitivity to cultural factors, including an appreciation of the languages, ethnic groups, religious and local customs in the area of deployment'.[27]

The extra training required for aircrew remained unquantified, and despite misgivings such as those expressed in the *Daily Telegraph*, the momentum grew in mid-1993 for the use of air strikes in the former Yugoslavia to protect ethnic enclaves proposed in contemporary peace negotiations and to suppress increasingly prevalent ground fire in close proximity to UN forces. As Serbian forces tightened their blockade around Sarajevo and repeatedly shelled the airport and UN troops located on or near it, the 'Deny Flight' mandate began to acquire an offensive component.

Typically, confusion marked the first transitional step when on 10 June NATO ministers, meeting in Athens, offered aircraft to defend UN troops. While NATO Secretary General Wörner referred specifically to troops in 'safe areas', US Secretary of State Warren Christopher said that the offer covered all UN forces in Bosnia if they were attacked and asked for help. A NATO statement ambiguously referred to 'air cover to the UN force in the performance of its overall mandate'. The British Foreign Secretary Douglas

Hurd agreed with Christopher; French minister Juppé restricted the offer to troops in six Muslim enclaves.[28] NATO military staffs at Headquarters Allied Air Forces Central Europe, tasked with co-ordinating the Alliance's offensive effort and establishing a command and control net, were not surprisingly unimpressed by the ambivalence of their political masters.[29] Nonetheless, preparations continued, including the identification of the requirement for the training of UN ground forces in forward air-control responsibilities.

By mid-July a mixed Alliance force including USAF A-10s, AO-10s, AC 130s and EC 130Hs, RAF *Jaguars*, French Air Force *Jaguars*, RNLF (Dutch Air Force) F 16As, USMC F/A 18s and USN F/A 18s and A6s was assembled at various bases in Italy and on the USS *Theodore Roosevelt* in the Adriatic, with in-flight refuelling support from the USAF and the RAF. By early August no agreement had been reached between the UN and NATO on command and control. On 3 August, according to Hurd, the NATO Council agreed to prepare plans for air strikes 'subject to arrangements for the UN to be involved so that our [British] troops are not at risk, and subject to progress or lack of progress at the Geneva peace talks.'[30]

Reports began to emerge of disagreement between the USA and her NATO allies not just over command and control, but over strategy and tactics. The USA wished for extensive freedom of action, under the overall command of USN Admiral Jeremy Boorda, NATO CINCSOUTH, to launch air strikes on a wide range of targets, including Bosnian commanders and 'those responsible, Bosnian Serbs and others.'[31] The major potential beneficiary of such action, Belgian Lieutenant-General Francis Briquemont, commanding UN Forces in Bosnia made his opposition clear: 'He warned that air strikes against the Bosnian Serbs surrounding Sarajevo could complicate the situation on the ground and invited supporters of the idea to take a hard look at his map. These show the Bosnian Serb army very close to Sarajevo, which is completely hemmed in, and overlooking the airport runway. If it advances further, there is a risk that air attacks could damage the city itself, and its vital airport.'[32]

Finally, agreements reached in the NATO Military Committee during the weekend of 7–8 August were approved and announced by the NATO ambassadors the following day. The extent of the previous disagreement was reflected by the tortuous procedures to be followed before air strikes could be launched.

Three originators of air strikes were authorised: a NATO member state, the United Nations or the NATO military authorities. The request would then go to the NATO Council, comprising either foreign ministers or ambassadors in Brussels, who would take account of the negotiations in Geneva and the situation on the ground in Bosnia. A unanimous decision would be required and the question would then go to the UN Secretary-General in New York, who would, in turn, consult the negotiators in Geneva as well as the Security Council. Operational decisions would be made by French General Jean Cot, the French officer in charge of UNPRO-FOR and Admiral Boorda, either of whom could block a decision, which would then be referred back to NATO and the UN. A number of 'triggers' for action were identified, relating to the 'safety of supply routes, recon-nection of energy and fuel supplies and access for aid convoys.'[33]

It will be recalled that among the characteristics of air power are rapid responsiveness and high speed. It would be difficult to imagine a com-mand and control structure more unwieldy, obstructive and operationally irrelevant to the needs of close air support than these procedures approved by the NATO Council. One US military planner, apparently without irony, observed that 'FAC (Forward Air Control) may not be requested for the expanded role debated by NATO. It will be an interdiction role with targets predetermined rather than called in by in-theatre units. Targets will not be time sensitive and precision guided weapons would be the desired approach.'[34] The views of British or French troop commanders on the ground, vulnerable to Serbian heavy weapons were not, apparently, solicited.

The operational manifestation of the NATO Council's labyrinth did not offer any easier passage. Tactical Air Control Parties (TACPs) were attached to UNPROFOR commanders on the ground. Britain provided an Air Operations Co-ordination Centre which was established in UNPROFOR headquarters at Kiseljak, Bosnia. Requests for air support would pass from the TACPs, via Kiseljak to the NATO Combined Air Operations Centre at Vicenza. In theory, the request still had two levels of approval to scale, in Brussels and New York. Then on its descent a further decision (assuming the request had originated from forces under the com-mand of General Cot) would be needed from Admiral Boorda. By the end of August, the allocation of aircraft was made at Vicenza by a daily task-ing order, reflecting the Coalition procedures in the Gulf. It covered some 20 close-support training sorties by a variety of aircraft, using a minimum of four communication channels, and transmitted to 20 recipients. Presumably in actual combat urgent calls for assistance from TACPs would take priority over preplanned missions, but exactly how, and by whom, pri-orities would be determined seemed uncertain in such a complex system with duplicate command chains.

More positively, the time taken to cobble together a politically accept-able command structure was well used by the operational staffs to add on the '10 per cent' to NATO air combat training required by the demands of peace-enforcing. Between July and September, more than 1,500 offensive training sorties were flown, supported by British, French and US tankers, EC 130 command, control and communications aircraft and AWACs. Crews became familiar with potential target areas and restrictions on weapon delivery. For example, all weapons were to be delivered 'under full positive control' by the aircrew; cluster weapons would not be used. Ground rules of engagement were extremely strict, taking into account the need to prevent collateral damage or injuries. One young pilot succinctly identified the nature of the operation: 'This is a true "trial by television" situation and we cannot afford to make mistakes when dropping live ordnance.'[35]

One circle remained to be squared in December 1993. However liberally interpreted, UN Security Council Resolution 816 authorised enforcement only of the 'notify' zone; it did not give a mandate for the use of air power against Serbian ground targets other than airfields. Any application to the Security Council for such action would face the risk of a Russian veto: hence the need to incorporate the Secretary-General in the more nebulous authorisation sequence and to beg the question of what could happen if he in turn had to seek Security Council approval.

By the end of 1993 the situation on the ground in the former Yugoslavia was depressingly familiar. Bargaining positions at interminable peace conferences reflected the territory gained or lost by the combatants. UN troops discharged their thankless task of persuading local brigands to allow humanitarian activities to continue with improbable depths of dogged persistence and varying degrees of success. Meanwhile, above their heads, NATO aircraft roared and dived in a show of sound and fury with little more significance than Macbeth's idiot's tale.

Action

In January NATO sabres were rattled again as Serbian artillery attacks on Sarajevo intensified. On 11 January a NATO Summit communiqué stated 'We reaffirm readiness to carry out air strikes to prevent the strangulation of Sarajevo . . '[36] Predictably, Radovan Karadjic, the Bosnian Serb leader, said that threats of air strikes could jeopardise the peace process and create new difficulties.[37] NATO was not abashed by this threat and reaffirmed its determination, this time to use air power to relieve Canadian forces near Srebrinica and to open Tuzla airport. To nobody's surprise, nothing happened.

On 21 January Secretary-General Boutros-Ghali made an unremarked but very important statement: that he would approve the use of air power in the former Yugoslavia if so requested by his special representative there, Yashushi Akashi. He also asked Mr Akashi to draw up a detailed plan for a possible military operation.[38] Almost by an imperceptible stroke, Mr

Boutros-Ghali had shortened and simplified the command and control chain, because it was to emerge three weeks later that actual authorisation for air strikes had been delegated down to Mr Akashi who was working in close contact with UN and NATO military commanders in-theatre.

Meanwhile, one Serbian Commander, who apparently had not looked up into the skies very much nor studied the progress of recent conflicts in the Middle East, became preoccupied with two SA-6 mobile launchers under his command. 'We control this air', he claimed, 'and no-one should forget that we have modern technology to detect any flying objects and we also have modern means to shoot down any plane. We will not allow planes to land at Tuzla Airport.'[39] He was failing to distinguish between C-130s, *Noratlas* and F-15Es and F-16s carrying laser and anti-radiation weapons. It looked, however, as if the bragging of Lieutenant-Colonel Milutinovic would never be tested.

And then, in February 1994, the environment in Bosnia dramatically changed. Indeed, the first move was associated with the arrival in Sarajevo of a new ground commander, British Army General Sir Michael Rose, to replace Belgian General Briquemont, on 24 January. He had scarcely time to demonstrate a very strong character before a Serb mortar exploded in the Moslem open market in Sarajevo on 5 February killing 68 civilians and wounding 200 others. Even by Bosnian standards the images on the world's television screen were horrendous.

On 7 February Mr Boutros-Ghali asked NATO to prepare plans for air attack on Serbian artillery threatening Sarajevo.[40] On 9 February the NATO Council issued an ultimatum to the Bosnian Serb Forces, demanding that they withdraw, or place under UN control, heavy weapons ('including tanks, artillery pieces, mortars, multiple rocket launchers, missiles and anti-aircraft weapons') located within 20 km of the centre of Sarajevo, within 10 days . . .[41] Any heavy weapons remaining within the Sarajevo 'exclusion zone' after 10 days from 2400 GMT, 10 February 1994 would 'along with their direct and essential military support facilities, be subject to NATO air strikes which will be conducted in close co-ordination with the UN Secretary-General and will be consistent with the North Atlantic Council's decision of 2 and 9 August 1993 . . .'

Meanwhile General Rose began to supplement the NATO Council's ultimatum with forthright negotiations on the ground; a truce was arranged and Serbian forces began to withdraw. This was not another vague NATO threat but a specific ultimatum with definable objectives. No-one was arguing that it could be 100 per cent enforced, nor avoid the risks which had been endlessly rehearsed over previous months. The Russian government, under pressure from nationalist, Pan-Serbian opportunists, was very uneasy until with a *coup de théâtre* on 18 February it announced that 400

Russian troops already in-theatre would be redeployed to enforce the cease-fire in Sarajevo. The ceasefire held, the Serbian heavy weapons continued to be withdrawn and the deadline passed with complete Serbian humiliation tempered only by the public display of international Slav solidarity. The 100 tactical air controllers deployed in-theatre and the NATO aircraft above them remained at combat readiness. The sound was similar but the threat was now very powerful. So much so that on 11 February the fragility of UN co-operation was demonstrated when Hungary announced that it would terminate overflights by NATO AWACs aircraft if air strikes were made against Serbian artillery positions. The Hungarian Prime Minister said, 'Hungary will not take part. We have to live with Serbia and the Serbian people for hundreds more years. AWACs aircraft cannot be present in Hungarian airspace if air strikes take place. This is natural.'[42]

Whether Hungary was motivated by frustration that it was receiving inadequate compensation for an embargo against Serbia costing it £1 billion, or by concern for 400,000 ethnic Hungarians in Serbia was uncertain, but the lack of support for an escalation in military activity by a country which hitherto had been a most valuable partner illustrated the regional political sensitivities about the use of air strikes.

Three weeks later, the Bosnian Serb air force, if a handful of combat trainers merited such a title, committed the incredibly foolhardy act of challenging the 'Deny Flight' restriction. Six *Super Galeb* aircraft took off undetected from Banja Luka airbase and bombed armaments factories in the Bosnian Moslem towns of Novi Travnik and Bugojno before being located by the NATO AWACs. Two pairs of USAF F-16s on combat air patrol were vectored on to the *Galebs* which ignored orders to land and sought to escape by flying out of Bosnian airspace. Four were shot down and the other two managed to evade and return to Banja Luka.[43] This was the first occasion that NATO aircraft, operating as part of the NATO organisation, had fired their weapons in anger for 45 years.

It would be easy to overemphasise this sudden and dramatic impact of air power on events in Bosnia. Less than two weeks later a French soldier was killed, almost certainly by a Serbian sniper, but General Rose did not call for a retaliatory air strike because 'In this case he doesn't know the origin of the fire.'[44] Two days later other French troops were attacked by a tank and a 30mm anti-aircraft gun late at night on 12 March. NATO aircraft were scrambled but were unable to locate the attackers, partly because bad weather impeded visibility and partly because the attackers were believed to have withdrawn into a forest.[45]

On the one hand air power had undoubtedly acted as a catalyst on events around Sarajevo. A determined ground force commander, an unusually determined NATO, and a finite objective on a precise region and timescale, had stimulated Russian diplomatic activity and forced a Serbian back-off which might have longer-term implications for peace in the region. The swift execution of the Serbian pilots from Banja Luka reinforced a novel sense of Western decisiveness and gave a much needed reminder to all the warring factions that, if the West could keep its act together, air power could be an influential and force-levelling instrument. But the other constraints would remain. There were 180 NATO combat aircraft in-theatre on 24-hour readiness on ground alert, on the tankers or on combat air patrol by March 1994. But they could only attack with minimum force, with no risk of collateral damage, under FAC control and with positive target identification. There remained a low level threat from AAA and small arms and the weather inhibited operations for several days at a time.[46] There remained little scope for any sustained, decisive application of air power.

For over two years, assessments of and genuine concerns about the potential of air power to facilitate a resolution of the conflict in the former Yugoslavia were distorted by parochial interests or ignorance, or both: political wrangles within NATO; domestic politics in the USA; turf wars between armed forces faced with swingeing reductions and staking claims for their role responsibilities in peacekeeping; governments seeking peace dividends and loth to accept unexpected and apparently interminable new security burdens; and civilian audiences, overwhelmed by media coverage of atrocities demanding action, any action, from those same governments. There were also genuine fears, there were constraints and there were unexplored opportunities. Significantly absent was informed, objective, public debate on the role of air power.

Yet there was sufficient historical precedent to enlighten both air power policy and practice. While the circumstances of Bosnia may not recur in such a combination, many individual features almost certainly will, just as many features of the Bosnian conflict itself resembled those of earlier campaigns in which air power did become involved, and left lessons for the future. The role of air power in Bosnia, or rather the lack of it, and by inference its potential in future peacekeeping or peace-enforcing operations, may be analysed against that broader historical perspective.

The Peacekeeping Environment

There was a dramatic contrast between the operational circumstances of the Gulf and those of Bosnia. In the Gulf the political objective of expelling Iraqi forces from Kuwait was specific and finite. In Bosnia the political objective for the use of military force remained uncertain. In the Gulf, topography and to a certain extent climate favoured air power, with Iraqi ground forces largely deployed in desert areas and distant from non-combatants. Their reinforcement, resupply and evacuation routes were few, extended and vulnerable. None of those features was present in Bosnia or associated with Serbian forces. The Iraqi army and its umbilical command and control system emanating from Baghdad were clearly defined, uncontroversial targets. The war was very much in a traditional, conventional mould, albeit marked by highly-sophisticated technology ideally suited to the environment. In Bosnia, on the other hand, the Serbian forces operated with considerable local autonomy, had large, well-dispersed and concealed arms caches, could largely dictate their own weapon and ammunition consumption rates and were therefore far less susceptible to interdiction than the Iraqi forces.

These features of the Bosnian theatre presented quite different problems to air force planners, but in addition there were constraints on the use of air power which are likely to be met in all peacekeeping environments. The expression 'peacekeeping' is used here as shorthand for a number of activities in a continuum, including humanitarian assistance, protection, self-defence, peace-enforcing as well as peacekeeping. The constant factor in this continuum is the breakdown of regional or national legitimate authority, perhaps from internal disputes, or internal collapse from external pressure. For example, international humanitarian aid may be delivered when a national disaster strikes any region on a scale beyond the capacity of the victim-state to respond. When that state's authority is unquestioned, the environment will be benign and receptive. But when humanitarian relief enters a region already ravaged by conflict, sectional interests may oppose, threaten and disrupt it. Such humanitarian activity then takes its place in the peacekeeping continuum and becomes a consideration in all other 'peacekeeping' activities in the area.

The activities may occur independently, as, for example, in humanitarian relief, or as in Cyprus where air power is restricted to patrolling the 'Green Line', and monitoring an extended truce between Greek and Turkish Cypriot forces. The requirement for air power may increase along the continuum as, in Bosnia, where humanitarian activity required protection by troops who, in turn, required defence from the air against superior, hostile ground forces. Or activities could be concurrent, as in Somalia where humanitarian aid was being supplied in 1993 at the same time as punitive air attacks were launched on a Somali warlord alleged to be disrupting the humanitarian activities. In traditional air operations in conventional warfare, the chances of achieving the objective and the costs/effort required will be primary considerations. In peacekeeping however, of equal importance is the assessment of the likely knock-on effect of the air operation on any other concurrent activity in the peacekeeping continuum. As NATO Secretary General Wörner observed in November

1993, a lesson from Bosnia was to 'avoid situations in which your own troops become hostages.'[47]

There may also be the danger of retaliation against non-combatants in-theatre who may be identified with the powers responsible for the air attack. Concern about such retaliation was frequently expressed in Bosnia and Somalia in 1992 and 1993. It was not new. In 1920 the process known as 'Imperial Policing' by air of parts of the British Empire was extended to the Afghanistan-Indian border. RAF aircraft had already been used to 'pacify' Somaliland and were deployed in Iraq and other Middle East territories in the 1920s.[48] In 1923, the Imperial Government of India remained doubtful about the humanitarian implications of air attack on tribesmen and their villages and expressed concern specifically about atrocities committed against British Christians in apparent retaliation for such attacks. A number of letters passed between the Indian Government and regional authorities, including one from the Chief Commissioner, North-West Frontier Province, to the Government in Simla, responding in detail to suggestions of retaliatory atrocities and also mentioning an early example of hostile media manipulation:

It is my opinion that the crimes directed against English ladies have no connection whatsoever with aerial operations against the tribes. The first lady attacked in recent years was Mrs Wingfield who was kidnapped from Peshawar in March 1920. Up to that date no bombing operations had been undertaken against the tribes. The murder of Mrs Foulkes followed in November 1920 and no bombs had been dropped except on tribal lashkars in Wazirstan during the actual fighting. The Ellis and Watts cases (murder and kidnap) are ascribed to Ajab and his gang, and there have been no bombing operations anywhere near Kohat, Tirah or Parachinar. Ajab, from whom many letters have been received, has never mentioned tribal bombing as in any way prompting his crimes. The theory that tribal bombing is responsible for them is being supported from three sources: (1) Kabul and its state press; (2) Chamarkand and the Al Mujahid; (3) Indian extremists and their press. All three occasionally find an echo in the press of other countries including England. It is hardly necessary to expose their motives for explaining away the crimes in this way. They are afraid of the hold over the tribes the aeroplane gives us, and the allegation of frightfulness and its result is a good stick to beat the government with. I regard the careful dissemination of this theory from the above sources as a piece of cunning anti-British propaganda.[49]

Then, the sensitivities were those of a single government applying military force in its own interest. A further characteristic of air operations in the modern peacekeeping continuum is that they will have a supranational authority, usually the United Nations The implications of such authorisation is that air power must be applied with scrupulous regard to formal international agreements and in accordance with the principles upheld by the authorising organisations. In Mogadishu in 1993, US helicopter and fixed-wing attacks on urban targets were criticised not just because of their military ineffectiveness but because they conflicted sharply with UN principles. There were grounds in September 1993 for believing that the local warlord General Aideed's troops in Mogadishu did use women and children as 'human shields'. US helicopters fired on women and children in close proximity to an ambush of Pakistani soldiers, prompting a comment by Major David Stockwell, American spokesman for the UN forces, 'There are no spectators at an ambush. Women and children are considered a threat. They are considered combatants, whether they shoulder arms or not.'[50] As a result, international perceptions of indiscriminate US air attack and failure to comprehend the peculiar constraints of peacekeeping dominated world headlines, not the brutality of the Aideed provocative manipulation.

Individual governments applying air power, or indeed any other kind of military force, in the peacekeeping continuum are likely to be far more sensitive to criticism than when committed to conflicts involving national security or the projection or protection of clearly-defined national interests. Governments will frequently have a choice about whether to get involved in peacekeeping or not.

Britain has interests in international stability and the primacy of international law and diplomacy as arbiters of disputes, but the use of force in support of that general principle may be considered more apposite in some cases than others. For example, there were no doubts about the principles at stake after the Argentinian invasion of the Falklands. In the Gulf, however, there was a coincidence of national interest and international principle, but Britain was able to choose whether to participate in the UN coalition and how much effort to allocate. The introduction of a choice about participating in peacekeeping has several significant implications for the application of air power. A democratic government is likely to be particularly sensitive to the impact on domestic politics of events in peacekeeping. Friendly force casualties will quickly become significant. If they are associated with losses of advanced combat aircraft to relatively unsophisticated weaponry, as in the case of US helicopters shot down in Mogadishu, domestic political opponents may combine concern about casualties with criticism of governmental policies. Government determination may be weakened by media coverage of victims and collateral damage from inaccurate or indiscriminate air attack. Rarely will it be possible, as in the Falklands War, to control media access to target areas. Guernica, London, Warsaw, Dresden and several locations in Vietnam have tarnished the image of aerial bombardment. Even in the Gulf War, as has been noted, scrupulous Coalition policy to minimise Iraqi civilian casualties was temporarily impugned by the tragedy of the Al Amariyah bunker. Disaster is media friendly; disaster induced by military excess or incompetence anywhere in the peacekeeping continuum provides media headlines and is likely to erode public support.

As a result, peacekeeping is likely to be subject to more resource constraints, political control and narrow political sensitivities than traditional military activities. Failure on the part of airmen to recognise and accept such political realities and their operational implications would have serious consequences for the future procurement for and application of air power.

Consequently, governments will tend to be diffident in defining political objectives in peacekeeping whenever there is a risk of long-term commitment and an uncertain outcome. As a result, military staffs, as in the Bosnian theatre, may chafe at the lack of a clear political mandate towards which they should harness their military power. The need for a more flexible approach was explained in November 1993 by NATO Secretary-General Manfred Wörner:

> . . . the purpose of intervention is not necessarily to win a war, but to influence the behaviour of the party concerned. We need to have limited military options for limited political or diplomatic objectives. It is wrong to think only in categories of all or nothing . . .[51]

The Secretary-General was laying down broad principles, but the operational implications of that sentiment cascade all the way down to the individual sorties flown across the peacekeeping continuum.

In the Gulf War, with memories of 'incrementalism' in Vietnam still bitter, the Coalition high command deliberately amassed and applied overwhelmingly superior forces in the hope that Iraq could be defeated quickly and with low allied casualties. Considerable efforts were made by psychological warfare to induce Iraqi forces to desert, but the primary objective was to ease Coalition success, not to reduce Iraqi casualties. The final and most complex characteristic of peacekeeping operations is that reconciliation is the objective in all applications of force along the continuum. That implies seeking to reduce both friendly and hostile casualties as far as possible. That may entail a maximum demonstration of force but the application of the minimum. That in turn risks tactical planning and weapon choices which by minimising force could actually jeopardise friendly forces. All in all, it is not surprising that military commanders are frequently very loth to become involved in combat in a peacekeeping scenario.

Vulnerability and Casualties

In theory, every air power role could be applied to peacekeeping operations, particularly if a Gulf scenario were to recur which demanded the deployment of large-scale conventional forces. Indeed, in the nightmare eventuality of a state threatening or actually using nuclear weaponry in disregard of UN authority, a limited nuclear response to enforce compliance may come to be considered. Such circumstances would severely task Mr Wörner's principle of limited military options. It is fortunately more likely that air power will be called upon at lower levels of intensity. But from the outset of any contribution, a realistic appraisal of the limitations of and constraints on air power imposed by the characteristics of the peacekeeping environment would be essential. As has already been noted, resilience to friendly casualties will be a significant factor in participant determination.

Provision of humanitarian aid by air is usually politically non-contentious for the donor state. In Bosnia, however, it cost the lives of the Italian transport crew in 1992, shot down by an unidentified SAM. Transport aircraft are especially vulnerable when approaching or climbing away from airfields and to ground fire when taxiing or off-loading. On several occasions UN aircraft approaching or leaving Sarajevo reported illumination by SAM acquisition radars or other systems. Often flights in and out of the Bosnian capital were stopped completely because the airfield was either directly under fire or swept by cross fire.

The particular vulnerability of transport aircraft to anti-aircraft fire is not a novelty in the 1990s: spectacular failure at Dien Bien Phu and costly success at Khe Sanh are probably the best-known precedents since World War II. In peacekeeping, however, such vulnerability may be too high a political price for a government to risk. If so, ground forces must be deployed to secure the airfields and surrounding areas, whereupon dependence on airlift ceases to be either an easy or a non-contentious option. Alternatively, the airlift may be suspended or withdrawn altogether, in which case the political determination of the interventionists is called into question and the morale and determination of those not complying with UN authority is proportionately increased.

Combat aircraft may also be vulnerable to ground fire. One of the earliest claims for small-arms effectiveness was as poetic as it was inaccurate. Mullah Seyed Mohamed of Somalia was subjected to the British policy of 'Imperial Policing' by air in 1920. For four months the Mullah's forces were bombed and harassed by 12 Royal Air Force DH 9 aircraft. In March, he commented to a peace delegation, 'The British brought 12 birds against me, but they could not hurt me. Their droppings fell on the top of my white canopy but did me no harm. Four of those birds they had borrowed from the French. Six I have killed, and four the British have returned to the French. So they have only two left.'[52] In fact, all 12 aircraft returned safely to Britain and within 12 months the Mullah was dead and his private jihad extinguished. By 1932 the RAF had lost only 14 pilots killed and 84 wounded in air-policing operations,[53] but as the aeroplane became a more familiar opponent, so it became more vulnerable. In 1936, for example, three RAF aircraft were lost in one day to ground fire in Palestine.[54] After World War II anti-aircraft defences were further enhanced by radar and missile technology.

For several years the threat to aircraft in low-intensity operations continued to emanate primarily from unguided anti-aircraft guns. British pilots, for example, did not face SAMs until operations in Oman in 1975. In Indo-China, the French Air Force lost 650 pilots killed or missing in action,[55] most falling to the 37-mm AA and other unguided ground-to-air fire from mobile guns which were difficult to locate and suppress. After the militarily successful Algerian campaign, a senior French Air Force officer subsequently set out 'four essential points to be followed when using helicopters' in counter-insurgency operations:

The first one applies when you fly your troops from A to B. The enemy can be anywhere; in this type of war you never know where they are . . . you need . . . safe itineraries, which are flight paths over ground that is definitely held by friendly troops.

Point 2 is to fly high enough to avoid ground fire from the enemy . . . Considering the terrain and the type of armament the enemy had, 1,500 ft was about the minimum altitude for helicopter flight.

Point 3 is to have the closest possible cover by armed helicopters . . . this ratio is now one armed helicopter out of five, with weapons such as 20-mm cannon and two to four SS 10 or SS 11 missiles.

Point 4 is to maintain fighter bombers immediately available on call in the target area for airborne fire support.

I don't mean that nobody is shot at or shot down when you follow these points but you do minimise the enemy's chances against your own people.'[56]

These were protective measures against machine guns and other small-arms fire which was augmented when the Soviet-built, hand-held SA 7 became widely available to insurgents in the following decade. When the scale of fighting expanded to the proportions of Vietnam the vulnerability of a helicopter to ground fire was still reduced by defensive tactics and self-preservation. The USA lost 3,587 helicopters to hostile action, almost exclusively to ground fire. In terms of human tragedy the figure is horrendous, but expressed as an operational statistic from over 37 million helicopter combat sorties flown between 1965 and 1973,[57] it represents a loss rate of less than 0.01 per cent and at no time deflected US strategy in the theatre.

Circumstances in Afghanistan in the next major insurgency were very different. By 1979 the Soviet Union had done its homework on earlier helicopter operations. In the early years of the war in Afghanistan, heavily armoured Mi 24s and fixed-wing SU 25s, also equipped with self-defence flares, made a considerable contribution to tactical Soviet operations, but even then the contest was by no means one sided. Until 1986, the Mujahedin in Afghanistan used heavy machine guns, SA 7s and occasionally rocket-propelled grenades against low-flying Soviet fixed-wing aircraft and helicopters. They set up ambushes near air bases, along flying routes and in the vicinity of landing areas, tactics very similar to those employed previously by the FLN in Algeria. The Soviet Air Force countered by armed helicopter and fixed-wing fire support, again reminiscent of countermeasures in Algeria. Aircraft losses were insufficient to seriously disrupt Soviet air power used in a wide variety of roles. The employment of the helicopter in particular 'was the most dynamic and effective feature of Soviet operations in Afghanistan. Given the decentralisation of operations and the great expanse of largely inaccessible territory, it would have been impossible for the Soviets to maintain pressure on the Mujahedin and to defend and supply their dispersed garrisons without the helicopter. Helicopters provided mobility of combat power (which the insurgents no way could match), enhanced surprise, reduced reaction time, enabled Soviet forces to respond to rebel threats very quickly and provided the Soviets with their most effective means of exercising initiative through direct action.'[58]

Then in 1986 the air war and the Soviet military position in Afghanistan generally were dramatically changed by the acquisition by the Mujahedin of three new surface-to-air weapons: the US-built *Stinger* and UK-built *Blowpipe* SAMs and Swiss Oerlikon AA guns. Tactical surprise was apparently achieved and Soviet losses increased rapidly through into 1987, reportedly averaging one aircraft a day.[59] All helicopters and fixed-wing operations were severely affected, either by direct attrition, by compulsive high speed to evade AA, by the adoption of higher-level profiles or by direct cancellation of missions with resulting loss of combat efficiency; all induced by the synergy of low-level gun with low and medium-level SAM.

Despite strenuous Soviet attempts to interdict the weapon supply routes from Pakistan, and further modification to tactical flying patterns, the impact of the new surface-to-air defences not only impaired Soviet effectiveness but boosted Mujahedin morale enormously and further weakened Soviet resolve to stay in Afghanistan at all. By February 1989, when regional arms agreements came into force, about 1,000 *Stingers* had been despatched to the Mujahedin. They were probably responsible for the destruction of 300–400 Soviet aircraft. All published figures of losses originate from the Mujahedin side and therefore, like most similar claims, were probably inflated. Whatever the exact figure, the losses ultimately proved too much even for the USSR, which originally at least had perceived a national security interest to be at stake. Surface-to-air weapons had dramatically reduced air power's effectiveness. Moreover, the weapons which had done the damage were the products of advanced technology but were handled by irregular forces drawn from a technologically-underdeveloped society. Less obviously, but almost as important for future operations, was the increased impact of old-fashioned lead when aircraft sought to evade SAMs at low level.

Two other facts were noted which could have further, far-reaching implications for air power in peacekeeping operations. The first was the reported receipt by the Sandanista government in Nicaragua of Soviet-built SA 14 man-portable missiles:[60] a reminder that Soviet families of *Stinger* equivalents would also soon be on the world market. The second was the widely-reported belief that many *Stingers* either never reached their intended Muhajedin recipients, were sold by them on the international black market, or were captured by Soviet forces.

It would therefore be prudent to prepare for the presence of advanced surface-to-air weapons in any future peacekeeping operations requiring a contribution from air power. Even when the non-compliants are perceived to have little indigenous military sophistication there is unlikely to be a shortage of international suppliers. Embargoes may be difficult to enforce, and non-compliants may have already built up clandestine stocks.

Air-to-Ground Operations

In future peacekeeping operations therefore, sensitivity to aircrew casualties in a publicly-uncertain cause could coincide with the possession, or suspected possession, by the non-compliants of a number of modern SAMs, supplemented by an indeterminate and unpredictable amount of unguided, low-level light AA fire. The weapons will be man-portable or highly-mobile and capable of concealment by contours as well as vegetation or urban deployment.

Such a threat would complicate proposals to introduce air power anywhere on the peacekeeping continuum, except in peacekeeping when truces or settlement terms had been agreed. Even then, the risk of attack by dissident minorities would remain, as for example it did in Rhodesia from December 1979 to March 1980 when unarmed RAF helicopters were deployed in support of the ceasefire and amnesty agreements marking the end of the civil war in the country. As the fate in Bosnia of the Italian transport crew testified, even the provision of humanitarian aid could be construed by one faction as partisan support to another.

The risks of retaliation increase as air power comes to be applied offensively. It is to be hoped that in some circumstances a show of force alone would suffice to persuade non-compliant combatants on the ground to abandon their military activities; but there is little historical evidence to substantiate it, especially when combatants have been motivated by beliefs or kinship rather than by the traditional pastimes of pillaging and unruly behaviour. If they can do so, ground targets are likely to shoot back. As in Bosnia, rules of engagement may well prompt controversy among participants when a ground attack is being planned. The options range from granting immunity from retaliation to any weapon firing from cover among non-combatants, to pre-emptive attack on any known or suspect firing position. The former policy was adopted by Britain in Palestine in 1936,[61] when aircrew were forbidden to attack buildings from which they had been fired upon. The response is laudable in humanitarian terms but likely to be ultimately counterproductive. Thereafter proscribed individuals or equipment could take sanctuary in urban locations with impunity and once more the resolve of the interventionists would be called into question.

But unless the response from the air was instantaneous, accurate and restricted, collateral damage and casualties would ensue while the weapons team itself could swiftly evade retribution. Air attack under such circumstances could be counterproductive. It might, as in the early days of British Imperial Policing, induce compliance and erode support for the dissidents from a non-committed population. But all recent evidence from Vietnam to Baghdad suggests that a more likely response would be hatred of the intervening force and increased support for the dissidents, especially if the non-combatants have little or no political or military power. When the objective of the military action is inducement and pacification rather than conquest, the value of such application of air power is even more questionable. This is, however, not an argument against offensive air power in peacekeeping but simply against dependence on it to counter small, mobile targets in built-up or other areas where the risks of non-combatant casualties are high. It will usually be difficult if not impossible for air power to counter sniper or other small-arms fire and highly-mobile man-portable mortars. Their eradication will remain a task for ground forces.

Air power can be used as a force equaliser where non-compliants are using armour and artillery, co-ordinated, as in Bosnia, from well-known and lightly-protected command and control posts, to threaten friendly ground forces or positions. There is here a minor parallel with events in the Gulf where air power drastically reduced Iraqi ground force strength by direct attack, making the subsequent task of the Coalition ground forces much easier. In a Bosnian scenario, the threat from non-compliant heavy weapons could be neutralised by their enforced abandonment or withdrawal, not just by destruction. If a UN convoy commander, for example, was known to be in regular radio contact with ground-attack aircraft on combat air patrol, a non-compliant force may think twice before threatening the convoy with tanks or stopping it at a large, static road block.

In accordance with the principle of minimum force application, a warning of air attack should be followed by a threat, and, if compliance does not follow, a precise strike on tank, heavy gun or command post. Such targets would be vulnerable to PGMs launched, as in the Gulf, from heights above the threat envelope of AA defences, thereby coupling maximum target discrimination with minimum risk of friendly casualties.

In this scenario there is far less cause for concern if the offending artillery or armour is pulled back into an urban environment to avoid such air attack. As long as it has moved out of range of the original UN or other friendly target, it has been neutralised. It will continue to present a residual threat until a peace agreement is assured, but air power could be tasked with ensuring that it does not emerge from its sanctuary.

In the Gulf War several precise attacks were made on strategic targets in the city of Baghdad which caused little or no collateral damage or civilian casualties. There may be circumstances in peacekeeping operations when the potential impact of such an attack may outweigh the collateral risks involved. If, for example, there was incontrovertible proof that a neighbouring state was actively supporting non-compliants against UN authority, training camps, weapons-storage areas and even transportation links could be considered legitimate targets. If, however, non-compliants were acting independently with little more than external tacit support or engagement it is unlikely that air attack on 'sanctuaries' would be authorised. In the Balkan example, punitive attacks on Belgrade would have had little impact on the fighting in Bosnia and, would have inflicted further hardship on non-combatants and risked uniting non-committed or friendly citizens with active supporters of the Bosnian Serbs. On balance, therefore, in peacekeeping operations air attack against tactical or strategic targets in urban sanctuaries is likely to be counterproductive in the search for conciliation and compromise.

Away from towns and villages, air attack can contribute to dissuasion and dilution of the non-compliant's own resort to violence. For example, by denying sanctuary in areas remote or inaccessible to friendly ground forces, by denying opportunities for the amassing of large ground force units, and by harassing non-compliant insurgents when they are out of contact with friendly ground forces. In concept they would be similar to the air operations in Malaya in the 1950s, but they would have learned from the experiences of those colonial conflicts.

For example, one Royal Australian Air Force Squadron of eight *Lincoln* bombers dropped 17,500 tons of bombs in Malaya and was credited with killing just 16 insurgents in nine years.[62] But the presence of the bombers kept the insurgents on the move, denied them opportunities to regroup and to set up camps and frequently drove them into unwilling contact with friendly ground forces. So called 'rapid response' attacks were not much more destructive. A 30-minute response was insufficient to prevent the insurgents from 'melting away' before the aircraft reached the target area.[63] Even when insurgents were engaged, the jungle canopy precluded any accurate assessment of the attack and jet aircraft did not have the endurance to loiter in the area. In this campaign there was virtually no anti-aircraft fire to contend with.

Three subsequent observations on air attack in the Malayan emergency have particular relevance to air power in peacekeeping operations at the end of the century:

> . . . for offensive air operations to be successful, certain conditions must be fulfilled. To my mind, these are an identifiable target, its exact geographical location, and an attacking force capable of accurate navigation to the target and carrying a weapon suited to the target.[64]
>
> Every successful bombing operation I knew of, including the one in which 14 were killed was the result of a carefully planned, delicate operation involving an agent. That takes time and pinpoint accuracy. An agent has always been in on it; it has been an intelligence-type operation.[65]
>
> The role of air power I feel, is an excellent example of Army-Air Force co-operation. The Air Force contribution is not spectacular; air is definitely a supporting arm of the Army. As an airman I would say we have no independent role in these operations. We must work closely in conjunction with the Army and the civilian authorities.[66]

The modern jargon for Colonel Clutterbuck's 'agent' would be 'humint': the derivation of timely intelligence data from human, as opposed to technical sources. It is not only the world's air forces who study air operations. Insurgent groups are likely to maintain radio silence, moving wherever possible at night or in cover. They may be detected by infra-red sensors but, as in Malaya, they must still be swiftly engaged before they have an opportunity 'to melt away'. Even then, the preferred peacekeeping response to timely intelligence may be an ambush to disarm, rather than ambush by air-to-ground to destroy.

In most, if not all offensive air operations, close co-operation between ground and air forces will be essential. The modern equivalent of the civilian colonial authority will be the representative of the UN or some other body. Some air forces, for example the USAF, may need to modify their traditional sensitivity to operations which appear to impinge upon their 'independence', even to the extent of placing operational control of combat aircraft in-theatre under a foreign ground commander.

Indeed, experience in 'low intensity', counter-'insurgent' operations suggests that the primary function of air power is in support of ground forces. But, 'support of' is no more synonymous with 'subordinate to' than artillery is 'subordinate to' infantry. The two are complementary. Offensive air support reduces the effectiveness of the opposition, denies him firepower or numerical superiority and, it is to be hoped, discourages his pursuit of his own coercive option.

Tactical Air Mobility

While offensive air support is an enemy force reducer, the provision of tactical air mobility is a friendly force multiplier. Provided, for the reasons already advanced, that hostile AA fire can be suppressed, reduced or evaded, both helicopters and fixed-wing aircraft can make a considerable contribution across the peacekeeping continuum. Helicopters can provide infantry with mobility over inhospitable terrain to match or exceed that of non-compliant insurgents. Territory which can take 3-4 days to cover on foot can be overflown by a helicopter in 20 minutes. Heliborne troops can outflank and envelope while at the same time induce surrender or compliance, reducing the advantages to dissidents of topographical features and distance. Algeria and, before the advent of *Stinger*, Afghanistan provide comprehensive examples of such operations. Casualty evacuation, reinforcement and resupply and the speedy provision of highly-visible military support to an isolated civilian authority are further roles giving positive support to peacekeeping operations. The cumulative impact of the provision of air mobility is to reduce the number of ground troops required in any specified area. Even when a permanent military presence is considered essential throughout the region, the ability to reinforce rapidly by air would still reduce the total number of ground forces required. Moreover, in underdeveloped regions or areas devastated by conflict, the helicopter can be used to provide aid and hospital evacuation for the civilian population also, thereby enhancing other activities on the peacekeeping continuum.

Combined Operations

Even such a partial survey of the contribution of air power to peacekeeping operations illustrates that the volume of activity is not necessarily an indication of the complexity and extent of the planning required to produce it. Co-ordinating air attack and air mobility, especially where the same aircraft were used for both, would alone require a detailed command and control structure. But, in addition, armed reconnaissance is likely to be a prominent task.

The pre-1986 Soviet model of convoy escort in Afghanistan by 'leap-frogging' helicopters to see, and if necessary clear, the road beyond the next hill or ravine would obviously facilitate the distribution of humanitarian aid and the protection of attendant ground forces. Such a presence in Bosnia, with appropriate rules of engagement, would have given irregular disrupters another factor to consider. Such armed reconnaissance would also reduce the number of occasions when close air support was called upon to relieve an ambush on a convoy or friendly ground forces. Indeed, an overall military objective by combined ground, rotary and fixed-wing forces would be to deny the initiative as far as possible to non-compliant insurgents. But, as with the 'agent' in Malaya, close contact with intelligence sources on the ground would be essential to ensure that the armed reconnaissance would be made over territory sheltering the dissidents. Seldom if ever will an interventionist force have sufficient assets for unrestricted operations.

On several occasions in 'traditional' operations the insurgents have been able to seize an initiative, with dramatic and disastrous consequences, by counterattacking against airfields. Conversely, they have been able to inhibit air activity by bringing an airfield under fire. Dependence on main operating bases, in addition to forward rough field or barebase locations, for both helicopters and fixed-wing aircraft remains a feature of air operations, and even with increased emphasis on short take-off and landing attributes, will remain so. Dien Bien Phu remains the greatest single airfield disaster, but on several occasions since then insurgents have penetrated airfield defences: at Akrotiri in the Cyprus conflict, on several occasions in Vietnam, and repeatedly by the Mujahedin in Afghanistan. These attacks had no significant impact on British, American or Soviet policy, but were they to take place during peacekeeping operations their impact on participants could be politically serious. One may also speculate on the international reaction of the UN Coalition if one or more Iraqi *Scuds*, had struck Dhahran Air Base immediately after USAF F 15s had deployed there in August 1990.

In peacekeeping operations, however, airfield dependence may be turned into a powerful political advantage. Whenever ethnic factors have prompted UN intervention it is highly probable that neighbouring states, with the greatest interest in the outcome, are those least likely to be welcome as members of the intervening ground forces. They can, however, contribute by providing airfields and controlled airspace for use by the intervening forces; as by Saudi Arabia, Turkey and the Gulf States in 1990 and 1991, and by Italy and Hungary from 1992 to 1994. Thereby the interventionists benefit from sanctuary for strategic air lift into the theatre and for main operating bases for shorter-range aircraft within the theatre. Under such circumstances, airfields may be available for UN operations in the future rather more readily than some analysts of the Gulf War have assumed. Such availability would be of considerable value in enabling continuous airborne command and control of operations or uninterrupted combat air patrols.

On some occasions, however, airbases in-theatre may be in hostile, or politically hostile hands. If peacekeeping operations are resolving an inter-state crisis, or with possible third-party involvement in an internal conflict, as in the Gulf and to a lesser extent in Bosnia, then peacekeeping may also require conventional counter-air support. For all air activity across the continuum, complete control of the air is essential. For reasons already argued, it is likely that the major threat will be from the ground, but from the outset any potential air intervention must be deterred, and if necessary, neutralised. The imposition of an air-exclusion zone is most important, as long as it is capable of being enforced. Peacekeeping operations are therefore likely to require the presence in-theatre of combat aircraft capable of establishing control of the air: ideally, equipped to neutralise both ground-to-air and air-to-air opposition. A third party should be in no doubt about the fate of its own airfields and supporting infrastructure should its aircraft seek to interrupt peacekeeping activities.

The Balance Sheet

If the Gulf War marked the apotheosis of late twentieth century air power, in the Bosnian fiasco before February 1994 it reached an impotent nadir. Yet, provided the unusual characteristics of peacekeeping operations are fully understood together with their attendant constraints, air power can offer a great deal to governments deliberating whether to participate or not.

It is difficult to envisage peacekeeping operations which will not require troops on the ground. For reasons already explained, most air operations will require close co-operation with and from ground forces. Some states, however, may wish to discharge their responsibilities solely by air power, or by using air power to supplement a much smaller ground contribution than would otherwise have been required. Air power as a hostile force equaliser and a friendly force multiplier will continue to be politically and economically attractive.

Air power can be deployed and withdrawn with comparative ease, especially if operating from friendly bases in-theatre but outside the disputed conflict territory. This attribute may not be conducive to the long-term political commitment necessary to resolve and sustain a complex settlement, but it will be attractive to politicians wishing to demonstrate their international responsibility without risking involvement in a latter-day Vietnam or Afghanistan. It is well argued that air power cannot hold ground, but it can make it very difficult for hostile forces to do so and it may thereby dissuade recalcitrant political groups from having recourse to armed force, or persuade them to abandon it, in pursuit of political objectives. Air power, like any other kind of military power, cannot impose a political settlement, but it can help to create a peacekeeping environment in which a political settlement is preferable to continued conflict.

No opponent should be free to use heavy artillery, armour and static command posts to thwart any peacekeeping activity when friendly air power can be brought to bear. No safe havens, no reliable supply routes, no unthreatened external military support should be possible. Ambushes, road blocks, hostile assembly and deployment should all be constrained by tactical air reconnaissance and air-mobile infantry. Irregulars or others who have fired with impunity on civilians or UN ground forces should, if they fail to heed specific warnings, become vulnerable to attack from the air. Air operations can be mounted from secure bases outside the threatened territories. They can be started, increased, reduced, suspended or terminated within hours and without the complications of the insertion or extraction of large numbers of ground forces.

If, on the other hand, an opponent can take advantage of topography or the urban environment to conceal his whereabouts or introduce a risk of collateral damage and non-combatant casualties, or actually threaten to inflict heavy casualties by cheap but effective AA weapons, he does not need to defeat the interventionists but simply to raise the costs of their effort beyond the national political, military and economic price they are prepared to pay. That is the uneasy lesson for air power, and any other kind of military power, in a Bosnian scenario.

Such considerations are likely to influence the future application of air power at least as much as the dramatic successes of the Gulf War. They will continue to interact with the evolution of technology to present complex problems for force structures, training and resource allocation. By 1994 it looked as if only one country, the USA, could look towards the twenty-first century with any confidence of being able to apply air power across the entire spectrum of warfare from low-intensity to large-scale international conflict. If so, the implications for international security are considerable.

CHAPTER 7

'RUSSIA WITHOUT WINGS IS NOT RUSSIA'

Air power was a central feature in the 40 years confrontation between East and West. It was frequently prominent in conflict between client states beyond the central European arena. While Western, and particularly American air power looked set to build upon the triumphs of *Desert Storm*, its Russian counterpart fell into disarray. How far would Western governments need to take its possible resurgence into account when looking forward into the twenty-first century? By 1994 all forecasts had to remain heavily qualified, but after a catastrophic sequence of events from 1989 to 1993 there were signs of reconstitution in the Russian Air Force (VVS) which, if fully realised, would ultimately challenge Western aerial hegemony and therefore perhaps inhibit its application as an instrument of policy.

Mr Gorbachev's arms control offers were regarded with some suspicion among Western air forces because for several months they were accompanied by sustained Soviet Air Force (SAF) offensive combat training and deployments of an increasingly sophisticated and effective nature. The impression was of a confident, professional force learning to employ new generations of aircraft and weapons in accordance with the concept of operations explained in Chapter 3 above. Then the entire structure began to collapse. Events frequently interacted with a destructive synergism, but for analysis the threads may be identified as the withdrawal from eastern Europe, the trauma of *Desert Storm*, the disintegration of the USSR, domestic economic collapse, and corrosion within the military structure itself.

Withdrawal from Eastern Europe

In late 1988 the Soviet Air Force deployment in eastern Europe was assessed by the British MoD to be 700 fixed-wing and 750 rotary aircraft in the Group of Soviet Forces Germany, 70 and 150 in the Central Group, 230 and 130 in the Southern, and 120 helicopters in the Northern: a total of 1,000 and 1,140, respectively, in the region.[1] In East Germany alone, the SAF used 110 airfields and helicopter bases supported by 70 radar and radio-transmitting stations, with the headquarters of the 16th Air Army at Wittstock.[2]

During 1989, one after another the Communist regimes of eastern Europe collapsed. At an international military conference in Moscow in November 1989[3] a GDR admiral who had marched in the Berlin demonstration the previous week sought to assure his Soviet military colleagues that his German fellow demonstrators had not been calling for withdrawal from the Warsaw Pact but simply for democracy and freedom of movement. The scepticism in the audience was well founded. By mid-1990 the USSR had agreed to remove its forces from Czechoslovakia and Hungary by mid-1991, from Poland by 1993 and from East Germany by 1994.[4] In the event, all Soviet airbases were returned to Poland in 1992 and all but one squadron had left Germany by the end of 1993.

Even without any other complications, the impact of a redeployment on such a scale, completed for the most part in less than three years, on operational effectiveness was devastating. It was, however, accompanied by the dismantling of the Warsaw Treaty Organisation so that the air-defence network of radar, interceptors and missiles which had stretched like a seamless web from the forward tactical surface-to-air batteries, through the co-ordinated national sectors back to the Soviet heartland itself, was demolished. In Moscow, the concern was not so much with the sudden 'vulnerability' of erstwhile allies, but the disappearance of the air-defence glacis protecting the vulnerable western flank of the USSR itself. Offensive capabilities were equally incapacitated. As has been explained, the regiments deployed in eastern Europe had a vitally important role in the WTO's aerial preparation and subsequent all-arms offensive. A very high proportion of the SAF aircraft withdrawn from their forward bases did not have the range to reach back and sustain a threat to western Europe.

Where possible, aircraft were recovered to bases where similar types were already located, but the recovery and housing of servicemen and their families was a very different problem which caused widespread bitterness and resentment at all rank levels. Various figures for the military homeless were given. In October 1991 Lt.-Gen. Abrak Aiupov, Deputy Commander-in-Chief of VVS said that there were then 200,000 homeless airforce servicemen and families. He shared the belief of many colleagues that the withdrawals were taking place too quickly: 'Even three years would be acceptable'. He hated being seen as a propagandist when he visited the homeless and was unable to give them any hope for improvement in the foreseeable future. His personal irritation was aggravated by a need to allocate overstretched funds to land reclamation in Germany, 'to replace earth two metres deep', to remove 'all concrete and buildings' and to make payments to Poles for the transit of personnel and equipment by rail.[5] Yet despite so many difficulties, the Deputy Commander-in-Chief was in no doubt about his priority: 'To maintain alert'. That comment was made at the end of a most courteous and frank conversation three years after Gorbachev's first arms control initiative; 15 months after NATO's July 1990 Declaration; 11 months after the signing of the CFE Treaty; two months after the failed coup of August 1991, and, perhaps most significantly, nine months after *Desert Storm*.

The Impact of the Gulf War

The overwhelming Coalition victory in the Gulf War was, for the Soviet armed forces, and especially the VVS, the realisation of a nightmare. In May 1984, the then Chief of the Soviet General Staff and First Minister of Defence, Marshal N. V. Ogarkov, was asked by a *Red Star* reporter, 'What do the basic changes in military matters consist of today?' In view of the Marshal's position, and the use of the daily military newspaper as the medium for the message, it may be assumed that his answer represented the views of the General Staff. In fact, his sentiments were to be widely repeated, and developed, surviving a superficial eclipse during the period of lip-service to 'defensive defence' and reasonable sufficiency.[6]

In the *Red Star* interview, the Marshal observed that a 'qualitative leap' was taking place in conventional weaponry which would inevitably change the preparation and conduct of operations, 'in qualitatively new, incomparably more destructive forms than before.' He argued that 'automated search and destroy complexes, long-range, high-accuracy, terminally-guided combat systems . . . and qualitatively new electronic control systems [made it possible] immediately to extend active combat operations not just to the border regions, but to the whole country's territory which was not possible in past wars.'[7]

Previously, Soviet doctrine had held that destruction of enemy assets by conventional firepower could only be achieved 'successively, not simultaneously'. Now, because of the developments identified by Ogarkov, there was the possibility of simultaneous, and immediate, destruction throughout the enemy's depth.[8] Such a development presented a serious threat, in operational and strategic depths, to the rear services. One other authoritative observation in 1984 was equally prescient: 'The destruction of truck columns with material means, dumps and bases, railroad stock, transport aircraft located at airfields, large bridges and other targets in the operational and strategic rear may result in the disruption of the support of entire formations (divisions, brigades) and large formations (fronts, armies, corps).' Worse still, 'The situation is even more aggravated if the enemy succeeds in conducting a massive strike on communications and other targets.'[9] Such concerns were not to be substantiated in eastern Europe, but they materialised dramatically in the Gulf. It was hardly surprising that many Soviet commentators believed that they saw NATO strategy applied by largely NATO forces drawing upon equipment and weapons designed for use in Europe. Indeed, the nightmare may have been even worse, because Ogarkov and his contemporaries had believed that even with the application of new technologies, operations would still extend over many months, not a few weeks.[10]

The impact of the Gulf War, and especially the dominant period of *Desert Storm*, reverberated among Soviet planning and policy staffs for several months, with results which will be examined below in the context of potential VVS reconstitution. In January 1991, the then Commander in Chief of VVS gave an interesting interview to the VVS 'house' journal, *Aviation and Cosmonautics*. Internal evidence strongly suggests that it was completed before the outbreak of *Desert Storm* and subsequently 'massaged' to include references to it. The preamble to the interview and all the questions put to General Shaposhnikov were concerned with the implication of domestic events in 1990 for military aviation. On three occasions in the context of long, wide-ranging comments on the problems facing him, he 'mentioned' the Gulf, and each reference was fractionally out of context:

Between staff training and flying accident rates: 'Means to repel a massed air attack, the countering of 'Stealth' aircraft, with the widespread use of radio-electronic systems and other such measures have been developed.' Later, between concern about the sustained threat from US and other NATO armed forces and the CFE residue, 'Moreover, the war in the Persian Gulf area exacerbates the situation and the military power of Japan and South Korea is growing'; and finally, in between general principles of flying training and command responsibilities, 'We intend to conduct multifaceted tactical flying exercises reflecting the contingency of a mass air attack by an enemy seeking to knock out our airfields and gain air superiority. Emphasis will be upon planning the protection of our aircraft from such attack, the employment of electronic countermeasures and new methods of dealing with stealth aircraft.'[11]

Early Soviet military comments on *Desert Storm* were generally defensive and often contradictory, seeking to exculpate Soviet military advisers and technology from the debacle, accusing the Western media of exaggerated claims of success, castigating Iraqi incompetence and ascribing Coalition victory to overwhelming numerical superiority.[12] The com-

ments attributed to General Shaposhnikov, however, went to the heart of
real Soviet concern. At the very time that the USSR had lost her air defensive glacis the worst fears expressed by General Ogarkov and his
colleagues had actually been exceeded in the brevity and comprehension
of the immediate, simultaneous attack on Iraq. The Commander-in-Chief
knew better than most that his reassuring observations on the Soviet
Union's ability to respond to an attack were little more than whistling in
the dark.

In June 1991 the author addressed 150 members of the Soviet General
Staff in the Ministry of Defence in Moscow, on changes in NATO policy,
and, tangentially, the Gulf War. The first question received, in a polite but
antagonistic series, was 'In the light of the unequal CFE reductions and the
changed circumstances in eastern Europe, how would *you* provide for
Soviet air defence?'

The Disintegration of the USSR

The perennial Soviet paranoia about surprise attack, ambivalently fed by
memories of June 1941 and by the USSR's own concepts of concealment,
deception and surprise, was even further exacerbated by the events of the
following six months. In the aftermath of the failed August 1991 coup, the
Soviet Union itself began to disintegrate. The General Staff strove in vain
to preserve united defence forces within a Commonwealth of Independent
States (CIS). But in a matter of months the defences of Moscow had moved
from the western ramparts on the Elbe to the banks of the Dvina and
Dniepr. The process was subsequently summarised by Minister of Defence
Pavel Grachev:

> On the basis of the Warsaw Pact we created the first and main strate-
> gic zone, a springboard for further offensive action . . . [where] elite
> forces were concentrated . . . When the two Germanies united and the
> Warsaw Pact collapsed, the main sector of defence moved towards our
> state border . . . After rebasing part of our best forces, we had to use
> these forces to man the Belorussian, Transcarpathian, Odessa and
> Kiev Military Districts [MD]. Following Ukraine's instantaneous pri-
> vatisation of the three MDs on her territory, we are in an
> exceptionally difficult position. . . . The Moscow MD has effectively
> become a border MD.[13]

In other words, the majority of forward airbases, logistic depots, early
warning radars, command and control units and every other item in a co-
ordinated, military structure was either in ruins or beyond Moscow's
control. To aggravate the situation still further, many regiments redeployed

from eastern Europe were allocated to bases in Belorussia, Ukraine or the Caucasus area, while others, for example the two TU-160 *Blackjack* squadrons at Priluki, Ukraine, had been based there from the outset in the days of the monolithic USSR. In January 1992, Moscow air staff members assured Western journalists that the TU-160s were part of the CIS strategic forces, directly subordinated to the Chief of the Commonwealth Forces, while demands by the Ukrainian defence ministry for the transfer of TU-22 *Backfire* C missile carriers were refused.[14] Two weeks later, the Ukrainian Ministry of Defence confirmed that it was assuming command and control of the TU-160s, even though Ukrainian air force officers privately conceded that they lacked specialist lubricants and access to spares.[15]

Nor were the problems restricted to the western flank. In early 1992, one General observed, 'It's going to be difficult to defend ourselves in the event of a military conflict. The first strategic echelon is completely destroyed, and this is not a secret. The reason is that to create the forces of the first echelon we put everything into the border areas – Kiev, Carpathian, Baltic Military Districts, etc. That's why we wanted to include the air defences in the [CIS] Strategic Forces and count them as collective security means. But it unfortunately didn't happen, so everything collapsed. And, in the Transcaucasian district, we dismantled all radar posts because they were attacked more often than combat units. In other words, our defences, especially in the south are tremendously weakened. And, if we have to fight, this can only be done by forces deployed to the centre. The centralised defence system does not exist any more.'[16]

Of particular concern in Moscow was the loss to that system of a number of early warning radar stations which provided warning of ballistic missile, as well as aircraft attack. Even in an age marked by agreements between the USA and the USSR on nuclear weapon reductions, old Russian fears died hard and were probably further sustained by the proliferation of *Scud* derivatives and long-range Chinese systems at several points across the long Russian southern and eastern frontiers. Disintegration of the Union threatened to remove radars in Latvia, Belarus, Ukraine, Azerbaijan and Kazakhstan from the network, inevitably leaving large gaps beyond the ability of Soviet satellites to monitor reliably.

Such was the deterioration of relations between Latvia and Russia, for example, that the Baltic state was not prepared to make any distinction between Russian army troops on the streets of Riga and Russian air-defence force technicians operating the radar station at Skrunda. The advantages to Latvia of negotiating and benefiting jointly from the early warning network were completely outweighed by sensitivities over principles of sovereignty and practical difficulties of providing access.[17] Confidence in missile early warning is an essential ingredient in strategic nuclear deterrence and stability. Without it, alert states are reduced and the risk of miscalculation is increased. Such fears lay behind the rather vigorous warnings by Commander-in-Chief of Strategic Missile Forces General Yu Maksimov, that the early warning system, 'cannot be decomposed [sic] but only eliminated, thereby threatening life on the planet.'[18]

On 19 March 1992 Belorussia followed the Ukrainian example of November 1991 and announced that all air defence, tactical aviation and bomber regiments on its territory would become part of the Belorussian Armed Forces.[19] Similar action was taken within the Russian Federation itself by the Chechen Republic and the Caucasus Confederation, as well as by the other republics. Independent Russian armed forces were authorised by President Yeltsin's decree on 7 May 1992. Continuity was sought by entrusting the functions of command and control over the troops to the structures of 'the former Defence Ministry and the General Staff of the USSR.'[20] And so, in less than the span of an average Western military tour of duty, the General Staff in Moscow had been responsible for an international alliance, then the USSR itself, then the Commonwealth of Independent States, and finally, or at least for the time being, Russia alone.

The fragmentation of the Soviet armed forces among the republics during 1992 had particularly severe implications for air and air defence forces. Whereas ground forces were structured in comparatively discrete formations within military districts, Soviet air power was co-ordinated and integrated: across the Union tightly for air defence, loosely for the interaction between strategic assets, such as long-range bombers, transports, tankers and reconnaissance/AWACs, tactical aviation and army aviation. The cumulative impact of the fragmentation was described by VVS Commander-in-Chief Deynikin:

> In my opinion you could compare the current situation in the Army with the evacuation in 1941: the only difference is that in those days we could transfer to the depths of Russia all our property down to the last split pin. Nowadays however our best equipped formations, from the point of view of aircraft, have stayed on the territory of other republics of the former union. We are now obliged to begin laying the foundations of Russia's Air Force.[21]

Ukrainian 'nationalisation' of 24 TU-95Ms, 19 TU-160 *Blackjacks* and IL-76 Transports particularly impaired Russian strategic capabilities.

Political disintegration immediately began to dissipate the former Soviet Union's air power, but the ability of the Russian Air Force to rejuvenate was further impaired by the impact of that disintegration on the aerospace industry of the former Soviet Union.

Turmoil in the Aerospace Industry

The General Staff understood the implications for the Soviet defence industries of Marshal Ogarkov's analysis of significant trends in warfare, but
had been concerned about the state of the Soviet economy and its inability,
without its reforming and restructuring, to mass produce new weapons
technology. There is little doubt that Gorbachev's early calls for *glasnost*
and *perestroika*, designed to modernise the Soviet economy, and hence
provide the wherewithal to re-equip the Soviet armed forces, were welcomed by the Soviet military. Similarly, his diplomatic offensive designed
to reduce external expenditure and elicit Western economic assistance,
could at first be welcomed by the military-industrial complex.

The domestic miscalculations, the false starts and the implications of
diplomatic success but economic failure were not welcomed. From 1985 to
1992, the Soviet Union and its successor states moved from economic stag-
nation to collapse and a major casualty was the aerospace industry. As
previously explained in Chapter Four, the desired industrial base was
clearly specified by senior military officers: 'What is demanded today for
series production of modern weaponry, the newest combat technologies, is
not common or ordinary but the most modern machine tools, robotics, the
latest generation of computers and flexible production systems.'[22] Or
again, two years into the Gorbachev period, 'In the struggle for improvement in the technical equipping of the military, it is difficult to
overestimate the basic trends of scientific-technical progress: the further
priority development of machine-building, especially machine-tool manufacturing, robotics, computer technology, instrument making and
micro-electronics. It is exactly these trends which are today the basic cata-
lysts of military-technical progress.'[23] The aerospace industry should have
been at the leading edge of the technological expansion.

In fact, 'It was recognition that the Soviet economy was militarily over-
burdened that led Gorbachev to take action at the end of 1988 to reduce
budget expenditure on the armed forces.'[24] Eight Soviet ministries
employed over nine million people supported in non-industrial activities by
another three million. In addition, almost all industries were involved to
some extent in military production while the Ministry of Defence had its
own research, repair and maintenance establishments. Military demands
extended further into the economy because of a perceived need to be able
to mobilise in crisis to face the USA and NATO. Military standards were
therefore imposed on civilian trucks, civilian transport aircraft and engines
and on the nuclear, space and communications industries.[25] The defence
complex had first claim on national resources but prices for the products
were kept low by artificially-fixed input prices which bore no relation to
the costs involved. The labour force was stable and sustained by privileged

rates of pay plus comparatively high standards of housing, welfare and other social facilities. For example, the Sukhoi complex in Novosibirsk included 270 housing blocks, 20 nurseries, polyclinics, a rest home, a Palace of Culture, and a sports stadium as well as the 'normal' industrial provision of on-site free restaurants and medicare. 'Given the distorted price and cost structures and a multitude of channels for concealed subsidisation, neither Moscow-based officials nor enterprise managers had any real understanding of the true costs involved in producing weapons for the Soviet armed forces.'[26] Indeed, despite the magnitude of the state system, no-one knew exactly how many civilians were employed in the military-industrial complex: a fact which further complicated attempts by Gorbachev to reform it.[27]

Overall, according to one authoritative British analyst, 'Defence accounted for perhaps 70 per cent of all research and development carried out in the USSR, manufacture for about 30 per cent of the GDP, employing 12 million out of 42 million industrial workers. In total, defence expenditure probably reached about 30 per cent of the GDP during the last 30 years of Communist rule.'[28] The defence sector was the most capable part of the former Soviet economy, but it contained many endemic weaknesses. Much machinery, including high-technology Western imports was poorly maintained and misused. In the best factories, productivity per worker was only one-tenth to one-eighth of that in advanced industrial countries, with reject rates for electronic components, for example, several orders of magnitude higher and energy consumption five to ten times higher than in western Europe for similar production.[29]

With *glasnost* came the revelations of what those industrial weaknesses had meant for aircraft, weapons and maintenance. In October 1989, Colonel General V. M. Shishkin, Chief Engineer VVS, reviewed progress in the improvement of aircraft maintenance, including improved liaison between the Air Force and industry. Self-financing in industry had improved production quality but some equipment remained inadequate. Every aircraft had unreliable components; many hundreds of man-hours were wasted correcting faults. There was no collective responsibility for poor work and quality was not yet tied in to output for bonuses. It was hoped that an economic stimulus would produce tighter sanctions against shoddy work.[30] In the same journal a critical article identified design faults and technical weaknesses in the TU-160, although as it was being compared with the less than perfect B-1B at the time, this could be placed in the context of the teething problems of many combat aircraft.

No such benefit of the doubt could be given to other observations. They included a *Backfire* loss due to wing structural failure caused by 'a defect in the design and manufacture of the aircraft'; the need to spend 'enormous sums' to correct manufacturing weaknesses which 'continue long after' the 'warranty' period; lack of industrial competition which results not just in 'rouble losses', but also 'the lives of our pilots'; separate funding of science and production; constant changes in aircraft design without interchangeable parts, units and assemblies.[31] 'The seductive myth that in the field of aircraft construction we had nothing but excellence and an efficient system' was demolished as the Ministry of Aviation and its designers lost their protection from criticism.[32]

The aerospace industry was therefore not in the best of health even before the events of the late 1980s. Then, in rapid succession, the government cut back aircraft orders as a result of the CFE Treaty and reduced budgetary provision accordingly. Between 1988 and 1991 military procurement was cut by 29 per cent and R & D by 22 per cent.[33] In the same period the aviation industry was directed to begin conversion from military to civilian production. In 1990 it was ordered to provide 'an increase in commercial engine production by 9.1 per cent, in consumer goods by a factor of 1.6, machinery for light industry and the food industry by a factor of 1.3 and machinery for the agro-industrial complex by a factor of 2.2.'[34]

Industrial conversion on the scale envisaged in the USSR had no precedent; there were no guidelines. US experience after World War II was examined but there were more contrasts than similarities. The USSR had no 'pre-war' structure to revert to; there was no free-market expertise and, great as the USA's war effort had been, its proportional consumption of national resources was far smaller than that of the USSR's defence complex. Conversion was complicated by a simultaneous desire to introduce market principles into the command economy. How far could central directives be imposed and how far should new products be determined by market forces when no process existed for measuring the extent of market demand? Indeed, how far could any conversion be taken when the General Staff continued to insist upon a residual capacity to mobilise in competition with the USA which, they insisted, could increase its tank production to 50,000 within 12 months?[35]

Those conversion measures which were centrally directed were often illogical and counterproductive. The engine repair facilities at Rybinsk were inadequate to cope with a backlog of 150 engines, but the plant was directed to begin making macaroni. The Soyuz metallurgical research plant was tasked with tooling-up to manufacture equipment for the starch and syrup industry, rather than for much needed civilian aircraft engines; the Klimov engine factory in Leningrad was directed to build machinery for the shoe industry, which interfered with the MiG-29 engine production lines. Conversion was often perceived to be the production of inferior products at the cost of impairing the residual defence capacity. In one cameo, the general director of the MV Frunze aero-engine plant in Kuybyshev described what the 'policy' meant in practice. After expressing hopes that his factory could expand production of power drives for the gas industry, already earning hard currency by export, he complained about the lack of funding for retooling and expansion. But then:

> This year we are going to start making sieves for starch. This even sounds funny. After all, ever since 1912 we've been making aeroplane engines. And now they've decided to put the association to work on something else. The level we operate at today is a level it's taken us decades to reach. We've got specialists who can make any kind of engine conceivable. But now in addition they're going to have to start making starch sieves. People just don't want to go into this kind of work. You're going to have to drive them to it, because they pay you kopecks and it's ridiculously labour-intensive to boot. There's no mechanisation, no automation. We are going to have to start at square one here, just about back at the point where you have to cobble things out on your knee. How in the world can we be expected to make a good quality product if this is something we're doing under compulsion?
>
> I think it's high time we speak up loud and clear on the situation we are in when it comes to this conversion business. We should be building facilities that will specialise in the production of consumer goods, facilities capable of operating at high levels of labour efficiency and productivity. If our aircraft plants have to go on making products that they're not cut out to make, then not too far ahead there's going to be trouble. One very senior colleague took a look at how we were making gears for a high-precision aircraft engine and declared, 'You know, I'm not going to be accepting any engines from you, and I wouldn't issue any certificate for this product.' And he's right. After all, can you really make components for aircraft engines and other industrial products on the same machines? But in our case there aren't any other production capacities available.[36]

The speaker was, of course, representative of those who had a vested interest in the status quo of the defence complex but even after removal of the subjective tone, the practical implications of conversion on the factory floor and its potentially disruptive impact on the flow of equipment from factory to squadrons is apparent.

At the same time as defence funding was reduced, so managers were directed to charge 'market' prices for their products. At a procurement meeting in Moscow in June 1991, Defence Minister Yazov was allegedly asked the market price for the first time, and without warning, for the next batch of 50 SU-27 *Flankers* and associated equipment. He reacted angrily by cutting the order to 25 and blustering that if that was to be the cost of new technology he would preserve the existing force structure with its current weapons. He was not prepared to cut force size to pay for improved technology.[37] In 1992 the Air Force could not afford to buy any MiG-29s or SU-27s and the orders for helicopters and military aircraft in 1993 were expected to be less than 15 per cent of the total in 1991.[38]

The descent into industrial chaos was accelerated by the break-up of the USSR during 1992, compounding the impact on the VVS of the separation of Air Force units among the republics. While only 10 per cent of Ministry of Aviation industry lay outside Russia, 35 per cent of electronics-related production and research organisations, including radio, computers and radar, anti-aircraft, anti-missile, control and navigation systems, electronic components, microcomputers, lasers and telephone and other communications equipment, were located in other republics.[39] Two accidents of geography, the location of the main Antonov production plant at Kiev, in Ukraine, and the Ilyushin IL-76 factory at Tashkent, in Uzbekistan, will complicate Russian reconstruction of its military transport force; but the location of the SU-25 plant at Tblisi, in Georgia, is likely to be less disruptive if the VVS does, in fact, concentrate on the procurement of multi-role aircraft.

Meanwhile, the demise of the Ministry of Aviation in 1992 was followed by the competition of design bureaux and production establishments to secure government funding, exports and foreign co-operation. In early 1993 the Chief of the Russian Air Force Main Staff, General of Aviation Anatoliy Maliukov, was unable to give exact figures on the current and expected strengths of the Air Force, nor on the forthcoming Air Force budget. He was, however, fully aware of the importance of sustaining an indigenous aviation industry, 'The problem for Russian military aviation is mainly that we can't buy a new series of aircraft. Our budget barely leaves us in a condition to exploit our existing force, but in order that our aircraft industry doesn't completely die, we have ordered a few aircraft, literally just a few of several types: TU-160s, SU-24s and SU-27s. We haven't ordered MiG-29s or SU-25s.'[40]

The full significance of orders of 'a few aircraft, literally just a few' is apparent, when compared with reliable British estimates in 1980 of Soviet production of 1,300 combat aircraft per year. If the Russian Air Force is to regain its international power and prestige, it would have to be accompanied by a revitalisation of the aerospace industry.

Internal Corrosion

For most of the period of confrontation, Western assessments of Warsaw Pact air power were heavily dominated by quantification, known familiarly and in some areas disparagingly, as 'the bean count'. It was understandable. It was much more reliable to count the numbers of aircraft on an East German airbase than to evaluate the combined impact of combat effectiveness of individual Soviet aircrew, or work out the sum of intangibles including the minutes in each sortie allocated to specific tasks, or the efficiency of groundcrew, or the motivation of conscripts, or the impact of the political commissar, or qualities of leadership, or even under what circumstances and with what determination a Polish pilot would loyally support a Russian or East German colleague against a NATO opponent. A possible clue to Soviet expectations about the last question was given sardonically to the author by a Russian general in Moscow in July 1989, before the collapse of the Warsaw Pact, in the context of the CFE negotiations: 'Why do you assume we have an advantage in reinforcing the central region? Which would you rather do, fly across the Atlantic or march across Poland?' In the light of events since 1989, his cynicism may not have been misplaced.

The West knew the size and deployment of the Warsaw Pact air forces, and thanks to Afghan defectors, was also aware of the details of the air component in any combined arms offensive against NATO. Assessments of potential effectiveness had to be anchored in fact, and interpretations had to assume the efficient use of equipment. Defensive plans based on any other assumptions could have proved disastrously negligent in war. The dangers of threat over-assessment, as long as it stopped short of deification, were far less than those of underestimation.

From observation of Soviet training, and from study of Soviet journals, there were obvious weaknesses, by Western standards. Aircrew flying hours were relatively low; flying training was stereotyped: since 1970 commanders had regularly called for more initiative from their subordinates; there were constant rivalries and jealousies between squadron commanders and squadron political officers; maintenance was usually carried out, rather than simply supervised, by engineer senior NCOs and officers. Some of these 'weaknesses' were perhaps the price paid for alternative operating procedures. For example, if the Soviet Air Force intended to launch a massive pre-emptive attack and had to depart and return over the densest surface-to-air defences in the world, there was a lot to be said for conformity, tight ground control and predictability. Soviet pilots were not trained to handle 'one-on-one', and least of all 'one-on-several' air-to-air engagements. And if officers got their hands dirty, but there were enough of them, the absence of junior airmen was irrelevant. Mirror images, applying

Western standards and operational requirements to the Soviet Air Forces, could be misleading.[41]

When the spirit of *glasnost* released decades of pent-up criticism across the Soviet Union, servicemen happily joined in. There is now a welter of 'evidence' of problems and weaknesses in the Soviet armed forces, not least in the air forces. Two caveats should be applied when their cumulative impression is examined. First, anyone who has spent any time in a barracks or squadron crew room, or as a senior officer has stayed on late at a unit dinner night, will know that British servicemen can hold their own internationally when criticising the system, their equipment, their personnel management, and especially their senior commanders. Early servicing and operational problems with the F-15, F-16, *Tornado* F-3, and B-1B and recurring servicing difficulties in some other air force areas should induce caution about criticism in the Soviet press about their new aircraft. Second, *glasnost* was the new party line, and senior commanders who had previously been implementing a suffocating policy of secrecy and inhibition now paraded their virtues of openness and the encouragement of free speech. Just a touch, perhaps, of Mao's 'hundred flowers blooming' two decades earlier.

That said, the evidence was too extensive, too specific, too repetitive and too similar from too many rank levels for any caveat to be very significant. One common thread, however, should not be underestimated: underlying many criticisms were a sense of hurt pride, frustrated professionalism and a genuine desire for reform, rather than rejection or destruction. While still commanding the VVS Group of Soviet Forces Germany, in 1988, the then Lt.-Gen. Shaposhnikov publicly criticised his subordinate commanders for preferring slogans and exhortations to competence and responsibility. Commander and officer training were unsatisfactory, while senior pilots were actually losing rather than consolidating their flight competence, 'Today's training requirements demand a new approach.'[42] Fifteen months later, in his new position as First Deputy Commander, VVS in Moscow he repeated the need for 'an understanding of the new approach to combat readiness', involving, as usual, collective initiative, responsibility and the implementation of progressive ideas; in sum, 'a need for fundamental improvement to political and combat training.'[43]

The General's reference to a need for both 'political' and 'combat' training revision illustrated a dual responsibility which, in peacetime at least, had dogged the Soviet armed forces since the first commissar had been appointed to monitor the post-imperial tendencies of officers who had come over to the Red armies during and after the Revolution.

The full residual extent of the political officer's responsibilities were expressed by Colonel General of Aviation, Member of the Military

Council and Commander of the Political Directorate of the Air Forces L. Batekhin in February 1988. He emphasised the importance of individual party work with pilots which was being impaired by a preoccupation with paper work. Then, his account of the responsibilities of the political officer imperceptibly merged with those associated in the West with the squadron commander: 'There are far too many instances of unit checks not being done properly . . . of falsification of reports to conceal glowing errors; discipline problems are causing concern; some units are far too lenient with safety violations; there is apathy in planning and execution of flights, an inability to read instruments, bad interaction amongst crews . . . the level of accepted responsibility must be raised to ensure that the commander of the formation political department is responsible for all the most dangerous potential incidents . . . it is the local party organisations and individual Communists who will effect the changes in the air forces: changes in the organisation of flying, the content and methods in the new combat training documents, the new methods of tactical flying training . . .'[44]

This quotation illustrates the penalty paid by the Air Force for the political control by the Communist Party. It was a penalty which prompted oblique references, but seldom an overt criticism. Not surprisingly, because annual reports were written by the political officers. Promotion boards were manned by political officers. 'Why else', asked one young military trainee of the author in June 1990, 'do you think we have such rubbish up there?' 'If you don't include a political assessment on your annual reports, how do you maintain control of your officers?' asked a member of staff of the Lenin Military Political Academy. Until the paralysing grip of the Communist Party was loosed from the air force, exhortations from senior commanders for initiative, progressive thinking and individual responsibility would continue to be frustratingly and irritatingly ineffectual to those who did wish to improve professional standards.

The debilitating impact of 'formalism' spread throughout the unit's activities. Achievements were measured by periodic statistical returns. Exercises were carried out by more senior aircrew. Aircrew arrived on squadrons deficient in basic aircraft handling and combat manoeuvring. Senior pilots given responsibility for their juniors' development were often incompetent and blasé. Standards crews commented on 'first class' pilots who could not handle their aircraft properly. One *Fencer* crew failed a local tactical evaluation exercise because it could not locate the target, was not competent with its equipment, had poor liaison with its ground-crew and finally attempted to 'fix' its exercise grading.

Western audiences marvelled at the handling characteristics of the demonstration MiG-29 at Farnborough in 1989, unaware that other MiG crews were grumbling that no information on this experience was being relayed to junior pilots, nor for that matter was much else either. One helicopter squadron commander sent his crews away to another base to do their continuation training because he did not want anything to do with it in case something went wrong.

Flight safety was a constant preoccupation, with much to be preoccupied about.[45] In 1988, 75 per cent of incidents were alleged to be caused by human error: stalling, too low level, unauthorised changes in combat order, and mid-air collisions. The great majority of losses in Afghanistan were non-combat. Inevitably, and not unique to the Soviet air forces, there were two different points of view regarding cause and effect. One, usually associated with the Political Directorate, emphasised good discipline, lack of complacency and strict adherence to regulations, usually in a spirit of 'Socialist competition'. The other demanded that a pilot should become total master of his machine, claiming that an overemphasis on flight safety led to simplification and stereotype.

One splendid contribution to the debate came from a much-respected World War II test and fighter pilot, Marshal of Aviation, Hero of the Soviet Union, Alexander Silentiev: 'Why should pilots not enjoy their work to the best of their ability? They should not be stopped from understanding and using their machines completely, even future transport pilots who some say will not need aerobatics. The detractors of aerobatic flying say that it is not within the interests of flight safety. I say there is far less risk if every pilot has been taught to fly with total mastery of his profession.'[46]

Nor was human error confined to aircrew. Colonel General Shishkin, the VVS Chief Engineer, criticised low states of combat readiness, slipshod rectification, lack of supervision, unnecessary 'scheduled' maintenance, inadequacy of military college engineer graduates, weak discipline and poor liaison between engineers and aircrew.[47]

Problems were exacerbated by the arrival of squadrons of 'third and later generation aircraft', rendering traditional visual and mechanised fault location obsolete because of the density and complexity of the electronic equipment. New methods of fault diagnosis and repair were required, but the shortage of microcomputers, outdated instructions and 'artificial barriers' were impeding the introduction of new systems.[48] In passing, this engineer observer highlighted the interaction of industrial accounting and air force maintenance: 'Economically it is often not beneficial for a repair firm to adopt the [new] system because the number of spares used counts as production and any reduction affects the economic indices.'

Nonetheless, in February 1989 the then Commander-in-Chief VVS, Marshal Yefimov, could still confidently state that, 'Now, Soviet doctrine complicates combat training by insisting on defence capability through

improvements in qualitative parameters . . . The technology, its exploitation and training for it are the chief problems of the Air Forces.'[49] Then
came withdrawals from eastern Europe, economic collapse and defence
cuts. General Shaposhnikov, who replaced Marshal Yefimov in August
1990, was asked in January 1991 what he found 'unsatisfactory in the
organisation of military life'. He replied, 'It would certainly be easier and
quicker to list what satisfies me, so many problems have been accumulated.'[50] This interview with *Aviation & Cosmonautics* presents the single
most authoritative picture of the state of the air forces at the time, and
could have been substantiated with scores of contemporary articles and
comments. His salient points were the following:

> The struggle for power, the expanding political activity within our
> nation, have given rise to confrontation among various groups,
> nationalists, extremists, etc. [which] naturally affects the morale of
> service personnel and compels us to use non-orthodox approaches to
> the training of aviators . . .
>   . . . a surplus of aircrew and a shortage of engineering staff . . .
> without a satisfactory service infrastructure . . . exacerbated by the
> imbalance of the state economic supply mechanism . . .
>   . . . efforts to reduce the flying accident rate have not always led to
> the forecast result [caused by] unsettled domestic circumstances of air-
> men, the reduction of flying hours, morale-psychological tension and
> people's current lack of confidence . . . several dozen flying accidents
> [in 1990], of which 60 per cent were not answerable to faulty equip-
> ment . . .
>   The unforeseen policies of several Union Republics' governments
> have provoked a series of crimes by servicemen . . . the number of
> deserters has increased. Crime rate has increased by 20 per cent . . .
> several hundred men have been killed or received severe injury. This is
> fewer than in the preceding year but how can we have norms in such
> matters when it is human life we are talking about?
>   Union republics have interrupted conscript call-up – as a result we
> have units reporting a shortfall in personnel . . . we are now employ-
> ing soldiers of the Soviet army . . . levels of discipline and flight safety
> show no improvement in the Air Forces' higher training colleges . . .
>   . . . because of tardy deliveries of spares and components from the
> rear services of the Air Forces up to 300 aeroplanes and helicopters
> stand idle each day . . .

This last statement appeared to contradict an earlier comment that 'despite
the complex nature of contemporary equipment with its all-too-frequent

failures, the engineers and mechanics managed to sustain an aircraft serviceability state of 90 per cent', begging the question, 90 per cent of what?

This was General Shaposhnikov's survey in 1991. It preceded the withdrawal of squadrons from East Germany and Poland, the disintegration of
the USSR, the further collapse of the economy and the aerospace industrial
base, and the full evaluation of the Gulf War. It is reasonable to assume
therefore that the conditions described by the Commander-in-Chief had
deteriorated still further by the time he in turn handed over to Colonel
General Petr Deiniken, after the August 1991 coup, on his promotion to
Defence Minister of the USSR. It is, however, just possible that his frank
appraisal of the situation in January 1991 may come to be seen as a turning point in the fortunes of Soviet – later, Russian – air power. In addition
to its catalogue of problems, it also described remedial measures in hand
and identified a wide range of further requirements. Flying hours were
being more carefully prepared, instructional methods improved, new
instructions deployed, and 'qualitative' rather than quantitative parameters
imposed, i.e., by the content of training sorties rather than their endurance.
Temporarily, priority in hours was being given to junior rather than more
experienced pilots. Further withdrawals and redeployments would first be
modelled in command and staff exercises to avoid previous mistakes.
Personal responsibility for various withdrawal activities would be given to
specific directors.

Exercises and training would reflect current realities. Training for what
would be necessary in war, would depend on the independent activity of
generals and officers, reasonable initiative, resourcefulness and a wise
understanding of risks. The air forces' higher colleges had to be improved,
a continuous pattern of officer progression between operational duties
and higher education and training would be developed. The engineering
and other technical support services would be improved, although not
immediately because of the accelerated withdrawal of forces from outside
the country.

Altogether it was a tall order, especially as things were going to get
worse before they got better. Yet just three years later there were signs of
reconstitution. It would be a long time before Russian air power would
offer a serious international challenge, but in 1994 the first shoots of recovery were visible.

It was equally possible that the shoots would decay and die alongside a
seriously-wounded aerospace industry. Or, even if the industry were rejuvenated, Russian air power could remain stunted by the short-sightedness
of army-orientated doctrine. Even if both the industrial base and military
thought were to flourish, the air forces might revert to old Soviet habits of
rigidity, stereotyping, suffocation of initiatives, buck-passing and elevation

by mediocrity. On the other hand, there could be a restorative congruence of interests and events.

Reconstitution: the Aerospace Industry

Opposition to conversion from vested interests within the defence complex continued. They received strong support from the ranks of the opponents of President Yeltin's economic reforms, including Communist Party members, nationalists who associated Soviet power with the defence complex and those military who still believed an industrial mobilisation capability was required. But during 1993, an alternative conversion programme began to emerge, emanating from Yeltsin's reforming supporters who were also concerned about the social and economic impact of 'conversion'.

It was associated with Andrei Kokoshin, Yeltsin's Deputy Defence Minister, a well-connected, ex-national Komsomol official who had elected for an academic rather than a political career in the 1970s. He had specialised in international security and achieved an international reputation as a fluent English-speaking defence analyst and reformer. In late 1992 he chaired a new Council for Military Technical Policy, comprising scientists, designers, economists and enterprise directors of the defence industry.[51] The procurement priorities specified by the Council were the maintenance of the 'strategic deterrent', development of precision-guided munitions, communications and reconnaissance, early warning and control, mobile forces equipment, and 'the elimination of inherited imbalances'.[52]

Kokoshin had used *Red Star* previously to air his views on conversion: it had failed, targets had been given to enterprises without reference to capital costs or subsequent competitiveness. Such scientific and technical strength was concentrated in the defence industry that it could become a most important component of the market economy. Russia needed to standardise its military equipment: 26 types of surface-to-air missile complex, for example, compared with the USA's four. There was a need to determine which enterprises would leave the defence complex and be converted, and by implication which should be encouraged. In some cases, weapon production should be transferred from other CIS countries to Russia in order to ensure complete independence in the most important areas.'[53]

In explaining military-technical policy goals, Kokoshin appealed to several interests: more emphasis on the modernisation of existing armaments; a reduction in the numbers of varieties; increasing interoperability; enhancement of mobilisation capabilities; reduction in the number of R&D establishments and particular priority to the development of dual-purpose technologies with both civil and military implications.[54]

The Kokoshin strategy therefore sought to resolve the dilemma of how to reconcile national interests with free-market forces, by identifying those sectors which would find a market and coordinating them within national planning. In the same period he proposed the adoption of a National Industrial Policy in which a central role would be played by a restructured defence industry. It would provide for Russia's security and act as a 'loco-motive' for the country's economic revival. Ownership would be mixed, with both state and private capital.[55] By early 1994 the proposals were supported across the Russian political spectrum and, if they materialised, could procure weapons for the Russian armed forces according to practices familiar in the West. It would however not be easy. Many in the defence complex would see 'dual-use technology' as a comfortable successor to previous practices. Civilian products and by-products would continue to emerge from establishments whose priorities were military and a preserved capacity for mobilisation. It was doubtful whether there would be a large enough domestic market to absorb the products. If not, it was a hard com-petitive international market beyond the frontiers. A prominent analyst of the Russian economy observed in late 1993, 'There is a real danger that the Russian economy will be partially remilitarised on a new basis, and in the absence of a strong domestic market for the high-technology civil goods, or export sales, substantial state budget support may be unavoidable, with potentially damaging consequences for the country's economic revitalisa-tion.'[56]

Nonetheless, for the first time in eight years a coherent plan for indus-trial reconstruction had been outlined, with some prospect for consensus. If it were to be successful, the priorities it had defined were highly relevant to the reconstitution of Russian air power.

Air Force Plans

Within the overall strategy, and amid the optimistic sales pitches of newly-converted aerospace market entrepreneurs, a core programme of aircraft and weapons could be discerned.

In August 1991, General Shaposhnikov indicated that the Soviet Air Force would introduce upgrades of *Fulcrum* and *Flanker* in 'the other half of the 1990s' and asserted the right of both the USA and the USSR to maintain the modern defence industrial base necessary to develop aircraft such as the USA's B-2 and F-22. 'If the onward movement is stopped . . . application of people's talents will be closed. Are the Soviet Union and the USA prepared for this? I don't think so.'[57]

Soon after the August coup attempt the direction was reinforced by the Deputy Minister of the Soviet Ministry of Aviation Industry, Vladimir Laptev, who confirmed a programme for upgraded variants of MiG-29 and SU-27, 'parallel' developments of a new generation of combat aircraft, and continued production of SU-24 and TU-160. Production for the Soviet Air Forces of MiG-29 and SU-25 would cease, although both would be offered for export.[58] That view either had not reached Tblisi, home of the SU-25, or it was overlooked two months later when SU-25 chief designer Vladimir Babak announced at the Dubai Air Show that an all-weather version would enter service in 1992.[59]

These conflicting statements are typical of many reported in the Western aviation press between 1991 and 1994. Old Western habits of reporting of Soviet combat aircraft died hard. Whereas the 'dreamsheets' and aspirations of Western aircraft manufacturers, paraded annually at locations such as Farnborough and Paris, were usually subject to a stringent professional scrutiny, the claims of Soviet and subsequently Russian salesmen were frequently printed as fact or, at least, without reference to conflicting evidence elsewhere. Three quite different strands may be identified, with decreasing levels of credibility. The first comprises the comments by senior air force officers referring to purchases or programmes. These are generally consistent and began to be substantiated in 1993 and 1994. The second comprises comments by officials like Laptev, who re-emerged in 1992 after the demise of the Aviation Ministry as 'President of the Russian Aviation Industry Union' whose differing statements probably reflected unpredictability and modifications in procurement decisions. The third comprises statements from newly-commercial locations such as the Mikoyan Design Bureau, which in 1992 was reported as having 'a counterpart to the USAF's Advanced Tactical Fighter' 'poised to make its first flight', 'a truly fantastic aircraft' known as the I.42.[60]

There was, however, still some doubt in 1993 whether the I.42 programme would survive. Neither of two prototypes had flown 18 months after designer Belyakov's confident statements. Indeed, he was later driven to complain of lack of support from the Russian Air Force for the new fighter, as lack of funding had stopped work on the aircraft's engines. His criticism prompted a slightly ambivalent but authoritative response from General of Aviation Maliukov, Russian Air Force Chief of the Main Staff: 'We can help them [Mikoyan] with extra cash injections, but it is hard to look ahead. We might save this programme through a big investment, but we are in a complicated position because the SU-27 is in production and new proposed modifications are wide-ranging and in principle will satisfy our requirements . . . [but] . . . We're not going to kill the programme. We will try by all means to save this work and we have some more freedom in the form of non-budgetary funding which has not been available until now ... from sales of surplus equipment and possibly from outside investors.'[61]

Such a statement was in accord with the reconstitution programme associated with Andrei Kokoshin and Mikhail Malei, but it was still some way from a confident assertion that I.42 would see squadron service. The comment assumed even greater authority because of the content and tenor of the particular interview given to *Jane's Defence Review* by General Maliukov. He believed that a period of disintegration had been survived and that now 'more or less we know on what we can depend, which factories, which supply bases, which units . . . our thoughts are turned to building a powerful air force'. But serious problems remained: 'We can't buy a new series of aircraft. Our budget barely leaves us in condition to exploit our existing force, but in order that our aircraft industry doesn't completely die, we have ordered a few aircraft, literally just a few of several types . . .'[62] Significantly, according to the General, those types were TU-160, SU-24 and SU-27, not MiG-29 and not SU-25.

He said that priority would be given to variations of SU-27, including fighter bomber and reconnaissance variants. Amid conflicting claims and forecasts over a period of three years, the reality and importance of the SU-27 programme was beyond doubt by 1994. In November 1993 Vladimir Laptev confirmed the presence of a military aviation plan agreed with industry, government and air force authorising the financing of a number of core aircraft programmes, including two new fighters, a next generation intermediate-range bomber and assorted transports and helicopters.[63] The two prototype I.42s would fly with existing engines; the upgraded SU-27/35 fighters would enter service in 'two or three years'. The new intermediate-range bomber could have been a Sukhoi development of *Fencer*,[64] labelled T-60, or the SU-27-1B variant already clearly identified by General Maliukov. A critical piece of the jigsaw fell into place in December 1993 when the SU-27 'multi-role combat aircraft', two-seat derivative of the SU-27 emerged and flew from the Sukhoi test complex at Novossibirsk. Present were Commander-in-Chief Deynekin and First Deputy Defence Minister Kokoshin, in an event recorded and reported by Russian television.[65] Strong circumstantial evidence suggests that the SU-27 variations will be at the centre of Russian Air Force resurgence in the next decade, equipped with modern avionics, radar and weapon systems.

General Maliukov was under no illusions about the problems which still lay ahead in creating an air force which could exploit SU-27 and its contemporaries. Agreements still had to be reached with other Republics on the employment of pilots, engineers and aircraft, which were impeding the reassembly of divisions after the withdrawal from eastern Europe. Training units needed to be reduced and combat regiments increased to correct the imbalances left by CFE Treaty restrictions and withdrawals. There was a need to redeploy protective fighters to the southern flank. Electronic warfare capabilities required improvement. This particular comment might have been related to an exception to Russian *glasnost* about their aircraft programmes. US intelligence sources in September 1993 referred to an EW variant of the TU-22M *Backfire* which was apparently being concealed by the Russian Air Force from Western observers. General Maliukov did not include TU-22s in his 'shopping list'. High priority had to be given to transport aircraft, by purchase of AN-70 and a new design, the IL-106 from Ilyushin.

'The majority of our problems', he observed, 'are long-term, relating to combat readiness and air force capabilities. We have a new, quite imperfect arrangement . . . if we think about proper arrangement of the VVS about the defence of the country, we must create the correct grouping from a strategic and tactical point of view. This is a serious problem, which should be resolved, but has so far proved impossible because of the billions it demands.'[66] In sum, the objectives had been identified, the plans were laid, and difficulties remained. Now, funding was required.

Similar signs of the clarification of weapon programmes appeared during the 1992–94 period. The Vympel Design Bureau appeared to have survived the upheavals of 1989–92 and was consistently reported to be developing a family of air-to-air missiles for deployment with the SU-27 variants and I.42. They included the R-73, a short-range, highly-manoeuvrable 'dogfight' missile allegedly comparable to the British Aerospace Advanced Short Range Air-to-Air Missile, the R-77, a medium-range (120 km), semi-active, radar-homing missile, and the R-37, a 400-km, active terminal-homing weapon.[67] While the performance of these missiles still awaited objective Western analysis, there was no reason to doubt that the new generation of Russian aircraft would be well-equipped for air-to-air combat. But as General Maliukov observed, the cost of new aircraft and weapons was only part of the expenses incurred in rebuilding the air forces infrastructure. He was only referring to the VVS, not to the Air Defence Forces, which faced similar problems of a comparable magnitude after the collapse of the air-defensive glacis and redeployment of PVO regiments. While the Russian Air Defence Force (VPVO) had inherited 65 per cent of Soviet weapons and equipment, most of the best had been stationed along the Union's periphery and nationalised by Ukraine and other Republics. There were alleged to be no modern SAMs in the Volga, Urals or the Central Economic Region surrounding Moscow.[68]

The emergence of a new military doctrine in 1992 and 1993 for the Russian armed forces was accompanied by a proposed force-structure revision to be implemented by 2000 which would amalgamate the aircraft and VPVO with those of VVS and allocate VPVO ground troops to Ground Force military districts.[69] Strong VPVO opposition to the proposals was led publicly in January 1993 by Commander-in-Chief Colonel General Prudnikov, who referred to the failure of earlier decentralisation experiments and forecast substantially decreased air-defence effectiveness if they should be repeated in future.[70] His comments, however, were a better reflection of VPVO vested interests than the realities of Russian air defence.

Indeed, only one month previously the General had explained that VPVO units were being restructured to increase both their fire power and mobility. Another senior VPVO officer noted that there were over 400 key targets in Russia requiring protection against strategic attack of which 25 per cent were of primary strategic importance. His proposals for restructuring stemmed from the new 'draft' military doctrine, which required early warning, the ability to repel aviation and missile attacks and to deliver a retaliatory strike. 'We were also guided by the requirement for mobile forces capable of acting in any direction from where a threat of aggression could emerge.'[71]

In Russia's first major national military exercise, Minister Kokoshin was quoted: 'Only mobile air defence systems were tested and evaluated because these systems will play a key role with the Mobile Forces.' The Air Defence Troops of the Ground Forces took the lead in the joint exercise.[72] The proposed reorganisation could, indeed, fragment and weaken Russian air defences by dividing assets between VVS, Army and Strategic forces. On the other hand, if air defences are subordinate to VVS, with flexible operational control arrangements between air defence regions, as, for example, in the UK and western Europe, the impact of political disintegration will be reduced. It is likely, however, that Russian concern about her vulnerability to strategic air attack, especially by stealth configured aircraft, is likely to remain well founded for a long time.

The extent of that vulnerability and its likely extended duration were explained by the General Designer and Head of Russian ground-based, air-defence surveillance and acquisition radars, Dr Yuri Kuznetsov, in May 1993.[73] He claimed that Russia was not lagging behind the West in basic research and inventions, but could not match subsequent development and series production. Nonetheless, he asserted that Russian larger, mobile, air-defence radars mounted on self-propelled vehicles had no equal, being self-sufficient and capable of operating and evacuation in no more than five minutes without compromising their performance.

Dr Kuznetsov confirmed that Russia had pursued the development of metric band radars which were practically unaffected by clouds and high atmospheric moisture and which offered advantages against stealth configuration and shape. He also stated, however, that while metric wave radar might enhance detection, it was not suitable for tracking, illumination and fire-control radars. Moreover, metric band radars were not very accurate and were themselves vulnerable to jamming.

'It is undeniable', he concluded, 'that the introduction of stealth technologies has created a number of completely new air-defence problems.
. . . Conventional radar technologies are experiencing increasing difficulties
in their missions. This is a result of the increased threat level, particularly
due to the introduction of "stealth" aircraft and weapons, low-altitude
cruise missiles with manoeuvring warheads, and so on, as well as parallel
advances in EW activities and devices affecting air-defence radars (powerful, versatile, active jammers, anti-radiation missiles, and decoys). This
situation demands important development efforts to significantly improve
broad sector coverage and so on. Please note that some of these goals are
in contradiction with each other: hence the search for innovative design
solutions.'

This authoritative analysis underlined the longer-term ambivalence of
air power for Russian security. On the one hand, a rejuvenated aerospace
industry, protected and nourished as a national asset, could provide the
aircraft and weapons to enable the Russian Air Force to regain its previous
international position. On the other the enormous Russian land mass and
the number and geographical spread of strategic targets would continue to
leave the country vulnerable to omni-directional air attack, now and for the
foreseeable future, enhanced by stealth technology. The development by
Russia of its own stealth technology would be of little avail to reduce the
defensive margin.

Export Potential

General Maliukov suggested that the Air Force would be allowed to allocate profits from sales to fund procurement programmes, although there
would be fierce departmental competition for any hard currency income
from arms exports. It seems, however, that the groups involved with the
internal restructuring of the defence complex were also keenly interested in
exports. The ubiquitous Mr Kokoshin argued strongly for a unified export
system to remove competition between separate Russian agencies peddling
SU-27 fighters.[74] His ally and Yeltsin-confidant Mikhail Malei explained a
comprehensive export philosophy. 'The enterprises providing goods that
are capable of finding an outlet on the international and domestic markets
should proceed with production. For Russia, the sale of weapons and military *matériel* is a required and inevitable process in this respect.' He
argued that if Russia were to sell 'the most up-to-date *matériel*, the potential value of export deliveries may increase to approximately US$12 billion.
In this case, this will concern items which have no equivalent elsewhere in
the world, and also those that differ radically from available models.' 'It
would', he went on, 'prove quite profitable to sell products at a level of 15
per cent below the average world market prices. By "dumping" the price in

this way we can maintain or improve the cost competitiveness of Russian commodities.'[75] Such an export policy was likely to find favour with all shades of political opinion. Concentration on the aerospace industry would still allow large-scale reductions to be made elsewhere in the traditional and in many cases obsolescent areas of the defence complex without monopolising the high-tech resources required for the revitalisation of the domestic economy. Indeed, exactly as in the West, export sales of defence equipment would be used to reinforce the interaction of domestic military and civilian production.

The theory will not, however, be easy to substantiate in the cold world of the international arms bazaar. Yesterday's ten-feet tall Soviet threats are likely to become vulnerable targets of Western competition, whose own industrial future will increasingly come to depend on overseas sales. By the end of 1993 the author had already listened reasonably impassively to Russian complaints about competitors at international air displays 'unfairly criticising Russian products' and 'exerting political pressure' to inhibit Russian exports.

In 1992, Malei's principle of ultra-modern equipment sales was seen in action at Farnborough, with offers of the advanced SU-27/35 together with long-range, anti-radiation missiles. MiG-29 and SU-25 lines were kept open for exports while Iranian interest in TU-22Ms was also expressed in 1992. By 1993 a marketing offensive was fully under way, with comprehensive displays at international air shows in Dubai, Malaysia, France and Moscow. The MiG-29 was heavily publicised in Western military journals, emphasising its manoeuvrability, rough field performance, fire control systems, growth potential, low observable shape, and maintainability. Equal prominence was given to the *Antey* S-300 family of surface-to-air missiles 'based on large-scale application of the most advanced technologies and operational concepts . . .' The international lure after the events of *Desert Storm* was direct and specific. 'The missile is optimised for interception of tactical and "near strategic" ballistic missiles, aeroballistic missiles as well as long-distance, aerodynamic targets, such as stand-off jammers, high-altitude reconnaissance or ELINT aircraft or AWACs and JSTARS-type platforms.'[76] Western marketing professionals were impressed by both the presentation and selective content of the Russian campaign.

While some former Soviet markets such as Libya, North Korea and Iraq were politically undesirable in 1994, there was no reason to assume that Russian foreign policy would permanently exclude them from customer relations. Previous Western dealings with Saddam Hussein and other regimes were reminders that a coincidence of commercial, political and military interest could exert powerful pressure on moral scruples. The

Pacific Rim countries were likely to provide lucrative arenas for aerospace competition. By 1994 China and Malaysia had become customers for SU-27s and MiG-29s, respectively.

To achieve the success hoped for by Malei and his colleagues, Russian exporters would need to overcome the Gulf War factor in international perceptions - thereby providing a further reason for Russia to emphasise Iraqi shortcomings rather than Western technology – and to convince the more long-sighted purchasers that Russian industry would provide life-cycle support. After the industrial disintegration, India, for example, had to locate 3,500 supplies scattered round the Commonwealth of Independent States despite indigenous manufacture of items such as MiG-21s and T-72 tanks.[77] Nevertheless, in view of India's dire economic position, and continued security concerns in south Asia, potential price reductions such as those postulated by Mikhail Malei might still prove attractive.

One other, double-edged factor might affect Russian aerospace exports: the impact of co-operative ventures with the West. Allied Signal, Rockwell-Collins and Honeywell reached agreement with Soviet design bureaux for co-operative work on avionics for civil aircraft, while Rolls-Royce began supplying commercial aircraft engines. In 1992 GEC Ferranti raised eye-brows at Farnborough by hanging a Thermal Imaging and Laser Designator (TIALD) pod on an SU-27. In November 1993, Mikhail Simonov floated proposals for co-operation between the USA and Russia on future fighter developments.

Such co-operation could in the first instance jeopardise Russian research and development by introducing more advanced, Western technology to the production lines. But two previous occurrences are worth remembering. One was the gift of Rolls-Royce *Nene* engines to the USSR in 1946, which allowed Soviet engineers swiftly to catch up with Western engine technology. The second, perhaps apocryphal, relates to Lenin's observation that capitalists would sell him the rope by which he would hang them. Co-operation between Russian and Western aerospace industries may bring short-term financial reward to the West, but in the longer term, it will increase the competitiveness of the Russian product by narrowing the gap between the two.

In sum, therefore, many weaknesses would continue to beset the Russian aerospace industry. But many were susceptible to resolution by the injection of resources and the freeing of management from bureaucratic suffocation. By 1994 Russia appeared to have an overall plan for the Air Force which depended on both state and private enterprise and which combined interests across the political spectrum. If this were the case, the aerospace industry could survive both political turmoil and further national economic deterioration. If, on the other hand, political stability was restored and the economy began to recover, the industry would become even stronger. In either case, therefore, the necessary industrial base for a reconstituted Russian Air Force would exist.

Two other questions remained. If the air force was to recover its military strength, how would it be used? And second, how would it compare with its erstwhile opponents?

The Doctrinal Framework

Doctrine, as a conceptual framework within which to construct strategy, operations and tactics has always been essential to the evolution of the Soviet armed forces. After several years of uncertainty, a new Russian doctrine was clarified in 1993 which considerably elevated the role of air power, albeit with one possibly significant reservation. It marked the end of a period of uncertainty in which public repetition of slogans and proposals frequently obscured a continuous and often acrimonious debate between reformers and the more conservative members of the General Staff. The external, international presentation of a Soviet military doctrine being revised in harmony with Gorbachev's declarations of 'sufficiency' and 'defensive defence' was as carefully co-ordinated between 1988 and 1990 as ever any Cominform theme in older, darker days. Conferences were attended by fluent exponents of war prevention, political resolution of conflict, respect for national, territorial and ethnic integrity, and revision of resource priorities to defensive alignments and structures. In the face of attack, 'defence would be pursued strategically, operationally and tactically'.[78] Distinguished 'official' spokesmen, including Akhromeyev, Moiseyev, Gariev and Yazov, repeated the central theme, 'Military reform is being conducted in strict accordance with the demands of defensive military doctrine, taking account of the need to maintain the Soviet armed forces at a level of reasonable and reliable sufficiency. The composition, structure, equipment and training of the army and navy is changing; as are views on their use to repel an aggressor.'[79]

There was, however, no such consensus back in Moscow. At a conference in November 1989, primarily intended to clarify the role of the Main Political Directorate in the new era, one speaker ironically referred to discussions on 'how best we can fight on our own territory. I would rather fight on other people's, but life is life and now political restructuring is giving us an opportunity to think again.'[80] In the same period a senior Soviet Foreign Ministry official asked his Western colleagues, in the margins of a conference at Houston, to 'express disagreements [with the declared Soviet position on arms control] carefully, because there are opponents in Moscow who would be strengthened'. During the same week the author was asked by a Soviet general to relay a private message back to the Chief of the British Defence Staff asking him if he could seek an opportunity to make complimentary comments on the imminent Soviet doctrinal expositions at Vienna, as 'this would be extremely valuable for the reformers in Moscow against their opposition.'

In common with many other Western analysts, the author sought details of the practical implications for the air forces of the doctrinal 'revisions'. Nothing was forthcoming about the extent, the timing or the detailed content. Perhaps in due course Moscow archives will reveal how far, if at all, 'defensive sufficiency' was ever anything more than the 'naked idea' as alleged by Major General Lata of the planning division of the Russian General Staff in Prague in April 1993.[81] Nonetheless, more than military obduracy was inhibiting any meaningful doctrinal revision from 1989 to 1992. It is worth recalling that it took NATO approximately seven years to revise the Alliance's strategy to one of 'flexible and appropriate response'. Albeit 15 nations had to be persuaded to agree, but the environment outside NATO headquarters in Brussels was calm and stable.

Doctrinal re-evaluation took place in Moscow against a background of alliance collapse, Union disintegration, *Desert Storm* trauma, the end of a major threat, economic collapse, cuts in the armed forces, political reform, and massive internal problems in the armed forces themselves. The original doctrinal revision referred to the Warsaw Pact; the 'First Draft' of December 1990 was for the Soviet armed forces; the 'Draft Military Doctrine' of May 1992 was Russian. This last became the reference point for the reconstitution of the Russian Air Forces.

The new doctrine in many respects reiterated old Soviet fears about 'the striving of some states or coalitions of states to dominate the world community . . . their adherence to resolving disputed issues by military means . . . the presence of powerful groupings of armed forces in a number of states [coalition of states] and the continuing system of basing them near Russian borders which gives them a favourable military-strategic position . . . attempts to use means of political and economic pressure or military blackmail against Russia.'[82]

New concerns about Russian minorities in the other former Soviet Republics were trenchantly addressed: 'the violation of the rights of Russian citizens and of people in former Soviet Republics who identify themselves, ethnically or culturally with Russia. This can be a serious source of conflict.'[83] That rationale for interference in the other Republics as a possible platform for Russian aggrandisement overshadowed an adjacent and at least as important modification to previous concepts of deterrence. If in the course of war, an aggressor undertakes 'actions involving the purposeful disruption of strategic nuclear forces and the destruction of nuclear power and other potentially dangerous installations, even by conventional means, this will be taken as a transition to the use of weapons of mass destruction.'[84]

The Russian General Staff had noted the ability of air power to strike precisely and conventionally at strategic targets and Russian vulnerability to it. The answer was the threat of escalation to a nuclear response. The message was reinforced in the published 1993 version of the doctrine which abandoned earlier pledges that Russia would not be the first to use nuclear weapons.

The difference between public observations on the outcome of the Gulf War and its actual impact on Russian thinking was stark. Comments by Lieutenant-General Sergei Bogdanov, in October 1991 in Moscow were typical of the General Staff public view: that the war became a testing ground for new weapons; that Iraq's failure to pre-empt had been critical to the evolution of the campaign; that classical models of all arms on the battlefield had been made obsolete; positional defence was ineffective; the war was lost before it began because of Coalition superiority in information systems, C^3I and electronic warfare; there were too many 'coincidences', suggesting careful Coalition preparation and (by inference) an artificially-engineered crisis; that Iraqi equipment was obsolete and inferior; even its modern equipment was poorly handled; the Coalition had overwhelming superiority; but the role of air power in modern war was increasing; resource priorities between army, air force and navy required re-evaluation. And, in addition, 'If we become the target of offensive action, we shall not only use defensive means in response.'[85]

Military commentators without General Bogdanov's planning responsibilities were more outspoken. The strongest advocate of the new supremacy of air power was retired Major General I.N. Voroby'ev, a prolific analyst who before 1991 was usually associated with ground force topics. He saw a novel tactical and operational phenomenon: the 'electronic-fire engagement', 'which, with air, missile, naval and electronic strikes over a lengthy period was the main decisive component of the operation . . . leaving the ground forces with the task of merely completing the victory. Thus, one of the features of technological war is that in certain conditions, its goals can be accomplished even without ground forces invading enemy territory . . . Any army which adheres dogmatically to outdated stereotypes of warfighting . . . which does not keep up with scientific-technical progress . . . is doomed to defeat.'[86]

As in the West, the concession of victory to air power was a little too much for most khaki analysts to swallow. More typical were those who comprehensively and clearly identified the salient features of the Coalition victory: the concentration and strategic impact of conventional PGMs;

EW supremacy; tactical surprise; defence suppression, etc; but, 'Aerial bombardment could not alone destroy the Iraqi army and could not destroy Iraq's military potential or its nuclear potential. Only the defeat of the Iraqi main grouping as a result of the last offensive made Saddam seek peace unconditionally.'[87]

The new doctrine left no doubts about the General Staff's real fears, incorporating a Gulf War onslaught into the traditional scenario of an invasion of Mother Russia by identifying the characteristics of future war: '. . . the enemy invasion will not begin on land, but in air and sea space. It will be characterised by a number of operations and engagements with the involvement of strong air, air-defence and highly-mobile, assault landing groupings and naval forces to disrupt strategic deployment, disorganise civil and military command and control, and take individual Commonwealth states out of the war. Destruction of economic and military targets by precision weapons to a great depth will be accompanied by simultaneous or pre-emptive use of electronic-warfare equipment.'[88]

Consequently, priority would be given to early warning, to the repulse of air and missile attacks, to the ability to retaliate, and to mobile forces which can operate in any direction where security is threatened. Procurement priority would be given to qualitative factors, especially to advanced, precision, long-range and very survivable weaponry capable of supporting operations without closing with the enemy, and also to advanced equipment and command and control and intelligence-gathering equipment: all this to allow force reductions while still retaining adequate capability.[89]

In May 1992, Minister of Defence Grachev suggested a list of nine priorities to implement the guidelines of the doctrine. Of them seven were directly associated with air power : 'Equipment for highly-mobile forces; strategic weapons systems; air defence systems; military space systems; long-range, high-accuracy weapons; army aviation assets; reconnaissance assets; electronic warfare; command and control systems.'[90] On the same occasion General Grachev outlined proposals to create highly-mobile forces, deployed on a regional basis, capable of repelling an attack from any direction. Constant readiness forces would be capable of effectively influencing local conflicts, backed up by rapid-deployment forces and strategic reserves. Current theories for the conduct of military operations, which still retained 'an infantry-tank character', should be revised to take greater account of the role of aerial attack, including precision weapons. The whole restructuring would take place over some eight years but, cautioned the General, 'The time frame . . . may have to be seriously adjusted under the influence of conceivable developments in the internal political and/or economic situation in Russia, as well as international relations.'

Doubts remained among Western analysts about how far this was Grachev's own plan, and how far he had the support of General Staff. Or, indeed, exactly how large the various components of the mobile forces would be. One description, published in December 1992 specified five air-borne divisions, eight airborne brigades, six motor rifle brigades, one *Spetznaz* brigade, three SAM brigades, space communications, 200 SU-27s, 150 SU-24s, 64 SU-25s and approximately 200 IL-76s plus 720 helicopters to make up the Immediate Reaction Forces, while the reinforcing Rapid Deployment Forces would call for three heavy bomber divisions - approximately 120 TU-22Ms and one unspecified 'Air Army' as well as three radar battalions of 180 helicopters to support three army corps, one motor rifle division, one tank division and five rocket artillery brigades.[91]

Even allowing for slimmed-down force sizes, General Grachev's caution about implementation periods looked well founded. Two hundred IL-76s were required to airlift one 7,000-man division, yet after the disintegration of the Union, Russia was left in control 'of only two military transport aviation regiments, less than half of that of the former Soviet Air Forces.[92] Even with augmentation from Aeroflot, an airlift on a scale required by the 'Immediate Reaction' force seemed unrealistic. Similarly, the deployment of several hundred combat aircraft into the southern regions of Russia would call for considerable and expensive infrastructure expansion.

By 1994 several questions about the future application of air power within the context of the doctrine remained unanswered. Would command of the combat aircraft be devolved to regional ground force commanders with the attendant risks of fragmentation and subordination to local tactical considerations? Or would command be retained at higher level, delegating only control and therefore preserving cohesion and potential for operational level co-ordination? There were some clues, but no unambiguous answers.

On the same occasion that General Grachev explained the functions of the mobile forces, Colonel General Korolkov emphasised the contribution of air power:

The VVS must gain air superiority, destroy the enemy from the air to his full operational depth, and apply the principles of mass and centralised control ... The air campaign's basis will consist of combat operations to repulse an air attack and air operations in the theatre of military operations, conducted simultaneously with large formations (fronts, armies or fleets) of the other branches of the armed forces and even long-range air operations. Without these actions, the Ground Forces' grouping cannot be successful . . . Operations and battles are clearly acquiring a three-dimensional character with widespread use

of electronic warfare and high precision weapons. The tendency of the
disproportionate change in the weights of the branches of the armed
forces in achieving the goals of the operation and of the war itself is
clear to see. The role of the Air Forces will steadily grow. They must
become the nucleus of Russia's mobile armed forces.[93]

General Korolkov's language was diplomatic: asserting greater responsibility for air power, and, by implication, a greater share of resource
allocation, while at the same time relating the whole to territorial defence
by 'Ground Force groupings'. How far the full flexibility of Russian air
power would be exploited, or constrained by traditional thinking remained
to be seen. Marshal Ogarkov died in January 1994, living long enough to
see not only his prophesies materialise in the Gulf War, but also their
incorporation into Russian doctrine.

Russia with Wings
If determination by its commanders was the deciding factor, the recovery
of Russian air power would be speedy and, indeed, produce an even
stronger instrument than before the advent of *perestroika*. After all, that
was the objective from the outset. 'Russia without wings', said
Commander-in-Chief Deynekin in August 1992, 'is not Russia: it has had,
does have and will have them.'[94] During the following 12 months, high-
ranking officers became even more upbeat. While references continued to
social problems and the impact of withdrawal, disintegration and resource
constraints, greater emphasis was placed on the future. The conversion of
flying-training centres into combat divisions, taking advantage of an aircrew surplus to reduce training schools, replacing obsolescent aircraft by
those withdrawn from eastern Europe and 'the near abroad', extending the
duration and improving the quality of theoretical and flying-training
courses at the academies were some of the measures outlined. 'My recent
trips abroad as both Commander-in-Chief and as the man responsible for
reorganisation of Russia's Air Force have shown me much to attempt to
introduce in Russia.'[95]

   Further details of the future shape and organisation of the Air Force
were given to a Royal Netherlands Air Force audience in April 1993 by Lt.-
General (Aviation) Antoshkin, Commander of the Air Force of Moscow
Military District:

   The combat strength of the Air Force would be related to the requirements of the CFE Treaty (3,450 combat aircraft) and treaty
   obligations would be strictly observed . . . The main arm of the transformation of the Russian Air Force is the formation of operational

task-orientated Air Force groupings in various regions of the country, to maintain security and defend the country's interests . . . [envisaging] . . . a reduction in the near future of 20 per cent in the fighting and personnel strengths of the Russian Federation Air Force, . . . with an ultimate reduction of one-third by the year 2000 . . . [which] will then constitute up to 17 per cent of the armed forces of the Russian Federation . . . qualitative improvement will be achieved by re-equipping with multi-role aviation systems with precision all-weather systems . . . Efficient movement of aviation, troop transport and actions by mobile forces will be improved . . . Systems of basing and support of aviation and the development of the Air Force infrastructure will be improved . . .

The transformation of the Air Force is expected to be carried out in stages. During the first stage – until the end of 1992 – the concept of the formation of the Russian Air Force was drawn up and approved. During the second stage (1993–1995), the withdrawal of forces will be completed and Air Force groupings will be set up on the territory of Russia. There will also be a transition to a mixed (contract and conscript) Air Force manning system. During the third stage, after 1995, there will be further cuts in the Air Force to bring it down to the agreed level (250–270,000 people) and the fundamental reorganisation and construction of the Air Force airbase network will be continued. The implementation of a base-orientated system of aviation support will be started and the transfer to a new system of cadre training will be completed. The transfer to a mixed manning system will be continued.[96]

This was a formidable blueprint which would depend for its achievement on the favourable confluence of factors examined previously in this chapter. But a defence industrial complex which was declining could make contract service as an air force technician more attractive. Initial attempts to attract contract airmen in 1992 had disappointing results, but by May 1993 a substantial pay increase had induced sufficient qualified applications for the recruiters to choose among them. Meanwhile, despite continued difficulties with the quality of life, aircrew morale was responding to the advent of new aircraft, the ending of confrontation with its associated demands of long periods of alert, the prospects of foreign exchanges and probably the demise of the *zampolit*. Other problems, such as pilot surplus, continued, but would gradually diminish with manpower planning revisions and normal exits. Precedence in flying hours was being given to junior pilots.[97] This, as frequent comments in the military press indicated, lowered current operational levels and aggravated problems of flight safety, but it could also become a transient phenomenon with successful restructuring. One beneficial impact of the disintegration of the Union was the prospect of reduced ethnic tension and fewer training problems, although the air forces had been less affected by both than had the ground troops.

If, whether by national economic recovery or by protected allocation of resources the Air Force did begin to recover its material strength, its ultimate effectiveness would be determined by its success in overcoming one traditional, perhaps endemic, problem and in dealing with a new one : one which was very familiar in the West.

The first was the ability of the new generation of commanders who, after all, were still the products of the old ways, despite a sharp drop in age, to succeed in introducing habits of initiative and free thinking within the general requirement of military interdependence and discipline. The removal of the *zampolit* and the establishment of a single professional chain of command, with promotion determined by military competence rather than by political acceptance, would be one encouragement. The advent of modern technology which required independent aircrew judgement for its exploitation would be another. To the casual observer during the period 1989–94 there was a considerable outburst of outspokenness and initiative among young officers when they were on their own which tended to completely dry up when they were in the presence of their senior commanders. That, however, is a phenomenon not peculiar to the Russian Air Force. It may well be that contact with their Western counterparts will have a strong influence on them. Like General Deynekin, they too might return home from abroad with 'much to attempt to introduce into Russia.'

There were signs in 1993 that some operational activities were returning which illustrated continuity with the developments immediately before the traumas of 1991. In eastern Europe training had begun to involve packages of some 30 aircraft, including SU-24s carrying bombs and air-to-surface missiles, escorted by MiG-29s with SU-24E ECM support. 30 per cent of such training took place at night, with the final legs of the 'attacks' being flown at 550 kn at 1,000 ft. In the same period anti-AWACs exercises were flown, some involving as many as 60 aircraft. One account in *Red Star* in May 1989 indicated that this kind of package was designed to destroy the AWACs fighter screen as well as the prime target itself. At armament practice camps in the Soviet Union, combined attack and escort fighter packages, including up to 100 aircraft, practised radio silence, night all-weather operations in an ECM environment. Even when aircrew hours were dropping to less than eight a month, they were beginning to be used more proficiently.

In November 1993 an exercise was reported which 'involved at least 35 aircraft of six different types launched from three different bases in European Russia. During the two-day, 5,000-mile exercise, the aircraft simulated a conventional attack on targets in the Russian Far East, then returned to their bases.'[98] One exercise did not mean reconstitution, but this was a significant step, for three reasons. First, Commander-in-Chief Deynekin was personally associated with it; second, at least two IL-62 airborne command posts and one IL-A50 *Mainstay* AWACs were involved; and third, TU-95-MS and probably TU-160 long-range aviation aircraft were co-ordinated with tactical SU-24s and SU-27 escorts, all using in-flight refuelling. The exercise suggested that, despite the allocation of combat aircraft to 'regional groupings', a residual central command would exploit and concentrate all the resources required.

The exercise was also symbolic of the redeployed Air Force's ability to resume business. One should, however, bear in mind that the demonstration of a single capability to give an impression of total strength was an old Soviet Air Force PR habit. On the other hand, awareness of previous exercises had seeped out in the West via intelligence sources; now they could be discussed with their Russian participants on the bases from which they had flown.

The second problem had probably also been present for many years, but rapidly assumed much greater dimensions in the aftermath of economic collapse and political and strategic reorientation. Hitherto, any interservice conflicts were well-concealed and tempered by the enormous Soviet allocations of resources to defence. After World War I the Royal Air Force fought for its independence; after World War II, the USAF. After the 'Cold World War III' it was the time of the Russian Air Force. The Army was still too strong to challenge, but, as has been noted, the Air Defence Forces were quickly defending themselves against a VVS takeover.

At a conference held in the Russian General Staff Academy in May 1993 to discuss the future of the infant Russian armed services, Admiral Pauk produced three arguments to defend naval aviation which would have been instantly recognisable on any Western flight deck and equally quickly disdained in air-force crew rooms: amalgamation would disrupt joint training between surface, submarine and naval aviation; operating over seas is very different from operating over land; and the Navy, with 1,580 fixed-wing aircraft, could argue for control of VVS long-range aviation with a primary mission in support of the fleets.[99] General Deynekin responded not very obliquely a few months later to his interviewer in *Izvestia* who asked, 'What is the role of Russia's strategic aircraft? Do they patrol the coasts of the USA?' The General replied, 'Recently while patrolling the oceans, our TU-95 achieved visual contact of the US nuclear-powered carrier *Nimitz* in international waters 4,000 km east of the Japanese coast. We found it in the middle of a cyclone. It is not easy to locate a carrier; satellites cannot always do it. We are always professionally interested in such a ship, which is in effect a floating air base.'[100] Billy Mitchell would have been proud of that succinct demolition of the case for discrete naval aviation flying skills.

Officially, however, the Russian Air Force would comprise long-range aviation, military-transport aviation, front-line aviation and the reserve and cadre training command.[101] Russian air power would also be applied by the helicopters of Army Aviation, by the SU-27s, helicopters and possibly carrier-borne, early warning aircraft of the Russian Navy, and by the land-based regiments of Naval Aviation. The air-defence interceptors would probably amalgamate with the VVS within a subordinate air-defence command. The final distribution of the air-defence ground environment, guns, missiles and radars, between strategic district and air forces, remained uncertain.

In 1994 the political and economic future of Russia itself was uncertain, perhaps even more so than that of its air forces. There was political agreement across the spectrum that a core defence industry should be preserved, that the Russian armed forces should be reconstructed and that Russian arms, especially high-tech aerospace arms, should be exported. It was possible, although obviously not certain, that the reconstitution of Russian air power could take place despite political turmoil and economic dislocation.

When Russia begins to reassert her position on the international stage, air power could well become an influential instrument for a state that has abandoned the persuasion of ideology and is unlikely for many years to possess largess for diplomatic endowment. Perhaps the biggest difference from the pre-Gorbachev years will be the reassurance that the rest of the world will be able to keep a close eye on that air power as it recuperates. In the longer term, it is well within the bounds of possibility that Russian air power will challenge the position enjoyed in the 1990s by the USA.

CHAPTER 8

THE ERA OF DIFFERENTIAL AIR POWER

On the threshold of its second century air power had become an integral component of warfare. Fifty years had passed since field army Generals Montgomery and Rommel had, from very different perspectives, expressed the view that he who lost the war in the air lost the war. The Gulf War had substantiated the optimism of the visionaries, while the alliance of satellite-derived technology and target-acquisition sensors promised at last the ability to attack individual targets with precision at night and in all weathers. Airmen could approach the next hundred years with confidence. A wealth of experience provided guidance for realistic planning for the future.[1] And yet air power faced an age of uncertainty which in some respects was even more complex than in its years of infancy.

The old certainties of confrontation had entailed the risks of global annihilation, but for governments and their air forces on both sides they provided a reliable framework for procurement, policies, plans and procedures driven by a clearly defined threat. Any peripheral contingencies in central America, the South Atlantic, south-east Asia or the Middle East would be dealt with from resources established to meet the central commitment. Now, elsewhere in the world, old hostilities smouldered: in the Middle East, in several places in Asia, in Africa and even in eastern Europe. The old East-West protagonists, however, with the possible exception of paranoiac members of the Russian General Staff, had reclassified most threats as 'risks'.

The only certainty was that armed force would continue to be an arbiter of international disputes, but the Western countries in particular were likely to have an option whether to become involved or not, except when a threat to their core national interests was either reconstituted or emerged elsewhere, as in the Gulf. The implications of this 'optional' factor for air power will be examined below.

Meanwhile, economic constraints were curtailing all the defence budgets of the Cold War antagonists. In some Western countries deliberate conversion of resources to the civil economy was accompanied by economic recession, accelerating defence cuts. All the Eastern bloc was riven by economic collapse, which, associated with political realignment, rendered impossible even the extensive but comparatively orderly reduction of defence budgets achieved in the West. In the Third World, defence budgets would continue to compete for scarce resources in priorities determined either by the perception of regional threats or by the ambitions or pretensions of governments unconstrained by democracies. In every case, competition between defence budgets and other domestic expenditures would be sharpened, and within defence establishments, struggles between the armed forces for shares of dwindling funds would grow more intense.

The third factor of technology would impinge upon options for participation and on the allocation of dwindling resources. All forms of military power would be affected, but air power most of all. Not only have aerospace technology costs, like those of armies and navies, continued to grow, but the very complexity and extent of this technology will compel very difficult choices on even the most well-endowed governments and defence staffs.

These circumstances will determine the impact of air power on international security. The ability of airmen to anticipate, respond to and deflect them will vary considerably from state to state.

Differential Air power
Theories of air power have usually transcended national boundaries. Trenchard, Mitchell, Douhet, Wever and Tukhachevsky, for example, shared many ideas about strategic bombardment. In their generation the implementation of their ideas was within the capacity of several nations: Britain, the USA, France, Germany, Italy, the USSR and Japan among them. In 1994 there was probably greater international consensus about air power theory, but the capacity to apply it diverged so widely that a further qualifying adjective had become appropriate : 'differential' air power.

A state's capacity to apply air power as an instrument of national policy may be measured against four criteria. The first is the breadth and depth of its aerospace industrial base, capable of quantity production. Coincidentally, such a base will contribute to levels of national technological literacy and numeracy from which air force recruiters can draw. Second, within that industrial base is the capacity for research and development which can identify and exploit science and advanced technology. Third is the capacity and inclination of a government to allocate resources to an air force and thereafter be prepared to use it to protect or project national interests. Fourth is the size and quality of the air force or air forces themselves. Only the USA meets all those criteria and even the most cursory comparison with a handful of other states illustrates its overwhelming pre-eminence.

In February 1994 it was reported that the Pentagon's $252.2 billion budget request had been cut by 35 per cent, with a drop from 6.3 per cent of GDP in 1985 to 2.8 per cent in 1999.[2] This followed a 'Bottom-Up Review' in 1993 which had proposed a reduction from 16 to 12 aircraft carriers, from 36 to 30 tactical combat-aircraft wings and from 301 to fewer than 200 strategic bombers. These reductions would be the greatest in the US armed forces since the period immediately after World War II and would inevitably resurrect old interservice squabbles over roles and resource allocations.

For example, they swiftly exacerbated arguments between the USAF and the US Navy over responsibilities for long-range conventional attack and between the USAF and the Army over surface-to-air defences. One rare public outburst by an Army general illustrated the depth of feelings being aroused by the pressure of defence cuts and perceptions of encroaching air power. USAF Chief of Staff McPeak was reported as wanting 'a kind of wall-to-wall review of where we stand in the theater defence business across the board.'[3] Major-General Garner, Assistant Chief of Army Staff for Operations and Plans, Force development, responded by stating that he was 'tired of dealing with Air Force mythology' and that USAF 'arguments are worse than specious, they are fallacious.' The General continued by pointing out the USAF's failure to deal with tactical ballistic missiles, comparing the cost effectiveness of a *Patriot* battery with 'hundreds of aircraft on patrol' and encapsulated pent-up Army frustration at further cuts with 'If you spend $10 billion on an army you modernise a whole corps. Ten billion dollars on an aircraft programme is nothing. You could fix every problem in the Army for 10 per cent of the F-22 programme.'[4]

US Navy – USAF differences were expressed in rather more diplomatic language by the Navy's Director of Naval Aviation, 'We are not trying to compete with the Air Force on deep strike; I do not think that the Navy is trying to emulate the Air Force bomber mission.'[5] Any remaining doubts were removed later in 1993 with the cancellation of the USN's proposed replacement for the A6 bomber, as debate in Washington between the armed services became progressively more acrimonious.

Even after the cuts, however, US air power could be applied by 16 operational B-2 stealth bombers, 50 plus F-117 medium-range stealth bombers, 60

B-1s, 40 B-52s, over 4,000 F-14, F-15, F-16 and F-111 fighter/fighter bombers, supported by 500 in-flight refuelling tankers, 34 E-3 AWACs, 20 JSTARS, and several squadrons of dedicated EW aircraft. Their weapons would include three new families of stand-off air-to-surface PGMs, advanced cruise missiles, new air-to-air missiles, and new families of unmanned vehicles. A new, highly-supersonic, high-altitude reconnaissance aircraft was still unacknowledged, while the exploitation of satellite support for various activities continued. Despite concern about progress on the new C-17 transport, and about serviceability across the transport fleet, the USAF's airlift inventory included over 1,000 aircraft. In other words, the USA could project the full panoply of air power, across all roles and with appropriate weapons for each, in support of interests world-wide. The major defence debate to which all the armed services contributed, was whether they could fight two 'medium-level' conflicts at the same time or whether they would need to concentrate on one while 'holding' on the other.

Three other air forces tried to discharge all roles. Sample comparisons are self-explanatory. The RAF front-line strength included 150 strike attack aircraft – none of them with integral PGM delivery systems – and 90 air-defence interceptors. There were no specialist defence suppression or ECM aircraft, 17 specialist tankers and approximately 30 transport/tanker variants in a total fixed-wing transport force of 73 aircraft. Three light carriers could deploy 24 fixed-wing combat aircraft. Britain's total defence budget in 1993 was the equivalent of 35 billion dollars.[6] The French budget for 1992 was 35.4 billion dollars, of which 13.2 per cent was allocated to the Air Force. Nuclear strike, air defence, ground attack and reconnaissance roles were provided for, supported by 11 tankers, three electronic warfare and four E-3F AWACs aircraft. Two carriers deployed 37 strike attack and eight interceptor aircraft. Russia, the third country theoretically at least prepared to exploit air power to the full was examined in Chapter 7. The United States' capacity to project air power was 20 times greater than that of the two other major Western exponents. No other country could match either the quantity or, increasingly significant for the future, the quality of its equipment. Near the other end of the scale in Europe was Denmark, with a defence budget in 1993 of $2.21 billion and a combat air strength of 60 F-16s.[7] Even with highly-professional people and strong, intelligent command the application of air power by the RDAF was restricted to air defence and air-to-ground support.

Contrasts with leading Third World countries were equally stark. In 1993 India's total defence budget was $6.3 billion. Its air force was numerically strong, listing 700 combat aircraft,[8] but lacked in-flight refuelling, early warning and electronic warfare and had only limited night/all-weather fighting capability. China, on the other hand, deployed over 5,000 combat aircraft from a defence budget declared in 1993 to total $6.77 billion.[9] In 1994 the large majority were still obsolete or obsolescent and, like those of India, lacked sophisticated force multipliers. This situation, however, is changing, and Chinese air power potential will be examined below in its Pacific Rim regional setting.

The USAF's own views on the future of air power were summarised in a report prepared by the USAF Association in late 1993. The authors freely acknowledged that the real issues in the contemporary debate about 'Roles and Mission' were, 'funding issues, clothed in the robes of roles and missions. Prior to the emergence of military aviation, disputes were ineptly solved by the logic that if it happened on land, it was the Army's, and if it happened at sea, it was the Navy's . . . Vestiges of this thinking are still embedded in defense policy. For instance, since the Air Force evolved from Army ancestry, its primary missions are all over land and roles at sea are "collateral". . . . The land-sea formula does not fit the aeroplane . . . We think it fair to say that at the center of the roles and missions debate – and the budgetary debate that underlies it – is air power, and that the crux is long-range air power. . . . All of the services respect air power. Across the spectrum of conflict, the nation now looks to air power as the initial and possibly (given the circumstances) the preliminary instrument of US force qualification. Air power is now widely recognised for the rapid results that it can now achieve, with minimum exposure, casualties and force attrition . . .'

The authors went on to castigate 'single-dimension' strategies as misguided, asserting that there was a need for a balance of land, sea, air and air space forces. 'Nevertheless, it is short-sighted not to recognise that careful, timely use of air power has emerged as a principal element in any multi-dimensional strategy – not necessarily the principal (that depends of the circumstances), but certainly a principal element . . .'

Four comparatively recent developments, they argued, had combined to reinforce the basic air power attributes of speed, range, flexibility and the ability to transcend natural boundaries. Those developments were stealth, accuracy, battle management and assistance from space. While the Air Force had no claim to a monopoly on air power in the air attack role – 'naval carrier-based aircraft provide useful options' . . . 'the rapidly available deep reach, the penetration capability and the sustained and heavily concentrated firepower of longer-range, land-based aircraft will make them the force of choice.'[10]

This clear and assertive definition of the primary position of air power in US defence policy, even to the emphasis on 'long-range operational air power' had its roots in events and ideas already examined in this study. Now, however, the ideas can only refer in the near future to US air power, with perhaps longer term competition from Russia, China and possibly Japan.

In considering the future impact of air power on international relations, there will obviously be two sets of circumstances : those in which US air power is involved, and those in which it is not. And if US air power is to be deployed in a conflict, on whose side?

Unpredictable Scenarios

It is impossible to permutate all the possible scenarios, with and without US participation, but the implications for air power of such unpredictability can be identified, for both the USA itself and for other aspirants to air power exploitation.

The air power strategic environment since 1945 may be compared to the swing of a pendulum (see page xiii), where the arc depicts characteristics rather than chronology. At one extreme is the 'Gulf Scenario', where a large number of factors coincide to create virtually ideal circumstances for the application of air power. At the other end of the swing is the 'Bosnian Scenario', where the opposite is the case. In between lie the major conflicts or specific applications of air power. That pendulum will continue to swing and, as before, will swing erratically and stop unpredictably at any point on the arc, just as the pendulum of warfare has always done.

Since the demise of the central confrontation between East and West, and until the formulation of new alliances, coalition partnerships will be equally unpredictable, as will opponents. Partners may be flying MiG-29s and the opponents F-18s. The RAF has fought against French- and US-built aircraft and weapons in its last two conflicts. Future Western partners may have to avoid *Patriots* as well as SA-12s.

The potential objective of the partners is likely to determine the extent of their commitment. To eradicate an international threat? To discourage potential aggression? To constrain? To restore a balance? To destabilise a regime? To eject forces from illegally-gained territory? The evaporation of ideology as a factor in confrontation may not be permanent. Europe has been fortunate to repeat the intensity of sixteenth century ideological confrontation for 50 years without the chaos and bloodshed of the Wars of Religion. Events in Bosnia and elsewhere in Europe, quite apart from more obvious sources of tension in North Africa and the Middle East, are reminders that pragmatism and rationale can still be readily consumed by unquantifiable passions. The presence of such features in a conflict will swing the pendulum well over to the right.

Predictable Features

While the permutation of scenarios may be difficult to predict, their operational characteristics were already emerging in 1994. First is the impact of international competition selling state-of-the-art military technology. Among the major arms exporters, France has usually given priority to export considerations in procurement policy. Britain has sought to reduce unit costs for her own armed services by extended production runs for export; the Soviet Union used arms exports for political purposes; while the USA could sustain her defence industry by the scale of her domestic requirement, leaving arms exports to be focused for political purposes and additional commercial benefit.

By 1994 Russia was clearly giving priority to exports of aircraft, surface-to-air missiles and associated systems at prices below those of competitive equipment from the West. Reductions in the US armed services meant that US defence industries now had to export to survive. Previous British and US arms sales to Iraq and Iran, respectively, indicated that when commercial opportunities conflicted with moral scruples there was likely to be only one winner. One way or the other, states whose international image was not quite acceptable could be expected to acquire advanced military technology. In addition. states such as Brazil, China, Taiwan, Japan and South Korea were developing their own defence industries and could complicate the international arms bazaar still further.

Consequently, while few countries are likely to create large air forces, or comprehensive larger-scale surface-to-air defences, they will increasingly invest in smaller amounts of sophisticated technology. The gap between Western aerospace technology and the rest, demonstrated so brutally in the Gulf, will narrow. Depending on the factors previously noted, Western air forces may preserve advantages but the differential will move progressively further up the technological scale.

As a result, air warfare will usually take place in an electronic environment affecting communications, navigation, target acquisition, weapon delivery and precision guidance. Low-level operations are likely to continue to be problematical, with the traditional difficulties of high-speed target acquisition and identification in adverse topographical and climatic conditions further aggravated by the widespread deployment of man-portable low level SAMs such as *Stinger* and derivatives of *Blowpipe*, plus any further Russian developments. By 1994 the threat posed by such weapons to transport aircraft had already affected the course of UN operations in Bosnia and the Russian airlift in Georgia. They will need to be considered when planning for future deployment and support of army and air force contingents 'out of area'.

The certainty of 'alternative' lessons being drawn from the Gulf was mentioned previously. The prospect of the USA asserting a monopoly of unchallenged superpower is not regarded everywhere in the world as necessarily a good thing. Nonetheless, it is highly probable that US air power will provide the leading edge of the monopoly. Not surprisingly, therefore, those countries which have not usually been found among the USA's allies have looked at the Gulf from a different perspective: how to blunt such projection in the future.

Indian Brigadier V. K. Nair has suggested some unwelcome features which could be introduced into scenarios loosely based on the US-led Coalition strategy in the Gulf. They include concentrating air force attacks on 'critical soft targets', such as AWACs, JSTARS and refuelling tankers, which even if successful would compel them to operate at greater defensive depth and thus degrade coalition/USAF activities. Special forces raids should be mounted against USAF forward bases and logistic concentrations. Losses would no doubt be high to the infiltrating troops, but results could be disproportionately significant. Shoulder-fired defence missiles should be given high priority and infiltration teams should also be equipped with them to threaten air transport and other movements. Even such a threat would prompt the diversion of resources to counter it. Above all, however, the potential opponent of the superpower should not passively await its fate. Military commanders must be permitted to apply their critical resources before, during and after the hostilities.[11]

It is expected that such measures would be taken by India in defence of national security rather than to further aggression, but other countries may not be so responsible or sensitive to international consensus. Brigadier Nair's perceptive analysis is based on two military principles common to all kinds of warfare : offensive action and the exploitation of enemy weakness. He also stimulates a politico-military discussion by implying that a traditionally defensive country seeking to uphold international law could under certain circumstances launch a pre-emptive strike: another principle not unknown to war in all three dimensions.

Optional Warfare

The underlying rationale for Brigadier Nair's analysis was mentioned in Chapters 5 and 6. It was impossible to contemplate military defeat of a superpower, but it might be possible to raise the risks to an unacceptable level. Obviously, risk evaluation – the balance of potential gains against costs and penalties – has, at least in theory, been a traditional activity of defence and foreign ministry staffs. Now, however, a new era of optional warfare has for many countries replaced the need to prepare to defend territorial integrity and national security.

After the overwhelming success of *Desert Storm*, those who had forecast thousands of friendly casualties, inextricable commitments and ecological disaster lost a certain amount of credibility. Almost a decade previously, the decision by the Thatcher government to go to war over a handful of bog-covered islands occupied by a few hundred insular ex-Britons over 8,000 miles away startled most of the world's governments, not least of Argentina and the Soviet Union.[12]

But in Bosnia, in the heart of Europe, circumstances and responses were very different. Excluding all the difficulties of political objectives, national rivalries and the unpredictability of military options, there was an underlying unwillingness among potential participants to incur casualties and costs when there were no compelling national security or commercial reasons to do so. Whenever a state has an option whether to participate in a conflict or not, all military considerations acquire a slightly different perspective, but especially those associated with the application of air power.

On the one hand, air power is the instrument of least commitment. As explained in Chapter 6, it can reach into a conflict zone from outside, either for direct air attack independently of ground forces, or in support of them. The USA has global reach, but medium powers such as Britain require, at the least, in-flight refuelling support closer to the theatre of operations. Such use of air power avoids the commitment of ground forces with their associated need for logistic support, basing and greater casualty risks. In the event of failure, cessation of air activity is far less politically visible than the extraction of ground forces under unfavourable or even ignominious circumstances. Moreover, even with the emergence of stronger regional air defences or other counters, air power will remain an instrument of Western superiority for some time.

But in optional warfare, domestic opinion may divide along party lines about participation in principle and about methods in particular. Even a low casualty rate which included individual aircrew and highly-expensive equipment might prompt speedy dissension. Indeed, how important would a conflict have to be before the USAF risked one-twentieth or even one-tenth of its B-2 force?

A totalitarian state may indulge its options more readily than a government accountable to an electorate. The presence of a free press will ensure that at least some political mileage would be sought by the opposition from a military setback. Moreover, air power will always carry with it the skeletons of Guernica and Dresden. No matter how precise the weaponry and professional the aircrew, every so often a weapon system will fail and non-combatants will die. Not only will the free press report such occurrences back at home, but internationally as well. The 'CNN factor' will be exploited to the full by all those who believe that air power is inhumane, somehow unfair and 'yet again' indiscriminate and hence, in sum politically counterproductive.

There may be however, a risk of over-emphasising the CNN factor in the application of air power in modern conventional conflicts. For example, some commentators have suggested that if the British public had been aware of the extent of the impact of RAF Bomber Command on German civilians in World War II they would have given greater support to the denunciation of the policy by individual politicians and churchmen. A timely reminder of the realities of British public opinion in the period was given in a BBC television programme in February 1994 on the RAF 'Dambuster' raid against three dams in the Ruhr in 1943. The British government dispensed with the usual security procedures and swiftly published details of the attack, emphasising the destruction and havoc wreaked by the millions of gallons of released floodwaters. The success was received with public jubilation and 617 Squadron passed into international mythology.

Whenever 'collateral' damage or deaths can be explained by national necessity, accident or genuine mistake, the adverse effect on air strategy or policy is likely to be minimised in both weight and duration. One's own casualties will continue to be regarded as much more important, however unpalatable such a position will seem to more sensitive consciences. Moreover, it is to be expected that democratic politicians will in due course learn to exploit the international media with the same facility that they usually accommodate their domestic outlets.

In sum therefore, air power is likely to become a favourite instrument in optional warfare, minimising friendly casualties, providing a wide range of offensive options, capitalising on technological superiority, susceptible to the fine tuning of volume and duration, and able to be started, interrupted and halted without concern for 'in-country' logistic support or protection. How far it may be seen as demonstrating a tacit unwillingness to become 'seriously' involved in a conflict over a protracted period will depend on the circumstances of the scenario and the relative values of the interventionist state. The critical contribution of air power is that it allows the options to be selected.

Maximising the Minimum
In the last resort, of course, air power's impact in any warfare, optional or otherwise, would be determined by the resources available to apply it. In the 1990s all air forces faced one particular problem, albeit for different reasons. The problem itself was familiar : how to achieve maximum cost effectiveness. Or, as Trenchard's script-writing staff officer had expressed it in 1922, 'the expansion of the power of *matériel* and personnel without increasing either.'[13] Now, however, there were various additional reasons to resolve the problem. The USA wished to protect capabilities in the face of defence cuts. European states had the same motivation, plus a desire to

avoid total dependence on the USA. Ex-members of the Eastern bloc wished to salvage something from the wreckage of their security structure. Third World countries wished to strengthen their regional positions and, if possible, reduce their vulnerability to longer-range pressure or intervention.

Consequently, several differing routes were chosen by states to maximise their resources to be allocated to air power. They may be examined under two interrelated headings : co-operation and force multiplication.

The concept of co-operation in warfare is as old as warfare itself. The construction of alliances in which the product was greater than the sum of the parts has been a goal of diplomacy down the ages. With rare exceptions the alliances were *ad hoc* and restricted to military co-operation during a period of hostilities. The age of air power has, however, seen several refinements on the theme. The extended period of East-West confrontation encouraged habits of peacetime co-operation which were probably more extensively developed among air forces than among armies or navies, but even then NATO and the Warsaw Pact conformed to the traditional pattern of co-operation in the face of a specific threat in a specific region. Other contemporary forms of co-operation are likely to have a more far-reaching influence on international, and differential, air power.

Industrial Collaboration

The interrelationship of Russian air power and the aerospace industry has been examined in Chapter 7. In 1994 there were equally significant contemporary developments in the West.

In his post-World War II report to the Secretary of War, General Arnold encapsulated the contribution of industry to air power:

> Air power is not composed alone of the war-making components of aviation. It is the total aviation activity - civilian and military, commercial and private, potential as well as existing. Military air power – or air force – is dependent upon the air potential provided by industry which in turn, thrives best in an atmosphere of individual initiative and private enterprise. Governments can do much to increase this air potential by judicious use of its co-ordinating and planning powers.[14]

The requirement for a national aerospace industry to support the projection of national air power remained an important principle in 1994, but in practice it had been diluted by various levels of international collaboration.

In the United States, military aircraft and weapons production was still supported by a high proportion of indigenous components, although unconfirmed reports alleged dependence on Japan for many kinds of

microprocessor. The US Marine Corps AV-8B was of British basic design
and flew with British engines. Sections of the LANTIRN navigation and
target acquisition system and the Head Up Display unit for F-22 also originated in the United Kingdom. High-value systems, however, such as
AWACs, JSTARS, F-117 and the stealth family were unmistakably products
of the USA's own aerospace industry, as were the *Patriot* and the *Stinger*
SAM. As a result, international collaboration had not been a significant
consideration in US air power procurement.

The situation in Europe was very different. In the 1970s Britain and
France collaborated to produce their primary day/clear weather
strike/attack aircraft, the *Jaguar*. Later, Britain, Germany and Italy collaborated to produce the most important all-weather strike attack aircraft
in their inventories. Including exports, 992 *Tornados* of different variants
were produced. Of those, 407 were purchased by the UK.[15]

In 1979 Britain, Germany and France began studies on a collaborative
fighter for the 1990s. Fifteen years later, *Eurofighter* 2000 flew for the first
time. By then France had dropped out of the partnership to design and
build the *Rafale*, while Britain and Germany had been joined by Spain
and Italy. The first EF-2000s were due to enter RAF and Italian service in
2000, and the German and the Spanish air force two years later. The vicis-
situdes of the EFA/EF-2000 programme illustrate most of the advantages
and disadvantages of international collaboration.

In theory, agreement on the specification for an agile air superiority
fighter should be easy to reach. A British House of Commons Defence
Committee report in 1992 confirmed that the 'next generation RAF fighter
would have to be capable of delivering high speed, beyond-visual-range
missile attacks, and of performing well in close combat using both short-
range air-to-air missiles and a gun. The essential characteristics required by
a fighter in both those forms of engagement was "agility", i.e., to be capable of very high rates of climb, roll, turn and acceleration at both sub-sonic
and supersonic speeds. Agility was required in beyond-visual-range engagement to maximise its chance of a "kill" by rapidly gaining height and/or
speed before firing its missile, and then to take drastic evasive manoeuvres
to escape the opposing fighter's missile. Agility was also required in close
combat to maximise the chance of obtaining a firing opportunity'.[16] The
report went on to note other important requirements, including range and
endurance, high-performance radar and low radar cross-section, fully integrated weapons, avionics and mission management systems, short take-off
and landing and high reliability and low maintenance.

This was a formidable specification, but one on which most air forces
would have been pleased to agree. In fact, France also wished to operate the
fighter from her aircraft carriers and disagreements over weight and

allegedly design leadership led to France's leaving the five-nations consortium in 1985. Already the programme had been slowed down by the need to establish consensus.

British studies have shown that collaborative programmes have tended to take longer to develop than national ventures, but the evidence is not conclusive. Delays have been estimated at two to two-and-a-half years or an extra 10 per cent to 20 per cent, with specific examples of 62 months for US national programmes, 83 for British and 100 for collaborative projects. On the other hand, the British MoD in 1991 believed there was no hard evidence that British collaboration programmes took longer than national ventures.[17]

It is intellectually precise to say that a national programme might have been delayed as long as a collaborative one, but the former would be immune to delays caused by disagreements over specification, work-sharing, the placing of contracts internationally,[18] and by political considerations in more than one country.

Work-sharing in the development plan of EFA/EF-2000 was agreed in proportions related to the potential national uptakes from production. The original plan was for 765 aircraft, of which Britain and Germany would take 250 each, Italy 165 and Spain 100. Work was shared 33,33,21 and 13 per cent, respectively.[19] By 1994, however, the total had been reduced to approximately 600, with the German share reduced to 140, Italy to 130 and Spain to 85. Work-sharing was a mixed blessing. Its considerable advantage was that it gave a highly-visible stake in national defence to indigenous industry. In the UK, for example, even during pressure for a post-Cold War 'peace dividend', strong all-party and trade union support for the EF-2000 programme was sustained. If, on the other hand, foreign industry had been seen to be benefiting from British defence expenditure, such broadly-based support would have been lacking.

There were also penalties. The work-sharing ratio applied to airframe, engine, engine accessories, avionics/armaments and general equipment areas, 'so as to provide a balanced spread of technology and a cost effective distribution of work.'[20] Those two objectives could be difficult to reconcile, for example, when one country, Britain, had a highly-developed and competitive electronic industry which Spain, in comparison, lacked.[21] Whereas the *Tornado* bomber variant had a software capacity of fewer than 100,000 direct source instructions, EF-2000 was contracted to have a capacity to grow from 800,000 to 1,600,000 without a change of hardware: statistics which illustrate the complexity of the fighter and the conflict between securing value for money and allocating work-shares by national proportions, regardless of national capacity.[22]

As with programme delays, so comparative costs between national and collaborative programmes are difficult to quantify. Collaboration must induce some comparative inefficiencies: arbitrary work-sharing, duplicated locations, international transport of components, and costs of international management among them. One theory holds that 'on collaborative aircraft programmes, development costs increase in proportion to the square root of the number of participants', but 'even so, each partner saves 50 per cent of the costs of an independent national development.'[23]

There is general agreement among politicians, government officials and specialist defence analysts that collaboration, despite some inefficiencies, does reduce excessive and wasteful competition in R & D, achieves economy in scale from longer production runs, which, in turn, induces a more competitive export. Furthermore, 'a strong element in the UK's approach to collaboration has been the desire to develop an effective European alternative to what it has feared would otherwise become US domination of the armaments market.'[24]

That fear was well founded. A letter to the US State Department from a senior executive with McDonnell Douglas at the time of the negotiations in 1992 about an F-15 sale to Saudi Arabia, and subsequently 'leaked', contained some very perceptive observations about the interaction between arms sales, arms control and foreign policy.

The writer expressed concern lest Saudi Arabia should buy EFA (EF-2000) instead of the F-15 because, 'the Saudis would be able to configure their EFAs to their own specifications, and the capabilities of those aircraft could be significantly enhanced in the future without US knowledge, consent or control'.

On the other hand, he argued, 'the sale of the F-15 to Saudi Arabia would significantly impair the ability of Europe's combat aircraft industry to develop a next generation fighter that would be sold freely in the Middle East. As a result, this scenario would greatly improve US control over military aircraft operated by other countries and ultimately enhance US competitiveness in the European defense market. The historic significance of this opportunity for the US Government should not be underestimated . . . The serious weakening or even elimination of foreign competition helps the US to retain its lead in a strategically vital industry, but perhaps more significantly could empower the US to act unilaterally in the future to effectively control the supply of arms to other nations.'[25]

This was not, of course, a statement of US policy, and presumably part of a lobbying campaign, but it very clearly identified the international implications of a potential US air power monopoly.

Collaboration also encouraged interoperability and standardisation of equipment, even though national weapon choices, and in the case of EF-

2000, installation by Italy and Britain only of a defensive aids suite, could constrain the principle in practice. Once commitments had been entered into, they could prove very expensive to abandon. The EF-2000 programme passed through a crisis in 1992 when German Defence Minister Rühe launched a strong attack on it, but found that the penalties of withdrawal were likely to absorb more than any savings accruing from a 'cheaper' alternative. Such an alternative would inevitably have had reduced performance. It took some time for some politicians and analysts to understand that by the time EF-2000 entered operational service it could be called upon to face not just MiG-29s and SU-27s, the originally envisaged opponents, but F-16s, F-15s and F-18s, plus indigenous Third World fighters, all sold on the international market. When air superiority was essential to the success of all other military operations, as most armed forces professed to believe, then economies sought by a reduction in capability could prove to be both illusory and disastrous.

If moves towards common European foreign and defence policies were to continue, the availability of a European combat aircraft at the hub of air power application would achieve even greater significance. The alternatives were to rely on the USA for the provision of air superiority, buy from the USA or buy from Russia. Reliance on the USA would widen the air power differential and further constrain independent European options. Purchase from the USA would erode the European aerospace industrial base and risk US market domination. Purchase from Russia would incur all the disadvantages of 'buying American' without the compensation of shared political interests and with the further risk of dependence on uncertain foreign sources.

Consequently, while the penalties of design compromise, delayed entry into operational service and increased development costs all prompted concern at various times over the EF-2000 programme, support in Europe for collaboration aerospace projects remained strong. The alternatives were politically, economically and militarily unacceptable. It would be difficult to envisage any credible European security policy in the second century of air power without a credible aerospace industrial base to sustain it.

Collaborative Assets

Collaborative production of the Panavia *Tornado* led to a further European co-operative venture: the establishment in 1979 of the Tri-national Tornado Training Establishment (TTTE) at Cottesmore in the UK. The concept of co-operative flying training was not new : for several years NATO crews had completed basic flying training in the USA. The different TTTE objectives were implicit in the Memorandum of

Understanding signed in 1979 by governmental representatives of the UK, the Federal Republic of Germany and Italy: '. . . having considered . . . the advisability of increasing co-operation and mutual understanding with the aim of achieving standardisation of weapons, tactics and techniques and the greater interoperability of their forces . . .'[26]

TTTE was intended to foster co-operation within the NATO alliance, but the value of such co-operative combat training will actually increase in a period when short notice, *ad hoc* coalition air power may be deployed. Maximisation of facilities offers opportunities to reduce costs to the participants. At Cottesmore, capital expenditure, maintenance and aircraft operating costs were allocated in proportion to the relative sizes of the national flying programmes. In 1990, for example, the proportions were FRG 47, UK 41 and Italy 11 per cent. Each country was to provide aircraft 'in numbers based on their national training requirement and the training syllabi. The aircraft will be integrated into a common pool at TTTE and will be flown as far as possible at a consistent rate. The aircraft will remain the property of the parent nation at all times.'[27]

By 1990 over 2,000 aircrew had graduated from the unit, at the hands of German, Italian and British instructors. Inevitably there were lessons to be applied to future similar ventures. National variations in weapons and other equipment fits constrained full standardisation, but, on the other hand, all crews flew each other's aircraft. Mid-life updates to the national aircraft varied according to national budgetary pressures and concern was expressed about divergence in equipment increasing to the extent that operation of a common fleet would become impracticable.[28] TTTE also absorbed different basic flying backgrounds and operational procedures so that in due course the crews would benefit when flying joint operations. Similarly, while groundcrews remained in national components, future squadron deployments would be facilitated by TTTE experience. The advent of EF-2000 would seem to offer opportunities for similar asset sharing.

Quite apart from such specialist activities, NATO air forces regularly trained together. Allied practice interceptions and evasions took place on a routine basis, reinforced by squadron exchange visits and individual exchange officer programmes. Regular large-scale exercises were flown and all NATO squadrons were subject to the same rigorous tactical evaluations by allied staffs. Of particular importance were the large 'package' exercises flown in electronic combat conditions at Nellis AFB in Nevada where potential scenarios could be realistically simulated. These habits of co-operation paid handsome dividends in *Desert Storm*. In the 1990s, however, there was the need for an imaginative rethinking about co-operative combat training. For example, rapid deployment to bases lacking the support facilities enjoyed in NATO, or co-operation with non-NATO air forces, or the rapid construction of international packages with various components. Among many different features, *Desert Storm* and Bosnia both gave time for international operations to be rehearsed in-theatre for several months before they had to be applied. Such would not always be the case and air staff would have plenty of scope for imaginative training-exercise planning and overseas deployments in preparing for 'optional' warfare.

Three years after the formation of the TTTE, a further experiment in asset sharing was begun with the formation of the NATO Airborne Early Warning (NAEW) Force, at Geilenkirchen in Germany in June 1982. By 1985 a fleet of 18 E-3As had been delivered, operating with crews drawn from all NATO members except France, Spain, Iceland and Britain. Britain, after the failure of its indigenous AEW programme, purchased seven E-3Ds and from January 1992 assigned them to NATO commanders to work alongside the NATO squadron. Subsequently, NATO AWACs deployed to Turkey during *Desert Storm* and to the Adriatic during the Bosnian saga. The precedent of the NAEW squadron in co-operation in a high-value asset may be an example for the international purchase of other systems, perhaps including JSTARS or other reconnaissance systems. Again, however, lessons learned from the NAEW experience would need to be applied. Forty per cent of the funding for the squadron was provided by the USA.[29] If NATO as an alliance should commit air power to a conflict or crisis in the future, it may be assumed that US high-value assets would be used. Logic would suggest therefore that purchase by any European combination should be under the auspices of the Western European Union (WEU) to complement NATO rather than duplicate US assets already available.

Before another high-value asset was purchased, detailed plans would be required to avoid repeating early problems in NAEW over manning and maintenance. The total NAEW manpower complement was 840, with national numbers assigned and command positions allocated in proportion to national funding contributions. Discipline, pay and conditions of service all remained under national control. It was not possible to co-ordinate in-flow and out-flow of individuals and national experience levels fluctuated considerably. Sixty per cent of groundcrew were NATO-hired civilians, thereby providing maintenance continuity, but arrangements for transition to war and crew reinforcement remained uncertain for a prolonged period. National constitutional restrictions on German aircrew in operations beyond NATO boundaries initially complicated crew allocation to NAEW operations associated with Bosnia.

Ultimately, however, the NAEW programme became a notable success, offering an example for future co-operative efforts. The field of reconnaissance would be a good candidate: always the air power Cinderella, never enough assets, similar military requirements, advanced technology required for sensors, communications and interpretation and, of particular importance in the context of differential air power, within the capacity of European aerospace companies. A reconnaissance force could include UAVs, fixed-wing aircraft and satellite systems.

The potential contribution to many kinds of military operation would be considerable, but it would not be a simple concept to translate into action. It should, moreover, be speedily examined by WEU planning staff, because the NATO precedent took some time to establish:

> The NATO (EW) success story however, did not materialise overnight. It was instead the result of an often difficult process played out in the capitals of 13 NATO nations over a period of several years. Many factors contributed to the accord, not the least of which was a workable agreement to share production contracts roughly in proportion to each country's contribution to the programme. Even then, it took over two years to hammer out each nation's share of the programme acquisition and of the operations and support budget . . . The result was the establishment of the first fully integrated multinational allied air force in history. Specialists from 11 nations worked side by side in the aircraft, on the hangar floor and in the many facilities which directly and indirectly support the NAEW mission . . .[30]

A Co-operative Security Regime in Europe

For a state to co-operate in an international reconnaissance unit, or units, it would need to have identified common security interests : the critical factor underlying NAEW co-operation and threatening it when the aircraft moved beyond Germany's declaratory security position. Air power has introduced a novel factor into international security which prompts concern everywhere but seldom stimulates realistic action to resolve it. One particular co-operative response would emphasise common security interests and could facilitate the reduction of several regional tensions.

The boundaries of territorial and aerospace security are not identical. Over the centuries, territorial integrity could be defended at one's frontiers. In theory at least, earlier generations of hostile aircraft could be intercepted at the boundary of one's national airspace and an attack would be neutralised. Now, the surface-to-surface ballistic missile, and the air-launched stand-off missile both call for defensive response beyond one's own national aerospace boundaries. As *Patriot* operations demonstrated in the Gulf, a missile which breaks up on intercept can still do a great deal of damage. If the missile is delivering a mass-destruction warhead it is imperative that it be intercepted, like the missile-launching aircraft, before it overflies one's own territory. It is no coincidence that Russian air force officers were especially strongly opposed to the withdrawal of ex-Soviet forces from the Baltic states, where the Skrunda air defence radar complex was a central link in Russia's western air defences. Similarly, for 40 years RAF interceptors prepared to attack incoming Soviet aircraft several hundred miles out over the North Sea and north-east Atlantic, with UK air defences closely co-ordinated with those of Norway, Denmark, Germany and the Low Countries.

Happily, that co-operation, integral to the NATO alliance, remained in place after the end of confrontation. In two other areas, however, problems of aerospace security could, if left unresolved, exacerbate potential sources of conflict on the ground. If, on the other hand, those problems could be resolved co-operatively, a habit might be developed which could be applied to less tractable tensions in each region.

In central and eastern Europe (CEE) the strategic legacy of the Warsaw Pact includes obsolete military structures irrelevant to contemporary and probable future regional security requirements, in a period of political and economic uncertainty in which traditional sources of conflict have re-emerged. CEE air forces were dependent on the Soviet Union for combat aircraft, weapons and the ground components of air defences. Since the collapse of the USSR, maintenance has been impeded by non-availability or the high costs of spares. Force structure, unit deployment and especially air defence orientation were subordinate to the dictates of the Soviet General Staff and directed solely towards the West. As described in Chapter 3, an air-defence continuum spread from the forward ground forces back over the WTO to the USSR.

Ground formations can be redeployed to face threats from new directions, and aircraft in particular can operate in any direction from one base, albeit with constraints on endurance and range if they are much further away from a 'new' threat. But, when air defence must begin over neighbouring territory, the precise locations of early warning ground radars and aircraft become extremely important.

In addition to tensions within CEE arising from ethnic sensitivities, minority problems, boundaries and suchlike, the xenophobic-revisionist utterances of Mr Zhirinovsky and his extremist Russian colleagues in 1993 and 1994 reinforced CEE perceptions of vulnerability and insecurity. Faced with conflicting priorities for resource allocation and political alignment, but conscious of the sources of contagious instability, most states in CEE had five options in deciding how to react to the air aspects of their strategic legacy.

The temptation to do nothing would be strong but counterproductive. Neutrality has never been an option for the defenceless. Even small but modernised air forces could inflict heavy damage on ground forces and civilian targets if unopposed. A second option, unilateral defensive provision, would not guarantee security. There would be no shortage of salesmen, especially from the West offering state of the art defence systems. But they would need to be supported by equally modern combat aircraft with their associated maintenance and training systems. Not only would such unilateral provision consume a high proportion of national resources, it would risk stimulating confrontational or competitive military preparations among neighbouring states. Were potential sources of conflict already existing, a regional arms race would ensue and the product of the investment would be destabilising rather than the opposite.

The preferred solution in CEE was to seek great power support, i.e., from NATO. The North Atlantic Co-operation Council (NACC) welcomed CEE countries and stimulated many forms of co-operation and assistance, but in 1994 the prospect of formal security guarantees by NATO to individual CEE countries still seemed remote. The dominant mood in western Europe on the collapse of Communism was one of relief, followed by a desire to reduce defence expenditures, not sustain them. There was no public support for giving military guarantees to CEE states against each other nor against a resurgent Soviet Union. Even in the face of perceived Serbian aggression in Bosnia, destabilisation in CEE was seen as a potential contagion which should be contained by diplomacy, counsel and practical, non-military assistance. Alternatively, should a CEE state look back to the USSR for security guarantees, the subsequent *frisson* in western Europe and among other CEE states can be readily imagined.

A fourth option of regional co-operation, for example, between the Czech, Slovak, Polish and Hungarian air forces, would confer more advantages: joint exercises, simplification of air-defence redeployment to 'outer borders' and closer integration of civil and military air traffic among them. But in the longer term, however, the concept of 'regional' air security within CEE is flawed. The practical effect of such a zone would, in the case of the example given, be to create a new frontier running north-south from the Baltic to the Danube. It would do little or nothing to enhance Polish security *vis-à-vis* Ukraine or Hungary's with Romania. Costs of force redeployment would be reduced in the vertical tier but the nature of the total defensive reorientation could easily be misrepresented as divisive and threatening to those states not included. Moreover, the problem of extra-territorial defensive depth in the skies to east and west of the grouping would remain unresolved. By definition, any such regional grouping would contribute little to the security of states excluded from the arrangement and the longer-term impact on CEE would, like the previous options, detract from, rather than enhance stability.

The fifth option originates from the problems presented by the nature of modern air power itself. Rivers and mountains continue to mark national frontiers but they have lost much of their value as protection for the territory behind them. Not only do modern combat aircraft have the speed to achieve surprise; many have the reach to outflank entire lengths of frontier defences, to cross neutral skies and attack strategic targets from flank or rear. For example, during confrontation there was always concern that WTO airforces would sweep south-west across Austria and Switzerland before attacking NATO's central region from the south. The neutral integrity of those countries was never in doubt, nor their intention to defend their airspace to the best of their ability, but the physical problems of high-speed interception in restricted airspace with little time were acute.

In today's CEE, several states could have a strategic interest in the same area of sky : the skies above Slovakia are a good example, south-western Ukraine another. Russian sensitivity to the air approaches over the Baltic states dates from the period when they were potentially a main avenue of attack from NATO's medium-range bombers flying towards Moscow. The problem is how to reconcile national security with neighbouring airspace sovereignty. The answer lies in a co-operative air-security regime.

The first step would be to extend co-operation in peacetime air traffic control to the monitoring and notification across national boundaries of military flying. In the United Kingdom over the last 30 years legitimate military interests have been confronted with ever-increasing civil traffic expansion but an effective joint-control organisation is now, as elsewhere in western Europe, in place. Despite such integration, the secure autonomy of the UK air-defence system was never compromised or constrained. Such Western examples could be studied and adopted for use in CEE, progressively reducing military control of air traffic.

If similar structures were adopted, or even when the principle is adopted, the way would be open for the extension of a joint civil-military control and reporting network linking ex-NATO, neutral, CEE and CIS states. The gradual evolution to a fully-automated information transfer system across several national boundaries would be lengthy and expensive but the provision of a manual interface between the existing systems would not. If the interface were to be reinforced by international exchange postings between military personnel the potential for co-operation would be accelerated. To ensure complete integration such exchanges should be omnidirectional. For example, from the Czech Republic at least with Slovakia, Germany, Poland, Austria and possibly with Hungary also, and extending north and south to include Sweden and Switzerland.

There would undoubtedly be military reservations to such a proposal. Exchange postings would be seen as intrusive intelligence-gathering opportunities, especially in the most sensitive areas of early warning, fighter strength, readiness states and reaction procedures. If that perspective were to be justified, then obviously the opportunities for surprise air attack would be enhanced rather than diminished. Western experience illustrates, however, that it is quite possible to isolate such sensitive areas within the total system. What would be very difficult under such a co-operative regime would be to prepare and mount a surprise air attack. The expulsion or isolation of exchange officers would in itself become a threatening and destabilising activity. In other words, as in all co-operative security regimes, there is a balance of advantage to be secured by both sides whereupon the absolute but unachievable concept of security is exchanged for a comparative practical level which accepts a fragment of mutual vulnerability.

Under such circumstances, air power would not be excluded from the armoury of national security, but its destabilising potential in a surprise attack would be considerably reduced. It would not be necessary to wait for an over-arching pan-European system to be debated and created. A series of local initiatives would build the structure upwards, leaving problems of system integration to be overcome by international, co-ordinated investment. Existing ex-Soviet obsolescent installations could be included in the programme.

Thereafter further steps could be taken. Joint air-defence exercises could be organised, with different partners against different geographical axes. No doubt some would generate more enthusiasm than others, and some would require longer and more delicate preparation. As with the exchanges, each would involve exposing some defensive preparations to a neighbour and, again, the balance of security advantage would need to be weighed by national air staffs. Meanwhile, moves to reconstruct national air forces away from the old Soviet model should proceed with caution. While Western training and progressive military education should be examined for their relevance, the slavish adoption of structures, equipment and philosophies anchored in very different political and economic environments should be avoided.

Air forces cannot be left untended on the ground without suffering degraded effectiveness and morale. In a climate of very constrained economic and manpower resources it may be necessary to accept a further period of aircraft and weapon obsolescence and a general reduction in air force size to allow the concentration of residual resources on high rates of serviceability and acceptable numbers of flying hours for the remaining aircraft and crews.

There is much in common with the contemporary position of CEE air forces in 1994 and the British Royal Air Force 70 years ago. The then Chief of the Air Staff deliberately directed resources towards less glamorous items of infrastructure, rather than front-line equipment. The modern parallel would be CEE investment in English-language training to enable military aircraft controllers to work alongside their civil counterparts, in the joint location of civil and military aircraft controllers, in forging links with neighbouring military command and control systems, and in programmes to facilitate exchange schemes for officers with neighbouring states. Moreover, all would be legitimate objects for international assistance and probably be viewed favourably by the NACC.

Equipment modernisation would by comparison move more slowly, taking advantage, it may be hoped, of the confidence-building measures implicit in the co-operative initiatives. National perceptions would vary considerably, but general guiding principles might well include providing mobile elements in C^3 systems and dispersal opportunities for combat aircraft in times of tension. Hand-held or small mobile SAM systems to inhibit hostile air intervention in low-intensity conflict might be preferable at first to the more superficially attractive but far more expensive options of modernising front-line aircraft.

The cumulative impact of these measures would enhance national security in two ways. First, they would encourage a regional environment in which habits of co-operation began to intrude upon more traditional independent, and ultimately counterproductive, approaches to defence. Second, if co-operative measures should break down, a state which had allocated resources to such defensive deployment would seriously complicate any aggressor's plans to use his own air power offensively and decisively. In both cases hasty escalation from disagreement through crisis to conflict would be inhibited, giving more time for bilateral diplomacy, more opportunity for mediation by external agencies and in extremis more facilities for the insertion of peacekeeping forces on both sides.

An aerospace security regime will not of itself bring peace and security to CEE. The legacy of thousands of years, not just of a confrontational hiatus, is far too complex for that. It could, however, reduce the possibility of air power being used as an indiscriminate instrument of coercion to resolve disputes among the inheritors. Agreements reached in the air environment may stimulate more co-operative approaches to conflict resolution on the ground where confrontation has been more direct, more deep-rooted and more bitter.

An Option for the Middle East
Outside Europe, few regions have seen such repeated and bitter conflict as

the Middle East. In early 1994 there appeared to be an opportunity for progress towards resolution of the Arab-Israeli dispute. At its heart lay territory, settlement, boundaries, access, sovereignty and refugees. Yet there remained another potential, quite discrete source of conflict : control of, and access to, regional aerospace. Sooner or later, an aerospace security regime would be required in the region, and some of its features could be similar to those proposed for CEE.[31]

Since the early 1960s Israel has depended heavily on her air force (IAF) to offset a perceived numerical inferiority in ground forces and threats emanating from the north, east and south-west. As explained in Chapter 2, the IAF has sought to sustain superiority by closely co-ordinated technological advantage, rigorous operational training and doctrine which incorporates defensive and offensive operations. For several reasons, air power was impinging even more heavily on the strategic environment of the Middle East in the early 1990s.

Modern combat aircraft can launch PGMs at high speed from many directions while 100 km or more from their targets. Yet the distance from Tel Aviv to Damascus is scarcely 200 km; between Damascus and Amman slightly less; from Tel Aviv to the Jordan-Iraq border 400 km. The West Bank territory is 60 km wide and 100 km long. A serious security problem arises in this region from the international fact that defensive frontiers in the sky are no longer commensurate with those on the ground. The need for aerial security in depth reinforces the conflict between national sovereignty of airspace and the legitimate right of a neighbouring state to self-defence.

The conflict of interest is aggravated by the power of PGMs to decapitate and paralyse command and control systems, thereby raising the potential value of a surprise air attack, either as an independent move or as a precursor to a ground offensive. If agreements should be reached on ground forces in the region, a lack of agreement on aerospace issues will become disproportionately more destabilising. As several conflicts in the area have demonstrated, air power can inflict heavy damage on ground forces, in addition to striking political, strategic and economic targets of great national importance with far-reaching consequences.

Israel has on several occasions faced an Arab coalition which has included states not contiguous to her. Conversely, Israeli aircraft have attacked longer-range targets in Tunisia and Iraq as well as those closer to home in neighbouring countries. In the Gulf War, Israel was attacked by *Scud* missiles launched from Iraq. Clearly therefore, an aerospace security regime in the Middle East must not be confined to the skies above the West Bank and Gaza ; it must ultimately encompass at least Jordan, Syria, Lebanon and Iraq. At the core of the relationship is the airspace over Israel itself, over the territories of West Bank and Gaza, and over Jordan, Lebanon and Syria.

Israeli dependence upon air power for her national security prompts a need for reliable surveillance and early warning in skies well beyond her frontiers; for aerial reconnaissance on overland approaches to her territories; for unimpeded flight over the occupied territories and for uninterrupted, rigorous training at all altitudes. Her neighbour Jordan, on the other hand, has faced a threat of attack from several directions in recent years and, while possessing only a small and obsolescent air force, has declared that any infringement of either territory or airspace would be opposed. Syria has re-equipped her air forces after the Beka'a disaster of 1982 but has placed greater emphasis on ground forces in her confrontation with Israel. Nonetheless, Syria could become a customer for revitalised Russian aerospace exports if a regional arms race was to be restimulated.

The first steps towards a co-operative aerospace security regime in the region would be similar to those in CEE: the stage-by-stage establishment of a co-operative air traffic control system with military and civil aviation components. In the foreseeable future, the majority of flights in the region will be of military origin, but, as peace returns, the growth in civil commercial traffic will be rapid. The creation of a joint military air traffic organisation (JMATO) based on existing air-traffic control centres and systems would require comparatively little capital expenditure, depending primarily on procedural revision. At present all major ground radar installations are military establishments. Two primary innovations would be required : one to establish routine communications between centres in Israel, the West Bank and in Jordan; the second to incorporate civilian air traffic controllers into the management system.

These three centres would link with the Damascus Flight Information Region (FIR) to the north and with neighbouring FIRs in the south-west and south-east. Each centre would be responsible for circulating notifications of air movement (NOTAMs) covering all civilian and military flights. It may be hoped that the proportion of military to civil flights in the area would gradually change as the peace formulae began to work, when the manning and command structure of a JMATO could be amended progressively to reflect that change.

In the early days of the organisation, when fears and suspicions are still being discarded, it is essential that accidental sources of conflict be eliminated. Notification of exercises and changes to flying patterns would be made via JMATO and priority should be given to the creation of a common emergency procedure to identify and notify unusual occurrences. In that way an aircraft straying off track by accident or because of emergency could be swiftly distinguished from one which had, for example, been hijacked or flown with malicious and provocative intent.

Internal security organisations would be responsible for preventing the unauthorised use of unconventional aircraft, such as microlites and hang gliders, as well as helicopters and fixed-wing aircraft. Events in the UK, however, have demonstrated that determined terrorists can evade the most conscientious and effective security forces and therefore the need to establish an airspace 'hot line' should be given the highest priority, however remote the possibility of such incidents may seem.

Once JMATO has been established, several other problems would become manageable. Of immediate political and commercial value would be the creation of two civilian airline corridors: one running east-west from Tel Aviv via Jerusalem to Amman, and the other linked to the first one running north-south above the Jordan Valley to Eilat/Aqaba. In due course the former would be continued eastwards from Amman and the latter northwards to Damascus. The height, depth and width of those corridors would be agreed by the participants, taking into account the usual factors of flight safety and military requirements. Additional ground navigational installations would be required in the region, but their cost would be quickly recouped from the expansion of civilian traffic, including, ultimately, overflights from Europe.

It would be hoped that the Palestinian authority in the West Bank would accept the presence in the West Bank airspace of designated military flying training areas for the IAF. Current air-to-ground firing ranges would be closed, but high-level, air-to-air interception training, low-level navigation training routes and helicopter transport corridors should be negotiated. Financial compensation could be included in negotiations. As in western Europe, the ecological impact of low-flying should be recognised and low flying routes restricted to uninhabited or thinly inhabited regions. It is not too fanciful to envisage in the longer term, with the growth of international stability, the IAF negotiating training facilities in the desert areas of neighbouring states.

In due course, this structure would facilitate the resolution of more sensitive aerospace issues, including surveillance and shared information, overflights in crisis and conflict, the deployment of SAM batteries and the infringement of airspace by ballistic missiles from states not party to the security regime. Like the overall peace process itself, the resolution of air-related disagreements is likely to take a lot of time and patience. The alternatives are at best the continued haemorrhage of resources into defence while stimulating such competition that no-one's security is actually enhanced. At worst, another Arab-Israeli war which could leave both 'victor' and 'vanquished' in barren lands.

Aerospace Insecurity

While there were some prospects in the Middle East and CEE for the harnessing of regional air power to co-operative security regimes, several states on the Pacific Rim were enhancing their air power unilaterally. There were sources of conflict, there was economic expansion and there was no overarching regional security structure. Circumstances here suggested that air power could ultimately become an arbiter in conflict rather than a contributor to stability.

With the exception of India, where defence spending fell substantially between 1987 and 1992, the countries of the Pacific Rim: Japan, China, South Korea, Taiwan, Thailand, Malaysia, Singapore and even Brunei all increased defence expenditure in real terms.[32] A high proportion of this increase in 1992 and 1993 was allocated to the purchase of aerospace products and services.[33] Several general reasons were advanced for this phenomenon at a time when relaxation of tension between East and West was being accompanied by defence reductions elsewhere. They included: preparation for uncertainties when the USA reduced its regional presence; the need to replace obsolescent equipment; the opportunities afforded by expanding national economies to spend more on military hardware; persuasion from military establishments, especially in China and Taiwan; and the favourable market opportunities stimulated by a low-priced Russian export policy.

There did appear, however, to be one catalyst : China, which during the 1980s moved to secure possession of a number of disputed islands in the South China Sea, including the Paracels, which were disputed with Vietnam, and the more southerly Spratlys, subject in whole or part to claims by China, Taiwan, Malaysia, Vietnam and the Philippines. The islands have a strategic significance in that some are big enough to sustain airbases, but most importantly they are believed to straddle potentially rich oilfields. China also has historical claims to the area and regards it as the strategic approach to her south-western flank.

Chinese declaratory policy has been ambivalent. In February 1992 a new law was passed that identified the South China Sea as part of China's 'inland waters' and empowered China 'to order the eviction of all foreign military vessels or vessels of foreign governments that violate China's laws in the area.'[34] Later that year, at an ASEAN meeting in Manila the Chinese Foreign Minister called for joint development of the area, at almost the same time that an American oil corporation prospecting a Chinese concession along the Vietnam shelf received a pledge that the developer would, if necessary, be protected by the Chinese Navy.[35]

On the other hand, Chinese force modernisation was unambiguous and focused. During 1992 and 1993 the Chinese Air Force began to take delivery of 72 SU-27s and 24 MiG-31 *Foxhounds* from Russia, with six IL-76 transports expected to be converted to in-flight refuelling tankers with drogue systems bought from Iran. By coincidence, the Russian deal stipulated that these aircraft were not to be based near the Russian border, so their deployment to the south-western island of Hainan, on the South China Sea, was useful for both parties.

Meanwhile a number of contracts were signed with Israeli companies for electronic warfare equipment, including radar warning receivers, electronic intelligence systems, jammers, fire-control radars and phased array airborne radar antennae. Other co-operative products were believed to include day/night imaging pods and infra-red line scanners.[36] Several reports, unsubstantiated by 1994, suggested that China was also seeking to buy an unwanted aircraft carrier from Ukraine.

By global standards, the differential with Chinese air power remained considerable, but already by 1994 she had established regional dominance and, apparently on the threshold of massive economic expansion, could continue to increase first her defence budget and subsequently her own aerospace industrial base. The Spratlys were situated 1100 km south of Hainan Island, within range of in-flight refuelled SU-27s. Provision of airbase facilities on the Spratlys themselves would permit Chinese air power projection across the entire South China Sea.

Across the Straits of Taiwan, the Republic of China proceeded with the development of its own *Ching Kuo* fighter and took delivery of 60 *Mirage* 2000-5s and 150 updated F-16A/Bs. Thailand was reported in 1993 to be considering the purchase of *Harrier* II Plus aircraft from which to launch anti-shipping missiles. Japan meanwhile continued to increase its 'self-defence' budget in real terms by 3 per cent in 1992 and 2 per cent in 1993.[37] It provided for continued development of its indigenous FS-X F-16 equivalent, a further 43 F-15s and four Boeing E-767 AWACs, together with a wide range of weapons and systems improvements.

One of the most significant developments, however, was numerically one of the smallest. In 1993 Malaysia bought 18 MiG-29s and 8 F/A-18s. Several countries had previously purchased aircraft from both East and West, but not at the same time. No official Malaysian statement about prices was made, but a figure of $20 million for each MiG and $30 million for each F-18 was authoritatively reported.[38] For the former the transaction involved a partial barter scheme with palm oil, while the latter was accompanied by very favourable credit conditions.

Operationally, the purchases looked a mixed blessing. It was also reported that the Malaysian government had sought information on *Harpoon* anti-ship missiles, *Maverick* air-to-ground, AIM 7M *Sparrow* and AIM 9S *Sidewinder* air-to-air missiles. If Malaysia could afford such weapons, it would have a small but extremely well-equipped night/all-weather combat force. On the other hand, whether it could manage and sustain the ground support for such a spread of equipment, or indeed whether the Russian aerospace industry despite its reconstitution would be able to provide life cycle support, were questions still to be answered. A reported offer by India of maintenance and spares support for MiGs might also be difficult to sustain in the longer term because of that country's own dependence on Russian sources for some MiG-29 components. Nonetheless, the Russian export drive had achieved its first open-market Third World success. Western competitors had been warned.

It would be easy to over-emphasise the destabilising potential of these convergent circumstances in the Pacific Rim region. As the *Economist* observed in 1993, 'Apart from the Koreas, there is no place in Asia where ethnic discord or international hostility could plausibly lead to a big war in the near future.'[39] Already by 1992 one commentator had implausibly alleged that 'The PLA Air Force is now in a position to ensure virtually continued, round the clock air coverage and combat air patrol over the [Spratly] Islands during a crisis or a conflict.'[40] That assessment took no account of the months, if not years needed by China to train aircrew and groundcrew for her newly purchased *Flankers;* of the hours of training needed to refuel in-flight reliably and consistently; of the number of tankers required to maintain airborne CAPs 1,100 km from base – quite apart from their own vulnerability and no account being taken of the early warning and control necessary to co-ordinate such an effort over such distances. In sum, such analysis failed to distinguish between numbers of aircraft and their dependence on other components to achieve their much longer term operational potential.

Having said all that, the Pacific Rim would be an interesting arena for air power analysts and, possibly, ultimately for applicants. It was an arena in which air power was likely to be yet again a dominant influence. Any conflict between the regional powers would, in the air at least, be likely to be short and intense. Any external power straying into such a conflict would find no easy pickings among these particular Third World air forces, although all but that of China would be vulnerable to superior numbers and the most advanced Western aerospace technology. How far the independent, unilateral attempts to enhance national security would succeed, when at the same time neighbours were taking similar steps, was also a question for the future.

Co-operation with a Patron

In the Pacific Rim, states were prepared to allocate resources from expanding economies to lay the foundations of expensive, high-technology air power. What prospects were there for states with scarce resources which could not afford to divert their most technologically competent people to operate and maintain such systems? Similarly, how could friendly external powers encourage local activities which would facilitate co-operation in emergencies?

In many parts of the Third World, dependence on a great power for one's own military security might be tainted with memories of imperialism. If, however, such a relationship were freely entered into, with advantages to both sides, and especially if there was a threatening neighbour whose political priorities appeared to be more Spartan than Athenian, how could a smaller, developing country facilitate the application of someone else's air power to enhance its own security? A number of measures could be taken with a minimal diversion of resources and probably with assistance from the 'patron'. None would involve permanent basing of foreign forces. In Chapter 5 the options available to a regional aggressor in the light of the Gulf War were examined. The objectives of the potential regional victim therefore should be to preserve access for the patron and slow down and complicate the progress of the enemy from across the frontier.

Speedy assistance would arrive by air, so the first priority would be to ensure that at least one airfield existed which was big enough to receive and operate friendly combat aircraft and heavy transports. It would be unwise to rely on the presence in-theatre of a friendly carrier task force, even if the potential combat area would be within range of carrier-borne aircraft. At least one civil airport should be expanded by the provision of duplicated runways and taxiways. Air traffic control facilities should be hardened and also duplicated. Fuel storage, pipes and refuelling hydrants should be increased, dispersed, concealed and hardened and placed underground wherever possible. Runway repair equipment and materials should be stockpiled and exercised periodically by reservists and civilians. If hardened aircraft shelters cannot be provided, dispersed and revetted hardstandings should be substituted.

Airfield defences should be based on hand-held, surface-to-air missiles, operated by ground forces whose peacetime cadre would be represented by the armed security forces now so familiar at most international airports. Such a combination of passive and active defences would place minimum demands on resources and highly-skilled manpower. In an infant democracy, such forces would have the additional advantage of presenting no destabilising internal threat. Nor could they be portrayed as provocative to neighbouring states. They would, however, seriously complicate any plans a neighbouring aggressor may have to stop friendly assistance arriving swiftly in a region. In alternative circumstances, they might deter unwelcome advances from outside the region.

If a small country did wish to allocate resources to the more visible instruments of air power, procurement priorities might not include the latest model MiGs or F-18s. For example, border-surveillance aircraft which would give early detection of potentially hostile movement would, in peacetime, support the civil power by identifying illegal traffic. In many parts of the world frontiers are not as accessible as those between Kuwait and its neighbours. A defender's military objective would be to slow down an invader, taking advantage of regional topography. That in many circumstances would be better achieved by ground forces deployed swiftly by helicopter and equipped with man-portable anti-armour weapons. The defender's assets should ideally include well-motivated people defending their livelihood and capitalising on local knowledge. Moreover, even the most sophisticated all-weather combat aircraft will for the foreseeable future have difficulty in locating light ground forces below dense vegetation, and therefore even if they were affordable would be inadvisable.

There is one further consideration in procurement priorities. If a patron is to be called upon at short notice, the greater the interoperability between its forces and equipment and the recipient's the better. Thus when attractive one-time good deals are being offered by the international aerospace salesmen, one should consider not just whom the weapons are going to be directed against, but also which friends one hopes will be alongside. That in turn prompts political and cultural considerations in addition to the more obvious ones of costs, long-term availability of spares and technical support.

In sum, several factors well away from the cockpit of a combat aircraft can help to reduce the air power differential for a small, less well-endowed country. A regional aggressor who seeks to apply 'alternative' lessons from the Gulf War can himself be constrained by relatively inexpensive 'counter-countermeasures'. Perhaps the most difficult task would be persuading one's own generals that the shiniest toys are not necessarily what the country needs.

Force Multiplication

Every kind of international co-operation to enhance the application of air power requires an underlying political alignment, which may be as unpredictable as the crises it is designed to confront. A primary objective therefore for all air forces must be to maximise cost effectiveness : to ensure that the product of its components is greater than the sum of its parts.

Principles of cost effectiveness are dangerous implements to apply to any kind of military force, not least to air power. Costs are usually quantifiable. Effectiveness can only be measured accurately in combat, by which time the evaluation may be irrelevant in defeat. Military effectiveness down the ages has been the product of factors tangible and abstract. The cost and most effective dimensions of a broadsword were readily quantifiable. The morale of the legionary, the leadership of the centurion, the fighting competence of the legion were, on the other hand, diffuse, fluctuating and dependent on many intangibles. One modern problem of enunciating defence policy by slogan – 'Front line first', 'Cut the tail and preserve the teeth', 'Value for money', and the rest is that the quantifiable factors can be entered neatly in the ledger. The intangibles are not responsive to such good clerical discipline.

The often quoted Trenchard dictum of 1922 has now acquired a modern paraphrase: 'Force-multiplication'. Trenchard, as an ex-soldier, had no doubts about the two components to be expanded : '*matériel*' and 'personnel'. Proposals for force multiplication in air power's second century should pursue a similar, synergistic duality.

Operational Cost Effectiveness

A further complication in the quantification of cost effectiveness is that it usually takes place in peacetime, while the only effectiveness which matters is operational effectiveness in combat. It should be self-evident, but protracted periods of peacetime operations may insidiously erode the distinction. For example, in the aftermath of the Gulf War the USAF began to experiment with 'Composite Wings' in which different types of combat, EW, tanker and other aircraft were co-located on one base. The concept was for a 'package' to train and work together in peacetime so that responsiveness and cohesion would be enhanced upon rapid overseas deployment in a crisis. Such a concentration on one base would increase costs because of the need to provide relatively small amounts of maintenance and groundcrews for several different aircraft and their supporting systems. But if the package had the requisite numbers and proportions appropriate for whatever scenario occurred – and that raised several different questions about the flexibility of prepackaged air power – then clearly the *operational* cost effectiveness would be very high.

A second example concerns the perennial argument, touched on previously in regard to the reconstitution of the Russian Air Force, over peacetime flight safety and the demands of combat on a pilot's skill. 'Train as you intend to fight' is a well-founded aphorism, but it threatens penalties in peacetime. How can one quantify the comparative costs of losing a number of aircraft and aircrew in peacetime, despite the most proficient supervision, because of aircrew pushing themselves or their aircraft just beyond their capacity, with another number of aircraft lost in combat because the exchange rate there between risk and destruction was very different and the crew's training had not prepared them for it?

The objective of force multiplication is to induce maximum cost effectiveness at the point of operational significance: in the weapon on the target; the missile intercepting the attacker; the equipment delivered or dropped when and where required; the opponent jammed; the intruder discovered and identified; or the fighter refuelled.

Force Multipliers

The implementation of force multiplication may bring difficult procurement decisions. Either the front line remains the same size and force multipliers are added, in which case defence costs rise, or force multipliers are introduced at the expense of the size of the front line. The first is likely to be unacceptable to governments seeking to reduce defence expenditure; the second will be perennially unpopular with air force commanders.

Nonetheless, it is in the front line itself that force multiplication must first be sought, by developing multi-role capabilities. In an ideal world with unlimited resources every air force would deploy role specialist aircraft, weapons and crews. By 1994 even the USAF could not afford that. Lobbying for the F-22 advanced tactical aircraft began to emphasise its air-to-ground potential; the B-2 bomber would deliver both conventional and nuclear weapons; while the 'specialist' A-10 lacked supporters and even the highly successful F-117 drew restrained criticism for its lack of operational flexibility. International priorities pointed to a multi-role future : SU-27 variants, F-15E, F-18, EF-2000 and even multi-role modified F-14s.

The advantages of multi-role aircraft are considerable, provided they are accompanied by multi-role weapons and multi-role crews. Thereby, the theoretical air power characteristics of flexibility can be fully exploited. A comparison may be made between the *Tornado* GR-1, which displayed considerable flexibility in the Gulf War by attacking airfields, bridges, fuel installations and ground forces at night and in all weathers, and the F-18, which did not have such offensive versatility but which could also be used as an air-superiority fighter.

Multi-role aircraft confer several operational advantages. They may be used in offensive or defensive scenarios; they facilitate the construction of force packages; they present multiple threats to an opponent; and they simplify and reduce support costs and volume by commonalty in spares, maintenance and groundcrew. For their flexibility to be fully exploited however they require multi-role weapons systems or weapons which are interoperable with integrated fire-control systems. They are by definition more complex and therefore more expensive to purchase than all but the most sophisticated specialist aircraft, such as SR-71 or JSTARS.

The purchase cost of a combat aircraft in relation to the total life-cycle cost varies considerably as a result of several factors, including obvious ones such as life duration and numbers of crew members. But the variation is usually between 33 per cent and 50 per cent of the total costs. Multi-role aircraft will produce long-term savings to offset increased unit purchase costs; multi-role aircraft plus precision guided munitions will not only effect economies in scale but, like the stealth technology of the F-117, drive savings deep into logistics, maintenance, manpower, training and infra-structure.

Sceptics will raise doubts over multi-role *operational* cost effectiveness, especially if design has led to compromises in air-superiority capability. It may be no coincidence that the best multi-role aircraft : F-15, F-16, SU-27, F-18 and EF-2000, were all designed originally as air-superiority fighters, with multi-role capability either secondary or subsequent.

The real penalties of multi-role dependence are less obvious but if not clearly identified, will inhibit maximum exploitation. The first is political: one squadron remains one squadron with the potential of several, but not all at the same time. Force multiplication does not mean double counting. Second, maintaining multi-role efficiency among aircrew requires more flying hours in total and possibly less for each role. Reduced specialist air-crew competence is a greater risk than constrained multi-role aircraft capability, but can be avoided. Israeli multi-role fighter squadrons, for example, allocate two-thirds of their flying hours to air superiority, and one-third to air-to-ground training, and all crews are expected to be dual-role capable. Conversely, crews may specialise within flights, flights within squadrons, or squadrons within wings, in which case the training require-ment will be contained at a cost of reduced flexibility. The alternative, of extending flying hours for everyone, induces penalties in aircrew work-load, air-frame life, fuel consumption, maintenance intensity and groundcrew manning. If in addition the multi-role squadron is also com-mitted to night/all-weather tasks, support costs and aircrew-manning requirements will increase still further. Nevertheless, while reducing life-cycle cost savings, the balance of benefits of the multi-role option could be expected to outweigh both the economic and operational limitations.

There are two other options for an air force which is facing stringent cuts and does not wish to pursue the multi-role path. The first is to preserve as many role capabilities as possible by specialist aircraft. That can only be done by progressively reducing the assets available for each: 'salami-slicing' which by reducing scale increases costs in exactly the opposite sequence to those achieved by multi-roling. This may be acceptable as long as only small national packages are likely to be required in the future in support of national policies. It does, however, risk reducing core assets, say in air defence, to the margins of viability.

The other option is to abandon roles altogether. The Israeli Air Force is frequently cited as a highly-efficient, cost-effective and consistently victorious air force. Several arguable factors can be set aside: financial support from the USA, heavy reliance on reserves, national resource priorities, and persistent inferiority among the IAF's recent opponents. The relevant factors are that Israel's territorial and numerical vulnerability has led it to construct what is virtually a tactical air force with two roles: air superiority and ground attack. It has no regular requirement for long-range maritime patrol, nor strategic airlift, nor long-range bombardment. On the two occasions that long-range air attacks were launched, against *Osirak* in 1981 and Tunis in 1985 its tactical aircraft were given extended range by a small number of tankers. Entebbe was just within range of its C-130s. A decision by any other air force to abandon roles altogether could only be taken sensibly after a reappraisal of national security and foreign policy interests. Even then, for reasons argued above, a multi-role residual force would almost certainly be preferable.

The most visible, single-force multiplier is the in-flight refuelling (IFR) tanker. It has a particular synergism with the multi-role combat aircraft. The latter, if developed from an air-superiority fighter, is unlikely to have the range of an earlier generation of light bomber, such as the *Canberra*. IFR converts the tactical fighter into a strategic, long-range participant. It sustains combat air patrols, enables indirect routing, extends interdiction and strategic penetration depth and increasingly is an integral component of front-line strength. Indeed, one of the few air power equations which lends itself to incontrovertible quantification is the comparative operational reach in all configurations of any 15 combat aircraft compared to 10 such aircraft with two IFR tankers available in support.

The second highly-visible force multiplier is AWACs. Its pivotal contribution to the Gulf War in controlling and concentrating assets has already been examined. It also fulfils part of the requirement for timely reconnaissance essential to ensure that priorities may be determined, sorties accurately directed and their impact speedily evaluated. Here there is a need to explore more fully the synergism to be obtained between unmanned vehicles and the traditional tactical reconnaissance aircraft. Carriage of the British Thermal Imaging and Laser Designator (TIALD) pod by *Tornado* GR-1 fighter bombers during and after the Gulf War over Iraq suggests further potential for multi-role exploration. Certainly, the smaller the combat strength, the greater the need to invest resources in reconnaissance.

The greatest, most obvious and most popular force multiplier is reduced vulnerability. It is also the most difficult to quantify and is always susceptible to technological or tactical surprise. It is even more important when front-line strengths diminish and aircraft and aircrew replacement costs increase. Defensive aids may reduce weapon load volume, but their value has increased in direct proportion to the effectiveness of the residual PGM weapons on board. In illustrating relative effectiveness during the evolution of air power, powerful examples are given of the destructive impact of one *Tornado* compared with one squadron of *Lancasters* in World War II. The corollary of that example is that the loss of one *Tornado* is the operational equivalent of losing one squadron of *Lancasters*. Not only is attrition reduction conducive to good aircrew morale and enhanced operational effectiveness, it leads to reduced expenditure on 'attrition' numbers in the original purchase orders.

The importance of survivability in an electronic-warfare environment should be so self-evident as to remove the need for explanation, but the relative allocation of resources and manpower to it in some Western air forces since 1945, including the Royal Air Force until the 1990s, suggests otherwise. One unambiguous lesson from the Gulf War was that survivability in future air warfare is inseparable from survival in electronic combat.

On the ground, the major force multiplier is serviceability and here at least most Western air forces are aware of its implications, if occasionally constrained by lack of perception in previous generations of aircraft and weapon procurement. While one PGM may have the destructive power of 25 'dumb' bombs, if one dumb bomb malfunctions the degradation is 4 per cent, but if the PGM fails the loss is 100 per cent. Serviceability is a compound of simplicity in construction, reliability in use, redundancy in system and easy accessibility for component repair and replacement. It is complemented by groundcrew skills. In this area, differences of interest between aerospace industries and air forces may be identified. Supply of spares and life-cycle support are frequently the most lucrative long-term features in an aerospace contract, while the interest of the air force is in reducing exactly those areas of activity. *Caveat emptor* could well enter the air power lexicon along with more familiar combat-orientated expressions.

On several occasions previously in this study the interdependence of ground environment and combat effectiveness has been emphasised. When Trenchard spoke of 'personnel' he was aware that the large majority of people in any air force are groundcrew, even though the combat risks are undertaken by the flying minority, except when airbases are under attack. So much so that when Trenchard was offered a stately home as a location for the embryonic RAF Staff College in 1922 he elected instead to place there his technical apprentice school.

Among the many resources which contribute to effective air power, only one – people – actually appreciates, rather than depreciates over time. It is not an automatic process. The lead donkey in Napoleon's baggage train experienced every victory with his master. At their conclusion, he was still a donkey. Learning by experience can be costly, painful and occasionally posthumous. Far preferable, and in the longer term more economical, is to learn from other people's experience: in training and in education. In the Royal Air Force, it takes between six and eight years to produce a technical senior NCO who will become the linchpin of ground servicing. It will take up to three years to train a pilot to first-tour combat standard. The Gulf War demonstrated without reservation the cumulative impact of skills, professionalism and dedication at all rank levels on the application of air power. Why, 2,000 years after the Roman legions should that sentiment need emphasising?

The fewer the resources available, the greater the need to recruit, retain and develop individuals to their greatest potential. Too often air forces are captivated by technology rather than its intellectual mastery. It was no coincidence that the US commanders in *Desert Storm* were not only imbued with their personal experiences in Vietnam, but were products of the most comprehensive military education and training systems in the world.

Clausewitz wrote, 'War is the province of uncertainty; three quarters of the factors on which action is based are wrapped in a fog of greater or lesser uncertainty. A sensitive and discriminating judgement is called for; a skilled intelligence to scent out the truth.'[41] That was in the comparatively straightforward days of warfare, before airmen added a new dimension and the fog became electronic.

With tight resource constraints, air force commanders have to avoid two extremes. On the one hand, they must not deploy a technologically-superior front line which is poorly led by narrow-minded people who will lack the intellectual muscle to anticipate tactical or strategic surprise, let alone have the flexibility to respond to it. On the other, there will be little point in producing the most highly-trained, well-educated, flexibly-minded leadership in the world if the front line will be overwhelmed by opponents whose equipment is superior in quality and quantity. Now, peacetime is also 'a province of uncertainty', difficult decisions about resource priorities will also call for 'sensitive and discriminating judgement'. Force multiplication begins with the ability to identify it.

The Need for Exorcism

After 100 years of theory and practice, air power had by the mid-1990s become a mature and sturdy partner in the military ranks. It was a little ironic that at the moment when air power had finally demonstrated its awesome capabilities, external circumstances should be compelling the most rigorous reappraisal of priorities in the allocation of dwindling resources and creating the most diverse and unpredictable operational environments. It was no consolation that armies and navies faced similar circumstances. Indeed, there was a danger of the resurrection of interservice, internecine strife reminiscent of the days of air power infancy, strife which impaired the healthy development of all three services in several countries.

Spirits from the past began to be invoked as substitutes for argument; skeletons rattled against cupboard doors; ghostly figures were resurrected as totems of doctrinal purity. If air power was to continue to evolve in its second century, and if armies and navies were to continue to benefit from its partnership it was time for an exorcism. The candidates were Douhet and his fantasies of strategic bombardment; zealotry which failed to distinguish between abstract air power and the real thing; residual parochialism in armies and navies and obituaries for the manned combat aircraft.

One of the most difficult tasks of the historian is to trace cause and effect. In the history of air power the writings of a prolific Italian and the subsequent application of similar ideas have combined to elevate Giulio Douhet to a pre-eminent position in the pantheon of air power theorists. As explained in Chapter 1, he had no influence on the Royal Air Force; his influence on the German and the Russian air force expired with the deaths of Wever and Khripin; the French air force lacked both the equipment and inclination to implement his theories; while in the USA the direct links between Trenchard, Gorell, Mitchell and the USAF were much more definable than the probable contacts between Gorell and Douhet via Caproni.

An excellent modern analysis, appropriately emanating from the USAF's School of Advanced Air power Studies, examined Douhet's theories in the light of modern PGM technology. The author acknowledged errors in Douhet's overestimation of the psychological and physical effects of bombing, including chemical weapons; in his lack of tactical awareness; in ignoring the need for an air battle to decide command of the air; in underestimating the strength of defensive air power; of being preoccupied with total war; in denigrating constraints of international law and morality; in underestimating the impact of surface-to-air weapons; in failing to relate air power to political objectives; in underestimating the continued requirement for ground and naval forces; and in denigrating experience from the past.[42]

After 100 years there is still no incontrovertible evidence that strategic bombardment has been decisive in breaking the determination of any opponent to carry on fighting. Even in *Desert Storm*, the most authoritative analysis concludes that the precision 'strategic' attacks on leadership and communications 'clearly fell short of fulfilling the ambitious hope entertained by at least some airmen that bombing leadership and C^3 targets might put enough pressure on the regime to bring about its overthrow . . .',[43] attacking oil refineries and storage in Iraq 'bore no significant results',[44] 'bombing alone therefore, failed to achieve the objective of eliminating the existing Iraqi nuclear weapons program . . .'[45] The same American survey summarises the 'strategic core' of the Gulf air campaign with an objectivity that should lay Douhet, even a precisely-guided Douhet, to rest for good:

> Regardless of the private hopes airmen may have had during the Gulf War that air power might achieve the coalition's military objectives without a ground campaign, the modest fraction of the air-to-surface attacks focused against the strategic core (15%)[46] had more pragmatic objectives . . . Planners wished to exert pressure from the outset directly against the heart of Iraqi power – an idea consistent with other strategic bombing campaigns. In some cases, as in the nuclear weapon program, the strategic air attacks were less effective than hoped or believed at the time . . . In other cases, as in Iraq's electric power system, the Coalition's immediate military objectives against the strategic core were achieved. In yet other cases, the bombing on leadership and C^3 targets, for instance, effectiveness cannot be clearly or precisely estimated . . .[47]

Four lessons may be taken forward from the first century about strategic bombardment, First, the initial shock on a civilian population is indeed highly likely to induce panic and poor morale; thereafter resilience is more likely. Second, if the populace democratically supports its government and its war aims, that resilience may turn to stubbornness and increased hostility to the attacker. Third, if the government is authoritarian and ruthless the impact of the bombardment on the population will be irrelevant. Fourth, only if specific targets are struck which have a synergistic impact on the opponent's physical capacity to continue the war will strategic bombardment justify the resources allocated to it.

Paradoxically, air power probably did determine the outcome of the Gulf War on its own, but as a result of strategic, operational, and tactical simultaneous synergism, not from any reincarnation of Douhet. By definition of the *Oxford English Dictionary*, Douhet was a zealot, 'uncompromising, or extreme partisan, fanatic'. In the face of early ignorant, bigoted and self-interested opposition from armies and navies, men of great vision and strength were needed to ensure that air power put down the roots from which ultimately *Desert Storm* was to spring. Then there was no alternative, now there is a century of hard evidence. It is time to place air power into the continuum of military history, to emphasise not just its unique characteristics, but the features it shares, to a greater or lesser degree, with other forms of warfare.

It also must be guided by, and relevant to, political objectives. It will be applied in different ways by different countries dependent on their different capabilities. Countries with threatening frontiers are not so much interested in long-range bombardment but close air support. Sweden, with a length of 1,000 miles and a width of 150 and a long history of armed neutrality, has very different requirements from those of Israel. Long-range bombardment was a natural priority for the USA whose potential enemies lay hundreds of miles over distant horizons. A coincidence of geopolitics, perceived threat, natural resources and technical capacity has produced the two most proficient exponents of air power: the USA and Israel.

Air power will be affected by the ebb and flow of technology between offence and defence as much as any other military instrument. Sooner or later air power will make its own contribution to the junk yard of military history : castles, cavalry, battleships and, imminently, the main battle tank.

Exponents of air power theory must remember to clothe the abstract characteristics in practical dress. Flexibility has been examined above. Ubiquity is equally demanding to substantiate. To exploit speed and concentration or force aircraft must be able to reach, locate, identify, acquire and destroy or neutralise the mission demands by night and in all weathers. A distinguished British airman, reflecting objectively on the considerable success of air power in the Gulf War observed, 'But until we can smart bomb through clouds or jungle canopy there will be limitations on the effectiveness of smart weapons. This is true in Europe, with its uncertain weather. The philosophy of going in at high or medium level and doing pin-point bombing, as we did in the Gulf to avoid ground fire, could not be applied to the same extent in Europe.'[48] That is the realistic voice of air power going forward into the next century : dominant, confident but aware of limitations.

The relationship of modern air power to the other components of military force was elegantly expressed by an influential USAF exponent and theorist, Colonel John Warden, who likened the relationship between armies, navies and air forces in war to the solo instrument in a concerto, where the composer having decided upon his 'objective', selects the appropriate instrument which, translating the metaphor, becomes the 'key force' in the music and in war. The instrument will vary from concerto to concerto; on some occasions it will be a soloist, on others it will harmonise, on others it will fall silent. 'Orchestration, not subordination or integration, is the *sine qua non* of modern warfare.'[49] The need now is for operational harmony, not cacophony. It is time for the zealots to fade away with honour. Their contribution is complete.

But while air power may have had zealots, the other services have not always been open-minded or moderate either. Even in 1994 a soldier or sailor who otherwise gave the impression of being well-adjusted, intelligent and well-read might ask, 'Why do we still need an independent air force?' To a certain extent it is the airman's fault that such ignorance persists. If air power is allowed to become synonymous with strategic bombardment, and any lesser application is perceived to be somehow inferior, and if the 'inferior' activity is in support of naval or ground force operations, it is hardly surprising that the advent of the ICBM and the diversification of warfare should resurrect old criticisms.

In fact, as explained in Chapter 1, the case for an independent air force originally rested on the wasteful duplication of resources, manpower and facilities in Britain when two air forces were competing for them. It was not the need to create an independent bomber force but the need to provide air defence which prompted the 1917 Smuts recommendation for an independent Royal Air Force. Those reasons remained valid in 1994, as Mr Perry and others in the USA were inconveniently noting, as resources dwindled and pressure for economies among the USAF, the USN and the USMC air forces increased.

The fact that the skies do not stop and start again over coastlines does not mean that air forces should command and control all air activities over land and sea. Coastlines do, however, define the interests of armies and navies, however much carrier-borne aircraft seek to move across them. For air power to achieve its maximum potential, it cannot be constrained by parochial interests whether from company, regiment, division, army or fleet.

The application of air power is now a profession of considerable complexity, demanding technological mastery, a sense of command, structure, speed, time, distance and impact in proportions quite different from those applicable on land or sea. Not greater, nor lesser, but different. It demands a discrete professionalism which must not be subordinated to the primary interests of another service; that route would lead directly to the subordination of air power itself to the detriment of all services. In personnel terms it could only offer a subordinate career and that in turn would lead directly to a reduced attraction for first-rate people. It would, in Colonel Warden's metaphor, condemn air power to the position of permanent second fiddle. When a violin concerto was required, there would be no one able to perform it. The ghosts of unbelieving soldiers and sailors should be exorcised and their spirits returned to their regimental and maritime associations.

And finally, the writers of the obituaries for the manned aircraft: they have variable pedigrees and their arguments are not always consistent. The biggest own goal in British defence policy occurred in 1957 when the Defence White Paper (the annual statement of government defence policy) of that year confidently asserted, 'Work will proceed on the development of a ground-to-air missile defence system, which will in due course replace the manned aircraft of Fighter Command. In view of the good progress already made, the Government have come to the conclusion that the RAF are unlikely to have a requirement for fighter aircraft of types more advanced than the supersonic P1, and work on such projects will stop.'[50] Thirty-seven years later the RAF still suffered from that decision, awaiting a new indigenous air superiority fighter and possessing no medium or long-range SAMs.

In the previous paragraph of that White Paper, the British manned bomber was condemned to similar oblivion, on account of the likely progress of ballistic missiles and missile defence. The 'unmanned' school received further boosts from the enforced descent of Gary Powers, the early impact of SAMs in Vietnam and the shock encountered over Sinai and the Golan Heights by the IAF in 1973. But airmen have not always made their counter-arguments convincingly. Even in *Desert Storm*, considerable publicity was justifiably given to the extinction of the Iraqi Air Force; not quite so much to the fact that subsequently, most operations were flown above 10,000 ft to stay out of range of SAMs and old-fashioned lead. Similarly, air forces have not been associated with the priority development of unmanned aerial vehicles (UAV). The expression 'There ain't no careers in UAVs' may be apocryphal, but is a recognisable sentiment. Air power is about the exploitation of the third dimension *by* man, not necessarily *with* man.

The roles of UAVs in the Gulf War were all forecast, with comprehensive analysis, by an eminent Chief of British Military Intelligence and air power theorist, Air Chief Marshal Sir Michael Armitage, in 1988.[51] They will continue to be employed in various EW roles, for direct attack, to launch weapons on command, in stand-off attack, and as decoys, in addition to the well-proven surveillance and reconnaissance roles. By 1994 considerable enhancement in range, payload and stealth characteristics foreshadowed wider employment. Indeed, it is probable that predictable, static targets will increasingly be targeted by unmanned vehicles, with an attacker choosing between the irrecoverable ballistic missile and the flexible, highly-controlled combination of aircraft or ship-launched cruise missile.

Satellites in the Gulf War also demonstrated their current and potential contribution to the application of air power. The application of GPS to aircraft navigation and weapon guidance could confer all-weather capabilities on PGMs, but a distinction should be made in the second air century between hopes and promises in all aspects of military technology. Satellite surveillance by optical, infra-red and radar technology will continue to provide strategic intelligence with associated constraints of weather, orbital frequency and positioning. Communications too will be facilitated in all aspects of warfare. In all cases, however, satellite activities will support and enhance traditional air operations, not replace them.[52]

In sum, the 'Who needs them?' argument rests on two premises: that the manned aircraft is too vulnerable, and that the man can be taken out of many of the combat-related loops.

Vulnerability has been touched upon earlier, and is a very complex issue. Three points are relevant. First, the acceptance of casualties is a function of arbitration by combat. 'Acceptable' attrition rates will continue to be a sensitive balance of force capabilities, morale, political acceptability and residual threat or objectives. The increased lethality of surface-to-air defences is offset by the increased effectiveness of individual aircraft and individual PGMs. Technological advantage may swing from ground-to-air and back again, but the aircraft will retain the advantages of exploiting the third dimension by concealment, deception, variable height, speed and direction. That said, low-level operations are likely to remain the least popular among combat aircrew in most environments in the foreseeable future.

Arguments about the need for a 'man in the loop' need to be placed in the context of likely operational environments. The second century of air warfare is likely to involve dense electronic combat, increasingly smart air-to-ground weapons, increasingly effective surface-to-air defences, long-range autonomous air-to-air weapons, mobile ground targets, concealed targets, the widespread use of decoys and deception: all in a rapidly fluctuating operational environment.

In the foreseeable future, UAVs and direct-attack missiles will be either preprogrammed or remotely controlled. The former will be inflexible, the latter will be slow to respond and dependent on preset sensors. Throughout the history of warfare, to be predictable is to be vulnerable; in electronic warfare to be predictable is to be neutralised before being destroyed. In rapidly changing surroundings, to be slow to respond is to become redundant. Sir Michael Armitage succinctly summarised the future direction and the synergism required for the UAV: '. . . both types of aircraft have a part to play in modern air warfare, and the unmanned aircraft, far from replacing manned versions are more likely in the future to act in their direct support. Meanwhile, the essential need to bring situational awareness and operational judgement to the scene of confused combat, means that manned aircraft are likely to remain the principal asset in the exercise of air power.'[53] That should be the epitaph for those who would compose the obituary of the manned aircraft, but exorcism is still rather an inexact science.

After 100 years of air power, from first thoughts to maturity, exponents do not need to be overly concerned about the occasional unreconstructed ghost. They do not need any longer to exaggerate air power's potential, nor to project universal 'lessons' from individual successes. By placing air power in the evolutionary process of warfare as a whole, unnecessary claims of superiority and unfounded fears of subordination may be abandoned along with the growing pains of infancy and adolescence.

In any dimension of warfare a mobile target will be more difficult to locate and hit than a static one. Some targets will be more heavily defended; others will be concealed. Decoys, deception and ambush may not accord with notions of chivalry, but they will continue to stimulate discomfort in opponents. The technology of air power will exploit some of these basic principles and be constrained by others, sometimes concurrently and sometimes not.

Success in *Desert Storm* will not guarantee air power sustained pre-eminence in its second century. That will depend upon its ability to offer governments a military instrument applicable across the spectrum of international security, from high-intensity to low-intensity operations, from national defence to the protection of interests, the protection of friends and the preservation of international law. It will stand or fall not by promises and abstract theories, but, like any other kind of military power, by its relevance to, and ability to secure, political objectives at a cost acceptable to the government of the day.

One enduring concept underlay all air power thinking and all operations from the first day of the century to the last, and will continue to do so. Any nation intent on going to war to pursue an interest or defend a principle must first secure the air above it. At least Douhet was correct about that, but Major Fullerton had said it 18 years previously: 'Command of the air will be an essential prerequisite for all land and air warfare'.

A British metaphor at the end of air power's first century, which may require translation for some readers, is of a batsman checking his guard and preparing to go for his second hundred. Or, to modernise General Hap Arnold's famous statement, present equipment is but a step in progress. Air forces must harmonise their equipment with their doctrine but keep their vision far into the future.

NOTES

Chapter 1

1. H.G. Wells, *The War in the Air*, 1908, Ch 5, cited in the *Oxford English Dictionary: Supplement*, 1972, p.49.
2. Jane's *All The World's Airships*, 1909, *OED*, ibid.
3. *The Aeroplane*, 12 April 1922, p.257.
4. Cited in *AP2000, Air Power Doctrine*, HMSO, London, 1993, p.13.
5. Ibid.
6. A reference to a definition and exposition of the concept of air power by R.A. Mason in *Air Power in the Nuclear Age, Theory and Practice*, by M.J.Armitage & R.A.Mason, Macmillan, London 1983, pp.2–3.
7. *The Air Power Manual*, Royal Australian Air Force Air Power Studies Centre, 1990, p.21.
8. *Air Power: A Concise History*, Robin Higham, Macdonald, London, 1972.
9. Cited in A.F.Hurley in the appendix 'Additional Insights' to *Billy Mitchell, Crusader for Air Power*, Indiana University Press, Bloomington, 1975, p.142.
10. R.F. Futrell, *Ideas, Concepts, Doctrine, Basic Thinking in the United States Air Force 1907–1960*, Air University Press, 1989, p.15.
11. John H. Morrow, *The Great War in the Air*, Smithsonian, 1993, p.4.
12. Peter L. Jakab, *Visions of a Flying Machine, The Wright Brothers and the Process of Invention*, Smithsonian, 1990, pp.43–44.
13. Futrell, op. cit. p.17.
14. Wells, op. cit.
15. CID Minutes of Meeting 14 July 1910, cited by Alfred Gollin, *The Impact of Air power on the British People and Their Government 1909–14*, Macmillan, London 1989, p.101.
16. Cited in Gollin, ibid., p.12.
17. *Journal of the Royal United Services Institution*, LII, 1908, p.1502.
18. 'Aeroplanes of today and their use in war', Captain C.J. Burke, *RUSI Journal*, May 1911.
19. Ibid. p.626.
20. Ibid. p.629.

21. Morrow, op. cit. p.19.
22. Cited in 'The British dimension', by R.A. Mason, in *Air Power and Warfare*, Proceedings of the 8th Military History Symposium, USAF Academy, 1978, p.23.
23. Hiram Maxim, 'Aerial navigation', *Century Magazine,* **XLII**, 6 October 1891, p.836, cited in Michael Paris, 'The rise of the airmen: the origins of air force elitism c.1890–1918', *Journal of Contemporary History*, **28**, 1993, p.1332.
24. Charles Gibbs-Smith, in *Air Power and Warfare*, p.54.
25. Paris, op. cit., p.127.
26. Parliamentary Debates (Commons), 5th Series, 2 August 1909, cited in Gollin, op. cit. p.79–80.
27. Ibid., p.76.
28. *The Birth of Independent Air power*, Malcolm Cooper, Allen & Unwin, 1986, p.5.
29. Cited in Futrell, op. cit., p.16.
30. 'The present status of military aeronautics', Major George Squier, *Flight*, 27 February 1909, p.304.
31. Cited in Morrow, op. cit., p.16.
32. Naval and Military Attaches' report from Berlin, December 1912, cited by Gollin, op. cit., p.232.
33. Philip S. Meilinger, 'Guilio Douhet and modern war', *Comparative Strategy*, **12**, 1993, p.330.
34. *Flight*, 4 March 1911, p.178.
35. *Flight*, 11 November 1911, p.989.
36. 'The origins of air warfare', D. J. Fitzsimmons, *Air Pictorial*, December 1972, pp.482–5.
37. *Flight*, 11 November 1911, p.989.
38. Reference to a *Daily Express* correspondent report in *Flight*, 30 December 1911.
39. Editorial, *The Aeroplane*, C.G.Grey, 17 August 1911.
40. Report of House of Commons proceedings, *The Times*, 31 October 1911.
41. Advertisement, *The Aeroplane*, 16 November 1911, p.559.
42. Quoted from *The Observer*, 20 January 1912, in *The Aeroplane*, 25 January 1912, p.76.
43. W. E. de B.Whittaker, 'Aviation in the Navy', *The Aeroplane*, 15 February 1912, p.151.
44. *A Short History of the Royal Air Force*, Air Ministry, London, 1920, p.10.
45. Statement to House of Commons, 4 March 1912, as reported in *The Aeroplane*, 7 March 1912.
46. See Morrow, op. cit. pp.40–5 for details of this disagreement.
47. War Office minute to Director-General of Military Aeronautics, 16 December 1913, cited in Gollin, op. cit., pp.201–2.
48. Gollin, ibid., Ch. 9.
49. Cited in Walter Raleigh, *The War in the Air*, Vol. I, Oxford, 1922, p.265.
50. Parliamentary Debates (Commons), 5th Series, 17 March 1914, cited by Gollin, op. cit., pp.277–9.
51. Memorandum to Mr Asquith, Asquith MSS, cited by Gollin, ibid., p.282.
52. *A Short History of the RAF*, p.421 and John Terraine, *The Smoke and the Fire*, Sidgwick & Jackson, 1980, p.44.
53. Morrow, op cit. p.364.
54. Ibid., p.312.
55. Lee Kennett, *The First Air War 1914–1918*, Macmillan, 1991, p.226.
56. Morrow, op. cit., p.196.

57. Ibid., p.344.
58. Memoranda to Director of Air Division, RNAS *et al.*, 1, 3, 5 September 1914, in E. Emme, *The Impact of Air Power*, Van Nostrand, 1959, pp.27–9.
59. Joint War Air Committee, Constitution, Functions etc., cited in Cooper, *The Birth of Independent Air power*, pp.46–7.
60. Morrow, op, cit., p.123
61. Cooper, op, cit., p.49–50.
62. Morrow, op. cit., p.185.
63. See Cooper op. cit., Ch. 7 for a comprehensive exposition of the problems facing the aviation industry and its inability to meet the 'surplus' forecast in the unification debates of 1917.
64. Raymond Fredette, *The Sky on Fire*, Smithsonian Edition, 1991, pp.39, 40, citing Hilmer Von Bulow, *Die Angriffe der Bombengeschwader 3 auf England, in die Luftwacht*, 1927, p.331.
65. Quoted by Squadron Leader C.J. Mackay, *The German Air Raids in England*, RAF Staff College, Andover, 1924.
66. Mackay, ibid., p.57.
67. Ibid. This correspondence is recorded in Ludendorff's *The General Staff and Its Problems*, pp.449–58 and partially cited in Fredette, op cit., pp.72–3. Mackay does not cite his source but the translations are identical.
68. J. A. Chamier, *The Birth of The Royal Air Force*, Pitman, 1943, p.140 (distilled from Raleigh and Jones, *War in the Air*).
69. Fredette, op. cit., pp.64–7.
70. Appendix II to Cabinet Minutes (WC233), 24 August 1917.
71. Cited in Cooper, op cit., pp.100–1.
72. See ref. 70.
73. US War Department Study, August 1918, cited in Morrow, op. cit., p.346.
74. RFC HQ Memorandum, 22 September 1916.
75. Alan Bott, 'An Airman's Outings with the RFC, June-December 1916', Elstree 1917, cited in Morrow, op. cit., p.169.
76. Morrow, op cit., pp.317, 318.
77. 'Dicta Boelcke', cited in Morrow, ibid., p.150.
78. Neville Jones, *The Origins of Strategic Bombing*, Kimber, London, 1973, pp.120 ff.
79. Report to Air Board by Lt.Cdr. Lord Tiverton, cited in Jones, ibid., p.146.
80. Cooper, op. cit., p.116.
81. See Trenchard diary extracts, cited in Montgomery-Hyde, *British Air Policy between the Wars*, RAF Museum, 1976, p.43.
82. Ibid.
83. Memorandum on the Bombing of Germany by GOC Independent Force, Royal Air Force, to Secretary of State for Air, 23 June 1918, Bracknell Papers.
84. Report on I.F. Operations 6–30th June, IFG/79, from Trenchard to Weir, 2 July 1918, Bracknell Papers.
85. Proposed Agenda Paper, IAAC, 20 July 1918, Bracknell Papers.
86. Memorandum (to Weir) on the Subjects for Discussion Proposed by the French Representative to the Third Senior of the Inter Allied Aviation Committee, by GOC Independent Force, Ochey, 9 July 1918, Bracknell Papers.
87. IFG/79, 2 July 1918. Bracknell Papers.
88. IFG/79, Report on October Operations, 1 November 1918, cross-referred to Table A, Weir Memorandum, 9 July 1918, Bracknell Papers.
89. IFG/79 Series, 2 July to 15 November 1918, Bracknell Papers.

90. Undated typescript among later 1918 papers. This is the only unreferenced document in the Trenchard Bracknell collection of which the earliest is 2 July and the latest 15 November. It is a flimsy, typed carbon copy of an unrecorded original with no indication of office routing. All the other papers originated from or were received in Trenchard's outer office.
91. Tenth Supplement to *The London Gazette*, 31 December 1918, p.135.
92. Cited in Montgomery Hyde, op cit. pp.44–5.
93. Trenchard interview in 1934, cited in Montgomery Hyde, ibid., p.45.
94. W. S. Churchill, 'Munitions Possibilities of 1918', Memorandum to War Cabinet, 21 October 1917, Section IV. Reproduced in Emme, *The Impact of Air Power*, Van Nostrand, 1959, pp.37–40.

Chapter 2
1. Collection of original letters and extracts in the Bracknell Papers.
2. The typescript copy of the Sykes Memorandum in the Bracknell Papers is identical to the text published as Appendix VII to *From Many Angles*, Harrap, 1942, pp.558–74, except for an introductory sentence in the typescript original. The 'Appendix' references, however, are to the typescript Appendices referred to, but not reprinted, in Sykes's autobiography.
3. *From Many Angles*, p.558.
4. Ibid.
5. Ibid., p.561.
6. Ibid., p.562.
7. Appendix B, typescript.
8. *From Many Angles*, p.265.
9. Appendix B, op. cit.
10. *From Many Angles*, p.265.
11. Memorandum on Air Force, Civil Aviation and Supply and Research Estimates for 1920–21 and following years to War Cabinet from Winston S. Churchill, Secretary of State for Air, Air Ministry, 24 October 1919, Bracknell Papers.
12. Permanent Organization of the Royal Air Force, Cmd.467, 1919, Appendix.
13. Memorandum, 24 October 1919, p.8.
14. Ibid., p.2.
15. CID 149C, cited in Montgomery Hyde, op. cit., p.101.
16. Cmd.467, op. cit., p.4.
17. Air Staff Memorandum No.43, S28279, 1929.
18. CAS Memorandum 1928, Cited by Williamson Murray in *Strategy for Defeat, The Luftwaffe 1933–1945*, Air University Press 1983, p.325.
19. Air Staff Memorandum 1929, op. cit., pp.5–6.
20. Interviews with Marshals of the RAF Slessor and Harris, at Rimpton and Bracknell, respectively, July 1977.
21. 'Air armament, training and development', lecture by Wg.-Cdr F.J.W. Mellersh, RAF Staff College, Andover, 11 May 1939, RAF Air Historical Branch, A/11/6, pp.37–8.
22. Ibid., p.53.
23. Extracts from Luftwaffe Service Manual No.16, cited in Richard Suchenwirth, *The Development of the German Air Force 1919–1939*, USAF Historical Study 160, USAF Academy, 1983, Chapter 12.
24. Manual No.16 para.10, cited in Suchenwirth, pp.12–16.
25. Ibid., para. 24.

26. Eye-witness report by General der Flieger Paul Deichmann, cited in Suchenwirth, pp.12-19.

27. Cited in Williamson Murray, op. cit., pp.8.

28. Ibid., p.11.

29. In 1977 Slessor observed to the writer, 'I suppose, on reflection, we were obsessed by the fear of a knock-out blow.'

30. Cited in Suchenwirth, pp.12–24.

31. Ibid., pp.12–20.

32. Alexander Boyd, *The Soviet Air Force since 1918*, Macdonald & Jane's, 1977, pp.110–12.

33. Horst Boog, *The German Luftwaffe Command, 1935–1945*, (MSS pagination), p.81. Published only in German as *Der Deutsche Lufte fuhrung 1935–45*, published by Deutsche Verlags Anstaldt, Stuttgart 1982.

34. Ibid., p.102.

35. Ibid., p.105.

36. Ibid., p.104.

37. Ibid., p.105.

38. Ibid., p.117.

39. Francis K. Mason, *Battle over Britain*, Doubleday, 1969, Appendix K.

40. Boog, op. cit., p.109.

41. C. Webster & N. Frankland, *The Strategic Air Offensive against Germany 1939–1945*, HMSO, 1961, Vol. IV, p.172.

42. Ibid., p.290.

43. Harris to Portal, 1 November 1944, ATH/DO/4, Air Historical Branch, Ministry of Defence, London, p.1.

44. Harris to Portal, 6 November 1944, p.1.

45. Harris to Portal, 12 December 1944, p.1.

46. Ibid., p.2.

47. Harris to Portal, 28 December 1944, pp.3–5.

48. Portal to Harris, 18 November 1945, p.2.

49. Harris to Portal, 18 January 1945, p.2.

50. Portal to Harris, 20 January 1945, p.1.

51. Portal to Harris, 8 January 1945, paras.15,16.

52. 8th Air Force, Commanders' Meeting Minutes, 21 January 1944, cited in McFarland and Newton, *To Command the Sky*, Smithsonian, 1991, p.161.

53. Ibid., p.190.

54. Spaatz to Arnold, 11 March 1944, cited in McFarland and Newton, ibid., p.221.

55. John Terraine, *The Right of the Line*, Sceptre 1988, p.682.

56. Williamson Murray, op. cit., p.284.

57. Philip S. Meilinger, 'Guilio Douhet and modern war', in *Comparative Strategy*, **12**, 1993, p.333.

58. General Omar Bradley, *Effects of Air Power on Military Operations: Western Europe*, report from 12th US Army Group, 15 July 1945, excerpts in Emme, *Impact of Air Power*, op. cit., p.241.

59. Cited in Emme, ibid., p.212.

60. General Carl Spaatz, 'Strategic air power: fulfilment of a concept', *Foreign Affairs*, April 1946.

61. Lord Tedder, 'Air Power in War', Lees Knowles Lectures, University of Cambridge, 1947, cited in Armitage & Mason *Air Power in the Nuclear Age, Theory and Practice*, Macmillan, 1985, p.1.

284 Air Power

2849849Air Power

62. W.S.Churchill, 31 March 1949, cited in Armitage & Mason, ibid.
63. See 'Air power in colonial wars', M.J.Armitage in Armitage & Mason, ibid, pp.46–82.
64. See, for example John A. Warden, 'The Air Campaign', NDU, 1988, p.13.
65. Armitage, in Armitage & Mason, op. cit., p.79.
66. Mark Clodfelter, *The Limits of Air power*, Free Press, 1989, pp.209–10.
67. See Armitage in: Armitage & Mason, op. cit., pp.223–43.
68. Ehud Yonay, *No Margin for Error*, Pantheon, New York, 1993, pp.45–6.
69. Interview in *Ma'ariv*, 23 October 1970, cited in Ehud Yonay, ibid., p.104.
70. Yonay, ibid., p.103.
71. Ezer Weizman, *On Eagles' Wings*, Wiedenfeld & Nicolson, London, 1976, p.103.
72. Interview with Yonay, ibid., p.118.
73. Liddell Hart received several testimonies from IDF commanders after the 1967 War attributing the adoption of Israeli strategy to his concepts. Excerpts were received by the present writer.
74. Yonay, op. cit., pp.208–13.
75. Yonay, op. cit., p.212.
76. Marouf Bakhit Nader, *The Evolution of Egyptian Air Defence Strategy 1967–1973*, MSS, King's College London, 1990, p.45, citing several Egyptian sources.
77. Yonay, op. cit., p.212.
78. See Nader, op. cit., for a comprehensive analysis of the Egyptian debate over the position of air defence in the nations' security posture and the rationale for the selection of the strategy for the October War . . . His account is based primarily on interviews with Egyptian decision makers in this period and on Arab sources.
79. Ibid., p.139.
80. Ibid., p.226.
81. Yonay, interviews with *Mirage* Squadron Commanders Even-Nir and Oded Marom, op. cit., p.305.
82. Nader, p.257.
83. For a detailed description and analysis of the air war, and superpower involvement, see 'Air power in the Middle East', by R.A. Mason, in: *Air Power in the Nuclear Age*, by Armitage & Mason, op. cit.
84. Yonay, op. cit., p.341.
85. See Benjamin Lambeth, 'Moscow's lessons from the 1982 Lebanon air war', in: *War in the Third Dimension*, ed. R.A.Mason, Brassey's, 1986 and Statistical Abstract, Combat Bureau of Statistics, *IDF Journal*, 21, 1990, p.26.
86. Benjamin Peled at an international symposium, Jerusalem, October 1975, cited in Nordeen, *Fighters over Israel*, Guild, 1991, pp.150–51.
87. Brigadier (Res.) Giora Furman, correspondence with author, January 1994.
88. Brigadier (Res.) Oded Erez, correspondence with author, January 1994.
89. Furman, op. cit.
90. Weizman, op. cit., p.179.
91. Rubenstein & Goldman, *Shield of David*, Prentice-Hall 1978, p.107.
92. Statistical Abstract, Combat Bureau of Statistics, *IDF Journal*, 21, 1990, p.26.
93. All figures and assessments are taken from US history of Congress Research Service Briefing Paper IB85066 Israel:US Foreign Assistance 27.1.94.

Chapter 3
1. *NATO Facts and Figures*, NATO Information Service, Brussels, 1989, p.4.

2. Bernard Brodie, 'The heritage of Douhet', *Air University Quarterly Review,* VI, No.2, pp.126–7.

3. Bernard Brodie, *Strategy in the Missile Age*, Princeton, 1965, pp.105–6.

4. Third Report to the Secretary of War by the Commanding General of the Army Air Forces, General H. H. Arnold, 12 November 1945, *Air Power and the Future*, Section 1. Extracted in *American Military Thought,* ed. Walter Millis, Bobbs-Merrill, 1966, p.445–6.

5. President H. S. Truman, Second Annual Message to the Nation, 6 January 1947. Public Papers of the Presidents of the US, US Government Printing Office, 1963.

6. Ibid.

7. See Perry McCoy Smith, *The Air Force Plans for Peace, 1943–45*, Johns Hopkins Press, 1970, for a definitive account of the 'parochial' motivation of the USAAF's Post War Division of the Air Staff Plans in the later stages of World War II.

8. Major-General St. Clair Streett, Deputy Commanding General, SAC, 25 July 1946. Quoted in *Ideas, Concepts, Doctrine : Basic Thinking in the United States Air Force 1907–1960*, R. F. Futrell, USAF Air University Press, 1989. Hereafter cited as Futrell.

9. US House of Representatives, Military Establishment Appropriation Bill 1947, Futrell, op. cit., p.214.

10. Memorandum, Spaatz to Arnold, ibid.

11. Forrestal Diaries, *Inner History of the Cold War*, ed. W. Millis, Cassell, 1952, p.313.

12. The four bases to be improved to 'VHB standard' were Marham, Lakenheath, Sculthorpe and either Poulton or Heathrow. Lt.-Col. J. W. Keeler, 'Locations of US Military Units in the UK, 16 July 1948–31 December 1967', cited by Col. D. W. Albrecht in unpublished thesis *Anglo-American Co-operation 1917–1992*, University of Cambridge, May 1992, pp.103, 106.

13. *Survival in the Air Age, A Report by the President's Air Policy Commission*, US Government Printing Office, Washington DC, 1948. Cited in *The Air Force and Strategic Thought 1945–51*, by David MacIsaac, Working Paper No.8, International Security Studies Programme, Wilson Center, Washington DC, 1979.

14. MacIsaac, Ibid.

15. Letter, Spaatz to Arnold, 23 July 1947, quoted by MacIsaac, op. cit.

16. JCS 1725/1 paras. 10, 11, 12, 1 May 1947, quoted in T. H. Etzold & J. L. Gaddis (eds.) *Containment: Documents on American Policy and Strategy 1945–50*, Columbia, 1978, p.302.

17. Walter Lipmann, *Redbrook Magazine*, September 1946, quoted in Lawrence Freedman, *The Evolution of Nuclear Strategy*, Macmillan, London, 1981, p.48.

18. See Futrell, op. cit., Ch. 5 for a detailed survey of this period from the USAF point of view.

19. General André Beaufré, *NATO and Europe*, Faber, London, 1967, p.22.

20. Defence Committee of NATO, DC 6/1, 1 December 1949, para. 5. Etzold & Gaddis op. cit., p.337.

21. Ibid. para. 7a.

22. US House of Representatives: Mutual Defense Assistance Act of 1949; Hearings before the Committee on Foreign Affairs, 81st Congress, 1st Session, 1949. Quoted by Futrell, op. cit., p.249.

23. Anglo-American Air Co-operation 1917–1992, D. A. Albrecht, Ph.D. Thesis, University of Cambridge, 1992, p.109, citing UK Air 8/1606, 'B 29 Airfields in UK 1948', Memorandum by the Minister of State for the Defence Committee.

24. Major H. R. Bronowski, 'A narrow victory', *USAF Air Force Magazine*, July/August 1981, pp.18-27.

25. Letter, General Kenney to General Whitehead, 9 August 1948. Cited by Bronowski op cit., p.34.
26. MacIsaac, op. cit., p.12.
27. JCS Harman Report, in: Etzold & Gaddis, op. cit., p.361.
28. Disconnected but very typical opinions expressed by Marshall Andrews, military editor of the *Washington Post* in a sustained anti-air power polemic *Disaster through Air Power*, Rinehart, New York, 1950.
29. D. Lilienthal, *The Atomic Energy Years*, p.391, quoted in Freedman, op. cit., p.51.
30. Col. W.H.Wise, 'Future of the tactical air force,' *Air University Quarterly Review*, Spring 1949, p.37.
31. Memorandum, Symington to Forrestal, 25 February 1949, cited in Futrell, op. cit, p.244.
32. Marshal of the RAF Sir John Slessor: address to the Royal Institute of International Affairs, London, March 1953.
33. W. Jackson & E. Bramall, *The Chiefs*, Brassey's, 1992, p.277.
34. André de Staerke, in: *NATO's Anxious Birth, The Prophetic Vision of the 1940s*, Hurst, London, 1985, pp.157, 159.
35. General Hoyt S. Vandenberg, in US Senate, DOD Appropriations for 1952, p.1272, cited in Futrell, op. cit., p.318.
36. Quoted in R.E. Osgood, *The Entangling Alliance*, Chicago, 1962, p.103.
37. The NATO Council decision was subsequently quoted in the British *Statement on Defence*, Cmd 9391, 1955, See Armitage & Mason, op. cit., Ch. 7. There was no reference in the NATO communique to nuclear weapons, but a need to retain levels of forces for the defence of the NATO area as planned.
38. NATO Final Communique, 14 December 1967, para.12. Reproduced in *NATO Final Communiques 1949–1974*, NATO Information Service, Brussels.
39. *Statement on the Defence Estimates 1985*, Cmd 9430–1, p.12.
40. *Statement on the Defence Estimates 1980*, Cmd 7826–1,p.5.
41. These figures were given by J.H. Hanson, 'Development of Soviet Aviation Support' in: *International Defence Review*, No. 5, 1980, p.683. While the financial estimates were subsequently found to be low, the numerical assessment of the deployment of aircraft to regiments was consistently accurate.
42. 'The character and importance of air operations in modern warfare', *Air Force & Air Defence Review*, Warsaw, December 1981. UKTRANS No.138, Soviet Studies Research Centre, Sandhurst.
43. *Materials from the Soviet General Staff Academy*, National Defense University Press, Washington, DC, 1989, p.325.
44. Ibid., pp.320, 325.
45. Ibid., p.324.
46. Ibid., p.333
47. General Don A.Starry, 'Extending the battlefield', *Military Review*, March 1981, p.32.
48. General Bernard Rogers, 'Greater flexibility for NATO's Flexible Response', *Strategic Review*, Spring 1983, p.12.
49. General Bernard Rogers, 'ACE attack of Warsaw Pact follow on forces', *Military Technology*, No. 5, 1983, pp.39–50.
50. John M. Collins, *US Soviet Military Balance 1980–1985*, Pergamon-Brassey's 1985, p.19.
51. Collins, ibid., pp.33–4.
52. Ibid., pp.38, 39.

53. Congress of the United States, Office of Technology Assessment, *New Technology for NATO*, Washington, DC, June 1987, pp.103–4.

54. A. Kokoshin, 'The Rogers plan: alternative defence concepts and security in Europe', *Economics, Politics and Ideology*, 13 August 1985, pp.3–4.

55. Marshal of the Soviet Union N.V.Ogarkov, 'The defence of Socialism: the experience of history and the present day', *Red Star*, 9 May 1984, p.2.

56. Major General I.Voroby'ev, 'Modern weapons and tactics', *Red Star*, 20 June 1984, p.2.

57. Air Chief Marshal Sir Anthony Skingsley, 'Interdiction and Follow-on Forces Attack', in: *Military Strategy in a Changing Europe*, B.H. Reid & M.Dewar (eds.), Brassey's, 1991. pp.213–14.

58. Collins, op. cit., p.131.

59. Steven L Canby, 'The conventional defense of Europe: the operational limits of emerging technology', Working Paper 55, International Security Studies Program, The Wilson Center, April 1984, p.4.

60. Ibid., pp.20, 21.

61. *Air-Land Battle Primer*, HQ USAFTAC/TRADOC, June 1978, pp.397–402.

62. Major James A. Machos, 'Tacair support for Airland Battle', *Air University Review*, May/June 1984, p.16.

63. Office of Technology Assessment, op. cit., p.135.

Chapter 4

1. For a summary of arms control negotiations in Europe see *Success and Failure in Arms Control Negotiations*, by April Carter, SIPRI, 1989, Ch. 9.

2. Para 23 of the 'Final Recommendations of the Helsinki Consultation (CSCE Document)', as quoted in *Confidence-building Measures within the CSCE Process*, Victor-Yves Ghebali, Research Paper No. 3, UNIDIR, Geneva, March 1989, p.3.

3. CSCE Document on Confidence Building Measures, Section I, para.2.

4. Ghebali, op. cit., p.9.

5. CSCE Document, Section I, paras 7, 9, 13.

6. Ibid., para 4.

7. Carter, op. cit., p.249.

8. Ghebali, op. cit., pp.31–2. Annex I to the document of the Stockholm Conference on Confidence- and Security-Building Measures and Disarmament in Europe, Stockholm, 19 September 1986, confirms this position.

9. Stockholm Document, para. 31.1.2.

10. CSCE/SC/WG8/3, Stockholm, 20 May 1985 (USSR, Bulgaria, Poland).

11. As reported in Journal of the CDE No.379/Rev.2. 178th Plenary meeting, 10 September 1986, p.5, para. (h).

12. John Erickson, 'The future of Soviet military doctrine' in: *The Lost Empire*, ed. J. Hemsley, Brassey's, London, 1991, p.105.

13. For a survey of this activity in early 1986 see Jane M. O. Sharp, 'After Reykjavik: arms control and the Alliance', *International Affairs*, 63 No. 2, Spring 1989.

14. As reported in *Pravda*, 8 July 1986.

15. Extract from text published in *Soviet News*, London, 18 February 1987.

16. Marshal Sergei F. Akhromeyev, Olaf Palme Memorial Lecture, Stockholm International Peace Research Institute, 29 September 1988.

17. Ibid.

18. Mikhail Gorbachev, United Nations Address, Novosti Press Agency, 8 December 1988.

19. Novosti Press Agency Publishing House, Moscow 1989.

20. Ibid., p.25, Table of 'Correlation of basic types of armaments'.

21. Marshal Ogarkov, as quoted in *Red Star*, 8 May 1984.

22. For a comprehensive survey of this period of transition in Soviet military thought, see *Soviet Military Doctrine : New Thinking on Nuclear and Non-Nuclear Strategy*, by Roy Allison, Centre for Russian and East European Studies, University of Birmingham, September 1989 and Philip A. Petersen and Notra Trulock, *A 'New' Soviet Military Doctrine: Origins and Implications*, Soviet Research Centre, Sandhurst, Summer 1988.

23. Major General M. Yasyukov, 'The military policy of the CSU: essence and content', *Communist of the Armed Forces*, No. 20, Moscow, October 1985.

24. Marshal S. Akhromeyev, *Problems of the World and Socialism*, No. 12, Moscow 1989.

25. Until 1989 the author was a serving officer in the Royal Air Force. He was not a participant in any official negotiations but was aware of the rationale behind the Western position and privy to many discussions on its formulation. He did, however, participate as a British government representative in a number of unofficial meetings between NATO and Soviet military, diplomatic and defence analyst specialists held in the UK and Germany during 1987 and 1988 on both arms control and confidence-building measures. Unless specified to the contrary, the following analysis of the Western position on air forces is based on personal awareness during that period.

26. Speech by L. I. Brezhnev, Tula, January 1977 as reported in *Izvestia*, 19 January 1977.

27. Vladimir Petrovski, Deputy Foreign Minister, Tass, 22 June 1987, cited in Snyder, 'Limiting offensive conventional forces', *International Security*, Spring 1988, p.49.

28. 'Air defense in a strategic operation', from the *Voroshilov Lectures*, Materials from the General Staff Academy, 2, p.41, NDU Press, Washington, DC, 1990.

29. Ibid., p.55.

30. This rather chilling possibility was hinted at on 27 June 1991 in Moscow to the author by a member of the General Staff's Operational Planning Group who, when asked how long the High Command had expected to take to reach the Channel, answered 'Three weeks, assuming we had neutralised your air forces.'

31. Throughout this period, the author was privy to regular intelligence digests which monitored the development of new Soviet aircraft, their deployment to squadrons and subsequent movement between airbases as well as participation in regular training exercises.

32. NATO, The Facts, 25 November 1988; WTO Figures, *Soviet News*, February 1987.

33. From 1986 to 1989 the author was Director General of Personnel Management for the RAF after four previous years in charge of Personnel Policy and Ground Branch Manning. He also maintained regular liaison with NATO commanders and colleagues in similar positions. All were experiencing similar difficulties in a greater or lesser degree.

34. Senior commanders subsequently began to take advantage of *glasnost* to vent their feelings publicly. See Ch. 7 for detailed examples.

35. 'Conventional forces talks: a place on the agenda for air power?', R. A. Mason, *Bulletin of the Council for Arms Control*, No. 43, April 1989, p.4.

36. The mandate signed by the 23 signatories at the Palais Lichenstein in Vienna on 10 January 1989, as quoted in *SIPRI Yearbook 1989*, p.422.

37. Ibid., p.421.

38. Ibid.
39. Ibid.
40. Position Paper provided by NATO delegations, Vienna, 6 March 1989, p.2.
41. Conceptual Framework of Agreement on Conventional Armed Forces in Europe, proposed by Bulgaria, Czechoslovakia, the German Democratic Republic, Hungary, Poland, Romania and the Union of Soviet Socialist Republic, 9 March 1989. Translated by the British Embassy, Vienna.
42. Ibid.
43. Ibid.
44. Grinevskiy, Plenary Session, 5 May 1989, US Delegation informal translation, p.2.
45. Plenary statement by General Tatarnikov, 9 May 1989, US Delegation translation, p.2.
46. Delegate sources to the author, after the plenary session of 1 May 1989.
47. NATO Press Service Communiqué M-1 (89)20, 30 May 1989, para. 49.
48. 'Declaration of the Heads of State and Government Participating in the Meeting of the North Atlantic Council in Brussels 29–30 May 1989', NATO Press Release, Brussels, 30 May 1989, para. 17.
49. See, for example, the analysis by Jane Sharp in 'Conventional arms control in Europe', *SIPRI Yearbook 1990*, pp.484–5.
50. IISS Conference at Barnett Hill, UK, 3–5 May 1989. A paper on 'Conventional arms control: air power constraints' by R.A. Mason, which set out the case for preparing a set of Western counterproposals received a positive reaction from the NATO and US political representatives at the conference and copies of the paper were retained for further study in Washington and Brussels.
51. As reported in *Aviation Week & Space Technology*, 5 June 1989.
52. NATO, The Facts, op. cit.
53. A disagreement observed by the author during private discussions in Moscow, 3–5 July 1989. Issues which later were to become serious obstacles to the treaty – definitions, land-based maritime aviation, training aircraft and above all PVO interceptors - prompted extensive disagreements among well-informed senior Soviet analysts and decision makers about how big a step should be taken towards the Bush position.
54. Negotiations on Conventional Armed Forces in Europe, Proposal Submitted by the Delegations of Belgium, Canada *et al.* to the Vienna Conference on 13 July 1989, Chapter I, p.2 Annex to *Atlantic News*, No. 2141, 15 July 1989.
55. Ibid p.4. Definitions and lists to support proposed ceilings.
56. Marshal Akhromeyev, address to the US House Armed Services Committee, 21 July 1989. Press release, Washington, DC, 21 July, p.12.
57. Ibid., p.11
58. *Problems of Ensuring Stability with Radical Cuts in Armed Forces and Conventional Armaments in Europe*, Kokoshin, Konovalov, Lamonov & Mazing, Novosti Press, Moscow, 1989, p.19.
59. GDR Press Release, Vienna 28 September 1989, para.2(a). Translated by the Institute for Defense and Disarmament Studies, Brookline, MA.
60. Ibid.
61. Ibid.
62. Ibid., para.4.
63. Ibid., para. 8 (a).
64. Ibid., para. 8 (b).
65. NATO Staff Briefing, Brussels, 31 July 1990.

66. Ibid.

67. Institute of Defense and Disarmament Studies, *Vienna Fax*, No. 21, 20 July 1990.

68. *Vienna Fax*, No. 22, 10 September 1990.

69. Not surprisingly, Western military appraisals of residual WTO capacity during this period became progressively more confident and pursuit of advantageous detail in the negotiations slightly less rigorous.

70. The present writer had several conversations in Europe and Washington during August and September in which such concern was expressed. Military opinion was fairly predictably divided between army officers, who had consistently emphasised the primary focus on ground forces, and air force colleagues, who feared that Soviet numerical superiority would be unrestrained and even extended as a result of unilateral national reductions in the West.

71. 'New from the negotiations', *Arms Control & Disarmament Quarterly Review*, No. 19, October 1990, p.32, UK Arms Control & Disarmament Research Unit, Foreign & Commonwealth Office.

72. *Treaty on Conventional Armed Forces in Europe*, Article II, sub-para. 1. (K).

73. *Protocol on Procedures Governing the Reclassification of Specific Models or Versions of Combat-capable Trainer Aircraft into Unarmed Trainer Aircraft*, Section 1, para. 2.

74. Ibid., and Section III, Procedures for Total Disarming.

75. *Treaty*, Article IV. 1 (E) and Article VI. 1 (E).

76. In figures issued in February 1989 (note 19 supra) the USSR had acknowledged a holding of 5,955 combat aircraft, excluding all combat trainers. Consequently in November 1990 NATO had expected a total in excess of 7,000.

77. At a non-attributable briefing in London on 30 November 1990 a senior British official expressed concern about the number of Soviet aircraft which had been either moved eastwards out of the ATTU area or redeployed to Soviet naval aviation during the previous 18 months.

78. *Vienna Fax*, 28 February 1991.

79. *Jane's Defence Weekly*, 30 March 1991, p.467.

80. A 'hangar queen' is the rather derogatory name for an aircraft, usually verging on obsolescence, which is progressively stripped of its components to service other, more modern aircraft until it has little remaining operational potential itself.

81. Article IV. 1 (E) and Article VI (E)

82. *Protocol on Procedures Governing the Categorisation of Combat Helicopters and the Recategorisation of Multipurpose Attack Helicopters*, Section I, para. 1.

83. Ibid., para. 3.

84. Ibid., Section III, para. 1.

85. Ibid., para. 2 and section IV.

86. Ibid., Section V.

87. Jane M.O. Sharp, 'Conventional arms control in Europe', *SIPRI Yearbook 1993*, p.591.

88. Tashkent Document, translated in *SIPRI Yearbook 1993*, pp.675, 678.

89. Approximation drawn from IISS *Military Balance 1993–94*, pp.98–106.

90. During frequent visits to Moscow between 1989 and 1993 the present writer, in many conversations with Soviet/Russian officers saw a gradual, if grudging, relaxation of hostility towards the West quite distinct from the belligerent irritation regularly expressed about the activities of some former Soviet republics.

91. *Treaty on Conventional Armed Forces In Europe*, Paris, 19 November 1990, as reproduced in *SIPRI Yearbook 1991*, p.472.

92. CSCE Document, Vienna, 4 March 1992, Section III, Contacts, paras. 20–33.
93. Treaty on Open Skies, Helsinki, 24 March 1992.
94. Reported in *Trust & Verify*, No. 39, 1993, p.2.

Chapter 5

1. *Conduct of the Persian Gulf Conflict, An Interim Report to Congress*, p.271, cited in *Gulf Lesson One – The Value of Air power*, by Wing Commander Gary Waters, RAAF Air power Studies Centre, Canberra, 1992, p.104.
2. Cited in *Storm over Iraq*, by Richard Hallion, Smithsonian Institution Press, Washington, DC, 1992, p.247; based on Department of Defense sources.
3. *Conduct of the Persian Gulf War, Final Report to Congress*, US Department of Defense, April 1992, p.241.
4. Cited by Hallion, op. cit., p.195.
5. Ibid., p.9.
6. Ibid. Appendix G, p.9. Schwarzkopf, *It Doesn't Take a Hero*, Bantam, New York, 1992.
7. *Aviation Week & Space Technology*, 25 February 1991, p.20.
8. Transcript of comments by Secretary of Defence Cheney on CNN, 2 March 1991, cited by Hallion, op. cit., p.252.
9. 'Desert Storm as a Symbol', Col. Dennis Drew, *Air power Journal*, Fall 1992, pp.6, 13.
10. 'The air war in the Gulf', by R. A. Mason, *Survival*, May/June 1991, p.225.
11. *The Gulf Conflict, a Military Analysis*, Lt.-Colonel Jeffrey McAusland, Adelphi Paper No. 282, IISS/Brasseys, November 1993, pp.63–4.
12. Ibid., p.50, citing Schwarzkopf, p.453.
13. *Air power: Desert Shield/Desert Storm*, US Air Force Internal Information Directorate paper, 1991, p.7, quoted by First Lt. M.M.Huxley in: 'Saddam Hussein and Iraqi air power', *Air power Journal*, Winter 1992, VI, No. 4, p.13.
14. *Final Report to Congress*, op. cit., p.45.
15. USAF *Gulf War Air power Study*, Draft Summary, April 1993, Section 6, p.2. Hereafter referred to as GWAPS.
16. Ibid., Section 8, p.5.
17. Ibid., Section 6, p.10.
18. *Final Report to Congress*, op cit., pp.142, 143.
19. Waters, op. cit., p.248
20. GWAPS, Section 8, p.5.
21. *Final Report to Congress*, p.F2, credits US logistics with the issue of up to 19 million gallons of fuel a day at the 'peak of operations', presumably during the land campaign. To that figure should be added the consumption of all Coalition forces not served by US units.
22. Ibid., p.T-89.
23. A figure derived from extrapolation of data given in Annex F to *Final Report to Congress*; in Waters, pp.215–7, and RAF Fact Sheets ASB2 7789, 1991, p.4.
24. Author's conversations with Coalition aircrew deployed to Dhahran.
25. *Final Report to Congress*, op. cit., p.F12.
26. Concern about such denial was expressed in a Congressional Staff Report in 1985: see *US-Soviet Military Balance 1980–85*, John M. Collins, Pergamon-Brassey's, 1985, p.137.
27. GWAPS, Section 8, p.7.
28. Benjamin S. Lambeth, *The Winning of Air Supremacy in Operation Desert Storm*, RAND, October 1993, p.2.

29. Air Vice-Marshal W.J.Wratten, 'The air war in the Gulf', presentation to IISS Conference, London, 11–12 April 1991.

30. Waters, op. cit., p.68.

31. BBC Newsnight, 20 August 1990.

32. Personal observation by visiting RAF officer reported to the author in January 1991.

33. Reported in *Sunday Times* (London), 27 January 1991.

34. Reported in *Flight International*, 24–30 April 1991, p.33.

35. Figures taken from *Final Report to Congress*, pp.145 and 272, and from *US Navy in Desert Shield and Desert Storm*, Office of the Chief of Naval Operations, Washington, DC, 1991, Table 2, p.D-9, cited in Hallion, op. cit., p.255.

36. *Desert Victory*, Norman Friedman, US Naval Institute Press, 1991, p.205.

37. *Aviation Week & Space Technology*, 27 April 1992, pp.18–20.

38. 'We must do better', by Rear Admiral R.D.Mixson, commander of Carrier Group Two in the Red Sea in *US Naval Institute Proceedings*, August 1991, p.39, cited in Hallion, op. cit., p.257

39. Report by naval observer USN Captain Steven Ramsdell, 14 May 1991. Cited by Hallion, op. cit., p.258.

40. GWAPS, Section 5, p.9.

41. Friedman, op. cit., p.212.

42. *Final Report to Congress*, p.306.

43. Ibid., p.T 196–8.

44. Mixson, in Hallion op. cit., p.257.

45. Hallion, ibid., pp.257 and 296.

46. Ramsdell, quoted in Hallion, op. cit., p.258.

47. Author's conversations with RAF planning staff, March 1991.

48. Air Weather Service, DESERT SHIELD, DESERT STORM Report No. 2, p.125, cited in GWAPS, Section 6, p.8.

49. Hallion, op. cit., p.154

50. Specific data on sortie curtailment is drawn from GWAPS, Section 1, p.19, Section 3, p.49, Section 6, p.8; *Final Report to Congress*, pp.196, 197, 228; and Hallion, op. cit., p.177.

51. GWAPS, Section 3, p.14.

52. *Final Report to Congress*, p.228; *Expert Witness*, Christopher Bellamy, Brassey's, 1993, p.79.

53. GWAPS, Section 2, p.24.

54. Cited in GWAPS, Section 4, p.18.

55. *Independent* (London), 7 February 1991.

56. GWAPS, Section 2, p.42.

57. Ibid., Section 4, p.19.

58. Ibid., Section 3, p.44 and Section 4, p.6.

59. Ibid., Section 6, p.9.

60. Ibid., Section 3, p.35.

61. The author flew in a stealth modified F4 at Wright Patterson Air Force Base in July 1971; parts of the aircraft were coated in radar-absorbing materials for testing. By then, the SR 71 was already fully operational, displaying several stealth characteristics in shape and technology incorporation.

62. In *Aviation Week & Space Technology*, 12 December 1990.

63. General Michael Dugan, 'The air war', *US News & World Report*, 11 February 1991.

64. Effect of CEP (Circular Error Probable: the radial distance from a point in which 50 per cent of all bombs are likely to land) on quantity: 90 per cent probability of hit.

DOD Briefing Notes, July 1991. There is evidence to suggest that the F 117s' bombing accuracy improved as the war evolved, e.g., Schwarzkopf, op. cit., p.415, 'in the first wave . . . just 55 per cent of their bombs on target.'

65. See Ch. 8 for discussion of future strategic bombardment.
66. AWACs operational details taken from *Final Report to Congress*, op. cit., pp.T40–42.
67. Friedman, op. cit., p.154.
68. Air Commodore J. Singh, *Air Power in Modern Warfare*, Lancer International, New Delhi, 1988, p.122.
69. Hallion, op. cit., pp.291–2, gives details of the F15Es.
70. *Final Report to Congress*, op. cit., pp.T84–86.
71. *Aviation Week & Space Technology*, 3 January 1994, p.53.
72. *Final Report to Congress*, op. cit., p.T153.
73. GWAPS, Section 2, p.19.
74. Schwarzkopf, *It Doesn't Take a Hero*, op. cit., pp.416–19.
75. McAusland, op. cit., p.38.
76. Schwarzkopf, op. cit., p.417.
77. GWAPS, Section 3, pp.26–32; *Final Report to Congress*, pp.223–6.
78. *Final Report to Congress*, pp.221–2.
79. USCINCENT SITREPS tabled by A.H.Cordesman, in Part 2 of Documents 'The War to Liberate Kuwait', Office of Senator John McCain, December 1991.
80. GWAPS, Section 9, p.4.
81. See, for example, *Desert Storm and Its Meaning, the View from Moscow,* Benjamin S Lambeth, RAND, 1992, pp.52–3.
82. NATO Political Committee Briefing Note, 2889/SIR560, by C.N.Donnelly, 31 August 1990, para.7.
83. W.J.Wratten, op. cit., p.203.
84. See Hallion, op. cit., pp.115–20.
85. 'The winning of air supremacy in Operation Desert Storm', transcript of address by Benjamin S. Lambeth to Zhuskovskii Air Force Engineering Academy, Moscow, 12 October 1992, p.15.
86. Hallion, op. cit., pp.247–8.
87. Group Captain N.E.Taylor, *Air Power Journal*, Summer 1993, pp.69–70.
88. Brigadier V. K. Nair, *War in the Gulf: Lessons for the Third World,* Lancer International, New Delhi, 1991.
89. Ibid., p.130.
90. The following hypothetical scenario details were drawn from a presentation given by the author to the United States Air Warfare Course, Montgomery, Alabama, entitled 'Reflections on the Gulf War, a view from the Little League', on 4 May 1992. In October 1992 he was presented with a copy of General Nair's book (ref. 88) by the author and was intrigued to see the latter's parallel suggestions. There is, of course, no implication whatever that India is cast in the role of regional aggressor.
91. Nair, op. cit., p.225.
92. Lambeth, *The Winning of Air Supremacy in Desert Storm*, op. cit., p.12.

Chapter 6
1. Interview with *Daily Telegraph* (London), 10 July 1992.
2. Ibid.
3. *Daily Telegraph*, 4 August 1992.
4. *Independent* (London), 5 August 1992.

5. Lawrence Freedman, *Independent*, 5 August 1992.
6. Downing Street sources, to *Daily Telegraph*, 4 August 1992.
7. *Independent*, 9 August 1992
8. UN Security Council Resolution 781, 9 October 1992, paras 1,2,4, 6.
9. See the comprehensive review of the contestants' ORBATS in *Jane's Intelligence Review*, October 1992.
10. *Aviation Week & Space Technology*, 23 November 1992.
11. *The Times* (London), 15 December 1992.
12. Ibid.
13. Exposition by USAF Major Muswell Stinnette, 433 Airlift Wing, Rhein Main AFB, in *Aviation Week & Space Technology*, 19 April 1993, p.58.
14. *Sunday Times* (London), 28 February 1993.
15. As reported in *NATO Review*, April 1993, p.5.
16. Text of North Atlantic Treaty, 24 August 1949, Articles 5 and 6, from *Treaties and Alliances of the World*, Keesing's, London, 1968, p.69.
17. *Royal Air Force News*, 14 May 1993.
18. Reported from Washington in London *Daily Telegraph*, 29 April 1993.
19. Ibid.
20. Ibid.
21. Ibid.
22. Ibid.
23. UN Security Council Resolution 794, 3 December 1992.
24. *Daily Telegraph*, 15 June 1993.
25. John Boatman and Barbara Starr, 'USA looks for answer to the ugliness of urban warfare.' *Jane's Defence Weekly*, 16 October 1993, p.25.
26. Douglas Fraser, 'Requirements in the field for effective UN peacekeeping', Paper presented to NDU/USIP Symposium at Fort McNair, Washington, DC, 11 December 1992, cited by Mats Berdal, *Whither UN Peacekeeping*, Adelphi Paper No. 281, IISS, October 1993, p.47.
27. Berdal, ibid., p.48.
28. *Independent*, 11 June 1993.
29. The author discussed the peacekeeping/peace-enforcing task with allied air staff officers during this period. They were extremely frustrated by the failure of the two agencies, the UN and NATO, for political rather than operational reasons to agree on either rules of engagement or chain of command. There was a strongly held belief that sensitivities about the security of ground forces already deployed in the theatre were masking much wider political ambitions and positions: specifically the traditional rivalry between France and the USA over the direction of military policy and strategy in Europe.
30. Douglas Hurd, BBC Radio interview, 3 August 1993.
31. Alan Phelps, *Daily Telegraph*, 5 August 1993.
32. Christopher Bellamy, *Independent*, 7 August 1993.
33. From a report on the North Atlantic Council decisions in Brussels on 9 August by Andrew Marshall, *Independent*, 11 August 1993.
34. Report by Barbara Starr and Charles Vickers of conversation with 'a senior US military planner', *Jane's Defence Weekly*, 14 August 1993.
35. Extracts from report by Joris Janssen Lok in *Jane's Defence Weekly*, 23 October 1993, p.32.
36. *Independent*, 11 January 1994, p.10.
37. *Daily Telegraph*, 11 January 1994, p.5.

38. *Independent*, 22 January 1994, p.4.
39. *Daily Telegraph*, 24 January 1994, p.6.
40. BBC report, 7 February 1994.
41. 'Decisions taken at the meeting of the North Atlantic Council on 9 February 94', reproduced in *NATO Review*, February 1994, p.11.
42. *Daily Telegraph*, 14 February 1994, p.8.
43. London press reports: *The Times, Independent, Daily Telegraph* and BBC, 1 March 1994.
44. *Independent*, 12 March 1994, p.11.
45. *The Times*, 14 March 1994, p.11.
46. Author's conversations with RAF in-theatre squadron commander, 9 March 1994.
47. Manfred Wörner, Secretary-General of NATO, at WEU Assembly, Paris, 29 November 1993; NATO Press Release, p.3.
48. For an excellent, well-balanced account and analysis of these early ventures in 'peacekeeping' by air power see P.A. Towle, *Pilots and Rebels*, Brassey's London, 1989.
49. Memorandum No.688-53-PS, dated Peshawar, 6 March 1923, from H.N.Bolton to Foreign Secretary, Government of India in the Foreign and Political Department, Sinta. In RAF Staff College archives, Bracknell.
50. As reported in *Economist* (London), 18 September 1993, p.68.
51. Wörner, op. cit., p.3.
52. Cited in 'Bombing the Mad Mullah 1920' Randall Gray, *RUSI Journal*, December 1980 p.46.
53. Towle, op. cit., p.19.
54. Ibid., p.50.
55. Armitage & Mason, *Air power in The Nuclear Age, Theory and Practice*, Macmillan, 2nd edn, 1986, p.287.
56. Lt.Gen.Y.P. Ezanno, in *Symposium on the Role of Air power in Counter-insurgency and Unconventional Warfare: the Algerian War*, Memorandum RM 3U53-PR, RAND, Santa Monica, July 1963, pp.37–8.
57. Colonel A.L.Gropman, 'The air war in Vietnam, 1961–73,' in *War in the Third Dimension*, Brassey's, London, 1986, pp.34 and 57.
58. S.R.McMichael, *Stumbling Bear, Soviet Military Performance in Afghanistan*, Brassey's, London, 1991, p.84.
59. DoD spokesman, quoted in *Aviation Week & Space Technology*, 13 July 1987, p.26.
60. *Jane's Defence Weekly*, 29 November 1986, p.1258.
61. Towle, op. cit., p.50.
62. Air Commodore A.D.J.Garrisson, in *Symposium on the Role of Air power in Counter-insurgency and Unconventional Warfare in the Malayan Emergency*, Memorandum RM 3651-PR, RAND, Santa Monica, July 1963, p.60.
63. Sqn.Ldr. A.Twigg, ibid., p.67.
64. Air Commodore P.E.Warcup, ibid., p.48
65. Col.R.L.Clutterbuck, ibid., p.54
66. Air Commodore P.E.Warcup, ibid., p.75.

Chapter 7

1. Figures collated by the author from authoritative RAF sources in February 1989.
2. Ulrich Brandenburg, 'The "Friends" Are Leaving', NATO, CND (93)100, 12 February 1993, pp.4–5.

3. Rear Admiral Shelev (GDR Navy), at Conference on New Thinking and Military Policy, Moscow, 13 November 1989.

4. For details of negotiations see Henry Plater-Zyberk, *The Soviet Military Withdrawal from Central Europe*, Centre for Defence Studies, Brassey's, August 1991.

5. Author's conversation with Lt.-Gen. A. Aiupov, Moscow, 2 October 1991.

6. For excellent studies of the evolution of Soviet military doctrine in the decade before the Gulf War see Roy Allison, 'Soviet military doctrine: new thinking on nuclear and non-nuclear strategy', Paper presented at MoD/University of Birmingham Seminar, 24 September 1989, and Philip A. Petersen & Notra Trulock, *A 'New' Soviet Military Doctrine, Origins and Implications*, Soviet Studies Research Centre, Sandhurst, Summer 1988.

7. *Red Star*, 9 May 1984, translated by the BBC Monitoring Service (SU/7639/C010).

8. From Voroshilov Academy Notes and Major-General Kuznetzov, cited in Petersen & Trulock, p.11.

9. Colonel General I. Golushko, 'The rear in conditions of the use by the enemy of high-accuracy weapons', *Rear Services & Supply*, No. 7, July 1984, p.18, cited in Petersen & Trulock, p.18.

10. See the references to Ogarkov, Gari'ev, Zhilin and others in Allison and Petersen & Trulock.

11. Colonel General of Aviation Ye. I. Shaposhnikov, Commander-in-Chief of the Air Forces, in *Aviation & Cosmonautics*, No. 1, 1991, translated by Air Commodore E. S. Williams, Soviet Studies Research Centre, Sandhurst, June 1992, UKTRANS 00504, pp.2, 3, 4.

12. For a comprehensive analysis of early Soviet response to the overwhelming success of Coalition air power, see Benjamin S. Lambeth, *Desert Storm and Its Meaning, The View from Moscow*, RAND, R.4164-AF, 1992.

13. Russian Defence Minister, Army General P. S. Grachev, *Izvestia*, 1 June 1992, p.1. Soviet Studies Research Centre, Sandhurst translation by J.B.K.Lough, August 1992, p.1.

14. Report in *Jane's Defence Weekly*, 25 January 1992, p.101.

15. *Independent* (London), 19 February 1992, p.10.

16. Colonel General Victor Samsonov, Chief of the General Staff of the CIS Unified Armed Forces, in *Red Star*, 18 March 1992.

17. The author observed this impasse at first hand in meetings in Moscow in June 1991 with political deputies from Riga and representatives of the then Soviet High Command. Not for the first time, nor the last, deeply-engrained mistrust on the one hand and military insensitivity on the other prevented what to the neutral observer seemed to be an eminently manageable problem with the prospect of favourable outcomes to each side.

18. *Izvestia*, 20 August 1991, cited in Stephen D. Shenfield, *Dividing up the Soviet Defence Complex: Implications for European Security*, Center for Policy Development, Brown University, May 1992, p.46.

19. *Nezavisimaya Gazette*, 24 April 1992, cited in *Commonwealth Defence Arrangements and International Security*, joint paper by Rogov *et al.*, for the Institute of USA and Canada and the US Center for Naval Analysis.

20. *Red Star*, 8 May 1992.

21. Colonel General of Aviation Petr Deynekin, Commander-in-Chief Russian Air Force, *Nezavisimaya Gazette*, 21 April 1993, Soviet Studies Research Centre, UKTRANS 529, translated by R. W. Dellow, p.1.

22. Major General M. Yaryukov, 'The military policy of the CPSU: essence and content, *Communist of the Armed Forces*, October 1985, cited in Petersen & Trulock, op. cit., p.24.
23. Colonel N. Goryachev, 'Know and capably apply entrusted weapons and military equipment', *Communist of the Armed Forces*, January 1987.
24. Julian Cooper, *The Conversion of the Former Soviet Defence Industry*, Royal Institute for International Affairs, London, May 1993, p.3.
25. This introductory industrial analysis draws heavily from Cooper, ibid., pp.1–4.
26. Ibid., pp.2, 3.
27. A meeting called by Mr Gorbachev on 2 October 1991 to assess the social implications of conversion was abandoned when senior officials were unable to quantify the scale of the problem. Conversations between the author and a participant at the meeting, Moscow, 2 October 1991.
28. Professor A. Kennaway, *The Economic and Industrial Legacy of Communism in Russia*, Conflict Studies Research Centre, Sandhurst, September 1993, p.6.
29. Kennaway, *Restructuring the Defence Technology and Industrial Base*, Conflict Studies Research Centre, Sandhurst, October 1993, pp.5–6.
30. *Aviation & Cosmonautics*, October 1989, pp.103.
31. Col. A. Manushkin, 'Penny-wise and pound-foolish or, more on the quality of aircraft we add to inventory', *Red Star*, 1 November 1990.
32. Cited by Dennis Marshall-Hardell, *The Reform of Flight Safety in the Soviet Air Force*, Soviet Studies Research Centre, Sandhurst, February 1993, p.41.
33. Cooper, op. cit., p.4.
34. V. Chuyko, Deputy Minister Aviation Industry, *Pravda*, 7 June 1990.
35. A senior Soviet reforming official in Moscow in June 1990, who quoted this figure to the author, was unaware that the generals' assertions could be discredited by reference to many Western open commercial, industrial and official sources.
36. I. Shitarev, in 'Editor's round table', discussion on conversion, with other senior officials in aviation industry, *Pravda*, 7 June 1990.
37. Eye-witness account to the author, Moscow, 26 June 1991.
38. Cooper, op. cit., p.9.
39. Shenfield, op. cit., pp.14, 15.
40. Interview with Col.General of Aviation Anatoliy Maliukov, *Jane's Defence Review*, 17 April 1993.
41. See, for example, Joshua Epstein, *Measuring Military Power, the Soviet Air Threat to Europe*, Princeton 1984, which combined penetrating analysis of Soviet practices and sources with an attempt to quantify them using Western operational experience and concepts.
42. 'Marked down by time', *Aviation & Cosmonautics*, March 1988.
43. 'Achieving greater combat readiness through caring for people', *Aviation & Cosmonautics*, July 1989.
44. *Aviation & Cosmonautics*, February 1988.
45. For an analysis of the interaction between flight safety and the reform movement see Marshall-Hasdell, op. cit., February 1993.
46. *Aviation & Cosmonautics*, September 1987.
47. Ibid., October 1988, Maj.Gen.L.Koshyrev, ibid., March 1988.
48. Ibid., November 1988, p.40.
49. Ibid., February 1989, p.1.
50. Ibid., January 1991, translated by Air Commodore E.S. Williams, Soviet Studies Research Centre, Sandhurst, UKTRANS 00504, June 1991.

51. *Red Star*, 11 March 1993, cited in Cooper, op. cit., p.28.
52. Ibid., 6 February 1993, cited in Cooper, ibid.
53. Ibid., 22 July 1992.
54. *Military Thought*, No. 2, 1993, p.8, cited in Cooper, op. cit.
55. For an extended evaluation of the Kokoshin initiative, see Cooper, ibid., pp.31–3.
56. Julian Cooper, 'The economies of the former Soviet Union, structural issues', paper presented to Seminar at University of Birmingham, 8 September 1993, p.5.
57. *Jane's Defence Review*, 27 July 1991, p.132.
58. Ibid., 28 September 1991, pp.564–5.
59. Ibid., 16 November 1991, p.930.
60. Ibid., 4 July 1992, p.6.
61. Ibid., 17 April 1993, p.15.
62. Ibid.
63. Ibid., 20 November 1993.
64. Russian sources for such reports cited in *Jane's Defence Review*.
65. Russian TV 19 December 1993, cited in *Jane's Defence Review*, 15 January 1994.
66. Ibid., 17 April 1993, p.18.
67. Ibid., 27 November 1993.
68. Major General Kozlov, VPVO, quoted in 'Russian air power, the first year', by Major Brian Collins, paper released by the office of the Special Advisor for Central and European Affairs, HQ NATO, October 1993, p.13. Hereafter referred to as Collins.
69. Collins, pp.11, 15.
70. *Red Star*, 26 January 1993.
71. 'Russian air defence forces', Major General A. Sumin, *Military Technology*, No. 7, 1993, p.27.
72. Cited in Collins, op. cit., p.15.
73. Yuri A. Kuznetsov, 'Russian air defence radar development', [interview], *Military Technology*, No. 5, 1993, pp.59–62.
74. ITAR-TASS 23 October 1992.
75. Mikhail Malei, 'The destiny of conversion that is Russia', *Military Technology*, No. 3, 1993, pp.53–5.
76. Advertising sections, *Military Technology,* Nos. 8 and 11, 1993.
77. Rahul Bedi, 'India's westward gaze', *Jane's Defence Review*, 9 January 1993.
78. See, for example, Lt.-General H.S.Starodubov, Deputy Director for Operations of the General Staff of USSR Armed Forces, in *Arms Control, Problems and Prospects 1990*, the proceedings of an international symposium convened in Texas by the Mosher Institute for Defence Studies, 4–5 January 1990, Texas A&M Press, 1990, pp.20–25.
79. 'Victory: memory and truth', Minister of Defence Marshal of the Soviet Union D.T. Yazov, *Pravda*, 9 May 1991, p.3.
80. Major-General Batenin, Moscow, 14 November 1989, at Conference on New Thinking and Military Policy, organised by V. I. Lenin Military Political Academy. Observed by the author.
81. A comment made in the presence of the author during discussions on European security at a conference on Military Doctrine and Military Reconstruction at Charles University, Prague, 15–17 April 1993.
82. From para. 6 of the 1992 Draft, cited in James F. Holcomb, *Russian Military Doctrine*, Soviet Studies Research Centre, Sandhurst, August 1992, p.2.
83. Ibid., para. 6e.

84. Ibid., para. 7d, cited in C.J.Dick, *Initial Thoughts on Russia's Draft Military Doctrine*, Soviet Studies Research Centre, Sandhurst, 14 July 1992, p.4.
85. Lt.-General S.A. Bogdanov, Head of the Operational-Strategic Research Centre of the General Staff, in a presentation to a conference on Urgent Problems of International Security, Centre for National Security and Strategic Studies, Moscow, 2 October 1991. From notes taken by the author.
86. 'Lessons of the Persian Gulf War', Major-General I.N.Voroby'ev, *Military Thought*, Nos. 4–5,1992, pp.67–74.
87. 'The Persian Gulf War, lessons and conclusions', Lebedev, Lyutov & Nazarenko, *Military Thought*, Nos. 11–12, 1991, p.109.
88. Draft Doctrine, para.10a, cited by Holcomb, op. cit.
89. Ibid., para. 13, cited in Dick, op. cit.
90. *Military Technology*, No. 2, 1993, p.17, extracts from conference paper given to a Military Scientific Conference at the Military Academy of the General Staff, 27–30 May 1992.
91. *Red Star*, 18 December 1992, cited in Collins, op. cit., p.24.
92. Minister of Defence Grachev, *Izvestia*, 1 June 1992, p.1.
93. *Military Thought*, July 1992, cited in Collins, op. cit., pp.31, 33.
94. *Red Star*, 15 August 1992, p.1.
95. Colonel General of Aviation Deynekin, *Aviation & Cosmonautics*, January 1993, pp.2–4.
96. From the script of an address by Lt. General (Aviation) N.T. Antoshkin, at the RNAF base Leewarden, 20 April 1993, translated by Suzette & Henry Plater-Zyberk.
97. Colonel-General Eugeni Zarudnyev, Director General of VVS Combat Training, in conversations with the author, Moscow, 28 May 1993, and conversations with VVS fighter pilots in the same period.
98. *Aviation Week & Space Technology*, 15 November 1993, p.51.
99. Admiral A. Pauk, *Military Thought*, July 1992, cited in Collins, op. cit., p.19.
100. Deynekin, *Izvestia*, 24 March 1993, p.6.
101. Ibid., *Red Star*, 15 August 1992, op. cit.

Chapter 8

1. The single most notable contribution to air power doctrine at the end of the century is *The Air Campaign, Planning for Combat*, by Colonel John A. Warden, National Defence University Press, Washington, DC, 1988. Many of Warden's prescient ideas may be seen in the Coalition air plans for DESERT STORM. Strong contributions to air power theory and analysis also emanated from the Directors of Defence Studies of the Royal Air Force, the Air power Research Institute of the US Air Forces, the Air Power Studies Centre of the Royal Australian Air Force, the Institute for Defence Studies and Analyses in New Delhi and from the RAND Corporation in California.
2. Report in *Jane's Defence Weekly*, 12 February 1994, pp.4–5.
3. *Jane's Defence Review*, 20 November 1993, p.32.
4. Ibid.
5. Rear Admiral Riley Mixson, Director of Naval Aviation, USN, *Jane's Defence Weekly*, 3 April 1993.
6. *Military Balance 1993–94*, International Institute for Strategic Studies, p.62.
7. Ibid., p.40.
8. Ibid., p.138–9.

9. Ibid., p.152–5.

10. 'A road map for US air power', from the USAF Association Advisory Group on Military Roles and Missions, reprinted in *Military Technology*, No, 10, 1993, pp.56–8.

11. V. K. Nair, *War in the Gulf, Lessons for the Third World*, op. cit., pp.225–8.

12. At a meeting with senior USSR Defence and foreign Ministry officials in 1989 the author was told that after the Falklands War the USSR took everything that Mrs Thatcher said very seriously, recognising in one sense at least a kindred spirit. Subsequently after 1991 when Russian concerns were being expressed about Russians perceived to be vulnerable in the CIS republics the author was accosted, 'Surely, after the Falklands, you understand how we feel . . .'

13. From the text of 'Sir Hugh Trenchard's Address' given at the official opening of the RAF Staff College Andover, by Air Vice-Marshal Sir John Salmond, 4 April 1922. *Aeroplane*, **XXII**, No. 15, 12 April 1922, pp.257–8.

14. From the 3rd Report to the Secretary of War by the Commanding General of the Army Air Forces, General Henry H. Arnold, 12 November 1945, extracted in Emme, *The Impact of Air power*, op. cit., 1959, p.305.

15. Hartley & Hooper, *Eurofighter 2000*, Centre for Defence Economics, University of York, 1994, Ch. 4, p.7.

16. *European Fighter Aircraft*, House of Commons Defence Committee Report, 11 March 1992, p.vii.

17. Hartley & Hooper, op. cit., p.9.

18. *European Fighter Aircraft*, House of Commons Committee of Public Accounts Report, 22 April 1991, p.26.

19. Defence Committee Report op. cit., p.xix.

20. Ibid.

21. Ibid., p.xx.

22. Ibid., p.xxii.

23. *The Economic Consequences of the UK Government's Decision on the Hercules Replacement*, Hartley & Hooper, Centre for Defence Economics, University of York, 1993.

24. *International Collaborative Projects for Defence Equipment*, HCP 626, MoD 1984, p.5, cited in Hartley & Hooper, ibid., p.18.

25. Lee Whitney, McDonnell Aircraft Company, Saint Louis, MO, July 1992, pp.3–5.

26. *Memorandum of Understanding (MOU) concerning a Tri-National Training Establishment for the Tornado Weapons System at Cottesmore in the United Kingdom*, between the UK, the FRG and Italy, 8 May 1979, Preamble.

27. Ibid., Article 3, para. 1.

28. UK MoD Air Staff Sources, 28 June 1990.

29. 'The NATO AEW programme: a Canadian perspective', C. Brando, *Canadian Defence Quarterly*, April 1989, p.25.

30. Ibid., p.28.

31. See 'Aerospace security in the Middle East, the way ahead', R.A. Mason, *Arms Control*, 14, No. 3, December 1993 for a complete analysis of aerospace security in the region.

32. See 'The Consequences of Arms Proliferation in Asia' Ro-myung Gong, Adelphi Paper No.276, IISS, April 1993, pp.42–61.

33. *Options for Defence*, ASEAN Special Report Plus, *Jane's Defence Weekly*, 22 February 1992.

34. Cited in 'ASEAN security dilemmas', Leszek Buszynski, *Survival*, 34, No. 4, Winter 1992–93, p.92.

35. Ibid., p.93.
36. 'China expands air forces', Prasun Sengupta, *Military Technology*, No. 8, 1992, pp.49–51.
37. *Economist*, 20 February 1993, p.21.
38. 'Malaysia splits fighter procurement', Ezio Bonsignore, *Military Technology*, No. 8, 1993, pp.51–3.
39. *Economist*, 20 February 1993, p.21.
40. Sengupta, op. cit., p.56.
41. *On War*, K. von Clausewitz, Book 1, Chapter 3, Princeton University Press, 1976, p.101.
42. 'Giulio Douhet and modern war', Philip S. Meilinger, *Comparative Strategy*, **12**, pp.321–38.
43. GWAPS, op. cit., Ch. 3, p.21.
44. Ibid., Ch. 3, p.21.
45. Ibid., Ch. 3, p.25.
46. Ibid., Ch. 3, p.10.
47. Ibid., Ch. 3, pp.32–3.
48. Interview with Air Chief Marshal Sir Patrick Hine, *Air Forces International*, No. 1, 1992, p.14.
49. Warden, op. cit., pp.146–7.
50. *Defence: Outline of Future Policy*, HMSO, London, April 1957, para. 62.
51. *Unmanned Aircraft*, Air Chief Marshal Sir Michael Armitage, Brassey's, London, 1988, pp.122–3.
52. See *Military Space*, Dutton, De Garis, Winterton & Harding, Brassey's, 1990, for an examination of the interaction between satellites and conventional air power.
53. Armitage, op. cit., p.124.

BIBLIOGRAPHY

Books

Aders, Gebhard, *History of the German Night Fighter Force, 1917–1945*, Jane's, London 1978

Air Ministry London, *A Short History of the Royal Air Force*, 1920

Albrecht, Colonel DW, *Anglo American Cooperation, 1917–1992*, University of Cambridge Thesis, 1992

Armitage, MJ. and Mason, RA, *Air Power in the Nuclear Age*, Macmillan, London 1986

Armitage, Sir Michael, *Unmanned Aircraft*, Brassey's, London 1988

Ball, Desmond, ed., *Air Power*, Pergamon, Oxford 1988

Beaufre, General Andre, *Nato and Europe*, Faber, London 1967

Bellamy, Christopher, *Expert Witness*, Brassey's, London 1993

Berger, Carl, ed., *The United States Air Force in South East Asia*, US Government Printing Office, 1977

Blank and Kipp, eds., *The Soviet Military and the Future*, Greenwood, London 1992

Boog, Horst, *The German Luftwaffe High Command, 1935–1945*, Stuttgart 1982 (in German)

Boyle, A, *Trenchard: A Man of Vision*, Collins, London 1967

Brodie, Bernard, *Strategy in the Missile Age*, Princeton University Press, New Jersey 1965

Boyd, Alexander, *The Soviet Air Force since 1918*, Macdonald and Jane's, London 1977

Chamier, JA, *The Birth of the Royal Air Force*, Pitman, London 1943

Clausewitz, K von, *On War*, Princeton University Press, New Jersey 1976

Clodfelter, Mark, *The Limits of Air Power*, The Free Press, New York 1989

Collins, John M, *US-Soviet Military Balance, 1980–85*, Pergamon Brassey's, Washington 1985

Cooper, J, *The Conversion of the Former Soviet Defence Industry*, RIIA, London 1993

Croft, Stuart, ed., *The Conventional Armed Forces in Europe Treaty*, Dartmouth 1994

Davis, Richard G, *Carl A Spaatz and the Air War in Europe*, Smithsonian, Washington DC 1992

De Seversky, Alexander, *Victory through Air Power*, Simon and Schuster, New York 1942

Douhet, Guilio, *The Command of the Air*, Faber and Faber, London 1943

Dutton, De Garis, Winterton and Harding, *Military Space*, Brassey's, London 1990

Emme, Eugene, ed., *The Impact of Air Power*, Van Nostrand 1959

Epstein, J, *Measuring Military Power, The Soviet Air Threat to Europe*, Princeton University Press, New Jersey 1984

Etzold, TH and Gaddis JL, eds., *Containment, Documents on American Policy and Strategy, 1945–50*, Columbia, New York 1978

Feuchtwanger and Mason, eds., *Air Power in the Next Generation*, MacMillan, London 1979

Forrestal Diaries, *Inner History of the Cold War*, ed. Millis, Cassell, London 1952

Fredette, Raymond, *The Sky on Fire*, Smithsonian, Washington DC 1991

Freedman, Lawrence, *The Evolution of Nuclear Strategy*, Macmillan, London 1981

Friedman, Norman, *Desert Victory*, US Naval Institute Press, Annapolis 1991

Futrell, RF, *Ideas, Concepts, Doctrine. Basic Thinking in the United States Air Force, 1907–1960*, USAF Air University Press 1989

Garden, Timothy, *The Technology Trap*, Brassey's, London 1989

Gollin, Alfred, *The Impact of Air Power on the British People and Their Government, 1909–14*, Macmillan, London 1989

Hallion, Richard, *The Rise of the Fighter Aircraft, 1914–1918*, Nautical and Aviation 1988

Hallion, Richard, *Strike from the Sky*, Smithsonian, Washington DC 1989

Hallion, Richard, *Storm over Iraq*, Smithsonian, Washington DC 1992

Hansell, Major General Haywood S Jnr, *The Air Plan that Defeated Hitler*, Higgins MacArthur, 1972

Hardesty, Von, *Red Phoenix, the Rise of Soviet Air Power, 1941–1945*, Smithsonian, Washington DC 1982

Hartley, Keith, *The Economics of Defence Policy*, Brassey's, London 1991

Hartley and Hooper, *The Economic Consequences of the UK Government's Decision on the Hercules Replacement*, Centre for

Defence Economics, University of York 1993

Hatchett, ed., *Arms Control, Problems and Prospects, 1990*, Mosher Institute, Texas 1990

Helmesley, ed., *The Lost Empire*, Brassey's, London 1991

Heydrich, Wolfgang, ed., *Zukunftige Einsatzaufgaben der Luftwaffe*, Ebenhausen, 1994

Higham, Robin, *The Military Intellectuals in Britain, 1918–1939*, Rutgers University Press, New Jersey 1966

Higham, Robin, *Air Power: A Concise History*, Macdonald, London 1972

Higham, R and Kipp, J, *Soviet Aviation and Air Power*, Brassey's, London 1978

Holden-Reid, B and Dewar, M, *Military Strategy in a Changing Europe*, Brassey's, London 1991

Hurley, Alfred F, *Billy Mitchell, Crusader for Air Power*, Indiana University Press, Bloomington 1975

Hurst, *NATO's Anxious Birth, The Prophetic Vision of the 1940s*, London 1985

Jackson, W and Bramall, E, *The Chiefs*, Brassey's, London 1992

Jakab, Peter L, *Visions of a Flying Machine. The Wright Brothers and the Process of Invention*, Smithsonian, Washington DC 1990

Jones, Neville, *The Origins of Strategic Bombing*, Kimber, London 1973

Joubert, Philip de la Ferte, *The Third Service*, Thames and Hudson, London 1955

Keesings, *Treaties and Alliances of the World*, London 1968

Kennett, Leo, *The First Air War, 1914–18*, Macmillan, London 1991

Kohn and Harahan, eds., *Air Superiority in World War II and Korea*, US Government Printing Office 1983

Kross, Walter, *Military Reform: The High-Tech Debate in Tactical Air Forces*, NDU, Washington DC 1985

Lambeth, Benjamin S, *Desert Storm and its Meaning. The view from Moscow*, Rand, Santa Monica 1992

Leebaert and Dickinson, eds., *Soviet Strategy and New Military Thinking*, Cambridge University Press, 1992

Levine, Robert A, *Flexible Flight: The Air Force Role in a Changing Europe, 1987–1991*, Rand, Santa Monica 1992

Lord, Christopher, ed., *Military Doctrine and Military Reconstruction in Post-Confrontational Europe*, General Staff of the Czech Armed Forces, Prague 1994

McFarland and Newton, *To Command the Sky*, Smithsonian, Washington DC 1991

McMichael, SR, *Stumbling Bear, Soviet Military Performance in Afghanistan*, Brassey's, London 1991

MacIsaac, David, *Strategic Bombing in World War Two*, Garland 1976

Mason, Francis K, *Battle over Britain*, Doubleday, 1969

Mason, RA, ed., *War in the Third Dimension*, Brassey's, London 1986

Mason RA and Taylor JW, *Aircraft, Strategy and Operations of the Soviet Air force*, Jane's, London 1986

Metz, David R, *Land-Based Air Power in Third World Crises*, US Government Printing Office, 1986

Millis, Walter, ed., *American Military Thought*, Bobbs-Merrill 1966

Momyer, General William M, *Air Power in Three Wars*, US Department of the Air Force 1978

Montgomery-Hyde, H, *British Air Policy between the Wars*, RAF Museum 1976

Morrow, John H Jnr, *The Great War in the Air*, Smithsonian, Washington DC 1993

Mrozek, Donald J, *Air Power and the Ground War in Vietnam*, Pergamon Brassey's, Washington 1989

Murray, Williamson, *Strategy for Defeat: The Luftwaffe, 1933–1945*, US Government Printing Office, 1983

Nader, Marouf Bakhit, *The Evolution of Egyptian Air Defence Strategy, 1967–1973*, King's College London, 1990

Nair, Brigadier VK, *War in the Gulf, Lessons for the Third World*, Lancer International, New Delhi 1991

Nordeen, L, *Fighters over Israel*, Guild, 1991

Osgood, RE, *The Entangling Alliance*, Chicago University Press, 1962

Overy, Richard, *The Air War 1939–1945*, Europa, 1980

Paret, Peter, *Makers of Modern Strategy from Machiavelli to the Nuclear Age*, Princeton University Press, New Jersey 1986

Plater-Zyberk, Henry, *The Soviet Military Withdrawal from Central Europe*, Centre for Defence Studies London, Brassey's, London 1991

RAAF, *The Air Power Manual*, Royal Australian Air Force Air Power Studies Centre, 2nd edition, 1994

RAF, *Air Power Doctrine*, AP 3000, HMSO London, 1993

Raleigh, Walter, *The War in the Air*, Oxford University Press, 1922

Richards, Dennis, *Portal of Hungerford*, Heinemann, London 1977

Rubenstein and Goldman, *Shield of David*, Prentice Hall, New Jersey 1978

Sabin, Philip, ed., *The Future of UK Air Power*, Brassey's, London 1988

Schwarzkopf, N, *It Doesn't Take a Hero*, Bantam, New York 1992

Schenfield, Stephen D, *Dividing up the Soviet Defence Complex: Implications for European Security*, Brown University, Rhode Island 1992

Showalter and Albert, eds., *An American Dilemma, Vietnam, 1964–1973*, Imprint Publications, 1993

Singh, Air Commodore Jasjit, *Air Power in Modern Warfare*, Lancer International, New Delhi 1988

Slessor, John C, *Air Power and Armies*, Oxford University Press, 1936

Slessor, John C, *The Central Blue*, Cassell, London 1956

Smith, Perry McCoy, *The Air Force Plans for Peace, 1943–1945*, Johns Hopkins Press, 1970

Stephens, Alan ed, *Smaller but Larger*, Australian Government Publishing Service, 1991

Suchenwirth, Richard, *The Development of the German Air Force 1919–1939*, USAF Historical Study 160, 1983

Sykes, F, *From Many Angles*, Harrap, 1942

Taylor, Philip M, *War and the Media*, Manchester University Press, 1992

Tedder, Lord, *Air Power in War*, Lees Knowles Lectures, University of Cambridge, 1947

Tedder, Lord, *With Prejudice*, Cassell, London 1966

Templewood, Viscount, *The Empire of the Air*, Collins, London 1957

Terraine, John, *The Smoke and the Fire*, Sidgwick and Jackson, London 1980

Terraine, John, *The Right of the Line*, Sceptre, 1988

Till, Geoffrey, *Air Power and the Royal Navy*, Jane's, London 1979

Towle, PA, *Pilots and Rebels*, Brassey's, London 1989

USAF, *Air Power and Warfare, Proceedings of the Eighth Military History Symposium*, USAF Academy, 1978

USAF, *Transformation in Russian and Soviet Military History*, Proceedings of USAF Academy Symposium, 1986, US Government Printing Office, 1990

USAF, *Gulf War Air power Study*, Washington, April 1993

US Congress, Office of Technology Assessment, *New Technology for Nato: Implementing Follow On Forces Attack*, US Government Printing Office, 1987

US Department of Defense, *Conduct of the Persian Gulf War*, Final Report to Congress, April 1992

USAFTAC/TRADOC, *The Air-Land Battle Primer*, 1978

Vallance, Group Captain Andrew, ed., *Air Power, Collected Essays on Doctrine*, HMSO, London 1990

Waddell, Colonel Dewey et al, *Air War – Vietnam*, Arno Press, New York 1978

Walker JR, ed., *The Future of Air Power*, Ian Allan, Shepperton 1986

Wardak and Turbiville, *The Voroshilov Lectures*, NDU Press, Washington DC 1989–90

Warden, JA, *The Air Campaign*, National Defense University, Washington DC 1988

Waters, Wing Commander Gary, *Gulf Lesson One – The Value of Air Power*, RAAF Air power Studies Centre, Canberra 1992

Webster and Frankland, *The Strategic Air Offensive against Germany 1939–1945*, HMSO, London 1961

Weizman, Ezer, *On Eagles' Wings*, Weidenfeld and Nicholson, London 1976

White, William D, *US Tactical Air Power*, Brookings, Washington DC 1974

Williams, ES, *The Soviet Military*, RUSI/Macmillan, London 1987

Williams, ES, ed., *Soviet Air Power: Prospects for the Future*, Tri Service 1990

Williams, William J, ed., *A Revolutionary War: Korea and the Transformation of the Postwar World*, Imprint Publications, 1993

Yonay, Ehud, *No Margin for Error*, Pantheon, New York 1993

Articles and Papers

Akhromeyev, SF, 'Olaf Palme Memorial Lecture', *SIPRI* 1988

Allison, Roy, 'Soviet Military Doctrine: New Thinking on Nuclear and Non-nuclear Strategy'. Centre for Russian and East European Studies, University of Birmingham, 1989

Bedi, Rahu, 'India's Westward Gaze'. *Jane's Defence Review,* 9 Jan 1993

Berdal, Mats, 'Whither UN Peacekeeping'. *Adelphi Paper* 281, IISS/Brassey's, October 1993

Bowie, Christopher J, 'Coping with the Unexpected: Great Britain and the War in the South Atlantic'. Rand, Santa Monica, 1985

Brandenburg, Ulrich, 'The Friends are Leaving'. *NATO Paper CND* (93) 100, 12 February 1993

Brando, C, 'The NATO AEW Programme: A Canadian Perspective'. *Canadian Defence Quarterly*, April 1989

Brodie, Bernard, 'The Heritage of Douhet'. *Air University Quarterly Review*, Volume VI, No. 2

Bronowski, Major HR, 'A Narrow Victory'. *USAF Air Force Magazine*, July/August 1981

Burke, Captain CJ, 'Aeroplanes of Today and Their Use in War'. *Journal of the United Services Institution*, May 1911

Buszynski, Leszck, 'ASEAN Security Dilemmas'. *Survival*, Winter 1992–3

Canby, Stephen L, 'The Conventional Defence of Europe: The Operational Limits of Emerging Technology'. Working Paper 55, International Security Studies Program, The Woodrow Wilson Center, April 1984

Carter, April, 'Success and Failure in Arms Control Negotiations'. *SIPRI Yearbook*, 1989

Collins, Major Brian, 'Russian Air power: The First Year'. HQ NATO October 1993

Cooper, J, 'The Economies of the Former Soviet Union, Structural Issues'. Seminar Paper, University of Birmingham, September 1993

Dick, CJ, 'Initial Thoughts on Russia's Draft Military Doctrine'. Soviet Studies Research Centre, Sandhurst, 1992

Drew, Colonel Dennis, 'Desert Storm as a Symbol'. *Air power Journal*, Fall 1992

Dugan, General Michael, 'The Air War'. *UN News and World Report*, 11 February 1991

Fitzsimmons, DJ, 'The Origins of Air Warfare'. *Air Pictorial*, Dec 1972

Ghebali, Victor-Yves, 'Confidence-Building Measures within the CSCE Process'. *United Nations Institute for Disarmament*, Paper No. 3, 1989

Gong, Ro-myung, "The Consequences of Arms Proliferation in Asia'. *IISS Adelphi Paper* 276, IISS/Brassey's, April 1993

Gray, Randal, 'Bombing the Mad Mullah, 1920'. *Journal of the RUSI*, December 1980

Hanson, JH, 'Development of Soviet Aviation Support". *International Defense Review*, 5/1980

Holcomb, James F, 'Russian Military Doctrine'. Soviet Studies Research Centre, Sandhurst, 1992

Huxley, Lieutenant MM, 'Saddam Hussein and Iraqi Air power'. *Air Power Journal*, Winter 1992

Karsh, Efraim, 'The Iran-Iraq War: A Military Analysis'. *Adelphi Paper* 220, IISS/Brassey's, Spring 1987

Kennaway, A, 'The Economic and Industrial Legacy of Communism in Russia'. Conflict Studies Research Centre, Sandhurst, 1993

Kennaway, A, 'Restructuring the (Soviet) Defence Technology and Industrial Base'. Conflict Studies Research Centre, Sandhurst, 1993

Kokoshin, A, 'The Rogers Plan: Alternative Defence Concepts and Security in Europe'. *Economics, Politics and Ideology*, August 1985

Kokoshin, Konovalov, Larionov and Mazing, 'Problems of Ensuring Stability with Radical Cuts in Armed Forces and Conventional Armaments in Europe'. Novosti Press Moscow, 1989

Lambeth, Benjamin S, 'The Winning of Air Supremacy in Operation Desert Storm'. Paper to Zhukovskii Academy, Moscow, October 1992

Lambeth, Benjamin S, 'The Winning of Air Supremacy in Operation Desert Storm'. Rand, Santa Monica, October 1993

Lebedev, Lyutov and Nazarenko, 'The Persian Gulf War: Lessons and Conclusions'. *Military thought* 11–12, 1991

McAusland, Lt Col Jeffrey, 'The Gulf Conflict, A Military Analysis'. *Adelphi Paper* 282 IISS/Brassey's, November 1993

MacIsaac, David, 'The Air Force and Strategic Thought, 1945–51'.

Working Paper No. 8, International Security Studies Programme Woodrow Wilson Center, Washington DC, 1979

Mackay, CJ, 'The German Air Raids on England'. RAF Staff College, Andover, 1924

Machos, Major James A, 'Tacair Support for Air Land Battle'. *Air University Review*, May/June 1984

Malei, Mikhail, 'The Destiny of Conversion that is Russia'. *Military Technology* 3/93

Marshall-Hasdell, D, 'The Reform of Flight Safety in the Soviet Air Force'. Soviet Studies Research Centre, Sandhurst, 1993

Mason, RA, 'Conventional Forces Talks: A Place on the Agenda for Air power?' *Bulletin of the Council for Arms Control*, London, April 1989

Mason, RA, 'Conventional Arms Control: Air power Constraints'. IISS conference, UK, May 1989

Mason, RA, 'Air power in Conventional Arms Control'. *Survival,* Sept/Oct 1989

Mason, RA, 'Commonwealth Security after the Gulf War'. Commonwealth Heads of Government Meeting, Baronage 1991

Mason, RA, 'The Air War in the Gulf'. *Survival*, May/June 1991

Mason, RA, 'Aerospace Security in the Middle East: The Way Ahead'. *Arms Control*, December 1993

Meilinger, Philip S, 'Guilio Douhet and Modern War'. *Comparative Strategy*, Vol 12, 1992

Mellersh, FJW, 'Air Armament, Training and Development'. RAF Staff College, Andover, 1939

Musial, 'The Character and Importance of Air Operations in Modern Warfare'. *Air Force and Air Defence Review*, Warsaw, December 1981

Ogarkov, Marshal NV, 'The Defence of Socialism: The Experience of History and the Present Day'. *Red Star*, 9 May 1984

Paris, Michael, 'The Rise of the Airmen: The Origins of Air Force Elitism c 1890–1918'. *Journal of Contemporary History,* Vol 28, 1993

Peterson, Philip A and Notra Trulock, 'A "New" Soviet Military Doctrine: Origins and Implications'. Soviet Studies Research Centre, Sandhurst, 1988

Rand, 'Symposium on the Role of Air power in Counter Insurgency and Unconventional Warfare in Malayan Emergency'. RM 3651-PR, Santa Monica, 1963

Rand, 'Symposium on the Role of Counter Insurgency and Unconventional Warfare: The Algerian War'. RM 3653-PR, Santa Monica, 1963

Rogers, General Bernard, 'ACE Attack of Warsaw Pact Follow-on Forces'. *Military Technology,* 5, 1983

Rogers, General Bernard, 'Greater Flexibility for NATO's Flexible Response'. *Strategic Review*, Spring 1983

Rogov et al., 'Commonwealth Defence Arrangements and International Security'. Institute of USA and Canada Moscow with US Centre for Naval Analysis, 1992

Sharp, Jane MO, 'After Reykjavik, Arms Control and the Alliance'. *International Affairs,* Vol 63, No. 2, 1989

Sharp, Jane MO, 'Conventional Arms Control in Europe'. *SIPRI Yearbook* 1990

Sharp, Jane MO, 'Conventional Arms Control in Europe'. *SIPRI Yearbook* 1993

Snyder, 'Limiting Offensive Conventional Forces'. *International Security,* Spring 1988

Spaatz, General Carl, 'Strategic Air power: Fulfillment of a Concept'. *Foreign Affairs,* 1946

Squier, Major George, 'The Present Status of Military Aeronautics'. *Flight,* 27 February 1909

Starry, General Don A, 'Extending the Battlefield'. *Military Review,* March 1981

Sumin, Major General A, 'Russian Air Defence Forces', *Military Technology,* 5/1993

UK Foreign and Commonwealth Office, 'New from the Negotiations'. *Arms Control and Disarmament Quarterly*

UK MOD, 'The Falklands Campaign: The Lessons'. HMSO, 1982

US Library of Congress, Congressional Research Service, 'Israel: US Foreign Assistance'. Briefing Paper 1B 85066, 27 January, 1994

Voroby'ev PN, 'Lessons of the Persian Gulf War'. *Military Thought,* 4 May 1992

Voroby'ev Major General I, 'Modern Weapons and Tactics'. *Red Star,* 20 June 1984

Whittaker, WE de B, 'Aviation in the Navy'. *Aeroplane,* 15 February 1912

Wise, Col WH, 'Future of the Tactical Air Force'. *Air University Quarterly Review,* Spring 1949

Wratten, Air Vice-Marshal WJ, 'The Air War in the Gulf'. IISS Conference Paper, London, April 1991

INDEX